David Handschuh

WTC

IN THEIR OWN WORDS

A HIGHLY DETAILED, IN-DEPTH LOOK AT THE RESPONSE TO THE WORST TERRORIST ATTACK ON AMERICAN SOIL ON SEPTEMBER 11, 2001

Exclusive Interviews with the Firefighters on the Scene at the World Trade Center Attack

EDITED BY HARVEY EISNER

WTC
In Their Own Words

Edited by Harvey Eisner

Firehouse® Magazine
Cygnus Business Media
3 Huntington Quadrangle
Suite 301N
Melville, NY 11747
Phone: (800) 547-7377
Firehouse.com®

Editorial Director: Steven Shaw
Project Coordinator: Joanne Godfrey-Kalfas
Art Director: Marianne Pardal
Creative Director: J.C. Suares
Designer: Kirsten Crock
Marketing Director: Kathy Magrane
VP, Custom Publishing: Steve Davidson

Firehouse Magazine
Publisher: Patricia Maroder
Associate Publisher: Jeff Barrington
Editor-In-Chief: Harvey Eisner
Managing Editor: Elizabeth Friszell-Neroulas
Associate Editor: Steven Shaw

Library of Congress Cataloging-in-Publication Data
ISBN: 978-0-615-48420-4

DEDICATION

This book is dedicated to the first responders who died in the line of duty
at the World Trade Center, September 11, 2001.

This book is also dedicated to the memory of my father, Joseph G. Eisner,
who took me to my first fire, the aftermath of a seven-alarm fire and plane crash in Brooklyn, NY,
December 1960 and to my mother, Carol, my brother, Carey, and friend Jean Rank.
They put up with me for years running to fires, traveling, visiting firehouses and
researching and writing about fires.

Harvey Eisner
June 2011

ACKNOWLEDGMENTS

Jeff Barrington, Thomas Buchta, Jack Calderone,
Mickey Conboy, Sean Conboy, Mike Coppola, Kirsten Crock,
Steve Davidson, Michelle Endres, George Eysser, John French,
Elizabeth Friszell-Neroulas, David Handschuh, Paul Hashagen,
Joanne Godfrey-Kalfas, Amy Kraemer, Claudia Jenks, Jack Lerch,
Larry Lynch, Kathy Magrane, Dan Maye, Todd Maisel,
Patricia Maroder, Mike Martin, Peter Matthews, Marianne McIntyre,
Jay McSherry, NASA, NIST, John Norman, Marianne Pardal,
Terri Petitt, Kathy Scott, Joe Scurto, Greg Semendinger, Steven Shaw,
Steve Spak, Steve Swick, J.C. Suares, Bill Tompkins, Steve White

I also gratefully acknowledge all of the brave men who shared their stories and all the firefighters nationwide who have welcomed me into their houses.

A portion of the proceeds from this publication
will benefit the following organizations:
FDNY Foundation
National Fallen Firefighters Foundation
UFA Thomas R. Elsasser Fund
Wounded Warrior Project

IN THEIR OWN WORDS

FOREWORD BY JOHN NORMAN

This book is a tribute to the heroes of September 11, 2001. As the 10th anniversary of that tragic day approaches, it inevitably stirs the memories of all who were old enough to be aware of the murderous attacks on New York City, the Pentagon and the defeated attack that ended in Shanksville, PA.

In the intervening time, much has been learned of events that transpired that day and in the days that followed. Many of those closest to the epicenter of the events had only two views of the events they were part of, the very large macro view of the overall scene (which took days to gather the true scope) and an extremely narrow view of their immediate environment and situations that they were dealing with personally. The World Trade Center incident was of such a large scale, with such diminished communications abilities and such an extended duration, that it was impossible to know what was going on just a block away.

Over the course of the last 10 years, I have been fortunate enough to sit among the survivors of the attack on the WTC; coworkers, colleagues and friends. As the shock wore off and we became accustomed to the terrible realities, stories would emerge of our various experiences. I was constantly awed at the tales of struggle, heroism, sacrifice and survival. It reminded me of my childhood, listening to the veterans of World War II, when they were finally at ease, telling their stories among themselves and other combat veterans.

Thankfully, *Firehouse® Magazine* has seen fit to capture some of these incredible stories and images for posterity. The interviews gathered here are true "oral histories," captured "in their own words," for future generations. That is a tremendous contribution to the historical record, and also a source of inspiration and understanding for future readers.

Of course, one of the most critical parts of that day will never be available, the words and thoughts of those who perished that morning. Radio transcripts and 911 recordings are all that remain from those heroes like Battalion Chiefs Orio Palmer and Ed Geraghty. For others, like Deputy Chief Ray Downey and Battalion Chief Larry Stack, the testimony of those survivors who witnessed their last selfless acts is all that remains.

As you reflect on their sacrifices, remember them as they were; firefighters, medics and cops who went into those buildings because people needed them, but also as loving sons, daughters, husbands, wives, fathers and mothers, who loved what they did, and in more than a few cases, enjoyed a good laugh while doing it and above all savored life.

AP Photo

AP Photo/Amy Sancetta

SFC Thomas R. Roberts/ NGB-PASE

CONTENTS

WTC IN THEIR OWN WORDS

Steve Scher

Todd Maisel

Photographer David Handschuh is removed after being injured in the South Tower collapse.

ON THE COVER:
FDNY Assistant Chief Gerard Barbara looks up at both World Trade Center towers as each burns after being struck by terrorists using jets to attack the buildings. Chief Barbara and 342 other firefighters died when the towers collapsed on September 11, 2001.
Cover photo by David Handschuh.
Cover design by J.C. Suares.

IN THEIR OWN WORDS

PREFACE BY HARVEY EISNER *Interviews in this book record only a portion of what happened that day.*

Peter Matthews

Right after 9/11, I started hearing bits and pieces of information about firefighters and companies who responded to the World Trade Center. I listened to many portions of stories about where the firefighters were and what they did that day and in the weeks and months following.

I started to keep a notebook that initially expanded to 16 pages. Over the last 10 years, those notes swelled to almost 30 pages of names, phone numbers and descriptions of where the companies had operated or what they had encountered. Listening to fire stories has always intrigued me. Telling fire stories to the American Fire Service is what I have done since 1979 with *Firehouse® Magazine*. After hearing about the courage and bravery of those firefighters, who took extreme risks in searching voids in the rubble, I decided to document history.

If someone 30 or even 100 years from now wants to know what happened on September 11, 2001 at the World Trade Center, the stories that these firefighters describe will fill them in on all the details as if they were standing right beside them. These stories, in the firefighters' own words, tell it as it really happened.

As I contacted these firefighters and told them what I planned to do, everybody was most cooperative. Many complimented me for undertaking a task that would capture the horror that these dedicated individuals had to face during probably the most difficult and dangerous day of their lives. I know so many people in the FDNY that speaking to those who operated at the site was fairly easy. I also knew, met or knew a relative of 93 FDNY personnel who were killed in the line of duty at the World Trade Center on 9/11.

As I interviewed the firefighters they might say, "Did you hear this story? Did you talk to so and so?" I asked many of these firefighters to speak to these other individuals for me to break the ice, so to speak. Many of these stories are published here today because of that teamwork.

To document the broadest collection of stories, I decided to interview firefighters who operated in many different areas around the 16-acre site. Instead of interviewing one entire company of five or six firefighters, I interviewed six firefighters from six different companies who worked in six different areas. It was like detective work, tracking down individuals. Many of these firefighters were promoted, retired, sick or working somewhere else after 9/11.

Peter Matthews

Firefighters report in after a collapse. Note all the dust and papers in street.

As I met firefighters who worked in various parts of the city, they suggested other firefighters who they had heard stories about and who I should talk to. Interestingly, I had met several of these firefighters many years before, but did not remember them. One chief said he worked in a firehouse for a portion of his career and recalled one of the firefighter's names, but could not remember the rest of the crew. I reminded him of all the other names and it was like old home week. We both knew the same people.

The book is divided into several sections. The history of the area and the 1993 attack are first. The 2001 attack and several maps of the building layout, elevator design and stairway routes follow. A map of the WTC area also appears to allow the reader to see and understand where the firefighters were operating on the site to eliminate any confusion.

The firefighters who responded to the first 10 alarms are next, followed by interviews with 13 firefighters who were in the hotel and survived either one or both of the towers collapsing. The next section details those firefighters who arrived on the scene just after the towers fell and those who worked in the days, weeks and months that followed. Next, we take a look at the damaged apparatus, donated apparatus and some of the special units put into service after 9/11.

Finally, we present the pictures of the 343 members of the FDNY who died in the line of duty and a memorial section capturing some of the funerals, memorials inside and outside of the firehouses, and street signs honoring the firefighters who died on 9/11.

A glossary of terms is on page 274 to help readers understand some of the firefighter terminology that appears in the book.

Harvey Eisner

World Trade Center History

By
Paul
Hashagen

When the Dutch West India Company established the first permanent European settlement in New York City in 1624, a grand new experiment in business, shipping and urban living began. Conceived as a private business venture, the outpost on the southeastern tip of Manhattan eventually became the greatest port on the Atlantic coast and then the leading trade center of the entire world.

LOWER MANHATTAN

Shortly after its establishment, the inhabitants of the city, then known as New Amsterdam, began a public works project reshaping the very land they lived on. Under the guidance of the colony's governor, Peter Stuyvesant, a small inlet from the East River was widened into a canal. Quickly this new waterway became lined with houses. By 1676, the Broad Canal, as it was known, had become so clogged and littered by debris from fruit and vegetable vendors that it was filled in and renamed Broad Street.

As time went on, marshlands were drained, meadows were built upon and older buildings gave way to the new. Even back to the earliest days of the colony, the people living on the island of Manhattan had no problem tearing down structures to make way for new ones. Maps drawn in the 1600s show the East River lapping up against the edges of Pearl Street on the eastern shore, and the North River (Hudson) being right up to Broadway along the western shore. Around the time of the American Revolution, the city even began to sell "water lots" to entrepreneurs looking to make additional plots of land by utilizing landfill. True to their Dutch heritage, New Yorkers created more and more land by pressing back the waters.

In August 1807, a young inventor named Robert Fulton pushed his steamship, the *Clermont,* away from the pier at Cortlandt Street (exactly adjacent to where the World Trade Center would later be built) and made the 150-mile trip up the Hudson River to Albany in 32 hours. This would help turn the steamboat into a commercial success and change the world of ships and shipping forever.

Battery Park, the public park at the very tip of Manhattan, was built on landfill owing to the repeated extension of the shoreline in the eighteenth and nineteenth centuries. Castle Clinton, the circular red sandstone fort, was more than 100 yards from shore on an artificial island when it was built in 1811. The land in between was filled in by 1855, joining the fort, now known as Castle Garden, to the island.

The same was true on both sides of the island, as the city spread to the north, the tip of the island expanded slowly outward as more and more land was reclaimed from the surrounding waters. The 1865 map of the city and the island of New York, created by Egbert L. Viele for the Council of Hygiene and Public Health, shows Manhattan Island with the street grid superimposed on it. On this map, the land added to the original island is highlighted clearly and half of the area within Liberty, Vesey, Church and West streets (the site of the World Trade Center) is labeled "made land." The original edge of the island along the North River was approximately where Greenwich Street is today.

The World Trade Center was the highlight of the New York City skyline, especially at night.

AP Photo/Mark Lennihan

Paul Hashagen Collection

(above) One of two engines made by Newsham, and sent to New York in 1731, in its shed adjacent to City Hall.

(below) This 1865 map of New York, created by Egbert L. Viele for the Council of Hygiene and Public Health, shows Manhattan Island with the street grid superimposed on it.

The West Side of lower Manhattan went through a number of changes as the usage of the land adjusted with the growing city. From the Battery to Chambers Street, west of Broadway, there were many old high-rise office buildings, loft buildings, warehouses and a string of piers that pushed out into the waters of the North River. The neighborhood morphed into the produce section of the city when the Washington Markets took over many of these Federal and Greek Revival buildings. This bustling area thrived for many years.

In 1908, two huge structures joined the neighborhood with the construction of the Hudson Terminal. These twin 26-story buildings, the new home and station of the Hudson and Manhattan Railroad, covered almost two square blocks and featured rental spaces, stores, 39 elevators and five subway lines. The main purpose of the structures was to connect railroad and streetcar terminals on the New Jersey waterfront with points in Manhattan. When it was completed, it was the world's largest office building. The buildings were engineering marvels of their day. A carefully planned system of gently sloping ramps allowed a steady uninterrupted flow of pedestrians from the street to the mezzanine level. (Some parts of the old station's track level were later incorporated into the World Trade Center.)

In 1921, Harry Sheck opened City Radio on Cortlandt Street, revitalizing the district of dilapidated warehouses. This new business of radios, tubes, antennas, knobs, wires and electronics continued spreading. During the next few decades, more than 100 stores popped up in the six-square-block neighborhood, including the largest collection of radio and electronic stores in the world. This area became known as "Radio Row."

Things had become so congested in the area, with the large produce markets, radio stores, office buildings and docks, that the West Side (Miller) Highway, an elevated roadway that ran from 72nd Street south to Chambers Street, was built in 1930. The area was packed with commuters, businessmen, teamsters, stevedores, longshoremen, shoppers and travelers.

Then, with the addition of the two under-river tunnels from New Jersey (the Holland Tunnel,

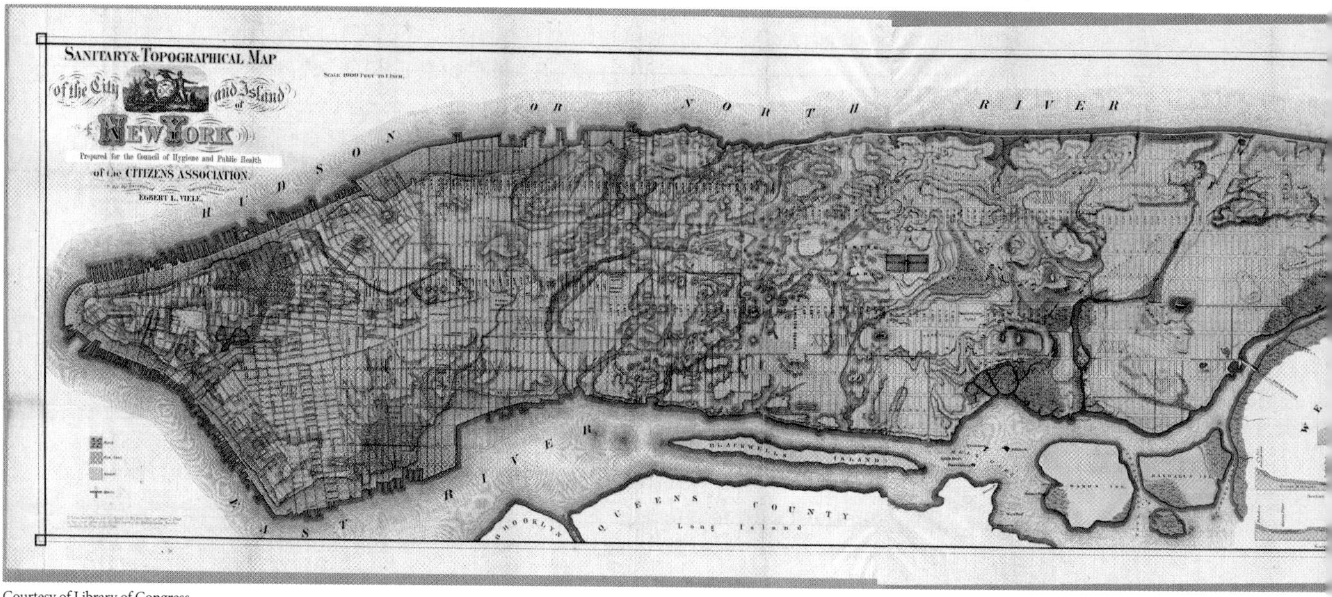

Courtesy of Library of Congress

Courtesy of the New York Public Library

Looking east along Cortlandt Street, toward Greenwich Street, men window shop in the famed "Radio Row" neighborhood.

completed in 1927, and the first of the Lincoln Tunnels, opened in 1937) and bridges from the outer boroughs, the Hudson and Manhattan Railroad steadily began to lose riders as the automobile became a preferred method of commuting. This and the age of the buildings in the area took its toll and the lower Westside neighborhood went into a steep decline.

In 1939, New York City hosted the World's Fair in Flushing, Queens. Among the popular exhibits was the World's Trade Center, a venue dedicated to the concept of "world peace through trade." Seven years later, Winthrop W. Aldrich, one of the exhibit's organizers, was now heading a new state agency with the proposed goal of creating a permanent trade exposition based in New York City. Despite all the research and preliminary planning done, the project was scrapped.

David Rockefeller, Aldrich's nephew, revived the idea as part of a major plan to revitalize lower Manhattan. A new entity, named the Downtown-Lower Manhattan Association, was formed by Rockefeller in May 1959. Their original proposals featured a huge $250 million complex to be built near the Fulton Fish Market on the East River. The centerpiece was to be a 70-story office tower and several smaller buildings.

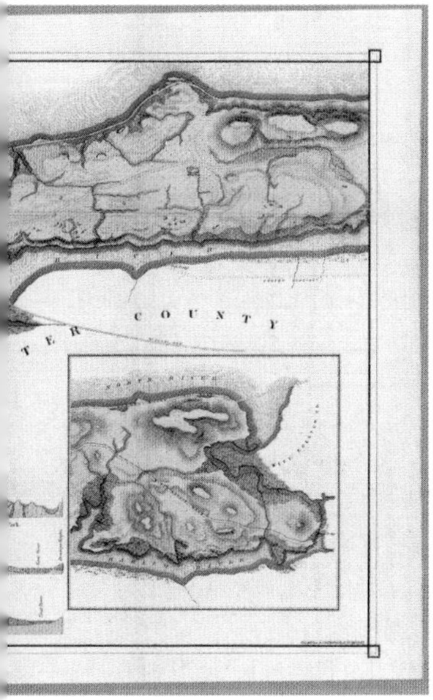

For added clout, Rockefeller brought in the Port Authority, which had just taken on the renovation of New Jersey's Hudson & Manhattan commuter railroad (the PATH train). The Port Authority decided to combine the two projects by moving the location of the World Trade Center from the Eastside to the west. This new location included the fabled "Radio Row" and a bitter battle began in the courts. The final ruling led to the destruction of an entire neighborhood.

The project began on March 21, 1966, with the demolition of 78 Dey Street. In all, five city streets would disappear from the maps with the completion of the World Trade Center project. One hundred sixty-four buildings, including the firehouses of Engine 6, Ladder 10 and Battalion 1, were among those structures. The new project, it was decided, would make the Trade Center the world's tallest building, surpassing the Empire State Building's 1,250 feet. The architect, Minoru Yamasaki, incorporated this idea in his design of two 110-story towers. To accomplish this, Yamasaki and his structural engineering design team devised a revolutionary concept of floor trusses radiating from a central core and tying into an exterior steel latticework.

The location of the project (itself largely built over existing landfill) would require a tremendous excavating operation and the building of a "bathtub" around the site to hold back the water table. The removal of 1.2 million cubic yards was needed to ready the site for footings, foundations and other underground work. As quickly as it was dug, the landfill was moved across the street and strategically placed along the shoreline until 23.5 acres of new land was reclaimed from the Hudson River (the present site of Battery Park City).

A formal ground-breaking ceremony was held on Aug. 5, 1966. The towers were completed within a couple of years and businesses started taking occupancy in Tower 1 in 1970 and Tower 2 in 1972. The finished seven-building complex added more than 10 million square feet of office space, hundreds of hotels suites, a major retail center, a busy transportation hub, and dozens of business and support services to lower Manhattan.

The 1,368-foot-high towers stood gleaming at the foot of Manhattan Island overlooking the Statue

DEMOLITION FACTS:

164
buildings were demolished

5
city streets vanished

AP Photo

(left) The new World Trade Center is shown under construction, August, 1969.

Kevin Tappe

(above) FDNY Super Pumper at multi-unit drill; hoses are attached to fireboat in Hudson River. World Trade Center Tower 1 is still under construction in the background.

CONSTRUCTION FACTS:

The foundations of the towers averaged a depth of 70 feet to find bedrock

1.2 million cubic yards of earth were excavated

192,000 tons of steel

425,000 cubic yards of concrete

43,600 windows (572,000 square feet of glass)

1,143,000 square feet of aluminum sheet

198 miles of duct work

12,000 miles of electrical cable

3,500 workers worked on the site

60 workers were killed during construction

of Liberty, Ellis Island, Wall Street and historic New York Harbor. Looking uptown, the sturdy 1,250-foot Empire State Building stood, the former record holder since 1931. This world record would again be eclipsed by Chicago's new Sears Tower in 1974.

THE 1975 FIRE

The controversial design and construction features of the towers themselves would not become an issue until the night of Feb. 13, 1975. Just before midnight, an employee of a cleaning company spread lighter fluid around a secretary's area of the Saunders-Meyers Company on the 11th floor of Tower 1 (North Tower) and ignited the accelerant. Flames immediately began spreading, fueled by the flammable liquid and the large supplies of paper and several large wooden desks.

The World Trade Center, being a Port Authority building, did not fall under the jurisdiction of New York City fire laws and despite appeals by the FDNY during the initial planning and building stages, the towers did not have a sprinkler system. The heat generated by the initial fire caused damage to the supports of the 12th floor and caused the failure of the exterior windows on the east wall of the building. Fire also raced unchecked through the plenum space above the occupancy and ignited the adjacent offices of a brokerage firm.

At 1158 hours, Box 67 was transmitted and FDNY units quickly responded through the empty streets of lower Manhattan. Members of Engine Company 6, who had lost their firehouse to the construction of the towers, entered a freight elevator and arrived at the ninth floor with their roll-ups (folded lengths of 2½-inch fire hose). The attack line was connected to the standpipe outlet on the 10th floor in stairway A and stretched to the fire floor on 11. With the windows out and the fire at an advanced stage, Captain Harold Kull and his men faced a tough situation.

"It was like fighting a blow torch," Kull said. "All

of my men got their necks and ears burned."

As the fire attack commenced, flames were working their way upward through a telephone equipment closet adjacent to the original fire area. This closet housed communication cables and equipment supplied by the New York Telephone Company (which two weeks later would suffer a major fire at a central office on Second Avenue and 13th Street. This fire injured more than 100 firefighters including some who had battled the WTC fire). Temperatures reached a point high enough to ignite the polyvinyl chloride insulation on the telephone cables, further intensifying the fire. Convected gases and heat in the 11th-floor closet raised the temperatures on the 12th through 16th floors to the ignition point, causing fires at these locations.

A second 2½-inch attack line joined the first and together pushed into the blazing fire area. Two additional lines, stretched from other stairs, supported this attack and controlled the spread to the point where the initial lines could move in. Meanwhile, the fire had spread to the 17th-floor equipment room as well.

Second-alarm units relieved the nozzle and search teams as their air supply expended. Third-alarm units stretched additional lines from the ninth through 15th floors to control the fire extending upward inside the telephone closets. The major fire had been contained within the 11th floor with relatively minor extension to the floors above. A total of 24 companies and 132 firefighters fought the fire. Sixteen firefighters were treated at the scene for smoke inhalation.

A month prior to this fire, the movie *The Towering Inferno* had been released. Commenting on the plausibility of skyscraper fires as depicted in the film, New York City Fire Commissioner John T. O'Hagan stated, "I'd sleep a lot better at night if the World Trade Center had sprinklers."

1993 ATTACK, EXPLOSION AND FIRE

In the early morning hours of Feb. 26, 1993, a three-vehicle convoy set off from Jersey City heading toward lower Manhattan. The middle vehicle was a yellow Ryder rental van carrying four large cardboard boxes that made up the largest improvised explosive device ever constructed on U.S. soil.

After weeks of careful preparations, the powerful homemade bomb was carefully loaded into the rear of a rental van by its makers. The terror cell, consisting of Islamic radicals, constructed the device while consulting manuals purchased in Pakistan. The 1,500-pound bomb was actually a slurry of urea-nitrate (a fertilizer-based explosive) and fuel oil, with waste paper added as a binder. Surrounding the boxes were four-foot red tanks filled with compressed hydrogen. One of the van's passengers held four containers of volatile nitroglycerine in his lap as the convoy traveled toward New York.

PREVIOUS FIRES IN WTC

342 FIRES FROM 1970 THROUGH 2001

- **47 fires activated one to three sprinkler heads and/or required the use of the standpipe hose for suppression. Only two required the evacuation of hundreds of people. No injuries or loss of life in these fires.**
- **1975 fire, one-quarter of 11th floor with extension through telephone closets from 9 to 19 floors**
- **COD and Commissioner O'Hagan predicted flow rates half of floor involved 1,250 gpm**

FEBRUARY 26, 1993 WTC ATTACK

- **Bomb exploded in second basement underground parking garage killing six, injuring 1,042 of which 15 who received blast injuries.**
- **Most of the 150,000 occupants evacuated the buildings.**
- **The evacuation took four hours and required 700 firefighters, 45% of the departments' on-duty personnel.**

Courtesy of NIST WTC Investigation

After a stop in Brooklyn, the group traveled to lower Manhattan. A few minutes after noon, the yellow rental van entered the underground parking facility of the North Tower of the World Trade Center, parking against the load-bearing south wall. One of the terrorists carefully placed a nitroglycerine container and a blasting cap into each of the four large boxes before connecting the fuse. After a final check, a cheap cigarette lighter ignited the fuse and the terrorists slowly walked away.

At 12:17, the burning fuse reached the bomb, setting off a tremendous explosion. A minute later Herb Eysser, FDNY Dispatcher No. 124, received the first phone call from a woman, her voice trembling with fear, reporting "...an explosion in the garage of the Vista Hotel." This and subsequent calls initiated the largest movement of apparatus in the history the FDNY to date. Just as Box 69 was being transmitted, the entire board lit up with calls reporting the explosion.

The quiet, snowy afternoon in lower Manhattan was now chaos. The blast tore through three floors of 11-inch-thick reinforced concrete. Hidden in the dense smoke was a jagged crater 200 feet long, 125 feet wide and four stories deep. On the B-2 level, various walls of elevator shafts and fresh-air plenums were severely damaged, allowing the dense clouds of smoke to move through the openings and upward through the cores of both towers above.

From their quarters on Liberty Street, members of Engine 10 and Ladder 10 heard the explosion and immediately responded around the block to the Vista Hotel. (The Vista Hotel is a 22-story hotel with 829 rooms.) Turning the corner onto West Street, Engine 10 pulled up to the luxury hotel and was met by a flood of people running from the structure. Two large overhead doors, feeding ramps to the lower levels, appeared damaged and light gray smoke was visible. Lieutenant Donachie transmitted a 10-75 signal (a working fire requiring the response of three engines, two ladders, an additional battalion chief and a rescue company).

As the first-arriving companies began to probe into the fire area, the damage slowly began to reveal itself. Voices could be heard crying for help through the smoke as the firefighters pressed on. Fire dispatchers were now receiving calls from people in the towers as smoke pushed up through the elevator shafts. Additional alarms were transmitted to supply the needed manpower to search the huge complex. Port Authority and NYPD officers augmented the fire department's searches as calls for help reached staggering numbers.

The true nature of the explosion was not known as the operation began. Initial reports indicated an electrical transformer explosion had occurred in the garage beneath the hotel. Firefighters would have to search through the heavy smoke and debris to find the location of the fires and determine what exactly had happened. The only thing for certain was a major explosion had occurred and that a tremendous amount of thick smoke was filling the complex. Fire commanders also knew the Port Authority Police Department's Operations Control Center on level B-1 had been heavily damaged. This was also the fire command station for Buildings 1, 2, 4 and 5. The complex's standpipe system was damaged and the fire alarm and public address systems were completely out of service.

As rescuers moved into the immediate blast area, dozens of dazed, injured and seriously burned workers were found. Moments after FDNY units arrived, lights within the towers blinked on and off, then a loud thud was heard seemingly from beneath West Street. Seconds later, the complex was plunged into darkness, reinforcing the erroneous assumption that this was a transformer explosion. (Several main electrical feeders to the complex, which were in close proximity to the explosion and fire area, were damaged. Water-cooled emergency generators quickly overheated and shut down, eliminating the emergency lighting.)

Surrounding the gapping hole, dozens of automobiles were burning adding to the already dense smoke. (In all, 124 parked cars were destroyed and 102 were damaged.) Four minutes after the 10-75 was transmitted, the alarm was upgraded to a 10-76 (working fire in a high-rise building). Fire commanders knew they were facing a major evacuation from the towers above and a serious fire with undetermined damage below grade. Additional fire companies would be needed quickly. At 1227

AP Photo/Val Mazzuka

hours, a second alarm was transmitted, three minutes later, a third alarm was followed quickly by a fourth.

On a ramp leading to the underground garage, Firefighter Kevin Shea of Rescue Company 1 was moving toward the sounds of voices calling for help when a piece of the concrete floor gave way beneath him. Shea plummeted more than 30 feet into the fiery blackness below. This would complicate an already mind-boggling situation. One firefighter recalled that as the smoke momentarily cleared across the scene, "It was unreal…like a movie set. Fires were everywhere. It reminded me of a *Terminator* movie."

Moments after Shea's fall, Battalion Chief Richard Rewkowski, who had been supervising several engine companies stretching a line from the hotel to the fire area, heard the Mayday on his radio. As they continued with the difficult stretch, Rewkowski was directed by Deputy Chief Steven DeRosa to the area of the trapped firefighter.

Leading the hose team down the stairs, Rewkowski used a guideline stretched toward the collapse location. The chief, Lieutenant McAllister of Rescue 1 and several firefighters carefully moved to the jagged edge trying to recon the exact location of the downed firefighter. Rewkowski said, "It was like looking into the crater of a smoking volcano."

The chief was faced with a very serious situation: disjointed voices still crying for help from the smoky recesses of the basement, numerous civilians trapped in the towers above, fires still blazing out of control below and one of his own men down — somewhere in the swirling cauldron below. Realizing the drop was beyond the reach of a portable ladder, they knew it would require a life-saving-rope evolution. This a dangerous operation on a clear day on a stable roof; in these conditions, it would be extreme, to say the least.

Outside in the street, fire commanders absorbed dozens of radio reports from firefighting teams, the team trying to reach Shea, updates from fire dispatchers and reports from escaping civilians. Building personnel reported in with damage assessments and local knowledge of the expansive complex. Police personnel added their reports from numerous locations above and below grade. Piecing these together, fire commanders tried to determine the scope of the escalating emergency. The need for search and rescue in the explosion area was a given. The evacuation of the structures (with no working elevators) and the various medical emergencies that would arise because of the stairway descents was also considered.

One major problem that had to be addressed as soon as possible was controlling the raging fires below. Commanders knew each and every facet of this complex operation would require skill, determination and a little luck – a commodity that appeared to be in short supply.

Back at the crater's edge, the remaining members of Rescue 1 (under the command of Lieutenant McAllister) and members of Squad 1 and Ladder 110 from Brooklyn, prepared for the rope evolution. Lieutenant John Fox was lowered by life-saving rope into the crater in hopes of finding Shea. After what seemed like a lifetime, the officer radioed back. He found Shea. It appeared as if Shea had broken both legs and was suffering other injuries, but was in fairly good shape. Other teams of firefighters converged on Shea from different directions. He was treated, placed

Police and fire equipment block the streets near the World Trade Center after the underground explosion on February 26, 1993.

TOWER FACTS:

200,000 visitors each day

50,000 people worked in towers

Sky Lobby Floors 44 & 78

WTC had its own ZIP Code: 10048

Each tower had 99 elevators and 6 freight elevators

in a Stokes basket and moved up to street level before being transported to a hospital with a broken kneecap, stress fractures to both feet and a broken nose.

As this was being accomplished, the severity of the smoke in Tower 1 was becoming clear as fire dispatchers received a staggering number of calls.

Not far from where the rope rescue was going on, members of Ladder 5, first due on the second alarm, were searching for reported victims trapped in a sub-cellar. They were moving across the rubble, crawling amid dangling wires, broken water pipes, burning cars and piles of shattered concrete. Nearby, an acetylene tank was burning, but the team continued past it toward the sound of muffled voices ahead in the smoke. They followed the sound to a pile of metal lockers and concrete debris. They dug frantically and uncovered an elevator pit containing 16 trapped workers who had been blown into the shaft by the initial blast. The injured were quickly removed.

Several dramatic rescues were made of individuals trapped on isolated sections of concrete hanging precariously above the gapping void. These victims were pinned beneath layers of building materials and were suffering from the effects of the dense smoke. Despite the quick response of the fire department, civilians trapped in these suffocating situations were running out of time.

A concerted effort began to place attack lines at the seat of the fire. With only four hydrants readily available, multiple hoselines were simultaneously put into position. With the only light available being from the fires themselves, the difficult and dangerous operation began. Eventually, the lines began to hit fire from a variety of angles and directions. As the smoke began to clear, nozzle teams were surprised to find they were not the only hose in operation. With the control of the majority of fire below, the perimeter of the crater started to become clear. It was huge.

On the streets above, the explosion was having a ripple effect across the city. First, most of the television stations in New York City were off the air since they utilize the antenna on the roof of the South Tower. One station did remain on the air and sent information to the city, especially those trapped within the smoke-filled towers. At one point, a television reporter erroneously advised the people within the towers to break the windows to allow the smoke to vent. Immediately, the streets below were bombarded with a shower of glass shards. This dangerous condition continued until the information could be re-reported. Subway service and PATH trains were halted due to the damaged PATH station on the B-4 level effecting subway service in lower Manhattan and across the river in New Jersey.

Inside the World Trade Center, the power loss placed the elevators out of service. Rescue workers had to climb stairs to reach those above. Within these many floors are offices, restaurants, cafeterias and the famous observation deck. With the wintry weather outside, the majority of the workers had chosen to remain within the towers for lunch. Each of the towers' 99 elevators also had to be checked for trapped occupants within the stalled cars.

Despite the damage, darkness, fires, smoke and the winter weather, FDNY members made rescue after dangerous rescue. People were removed from stalled elevators on the upper floors; they were rescued from beneath debris in the sub-basements and evacuated from every floor in the building. Many suffered smoke inhalation.

This operation was the largest movement of apparatus to date in the history of the FDNY. During the initial 24 hours of operations, there were 135 responding FDNY companies with approximately 775 uniformed members at the scene. The equivalent of 23 alarms were called for this emergency. Amazingly, the FDNY fought two other major fires, a second alarm on Rockaway Boulevard in Queens at 12:54 P.M. and a second alarm on Hancock Street in Brooklyn at 3:18 P.M. while operating at the World Trade Center.

In all, six civilians were killed and more than 1,000 were injured (mainly smoke related), with more than 450 of those treated at hospitals. One hundred five members of the department were injured while operating with five of those members being admitted to the hospital. Thirty-five police officers and one EMS worker also were reported injured.

Ten members of the fire department were awarded medals of valor for operations at the World Trade Center. Twenty-five companies were awarded unit citations for their rescue efforts.

The Twin Towers are the backdrop for Medal Day Ceremonies at City Hall.

Steve Scher

Visible from space, a smoke plume rises from the Manhattan area after two planes crashed into the towers of the World Trade Center. This photo was taken of metropolitan New York City (and other parts of New York as well as New Jersey) the morning of September 11, 2001. "Our prayers and thoughts go out to all the people there, and everywhere else," said Station Commander Frank Culbertson of Expedition 3, after the terrorists' attacks.

NASA picture taken from International Space Station

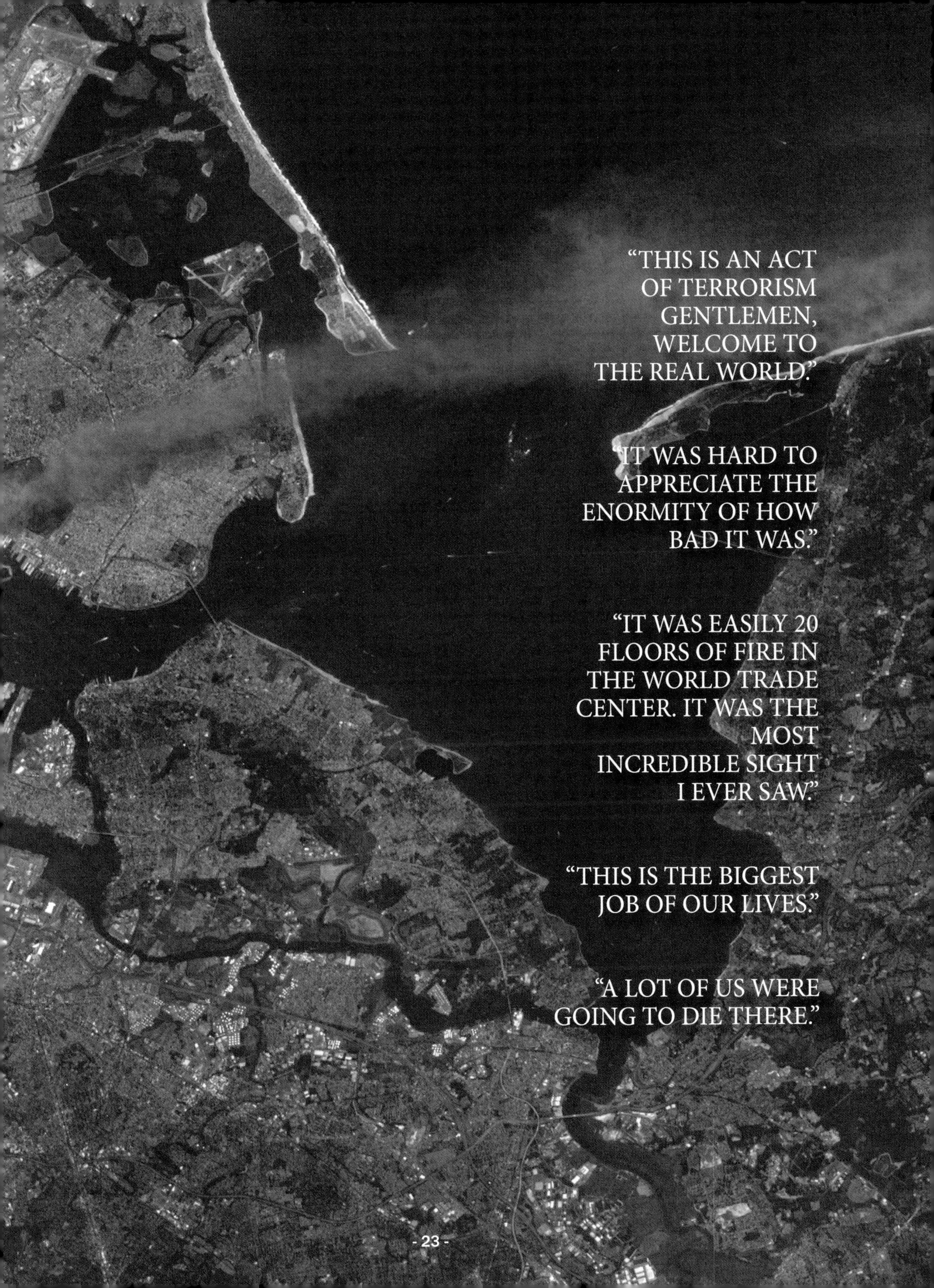

"THIS IS AN ACT OF TERRORISM GENTLEMEN, WELCOME TO THE REAL WORLD."

"IT WAS HARD TO APPRECIATE THE ENORMITY OF HOW BAD IT WAS."

"IT WAS EASILY 20 FLOORS OF FIRE IN THE WORLD TRADE CENTER. IT WAS THE MOST INCREDIBLE SIGHT I EVER SAW."

"THIS IS THE BIGGEST JOB OF OUR LIVES."

"A LOT OF US WERE GOING TO DIE THERE."

istockphoto.com

A photo of the World Trade Center and the World Financial Center, shortly before 9/11.

9/11 Attack

USE OF JETS IN ATTACK

At 8:46:30, five hijackers flew American Airlines Flight 11, a 767-200 ER twin engine, wide-body aircraft that could hold 23,890 gallons of jet fuel with 76 passengers and a crew of 11, into the north wall of WTC 1 at a speed of 443 mph. The jet was carrying 10,000 gallons of fuel. The total weight of the aircraft was estimated to be 283,600 pounds. The jet hit the exterior of the 96th floor. The aircraft cut a gash that was over half the width of the building and extended from the 93rd floor to the 99th floor. A wheel landed on Cedar Street 700 feet farther south. A second wheel landed another 700 feet away. The devastation took 0.7 seconds. Some survivors reported fallen ceiling tiles throughout the building all the way down to the concourse level. The pipes for the sprinkler system were severed. At least 166 windows were broken. Damage to the interior walls was reported from the lobby to the 92nd floor. It is estimated that 1,355 people from the 92nd floor to the 110th floor lost their lives due to collapsed walls in all three stairwells and interrupted elevator service to the upper 60 floors.

SECOND ATTACK

At 9:02:59 A.M., 16 minutes after the first impact, five hijackers flew United Airlines Flight 175 with nine crew and 51 passengers into WTC 2 at about 540 mph, about 100 miles faster than AA 11. UA 175 was a Boeing 767-200ER and had also left Boston for Los Angeles. It flew into WTC 2 carrying about 9,100 gallons of fuel. The plane brought about 14 tons of combustibles into the building. The aircraft disappeared into the building in a fifth of a second. The tower was estimated to sway 27 inches to the north. The center of the nose of the plane struck the 81st-floor slab. The entry stretched over nine floors from 77 to 85, rather than eight in WTC 1.

TIMELINE OF SEPTEMBER 11, 2001 TERROR ATTACKS

7:59 A.M.	8:01 A.M.	8:14 A.M.	8:46 A.M.	9:02 A.M.	9:40 A.M.	9:49 A.M.	9:59 A.M.	10:00 A.M.	10:29 A.M.	5:20 P.M.
American Airlines Flight 11, carrying 92 people, leaves Boston, MA, for Los Angeles, CA.	United Airlines Flight 93, carrying 45 people, leaves Newark, NJ, for San Francisco, CA.	United Airlines Flight 175, carrying 65 people, leaves Boston, MA, for Los Angeles, CA.	Tower 1 (North Tower) of World Trade Center is struck by American Airlines Flight 11.	Tower 2 (South Tower) of World Trade Center is struck by United Flight 175.	American Airlines Flight 77, carrying 64 people from Washington, DC, to Los Angeles, CA crashes into the Pentagon.	Federal Aviation Administration blocks airline takeoffs nationwide.	Tower 2 (South Tower) of World Trade Center collapses.	United Flight 93 crashes 80 miles southeast of Pittsburgh, PA.	Tower 1 (North Tower) of World Trade Center collapses.	7 World Trade Center collapses.

A fireball erupts as the South Tower is hit. Debris traveled as far as five city blocks. Getty Images

DAMAGE TO WTC 2

• Direct Structural damage from the aircraft included more severe damage to the core columns than in WTC 1.

• Jet fuel sprayed into the building interior that ignited widespread fires over several floors.

• Dislodging of sprayed fire-resistive material from structural members due to the aircraft impact and aircraft and building debris which enabled rapid heating of the unprotected structural steel.

• Sustained fires on the east side of the tower and an ample air supply.

• Weakened core columns that increased the load on perimeter walls

• Sagging of the east floors that led to pull-in forces on the east perimeter columns

• Bowed east perimeter columns that had a reduced capacity to carry loads.

• Of the roughly 6,000 people who started the morning below the 77th floor, all but 11 evacuated the building indicating sufficiently efficient movement within the three stairwells within the time available.

Information courtesy of NIST

INITIAL DAMAGE

• Structural damage from the aircraft.

• Large amount of fuel sprayed into the building interior that ignited widespread fires over several floors.

• Dislodging of sprayed fire resistive material from structural members due to the aircraft impact that enabled rapid heating of the unprotected structural steel.

• Open paths for fire spread resulting from the open plan of the impact floors and breaking of partition walls by impact debris.

• Weakened core columns that increased the load on perimeter walls.

• Sagging of the south floors that led to pull-in forces on the perimeter columns.

• Bowed south perimeter columns that had a reduced capacity to carry loads.

• Of the roughly 7,545 building occupants who started that morning below the 92nd floor, all but 107 escaped the building. Those left behind were trapped by debris, awaiting assistance, helping others or were just too late in starting their egress. For the most part the evacuation was steady and orderly.

COLLAPSE OF BUILDING 7

WTC 7 was built on top of an existing Con Edison electric power substation. It was located on land owned by the Port Authority of New York and New Jersey. Collapse of WTC 2 did not cause any structural damage or start any fires in WTC 7. Collapse of WTC 1 damaged exterior columns on the lower floors of the south and west faces and initiated fires on 10 floors between floors 7 and 30. Fires on the lower floors (floors 7 to 9 and 11 to 13) grew and spread since they were not extinguished either by the automatic sprinkler system or by the FDNY because water was not available. Fires were generally concentrated on the east and north sides of the northeast region beginning at about 3 P.M. to 4 P.M. The local fires on the upper floors (floors 19, 22, 29 and 30) were not observed after approximately 1 P.M. On September 11, 2001, WTC 7 endured fires for almost seven hours from the time of the collapse of the North Tower WTC 1 at 10:28:22 A.M. until 5:20:52 P.M. when WTC 7 collapsed. The collapse of WTC 7 was the first known instance of the total collapse of a tall building primarily due to fires.

2,749 PEOPLE murdered on 9/11 at WTC

1,125 STILL MISSING from WTC

Only recovered 124 WHOLE BODIES from WTC

Fires burned at site at temperature of 1,300 degrees Fahrenheit FOR SIX MONTHS

Building 7 lies in a heap of rubble. It almost fell straight down. Firehouse Collection

- **Building 7 was a 47-story office building north of the main WTC complex. It was built on top of an existing Con Edison electric power sub-station. The building endured fires for almost seven hours from the time of the collapse of the North Tower at 10:28:22 A.M. until 5:20:52 P.M. when it collapsed.**

- **The collapse was the first known instance of the total collapse of a high-rise building primarily due to fire.**

- **The collapse of WTC 1 damaged seven exterior columns on the lower floors of the south and west faces and initiated fires on 10 floors between floors 7 and 30.**

Courtesy NIST

FDNY ALARM BOXES (Unofficial Response)

BOX 8087 #1 WTC NORTH TOWER

Engine 4, 6,7,10, 24 Ladder 1, 8, 10, 15, Battalion 1, 2, Division 1, Safety Battalion 1, Rescue 1, Marine 1, 6, Battalion 4, 6, 7, Engine 5, Engine 9/Satellite 1, Engine 15, 28, 33, Field Communications, Ladder 6, 20, Special Operations Battalion 1, Engine 3/High-Rise Unit 1, Engine 16, Engine 39/High Rise 2, Engine 55, Ladder 5, Rescue 2, 3, 4, Squad 18, Hazardous Materials Unit 1, Ladder 3, Squad 1, 288, Car 36 D Father Judge, Battalion 11, Engine 1, 21, 34, 54, 65, 207, 226, Ladder 9, 18, Rescue 5, Marine 7, Battalion 8, 9, Division 3, Squad 252, Engine 26, 289, 274, Reserve Engine 508, Engine 162, Battalion 21, 19, Engine 263, Marine 9, Engine 236/15, 318/279, 286/10, Division 6/3, Reserve Engine 505, Engine 309/33, Squad 270, Reserve Engine 500, Ladder 47/6, 119, 117/3, 79/131, Engine 321, 278, 281, 247/240, Ladder 104, Ladder 122, 161, Engine 206/Foam 6, 290, Reserve Engine 518, Ladder 107/105, 153, Battalion 37, Engine 248, 254, Reserve Engine 514, Reserve Engine 511, Ladder 37/9, 165/18, Engine 250/5, Ladder 154/6, 111/1

BOX 9031 ADDITIONAL ASSISTANCE FROM BROOKLYN ON HIGH-RISE FIRE

Engine 205, Ladder 110, Battalion 31

BOX 9998 #2 WTC SOUTH TOWER

Engine 22, 40, 44, 53, 211, Ladder 11, Division 3, Battalion 10, 12, Ladder 2, 13, Ladder 16, Engine 23, 209, 212, 214, 216, 217, 220, 221, 229, 230, 235, 238, 279, Ladder 7, 12, 24, 118, Engine 47, 58, 74, 76, 91, Ladder 4, 21, 22, 25, 35, Car 10A, Squad 41, Engine 14, Ladder 124/5, Squad 61/18, Ladder 17/15, Battalion 26/7, Ladder 58/20

BOX 0050 ADDITIONAL MANPOWER FOR ALBANY/WEST STREET STAGING AREA

Engine 201, 240, 219, 228/205, 280, Ladder 113, 114, Battalion 32, Ladder 43, Engine 201, 210, 324/Satellite 4, 159/Satellite 5, 59, 93, 251/259

BOX 2033 ADDITIONAL MANPOWER FOR WTC STAGING AREA

Engine 35, 258, 259, 260, 261, 262, 294, 312, 325, Ladder 115, 116, 128, 136, 138, 163, Battalion 45, 46, 49,Engine 50, 64, 68, 83, 94, 84/16, 224, 231/24, 271/6, 305/3, 307/5, 310/55 Ladder 135/5, Battalion 38, 39

- **Numerous units were assigned to staging areas then re-assigned to boxes near the WTC.**
- **Numerous units relocated to cover empty firehouses and then were assigned to staging areas or boxes near the WTC.**
- **Engine 250/5 means Engine 250 had relocated to cover Engine 5 firehouse.**

FDNY STAGING AREAS

BROOKLYN-BATTERY TUNNEL STAGING BOX 1377

Engine 202, 204, 210, 224, 239 Ladder 101, 105, 131, 132, Battalion 40, 48, Division 11, Engine 201, 240, 249, 278, 281, Ladder 102, 113, 114, 122 Battalion 41/31, 42/32, Ladder 149, Ladder 161, Engine 233, 277, Ladder 104, Engine 264, 311, Ladder 133, Battalion 32, Engine 219, 228/205, 280, 282/204, 165, 241/224 246/235, 276, 211, 284/207, 318/279 160, Ladder 78, Engine 227, Reserve Engine 518, Ladder 148, Engine 247, Reserve Engine 519, Ladder 107/105, Battalion 58, Engine 290, 254, Ladder 153, Reserve Engine 514, Engine 206/Foam 206, 248, Battalion 37

QUEENS MIDTOWN TUNNEL STAGING BOX 7115

Engine 258, 259, 260, 261, 262, 312, 325, Ladder 115, 116, 128, 136, 138, 163, Battalion 45, 46, 49

ENGINE 35 QUARTERS STAGING AREA 3RD AVE-EAST 124TH STREET, MANHATTAN

Engine 35, 50, 64, 68, 83, 84/16, 94

SI FERRY TERMINAL STAGING BOX 8000

Engine 157, Ladders 83, 84, 85 Engine 164, 156, 166, 155, 162, Marine 9

BROOKLYN BRIDGE STAGING BOX 320

• Units responded to the Brooklyn Bridge after the WTC collapse closed the Brooklyn Battery Tunnel.
Engine 227, 241/224, 249, 276/211, 282/204, 284/207, Battalion 41/31, 42/32, Engine 246/235, Reserve Engine 515, Reserve Engine 519, Ladder 119, 148, Engine 152, 160, Ladder 78, Engine 155, 156, 164, Ladder 84, Engine 153, Ladder 149

BOX 0085 TRANSMITTED TO PROVIDE RELIEF

Engine 45/33, 218/55, 266/16, 328/3, Battalion 38, 39, reserve Engine 500, 317/207, Ladder 142/1, Engine 251/259

DIVISION OF TRAINING

• Units assigned to the Bureau of Training responded from Randall's Island to the scene.
• Numerous Bronx Ladder Companies relocated to downtown Manhattan Ladder Companies immediately after the first tower was hit.
• Mutual aid into city: New Jersey, Nassau County, Suffolk County, Westchester County.

IN THEIR OWN WORDS

AN INTRODUCTION BY HARVEY EISNER

In the worst terrorist attack on U.S. soil, hijackers crashed three planes into landmark buildings on September 11, 2001. Two jets crashed minutes apart into the World Trade Center in lower Manhattan. One jet crashed into the Pentagon in Arlington, VA, killing 184 onboard and on the ground. Another hijacked jet crashed near Shanksville, PA, killing 44. Originally, more than 5,000 people were missing and presumed dead at New York's twin 110-story World Trade Center towers. Following the collapse of both 1,350-foot-high towers, more than 400 members of all ranks from the New York Fire Department (FDNY) were unaccounted for. Numerous police officers from the New York Police Department (NYPD) and the Port Authority of New York and New Jersey were also missing.

The final death toll was 2,752, including 343 members of the FDNY, 23 officers of the NYPD and 37 officers of the Port Authority Police Department.

At 8:46 A.M. on September 11, 2001, FDNY units operating nearby at an unrelated incident witnessed a jet fly straight into the north side of 1 World Trade Center. That set into motion the largest FDNY response in history. More than 1,000 firefighters were dispatched to the scene. During the 1993 bombing at the World Trade Center, where 15 people were killed and 1,042 were injured, 750 firefighters responded on 16 alarms. The evacuation of 150,000 people during the 1993 incident took four hours. The 2001 incident required approximately 23 alarms in the first few minutes.

Sixteen minutes after the impact of the first jet, a second jet crashed into the south side of 2 World Trade Center. Because of the location of where the jets crashed on the upper floors in both World Trade Towers, hundreds, if not thousands, of occupants were trapped. The impact of both crashes dislodged fire-retardant material and destroyed the standpipe and automatic fire sprinkler piping, rendering fire protection features unusable. Each tower also sustained structural damage. Apparently, following the impact, only one elevator was working in each tower. Jet fuel ignited on the upper floors and dropped down the elevator shafts. People in the lobby were burned when the jet fuel ignited. As quickly as firefighters arrived, they were given assignments and were sent upstairs to remove as many occupants as possible. Other fire units staged in areas around the World Trade Center complex awaited orders. EMS units set up in various staging areas. Debris from the towers was falling to the street. Hundreds of trapped occupants jumped to their deaths from the upper floors of the towers.

The lack of working elevators led to a 70-floor walk up narrow stairways for firefighters

Peter Matthews

with civilians evacuating at the same time. This, along with a lack of water supply on the upper floors, caused a severe delay for firefighters to be in position to rescue and remove civilians and fight the fire on the upper floors of each tower.

At 9:59 A.M., the South Tower, 2 World Trade Center, had a complete and total collapse. A tremendous cloud of dust and debris blanketed lower Manhattan. First responders who weren't killed or injured took cover with civilians still in the area. Adjacent buildings were damaged and some were on fire. It took several minutes for the dust to partially clear. The order was given to evacuate the North Tower, 1 World Trade Center. Some firefighters heard the order and some apparently did not. Thirty minutes later, while some firefighters were evacuating, some still ascending and others still arriving on the scene, 1 World Trade Center collapsed and created another tremendous dust cloud visible from the International Space Station. More firefighters were injured, killed or simply ran for their lives, others were trapped. An exhaustive search that would continue for almost three weeks to rescue those trapped began. After approximately three weeks, the incident went from a rescue mode to recovery mode. Units operated around the clock searching for the remains of those killed in the incident. This 10th anniversary retrospective looks back at what the first responders saw and how it affected them. Their lives were changed forever.

We present the comments from those fateful days, IN THEIR OWN WORDS.

David Handschuh

Rescue 1 responds south on West Street approaching Chambers Street. They would arrive in under one minute. All aboard died within two hours.

WTC & Neighborhood Map

Several maps and diagrams are included in this book to allow the reader to follow the firefighters through the immediate neighborhood. Diagrams of the stairways, elevator configuration and lobby layouts of the Twin Towers, including the fire command stations, are also included.

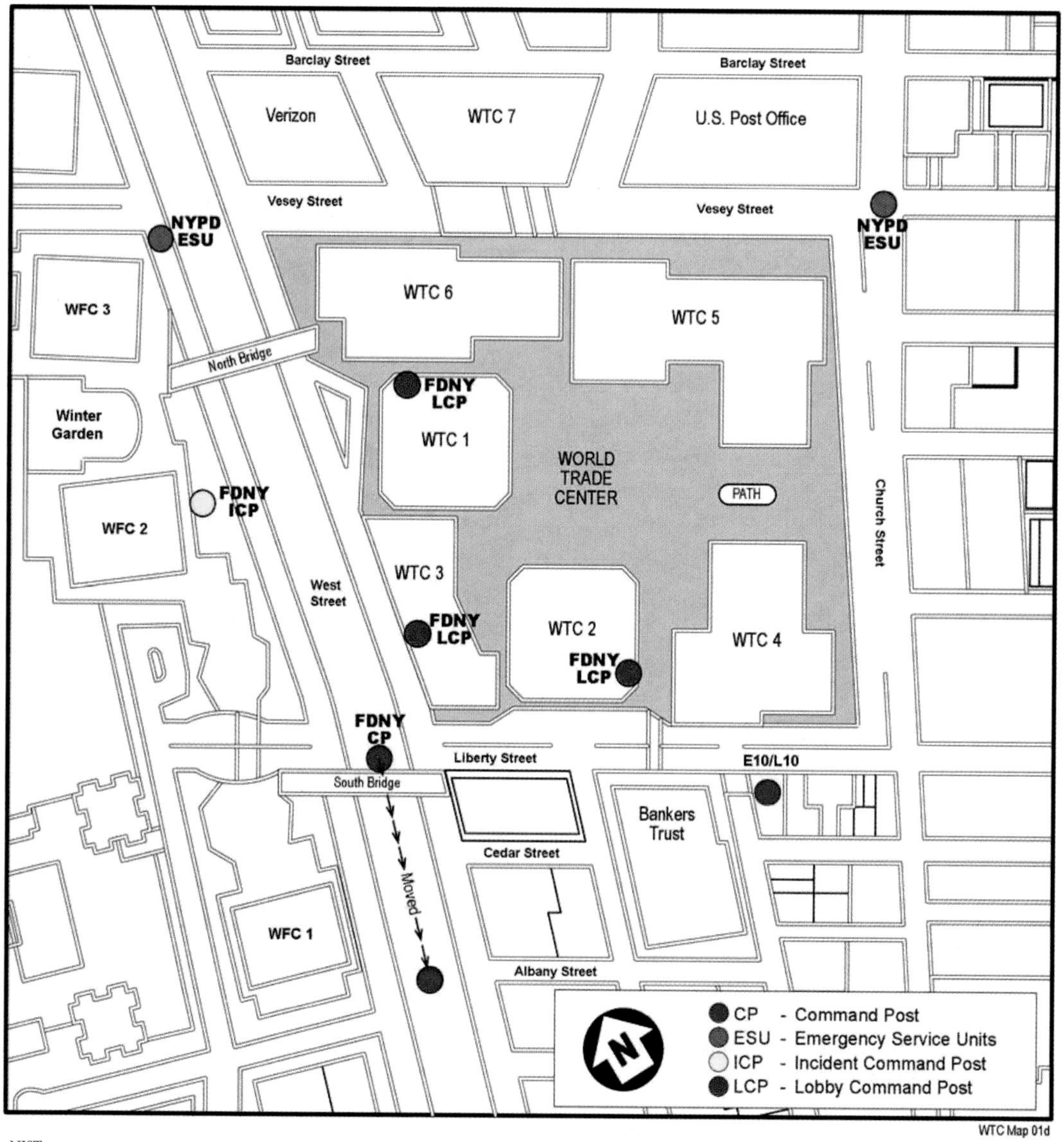

NIST

Here is a street and building map of the immediate area around the World Trade Center. The North and South Pedestrian Bridges are visible as well as the World Financial Center (Building 7) to the north and the various initial command posts. After the collapse, the command post was moved five blocks north to West and Chambers streets. This map can be used as a reference point when reading the firefighter interviews, which run from page 34 to page 246.

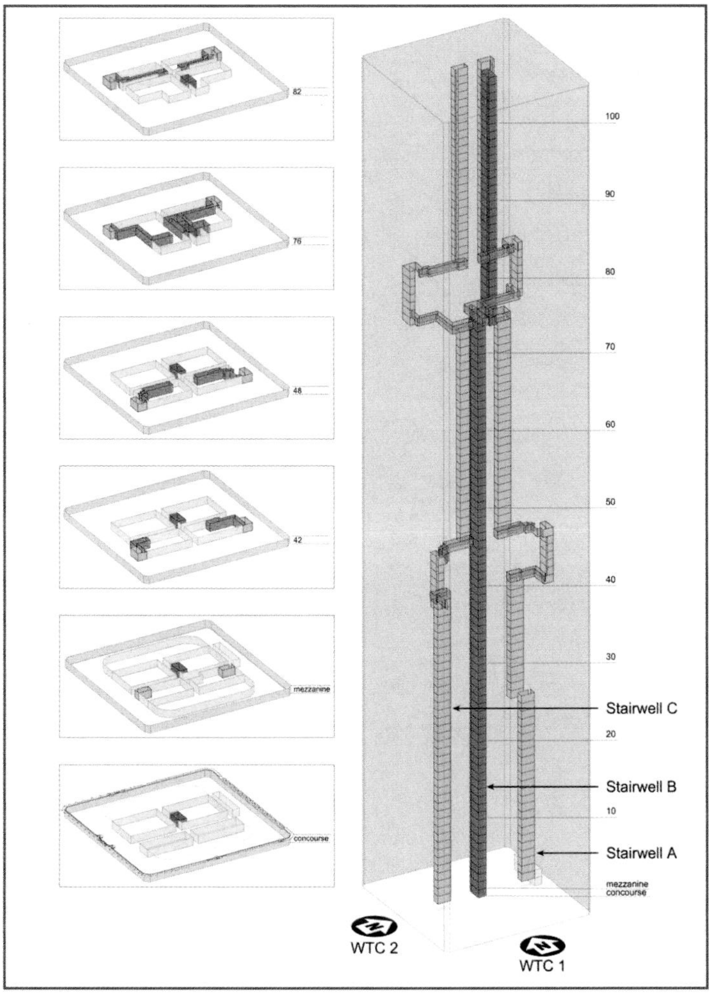

NIST

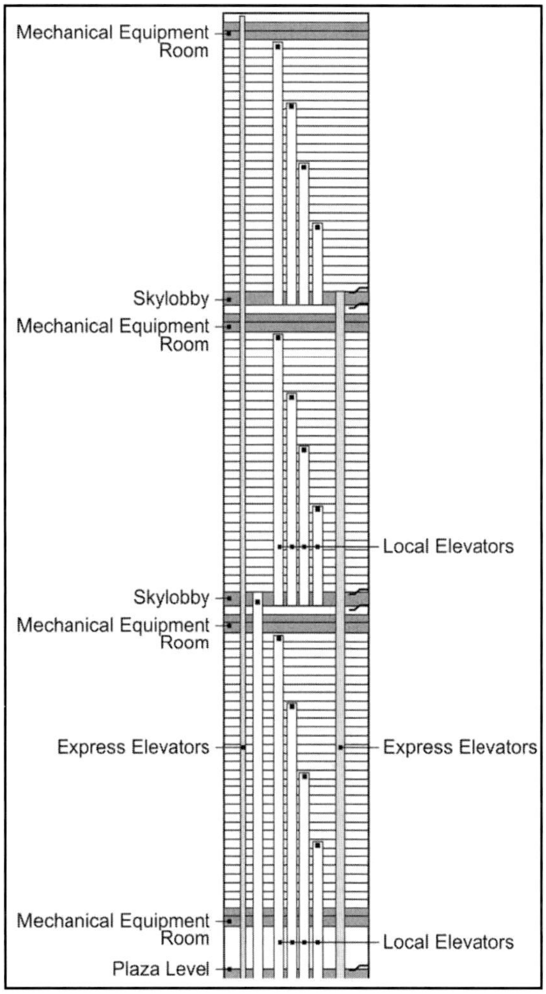

NIST

The A, B, and C stairways are visible in a cutaway view of the tower. The stairways were redirected around the mechanical equipment floors around 44 and 78.

The elevator scheme above shows that a person traveling to floors 1-44 would take a local. For floors 44-77, a person would need to go to the 44th and switch to a local. To obtain access to floors 78 through 110, an individual would go to the 78th floor and take a local. For the observation deck and restaurant, there were express elevators that went straight to the top. In all, each building had 99 elevators and a few freight cars. On 9/11, after the attacks, apparently only one elevator in each building was working.

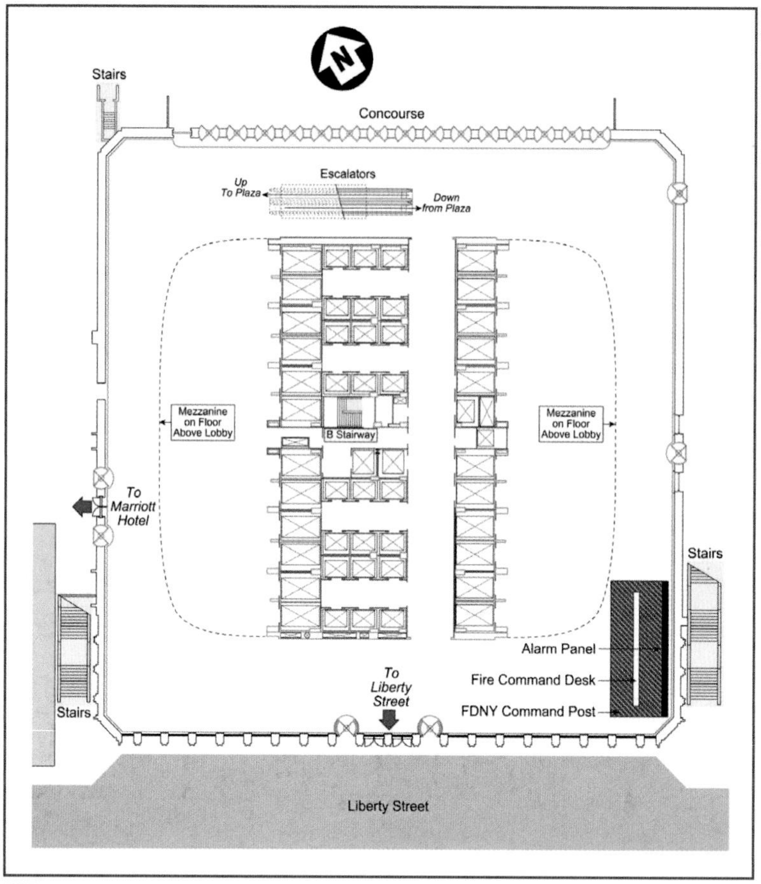

2 World Trade Center, the second tower to get hit, had its fire command station in the southeast corner of the first floor, close to Liberty Street. The B stairwell is visible in the middle of the elevator lobby.

NIST

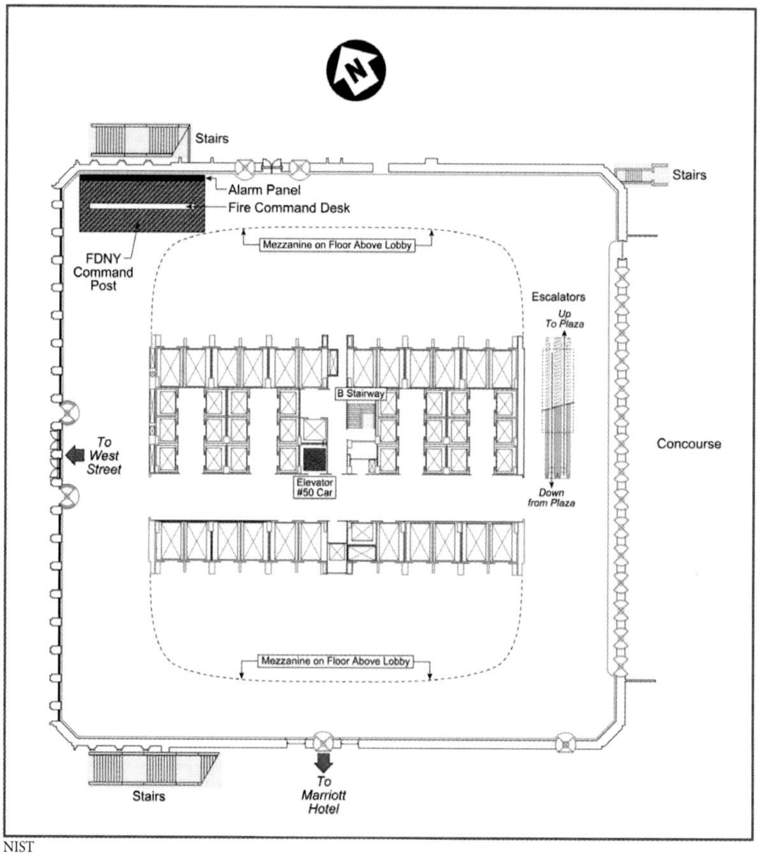

1 World Trade Center, the first tower built and the first tower to be attacked, had its fire command station located in the northwest corner of the first floor. Numerous people in elevators and in the lobby of the North Tower were burned when jet fuel spilled down the elevator shafts and ignited.

NIST

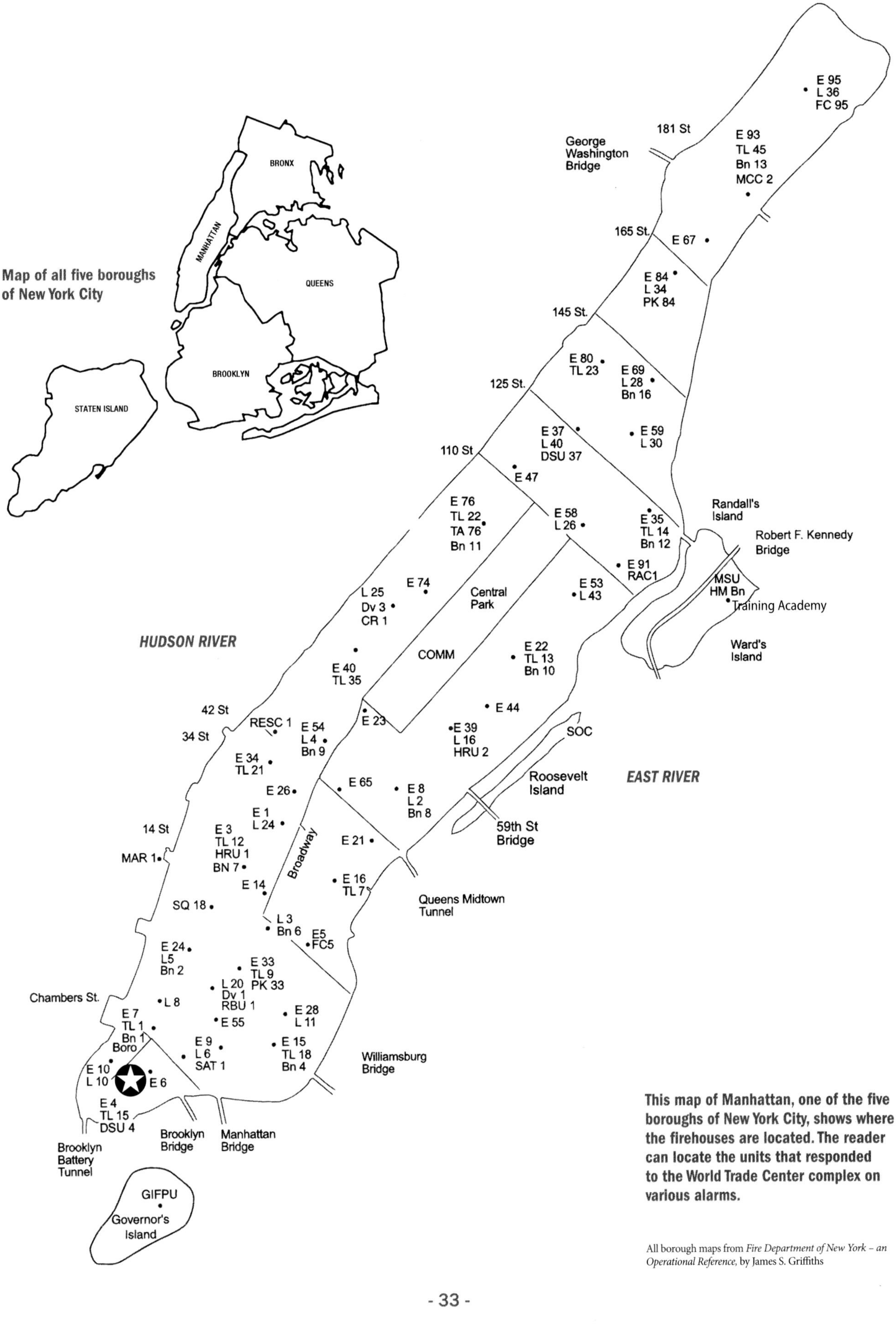

Map of all five boroughs of New York City

This map of Manhattan, one of the five boroughs of New York City, shows where the firehouses are located. The reader can locate the units that responded to the World Trade Center complex on various alarms.

All borough maps from *Fire Department of New York – an Operational Reference,* by James S. Griffiths

These maps show where the firehouses are located in the four outer boroughs of New York City.

BRONX

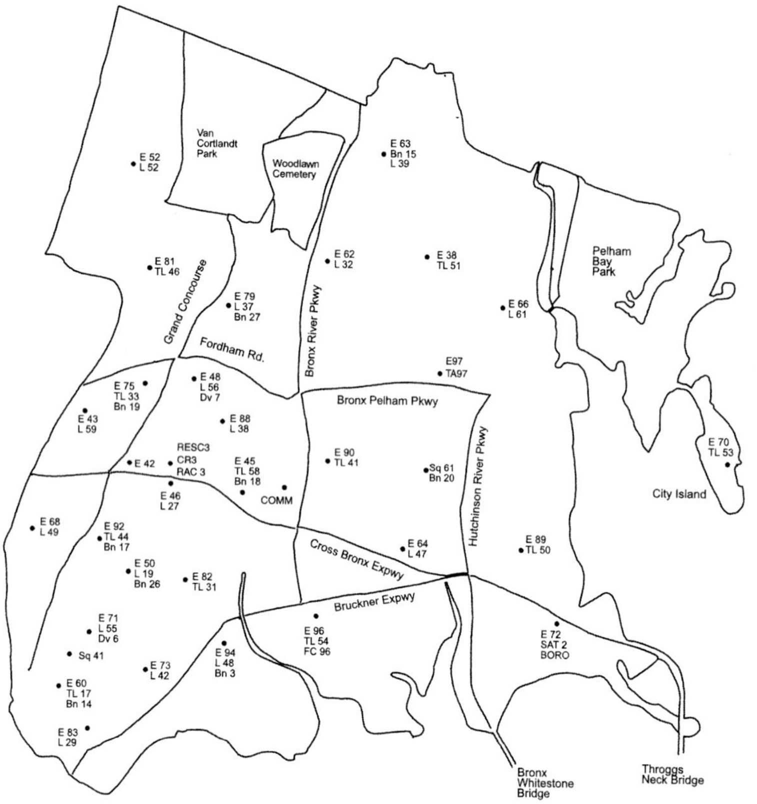

BROOKLYN

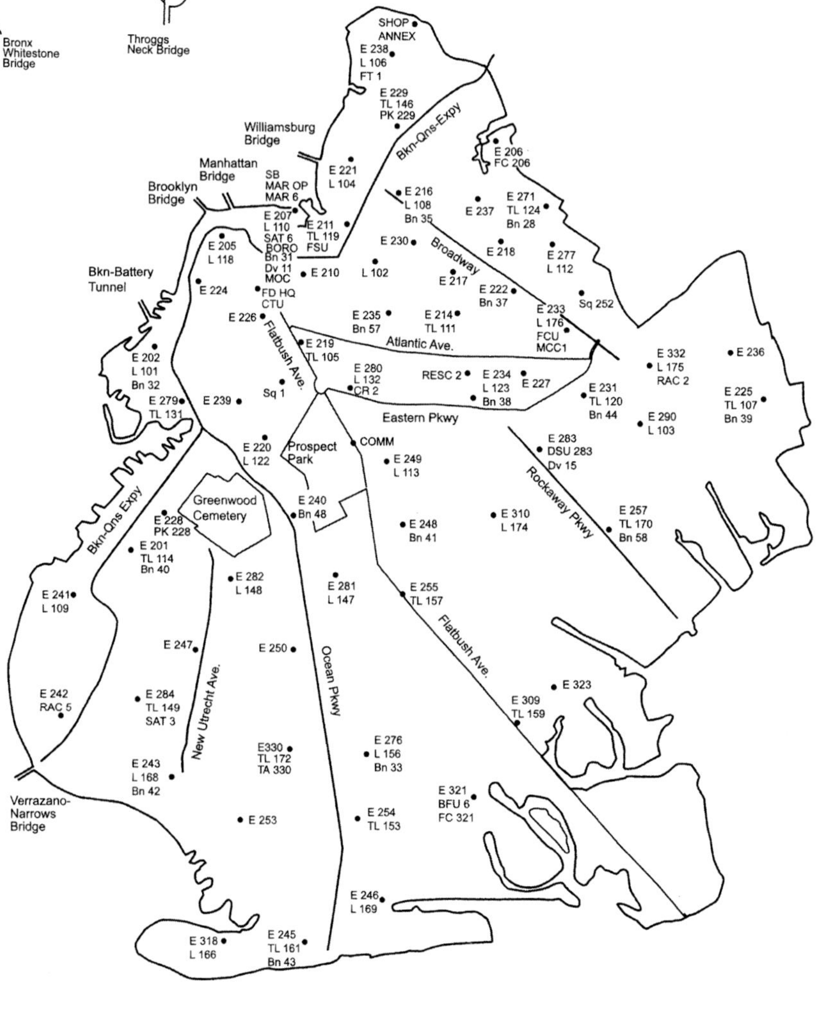

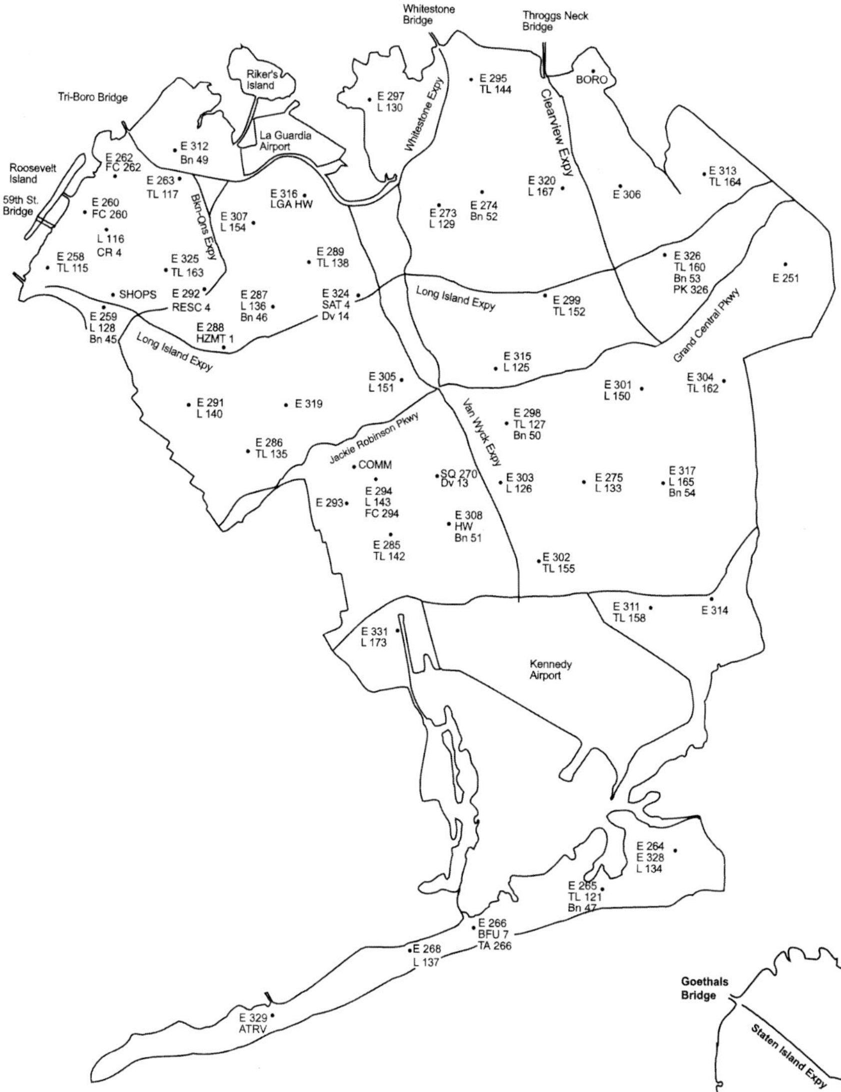

QUEENS

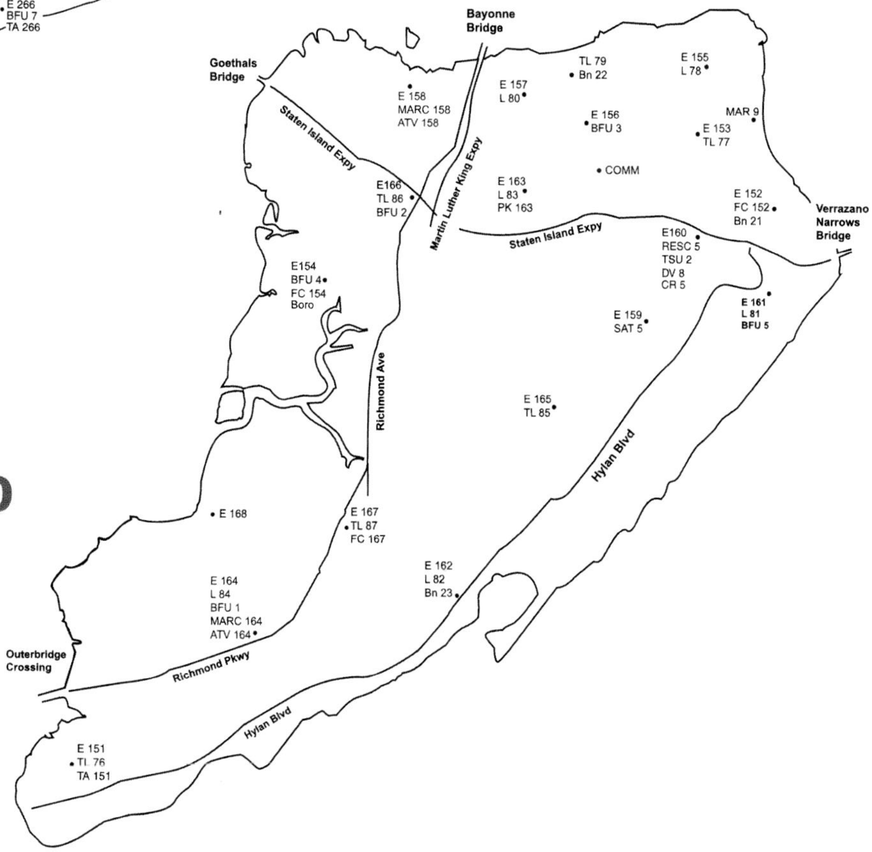

STATEN ISLAND

Up To 31

Firefighter Jim Curran
Ladder 8, Lower Manhattan

now Fire Department Operations Center

I was appointed on February 4, 2001. After probie school, I spent 14 weeks at Engine 34 and Ladder 21. I was assigned to Ladder 8 on July 28, 2001.

On September 11, we were slated to go out of service for our annual medicals at 9 A.M. We received a phone alarm at 8:25 A.M. at 313 Church Street for a natural gas leak in the street. The rest of the assignment was Engine 7, 55, Ladder 1 and Battalion 1.

We were still operating when we heard a plane fly right over us like it was going to crash. As we looked up we saw it fly into the North Tower. Lieutenant Vinny Holleran said let's go.

I put the tools on the rig and jumped on and responded to the scene. Someone said this is going to be a bad day. As we went south on the West Side Highway, there were already body parts in the way. There was a person in the middle of the street that was burned. In the lobby, several more people had been burned. One person had every stitch of clothes burned off except for their jacket.

We were one of the first ladder companies inside. Engine 7 and Ladder 1 were behind us. I said we're the first ones here, nobody else. Walking through the lobby, the marble slabs on the walls were cracked. Pieces were all over the floor. There was rubble, glass and several spot fires burning. A cop stopped the escalators so we could walk up. There was pink everywhere from the jumpers.

The members took two laps around the mezzanine level. The large freight elevator was not level in the shaft. It was decided that we were going to walk upstairs. It was hard to climb up the stairs. You had to turn sideways holding the can and hook. We stayed against the wall.

Apparently, when we were on the 16th floor the second plane hit the South Tower. Around the 18th floor, there was a call for oxygen for someone having chest pains. On another floor, someone else requested oxygen. A firefighter was escorting a member who was having problems.

A report came from a member of the Secret Service about the possibility of a third plane coming in. Everybody looked at each other. Somebody with a look of fear on their face said if the plane hits below us, we'll be cut off.

At the 23rd floor, the tower vibrated and shook side to side. The power went out on 30. At that time, we heard that there was a partial collapse on floor 65. At the 31st floor we could smell jet fuel. On the 35th floor I decided to call my mother. She works at Greenwich and Barclay streets. She told me the second tower had fallen.

Suddenly, someone yelled get off your phones! Get out now! We left our masks and tools. We were with Engine 7, 28 and 33 and Ladder 9. As we descended the stairs, John Tierney of Ladder 9 was two people behind me. We were in probie school together. At the ninth floor we switched stairways because debris was blocking the stairs.

Firefighters remove an injured person. In the background (from right to left) early in the incident. Engine 7, Ladder 8, Tower Ladder 1 and a tractor-trailor aerial park close to the North Tower.

David Handschuh

Greg Semendinger

The North Tower's upper floors burn as smoke and dust from the South Tower collapse still cover lower Manhattan.

The dust was three to four inches thick. Coming down no one ran. We were walking at a decent pace. One of the firefighters yelled that the South Tower fell. What are we waiting for?

Outside, we were standing under the North Pedestrian Bridge. The floors of the North Tower started to blow out. We all ran north. As we ran past the telephone building, the cloud hit us. We dove on top of each other. There might have been six of us on top of each other. After seven or eight seconds, the noise stopped. Most of us made it to safety. Those who ran south or west didn't make it.

After the cloud lifted, we went back to look for the lieutenant. He was killed. He had stopped to talk with someone in the lobby as we were exiting.

I finally left the scene at 11 P.M. I didn't go home until Friday. Our rig was destroyed. We received a replacement rig on Friday. They found our apparatus buried 35 feet below the ground on September 22.

At least four probies from my class were killed: Chris Santora, Engine 54; James Pappageorge, Engine 23; Dennis O'Berg, Ladder 105; John Tierney, Ladder 9. The next probie class was released before 9/11. Apparently, six probies were killed from the class that was appointed on May 6, 2001.

FACT

A FIFTH ALARM
calls for a minimum of
18 ENGINES, 7 TRUCKS, & 5 CHIEFS

On 9/11, 3 FIFTH ALARMS were
called in the first few minutes

***EDITOR'S NOTE:** In the following interviews, there are many references by firefighters who worked at the World Trade Center site to the debris left by the collapse of three buildings as "the pile." These references are in no way meant to be derogatory. We refer to the area as the World Trade Center or site.*

Direct Attack

Chief Joseph Pfiefer
Battalion 1, Lower Manhattan

now Assistant Chief, Counter Terrorism & Emergency Preparedness

I was with Engine 7, Ladder 1, Ladder 8 and another engine. It was a gas leak in the street, it was Church Street and Lispenard. The meters went off. They called Con Ed. Everything was checked. It was basically routine on a nice, sunny morning. I had one guy from a film crew riding with me. They were doing a documentary on the probie in Ladder 1. They had been there for weeks, whenever the probie worked.

We're standing in the street. The gas leak's all over and then we hear a plane going over, a very loud plane, which you never hear in Manhattan. We all look up and we see this commercial airliner flying by very low. We follow it and it goes right into the Trade Center. You could see it didn't veer off. It appeared to aim at the Trade Center, smashed into the upper floors, created a big fireball and then disappeared into the building.

I jumped in the car. Everybody else got into the rigs. I transmitted the second alarm for a plane into the World Trade Center. Twenty seconds after that, I transmitted a third alarm. I asked for the second alarm to report into the Trade Center and for the third alarm to stage at Vesey and West. I told them at that time it was a direct attack. 10 Engine came on after that. They were in quarters. They heard it too and then after I gave the second, they gave a verbal.

Traveling down West Broadway, we have a direct view of the Trade Center. We didn't have fire showing at that time. When I pulled up, which would have been on the west side of the building, I got out of the car and looked. There was no fire and there was no smoke at that point, at least from that view.

We walked in. There was glass, all broken, and there were a number of people burnt in the lobby. I went over to the command post and they didn't have exact information. They were estimating from calls somewhere around 78. But that was just speculation. The elevators were out for the most part. I sent companies to double-check that. That was also confirmed by the control panels.

(Deputy) Chief (Peter) Hayden came in just four minutes behind me. The game plan was to pair up the engines and to only take half the amount of hose. This way we could switch back and forth. And the trucks to get me some information. The plan was to do a rescue because we knew we had a lot of people trapped above, and people trapped in the elevators.

The First Division aide brought in the command board. Joe Callan, the citywide tour commander arrived. That was all officers taking part in directing people and keeping track of people. I sent chiefs up, the supervisors. We knew it was a long walk. If you average a minute a flight, it's going to take over an hour to get there. I got a report that the B stairs were crowded with people and some switched over to the C stairs.

Then what we heard was the jumpers actually hitting the canopy, which was where the battalion car was parked. A number of times, I had to send my aide out to the car to get a radio or turn on the repeater radio. The tracer has a repeater radio which operates on Channel 7 on our handie-talkies and we attempted to use that. I attempted to use that with (Battalion) Chief (Orio) Palmer. We tried to communicate to each other, since we were very familiar with the system and that failed. It did not work. We've done that before. We've discussed personally high-rise operations communications and so on. We've talked this through long before this and practiced it and tried things out, but it didn't work. Because that was going to be the command channel.

With any high-rise, you get some communications and you miss some. There were messages, urgent messages of firefighters having chest pains as they went up, but there wasn't a lot of need for handie-talkie communication because there wasn't any information to be passed either way. A number of times, we tried to contact people and we had difficulty. Then other times there was no problem, which was the typical high-rise. There was a lot of noise, but the Trade Center had a big lobby, so we were able to deal with that.

You've got a bridge coming across West Street. Right there is the traffic circle and then right there in the middle is the canopy. That's a large area. We came in and parked right underneath it, so it was actually a very good spot for us.

The jumpers were hitting that, but it must be some sort of plexiglass because they didn't go through, but it made a very, very loud sound. It was a concern. There's nothing we could about it. We tried to contact

Greg Semendinger

The North Tower burns, generating thick, black smoke before the South Tower was attacked.

people on the PA system. Basically, we wanted people to know that we were coming up, not to jump and that we're going to try to get to them. Obviously, the people on the floors where the plane hit, they were on fire. The choice was made for them, but we didn't want people to jump just because there's a little smoke there.

One of the things that really should be mentioned is that very early on, Mike Hurley, the fire safety director, asked about evacuating the other tower. I mentioned that to Chief Hayden and we both agreed that it should be evacuated. This is a matter of a couple of seconds. We told them to evacuate the tower and that was very early on, which proved to save a lot of people and that was way before the second plane hit.

We heard the noise. That was very similar to the other one, a very loud plane coming in, and then the explosion. I think we got the reports right away that a second plane just hit. That was almost instantaneous. At that point, Donald Burns said he would take command of the South Tower and Chief Palmer was going to go with him. I was going to stay with Hayden and Joe Callan and deal with the North Tower.

You could see some of the debris coming down into the plaza area to the mezzanine and then some stuff out on the street. But from our vantage point, we didn't have a great view, but we knew. Once they split, that became a separate fire. So we had two separate fires going. Somebody told me that they transmitted a fifth alarm for each, and then transmitted a second for Brooklyn. People confused which was Tower 1 and Tower 2. At one point, I wrote it on the desk.

There was a report of a third plane, but that really wasn't told too well to us and I couldn't get anybody to confirm it. That's when Chief Callan called people down. I was involved in a different part of the operation. I'm trying to get a hold of the helicopters and that wasn't working too well because I couldn't get an outside line or couldn't get through. I was trying to contact the police through the dispatcher, but we were having difficulty doing that.

Then, all of the people that came into the lobby left the lobby. They were going to set up a command post across the street, so a lot of our guys left. A lot of other people left. I'm not too sure what their reason was. Maybe they knew more than us. But the lobby kind of emptied out. Then the South Tower collapsed. Actually, let me just back up a second. My brother was a lieutenant at 33, and he reported in to me early on, on the second alarm. He came up to the lobby command post and we spoke a little bit. I told him what we knew and he didn't say much. He just gave me of a look of a real concern and then he took his company upstairs.

We weren't getting any more companies in at that point. At that stage, the other command post was being set up, so things were kind of being filtered before it got to us. Then people were being moved into the South Tower and the Marriott. By the time we got that report, nobody else was coming in.

When the other building collapsed, we heard a loud, rumbling noise, very loud, and I kind of knew the building, so we were able to push around the corner to the entrance of 6 World Trade. And then what happened, the whole area, debris came in. You could hear the debris coming into the lobby and the whole lobby went black. And we thought – at least I thought – that perhaps the elevators collapsed because we did get reports of problems with the elevators, so

Firehouse Collection

AP Photo/Matt Moyer

(above) In contrast to the previous aerial view, this is the view companies would see as they approached both towers.

(inset) A photo of Fire Department Chaplain Father Mychal Judge outside of the quarters of Engine 1/Ladder 24. Engine 90, who was relocated, goes on a run. The Father was assigned to the Church located across the street from the firehouse. He parked his Fire Department vehicle inside the firehouse and ate his meals with the firefighters.

we thought that might have collapsed and exploded into the lobby, or part of the plane fell off and came in, or part of the upper structure something came down, but never did we think the whole building collapsed. We knew something collapsed, but we never thought the whole building came down.

Everything is black. You couldn't see the hand in front of your face. And we're not too sure who's alive with us at that stage, so we're calling out to each other to see who's here. I called for an evacuation. I was able to contact somebody on the upper floor, one of the chiefs, and I told him to evacuate. I said that a number of times.

Also right around that point, I'm not too sure if it was before or after, we found Mychal Judge, Father Judge. I grabbed somebody's flashlight. I removed his white collar, opened up his collar and I checked for his pulse, and I didn't find any. I knew he was gone. Now, one of the interesting things with him is that he really died praying. If you saw the tape, that segment, you could see his mouth moving and you could see him, you know, before this in the lobby with us, very intently praying, very worried, which is a little different from him. You would at least get acknowledgment as you walked by him. He wouldn't interfere, but you would get a nod or something. He was very focused and very worried, almost like he knew what was going to take place.

We weren't too sure if the bridge was still there, so I told some of the people, including Chief Hayden and Chief Callan, because I know that they had the priest and it's slow moving carrying somebody, I said let me see if the bridge is here. I walked across the bridge with my aide, the camera crew, an EMT lieutenant and somebody else. I went all the way across. We found out the bridge was there, and then I tried to radio back and there was no answer. I had promised that I'd let them know, so we walked all the way back across the same West Street bridge, and I was able to make verbal contact with them. I realized they went out one of the side entrances, a side window onto part of the plaza area and that wasn't the best place to be so we went back the third time across West Street.

There was nobody there at that point. We come out, we're all full of debris and we can't really see everything from underneath that bridge. All we saw was the debris, a lot of paper and smoke filling the whole thing. So even when we got out, we still didn't know that the building collapsed.

From there, we walked out into the corner by West and Vesey and went over to Chief (Sal) Cassano (citywide tour commander), and Chief Hayden came. I was told to set up a command post a couple of blocks away. But before anything could be done, we heard a rumbling sound again and then people yelling to run. We ran maybe 50 yards the most. It was less than 10 seconds. The camera guy went behind the truck and I came up after him. He was a little faster than me, he didn't have all that gear on, and I wound up laying across, protecting him, because he had no helmet or anything. Then the white dust cloud came, engulfed us, immediately followed by the street now becoming black. At that point, I thought it was going to be it. We could hear things crashing and steel smashing down all around us and everything's black and I thought we were just waiting for the squish at that point.

I was maybe 20 yards up Vesey Street toward the river. We were on the side of 3 World Financial. We didn't get far. It was complete silence. And with the cement debris, it was like the first snowfall. The sound you hear after a first snowfall, that quiet, very still quiet, that's what it was like. After everything collapsed and stopped banging and clinking, there was no sound. There was no sound on the radio. There was no sound in the street. It was just still.

Then it started to lift a little bit. We stood up, but couldn't see anything and then we hear pop, pop, pop. We hear gunshots and somebody yelling get down, get down. Now we figured we were being shot at. We tried to hide behind another car. We found out later a police officer was taking out a window. We noticed some law enforcement having a guy in handcuffs, so we figured that was the guy that was shooting. In reality, it wasn't. At that point, the cameraman went one way and I went back to the scene.

People slowly started to come back. Guys from home came in. Chief (William) Blaich, he came down. I worked with him. His brother Charlie, two deputy chiefs came in. He took a section. Larry Burns, who was a chief here, retired, he operated out of 10 Engine's quarters. Tom Haring, who was also another chief here, the deputy. Nick Visconti came. What happened, just geographically people sectored it off pretty much like the four sectors you see now on the maps, but it was sectored off more by the name of the chief.

I was on the north side of the West Street bridge. We were getting reports of Jay Jonas, his Maydays. He was very calm, I'm trapped in the B stairs fourth floor. The thing is he had no idea what took place. We tried from beneath to get to him through the parking garage and that was no good. We were going to go in through 6 World Trade and that wasn't really working too well. The best part was hearing him, that he got out. That was incredible. We were very frustrated in figuring out where he was.

I watched 7. At one point, we were standing on the west side of West Street and Vesey. And I remember Chief (of Operations Daniel) Nigro coming back at that point saying I don't want anybody else killed and to take everybody two blocks up virtually to North End and Vesey, which is a good ways up. And we stood there and we watched 7 collapse.

I also remember trying to contact my brother on the radio and not being able to do that and I figure he'll find me, I'm the guy in the white hat. It's a lot easier to find me than for me to find him. When that didn't occur, I wound up walking the site, looking for anybody from 33. The rig was intact on the corner, but I couldn't find him or anybody else from 33.

(Captain) Dennis Tardio was coming down the C stairs in Building 7. At about the 9th or 10th floor, he met my brother Kevin, who told Dennis you can't get down these stairs, there was all sorts of debris. He directed him to the B stairs and, according to Captain Tardio, they got out of the building and 30 seconds later it started collapsing. If they would have continued in the same stairs, there was no way they would have been out. I'm not sure if my brother stayed there a little longer and directed more companies along with his guys or he was doing what firemen do, make sure all the brothers get out.

You get that sinking feeling in your stomach. My wife's at home watching the whole thing on TV, knowing I'm there, seeing the towers collapse, and she wound up saying to my aunt that she's a widow. It was very traumatic for her. She was picking up my kids at school and she broke down crying because I couldn't get any word out to her. Cell phones weren't operating. I couldn't get a cell site. I didn't get her. I had to go through my aunt. I couldn't get my parents. It was just kind of hit and miss with phones lines until after 3 o'clock. I was able to get word out. It was very emotional when I came home because I had worked for 40 hours. I got home around midnight. It was very emotional, a lot of hugs and tears.

It's kind of strange, Ladder 1, Engine 7. We were the first ones there. Only 10 beat us in, by seconds, and we were just able to make it somehow. I had two buildings fall.

Right Next Door

Firefighter Tim Brown
Rescue 3, detailed as supervisor in operations at the New York City Office of Emergency Management (OEM), Manhattan

now retired

When the first plane hit, I was in 7 World Trade Center, on the third floor. I didn't hear it. The only reason I knew something was wrong was because the power went out for about three to five seconds. I knew that there was a major interruption of power, and the power came back up because it was rerouted automatically by computers.

People who were sitting next to the windows facing Tower 1 all stood up and starting running away from the windows. I yelled what's wrong, and they said a plane just crashed into the tower.

Some sort of minor panic evacuation occurred in the cafeteria. The one escalator down was loaded up. I pushed my way through the crowd down to the lobby level, where I saw my boss, Calvin Drayton. He told me to go up to our office on the 23rd floor and make sure that the proper notifications were being made. We have a responsibility to notify a lot of agencies in a situation like this.

When I got up to the 23rd floor, I went to my desk and grabbed my police radio, fire radio and OEM radio. I went into our watch command, which is our communications center, to make sure they were prepared for the onslaught of calls we would be getting. I saw that the supervisor, Mike Lee, had things under control. I went into our emergency operations center to make sure that was being powered up. I ran into Mike Berkowitz, who is the supervisor in charge of that part of our operation. He said he had the manpower he needed to get it up and running.

I took the elevator back down to the lobby and proceeded to Vesey Street. There was a lot of debris and stuff burning in the street. I went to my car. I opened my trunk and took off my jacket and threw on a Mayor's Office jacket and a helmet and boots, and went back to the corner of Vesey and West Broadway, where I saw our Car 2 there, an inspector from the police department and (OEM Commissioner) John T. Odermatt. He was going to stay there at the exterior command post, which was the police command post. I told him I was going to meet Car 3, Calvin, at the fire command station in the lobby of 1 World Trade Center. I wanted to get a three-sided view of Tower 1 before I went up, so I ran into the plaza level and saw tremendous destruction. I saw a lot of stuff on fire. I saw plane parts, building parts, bodies – a very war-like scene.

Going toward the fire command station in number 1, I went by the escalators, which were loaded with many people evacuating the building. It was very orderly. Nobody was panicking. People were helping other people. These people were all healthy, they were not injured. They were getting out under their own power.

I went down a level, from the plaza level to the lobby level of 1 World Trade Center, where the fire command station was located. I ran into about a group of about 30 or so firemen. In that group, I saw my friend Terry Hatton, the captain of Rescue 1, who saw me and motioned for me to come over. I went over to him and gave him a hug, and he said I love you, Brother, it might be the last time I see you. We hugged, I kissed him on the cheek and he went into the stairwell. The other person I remember seeing there was Chris Blackwell from Rescue 3. I went over to Chris and he said to me Timmy, this isn't good. I said I know, Chris, be careful. I kissed him on the lips because that's what we always did to shock other people. It was the last time I saw Chris.

Then, a firefighter came into the lobby of number 1 and told us the second plane had hit. I didn't hear anything. Calvin told me to go to number 2, get with the command post there and help the fire department with their command and to let him know everything that was going on.

I went out through a broken window to the West Street side and ran as fast as I could. There was a lot of stuff crashing from above. At that time, I didn't know what a lot of it was, but apparently, some of it was people jumping. I ran down the West Street side and ran around to Liberty Street side and ran into number 2. The first person I saw in there was (FDNY Assistant Chief) Donald Burns. I asked him if there was anything I could do. He just gave me a poker face, as if to say you

Greg Semendinger

The South Tower collapses, spreading smoke and dust throughout lower Manhattan.

and I aren't going to be able to handle this. He said he already had a fifth alarm ordered for this building and we would have to wait for the troops to arrive so we can start helping these people.

I ran around the corner. Somebody grabbed me and told me there were people trapped in an elevator. I went around to where the elevators were and the hoistway door was open and I could see that about two feet of the car was showing from the top. I could see legs, I'm guessing about eight people. The elevator pit was on fire, so I started screaming at the Port Authority folks to get fire extinguishers, which we had difficulty doing.

As firemen started showing up in the lobby, I asked them to bring in their extinguishers and they started trying to put that fire out. I ran into Mike Lynch from Ladder 4, who I know is a young, very competent guy, and I said to Mike take care of this. And Mike said I got it, Timmy, go.

I went back to where the command post was in Tower 2 and the command board was not set up yet. I decided to go to the phones and try and call Washington to make sure we were getting air cover. We were told over the OEM radio that there was a third plane inbound for us and that we should be prepared to get hit again.

I was on the phones trying to call Washington, but I couldn't get through. The operators told me that the Pentagon had also been hit. Then I got in touch with SEMO, the New York State Emergency Management Office, in Albany and asked them for help. They said they were already in the process of getting us help from the military.

I went back to the command board, which was now being set up on the Liberty Street side of 2 World Trade Center, inside the lobby next to the doors. Now, civilians coming down in the stairwell were more severely injured. They were burned and bloody and broken, so we knew some of these people were coming down from those floors that were affected by the crash.

I got word back on my OEM radio that the

third plane was no longer inbound, that it had crashed and so that all gave us a sigh of relief. I noticed that the lobby was beginning to fill up with civilians. It was beginning to impede the evacuation down the stairwells of other people and I knew that we needed to get the lobby cleared. I asked the Port Authority to take people who could walk underground to 7 World Trade Center, where we had established a triage area. I took it upon myself to go find EMS, which is a decision that saved my life. I told Chief Burns that that's what I would be doing. I went out the doors back onto the Liberty Street side. There was stuff crashing all around.

As I got just outside the doors on the sidewalk, Mike Lynch yelled my name out and he was out at 4 Truck's rig. He was a chauffeur and he was trying to get the Hurst tool off by himself, but it was difficult, so he yelled to me for help. I started running toward him to help him, but before I got over to him, a younger fireman got to him first and helped him, so Mike said nevermind to me. He was taking that Hurst tool back inside to try and force the elevator car down so he could get the people out. That rig was later found below grade; apparently, they found it three or four levels down, so that's where Mike was the last time I saw Mike alive. I had worked with him in Ladder 4. I was fortunate enough to be able to tell his family that I witnessed him saving those people in the elevator and I'm confident that they had time to get many of them out to safety before Mike was killed.

I ran out across Liberty Street as fast as I could, knowing that people were jumping and things were crashing down from the building above me. I ran over to the pedestrian bridge at West and Liberty, where EMS was beginning to set up their staging area. I ran into (Deputy Chief) Charlie Wells from EMS and I said to Charlie that we needed help inside of the lobby of 2 World Trade Center, there were a lot of injured people. So he said Timmy, just give me a minute to get a couple of guys together and then we'll all go back in together.

I stood there underneath the pedestrian bridge with them. He got two paramedics. They put their helmets on. They got their jump kit and their stretcher, and about two minutes later we were running back across Liberty Street to the southwest corner of the Marriott Hotel. We ran to the edge of that and I wanted to take them along the edge very close to the building so that we would be protected from any falling debris.

As we got to that corner of the Marriott, it was the Tall Ships Restaurant entrance. The doors were wide open. There were people inside. We ran along the edge, which would be the exposure-4 side of the hotel. Just as we rounded the corner to Tower 2 to go in the deeper sidewalk – Tower 2 was set back farther into the lot – there was a tremendous roar above us. There was no question what it was. It was very obvious that the building was collapsing.

I know I did not even look up. I spun on my heels and as I ran by everybody, running for my life, I yelled to Charlie and the other paramedics to follow me because I knew where I was going. Then I retraced my steps back to the entrance of the Tall Ships Restaurant and ran into the lobby, hoping that this building would protect us.

As I ran into the lobby, it was crystal clear. And about two seconds later, it was pitch black. There was tremendous dust, tremendous wind blowing at me. People started to scream and the noise kept getting louder and louder. I knew I could not continue running forward, so I turned around again and started running back to the entrance where I had come in, but I realized I could not go out in the street because I would be killed by the steel that was falling. There was nowhere to run. The roar was getting louder. I couldn't see anything. I couldn't hear anything except the roar.

I got on my hands and knees and started crawling. I found a steel column and I knew that this would be my only hope. I grabbed onto the column, wrapped my arms around it as tight as I could and tried to become one with the column. This roar just seemed to keep getting louder and louder. The wind now was I'm guessing upwards of 75 miles an hour, maybe more. It was blowing my legs up in the air. It was hard to hold onto the column and not get blown out into the street. I lost my helmet. I lost my pager. I thought that this

Steve Spak

All that remains of the 22-story, 386-foot-long hotel is a small, three-story section after the second collapse. Note the debris on West Street.

would be my grave and I just sat there and waited to get crushed.

Surprisingly to me, the roar stopped. The wind slowed down and I began to realize that I was still alive. I still couldn't see anything. I stood up and started walking with my hands out in front of me toward what I thought was the entrance where I came in and I ran into a truck with its headlights on. And I still to this day do not know what that truck was. I thought that it was a box truck and the first thing that came to my mind was that it was a truck bomb, so I turned around and started running away from it yelling at everybody that it was a bomb, run the other way, it was a bomb.

So everybody started following me. There were I'm guessing 30 people around me as we began to be able to see a little bit. We ran into a rolldown gate, which I later heard had separated the restaurant from the hotel and that's the rolldown gate that they pulled down when the restaurant closed. The gate was down. We lined up on the gate and put our fingers under it and tried to lift. We got it up about two inches and then all these fingers came from the other side. There were people trapped on the other side of it. I was told that it was 131 Truck on the other side because they gave the same story I did.

We lifted the gate maybe two feet. From behind us a girl said we found a way out, follow us, so we all turned around and started following her. And this is still fright mode where everybody is still in shock and panic. There was a fireman outside on top of the rubble yelling to us to follow him, that he was outside and he knew where we could go to safety. Eventually, they got that rolldown gate up. It's not clear to me, but I think that when I left, it was up two feet and I heard that that is how they escaped. They came out and followed us out.

We ran out across the rubble toward West Street. I continued across West Street until I got to the World Financial Center. I wanted to get to the river and as far away from these buildings as I could. I tried to break through a glass door that was locked and I couldn't break through it. I had no tools. I was trying to throw a chair through it, but the glass was too solid.

At this point, I could hear my boss Calvin on the OEM radio calling for help and that brought me back to reality. I went back out onto West Street and ran north along West Street over all the rubble. I communicated with Calvin on the radio, I kept asking him where he was. I started to get a general idea where he was, so I started running north on West. I ran by Chief Feehan (First Deputy Commissioner William Feehan), who was standing amongst the rubble. I shook his hand when I ran by him and he told me to be careful.

As I ran north on West Broadway, people behind me started to scream, and I turned around and looked over my shoulder and watched as Tower 1 collapsed, knowing that my friends Terry and Chris and a lot of the guys were in there. We continued to run north because we didn't know how far that building was going to fall toward us. We were at West Broadway and Warren Street. Now it just became overwhelming emotionally. I was watching my friends die.

The Phone Calls Never Stopped

Dispatcher
John Lightsey
Manhattan

I began work at 7 A.M. That morning I was assigned to the Voice Alarm position. It had been quiet. There were a few EMS runs. At the same time Battalion 1 called on the radio the quarters of Engine 10/ Ladder 10 called on the voice alarm.

A light came on indicating their units and a tone went off. They said a plane hit the World Trade Center towers. Transmit the box (send a full first alarm assignment of at least three engines, two ladders and a battalion chief). Over the radio, Battalion 1 transmitted a second alarm (four engines, two ladders, deputy chief, battalion chief and numerous special units). The telephones started to ring. Chief (of Department Pete)Ganci responded and ordered a fifth alarm for a confirmed plane crash.

We looked at the board and map. We drew a line across 125th Street. We sent most of those companies to the fire. Brooklyn told us that they were sending a second alarm to a staging area near the Brooklyn-Battery Tunnel. We weren't concerned at that moment with relocations [sending one company from an outlying area to cover an empty firehouse near the incident].

When a second fifth alarm was ordered, we used a lot of companies from outside of Manhattan. We took the numbers and started assigning them. The incoming phone calls never stopped.

Two supervisors came in. I was switched to the radio position. It was non-stop between units calling on the radio and getting messages to broadcast. I was on the radio when a third fifth alarm was transmitted. I was very surprised to hear all the alarms being requested.

Once the second plane hit, it became long and drawn-out process. The South Tower collapsed. One of the Marine companies reported a major collapse. I stayed on the radio until 6 P.M. It was amazing that there was that amount of manpower that responded right away.

Dispatcher
Tyrone Connell
Manhattan

Flowers sit atop the bumper of Ladder 24. A civilian had left a message in the dust on the rig.

AP Photo/Amy Sancetta

That morning was my first day on the Manhattan radio. I had been in radio class. I heard Battalion say they had a plane into the Trade Center and transmit a second alarm. I looked around the office and asked if everyone else heard the same thing I had heard? They said yes.

A 10-60 was requested. Every car responding had a message. I switched to the alarm receipt dispatcher position. People calling in were asking advice. It seemed like they all called from above the 85th floor. I told the people to stay where they were; firefighters were on the way up.

When a person called I asked what room they were in and what side of the building that room was located. Most people were calm. One man called four or five times, he said he had a wife and three kids and didn't want to die. All the people wanted to know what to do.

The 911 phone lines, the tie lines with other agencies were all constant. After the second collapse, other people in the surrounding buildings were calling. People in the subways were reporting smoke.

You've Got What?

Firefighter John Jermyn Ladder 77, Staten Island (responded from near the Fire Museum in SoHo)

now retired

I was working light duty at the Fire Museum. I live in Staten Island. The Staten Island Ferry left at 8 A.M. and arrived at 8:30. It was a beautiful day. I took the subway up to Varick and Houston streets. As I reached the top of the stairs, I heard a woman say look at the fire. I said when did that happen? She said two to three seconds ago after the impact of a plane.

I was about one mile north of the Trade Center and I could look directly downtown to it. I could see a crater about 15 stories high. A gigantic fire ball was emanating from the building. You were thinking it was a small plane accident, but I knew it was a terrorist attack. I had responded there in 1993 for the previous attack. I thought what if they were successful in taking down the towers.

I called the fire dispatcher. The call got routed to another borough like Brooklyn or Staten Island. I identified myself, who I was, where I was. The dispatcher said, where are you? What did you see? Apparently the dispatcher did not have this information yet. I said this is major fire! A plane hit the upper floors of the North Tower! There is major impact of the North Tower. You are going to need a lot of units.

At that time I could hear the sirens from Engine 24 and Ladder 5 as they responded from their firehouse around the corner. I signed in at the museum. I had my fire gear and I thought it was going to be a huge incident and that there would be a recall of off-duty members. I called HQ and spoke to Fire Safety Education and Ladder 77. I told them of my intentions of going to the scene.

I drove a van downtown. As I passed Ladder 8, I stopped and picked up two to three firefighters. I arrived near the North Tower. The firefighters wanted to jump out. I said find your company or a battalion chief, don't just run in. They agreed and got out.

I was there in 1993 and remember the rigs were bumper to bumper. I said at the end of the day I'll have to drive the van home, so I drove north on West Street to a clear spot near Chambers Street. As I was leaving the van, Engine 220 was passing by. I used to be assigned to the ladder in the same quarters. One of the firefighters yelled for me to go with them. The covering captain put me on the

Ladder 3 (near right) and Rescue 1 (partially obscured) were destroyed where they were parked near the North Pedestrian Bridge.

Steve Spak

riding list. He said you have to stay with me.

I had missed the impact of the second tower. The guys filled me in. We were instructed to report to the command post of the South Tower. As we walked down West Street, there were a lot of jumpers coming down. We wound up in the middle of the street between Engine 10/Ladder 10 and the Deutsche Bank (Bankers Trust). The Captain said where is the command post? I said we walked past it on West Street. At that time we heard the pancaking of the South Tower collapse. Floor by floor. Thump, thump. I didn't look up. I knew what it was. I said you are not going to escape this.

The building was a quarter-mile high. Everybody started to scatter. The captain ran to the Deutsche Bank, the company followed. We made it under an overhang, but we were still outside. I wedged myself between beams on the exterior of the building. I figured that the tower was going to hit the Deutsche Bank and I would be gone.

In the dust cloud that followed, I had my mask on. I couldn't see or hear anything. I was anticipating a blast of energy in my face, but didn't experience it. The feeling I had was whether I was alive or dead. I heard a voice of the captain and one firefighter calling for the forcible entry tools to take out a window of the bank building. I was very happy to be reunited with them. We were in a protected area.

A janitor opened a door and you could see light into a loading dock. He gave us bottles of water. A few other firefighters were there. Some were injured, others were bleeding from the head. We talked about what we were going to do. The captain was pretty much blinded. One firefighter said we should search for survivors. Someone said if the South Tower came down, the North Tower is going to collapse. We all agreed to retreat. If the North Tower was going down, we didn't want to be near it.

I asked the firefighter who was bleeding to follow us. As soon as we got outside he went another way. We left the building and went south on Washington, west to West Street and were in front of 75 West Street when the North Tower came down. We were about four blocks away when we heard it come down. I started to feel like I was going into shock. What I saw of the body parts and the jumpers coming down, I had to shut it out and have tunnel vision. I followed the captain and continued to operate. He maintained the integrity of the unit. Inside 75 West Street, I called my wife and gave her contact info for all the members. My wife called my parents to tell them I was still alive after the second collapse so my parents wouldn't worry. That was a great comfort.

We wound up by the marina and went aboard the Tender Smoke fireboat. I had my eyes washed out and was given first aid. We helped stretch a 3½-hoseline from the fireboat through the Winter Garden to supply hoselines. As we were stretching the heavy hose my back went out.

A firefighter on the boat wanted to know who was operating the hoseline. I followed the hoseline to see what was on the other end. On West Street, I was standing 25 feet above ground level and there was a ladder truck below me. Steel beams were strewn everywhere. I saw firefighters with a Stokes basket extricating Chief Al Fuentes, who was in bad shape. They took him to New Jersey.

Years later it made me feel good that someone survived. It was a miracle. A firefighter pulled into the marina with his own boat. He said this is the new Pearl Harbor, the nation is under attack.

I eventually went back to the museum. There was a foot of ash on the roof. It started right up. I reinjured old injuries. I went to the emergency room at Staten Island Hospital. They were ready for mass casualties, but nobody came. I received great care.

My career didn't end up they way I thought it would be. It took a lot of wind out of my sails. I'm involved with the WTC Monitoring unit. A lot of people are in bad ways. We meet to help support each other. Many guys retired before their time. I miss the job terribly, but I figure we all would go back if they could. It was a horrible day. I never thought the towers would collapse. I thought we were going to put the fire out like we always do.

(opposite) Firefighter Jermyn was with Engine 220 and was standing in front of the South Tower on Liberty Street when it collapsed. They ran under the overhang of the Bankers Trust high-rise.

Greg Semendinger

At A Complete Disadvantage

Deputy Chief Peter Hayden Division 1, Lower Manhattan

Chief of Department, (now retired)

I was in quarters. I was continuing on. I worked the night before. I was in my office when I heard a plane coming in low. I looked out the window. I really couldn't see anything because the building lines obstructed the view, but I heard the crash and I knew right away what it was. I heard the radio right away. I heard (Battalion Chief) Joe Pfeifer, who was already out on the box before I even got out of the office, transmit the third alarm for a plane hitting the Trade Center and he set up a staging area at West and Vesey. I yelled to my aide, Chris Waugh, let's go, and we started out down toward lower Manhattan.

We went down Broadway, then down Canal and onto West. I saw a large column of smoke surrounding the entire top of the building. I didn't see any flame. I didn't see any holes or anything. All I saw was the top portion of it covered in smoke. I asked to verify the assignment with the dispatcher. He alerted me that a third alarm was in. I think he was saying that some rescue was not available, and did I need a third one? I said send them.

We parked out on West Street by Vesey. We walked in. There was debris coming down. There were a number of people out in the street who were burned. The front windows of the lobby were all blown out, broken. It was chaos. When we were moving to the lobby, there was a lot of damage in the lobby, some people screaming. All the marble tiles were off the wall and smashed on the floor. The people who were burned were conscious and walking, but they were pretty badly burned.

I went through a door. I don't know why, but I came in through the door. I went to the left. When I went in, the lobby was to the left. I met up with Joe Pfeifer. He started to brief me on what he had. We already knew that the other plane had struck. And we went through the problem that we were having. They were trying to find an elevator that was working. We were trying to delineate what was going to be the attack stairs, what stage of evacuation have we gotten to, any reports of evacuation and what assignments were made. Port Authority officials were on the scene. We told them to begin evacuating not only the north tower, but the whole World Trade Center complex, start moving everybody out and away.

We were getting a number of reports of people burned in the upper floors. We didn't have any specific floors at that time. We had given out assignments to proceed no higher than the 70th floor. The plane supposedly hit the 80th floor. He said don't go any higher than 70. That's where we were going to set up our operations post.

There was a lot of discussion on what was operating in the building after the initial assignments. We found out there weren't any elevators working. Not too long afterwards, we found out we had no communications from the building either. We were really at a complete disadvantage. We had no elevator. We had no communication systems.

We were getting a number of distress calls, both from our dispatcher and from cell phones. As we got the distress calls, we were giving specific assignments, if it was a specific report of a floor, of somebody trapped, or if we didn't have that, we had companies coming in and we were designating a group of floors for them to search. For instance, a battalion chief and three companies, you do floors 21 to 25, make sure everybody's down.

A number of the ranking officers arrived on the scene in a very short period from downtown Brooklyn into lower Manhattan. There was a discussion early on about the necessity to establish a command post remote from the lobby command post. We felt it was not a very good area to be operating in the lobby, and we agreed to establish a command post at West and Vesey. Eventually, that's where the command post was established by the chief of the department and Commissioner Feehan. Chief Callan, who was the citywide tour commander, remained in the lobby with Joe Pfeifer and me. We manned the lobby command post and directed the operations from there.

Sometimes I'd say Joe, get a company and send them up there. Some orders I gave out specifically. I don't think there was any set order in how it was done. We used the B stair as the main approach to be our attack stair. That's what we were using to gain access.

We had switched to a command channel, but I know there were reports, particularly from

David Handschuh

View from the street after the second jet hit the South Tower. Steel and debris erupt out of all sides of the tower. The hotel is at bottom left.

companies who were operating on the lower floors, that they had trouble getting some of the reports. Obviously, as they got higher, communications were becoming more and more difficult. I think that the highest level we had any reports from was somewhere in the low 50s.

We heard Maydays after the collapse of the South Tower. When the second plane hit the South Tower, we felt it. We didn't know what it was right away, but then somebody told us that a plane hit the second tower. We started calling everybody down in the North Tower after the second plane hit. We recognized the possibility of a collapse, but our thought process was that there was going to be a partial collapse, a gradual collapse after a couple of hours of burning, and we thought we had time to complete the evacuation and get everybody out.

We made a conscious decision early on that we weren't going to try and put the fire out, for a number of reasons. One, there was too much volume of fire. Second, the building systems were probably not functional. We had too many distress calls coming in. We didn't think the standpipe system was even going to be intact up there. We had to forgo the whole idea of trying to put any fire suppression efforts in there. This was strictly a search and rescue operation.

When the second plane hit the South Tower, Chief Burns left the lobby of the North Tower and went over to assume command of the operations in the South Tower. Only a few short minutes after that occurred, we felt it was wise for us to start evacuating this building and we started calling our people down, which was probably about 25 minutes before the North Tower collapsed.

When the South Tower came down, we didn't know specifically what it was. It was certainly a large event, let's put it that way. We knew something had happened. We didn't know whether it was an explosion. We didn't know if there was a partial collapse outside. I don't think anybody knew what happened, but certainly, if you were in the lobby of the North Tower, you were covered in debris.

We were covered in blackness. There were a couple of people killed. Father Judge was in the lobby. He was killed. We knew that some very calamitous event had just occurred. At that point, there were Maydays being given and orders to evacuate the North Tower, everybody out, but we had been doing that for 25 minutes. We had been telling guys to come down to the lobby. We realized nobody on the upper floors could hear us, but we were waiting for them to come down. But there still were civilians coming out of the building too at that time.

We started ordering guys down, but at one point later on, I was talking to Chief Downey about collapse. I remember the conversation well. I was saying the guys are not coming down. We're calling guys down, but they're not hearing us. Everybody was very concerned. We wanted to just get everybody down.

We had about 25 elevators. It was a mess. That was the only way to describe it. We knew we were in very deep trouble. They wanted to limit the number of people going in, but we lost control with that because of the off-duty guys coming in and going up

To establish a presence after the two collapses, Hayden climbed onto a rig. He had firefighters take a moment of silence. Accountability was achieved, orders were given out and control was regained.

Bill Bennett

the stairs. Our main focus was to answer the distress calls, to keep getting people coming down the stairs. But we started calling guys down – come on down, that's enough, especially after the second plane hit.

We were under attack. We knew we were in trouble, so we started calling people down. We had a report from OEM that there was possibility of a third plane coming in. That really put the antennas up for us because, number one, if a third plane does come in and hits these buildings, they're coming down for sure. Before we had the partial collapse, we were aware that timewise we thought we had a couple of hours. I think everybody envisioned the idea we're going to get everybody down and back everybody out a few blocks and watch this event, the top 15 or 20 floors fold in. That's what we thought. It didn't happen that way, though.

After the South Tower came down, it was about 15 minutes before you could see anything. You were in darkness in lower Manhattan. It was unbelievable. I went back out to see what the lobby was like and see if we could get out the front door, and I couldn't see anything. There was a lot of debris in the lobby. Then there was a fireman there, and a victim. And when we got a closer look at him we realized it was Father Judge.

Some of the guys picked up Father Judge and carried him up the escalator and out onto the mezzanine level, then out into the walkway. We walked around the outer area of Building 6 on the mezzanine level. We went down the escalator walkway down on Vesey Street. We carried Father Judge down there, then we turned him over to some firefighters and EMS. Then I walked back with Chief Callan. We walked back down Vesey, and I met Chief Cassano and a number of other chiefs at West and Vesey who had all assembled there thinking that's where the command post was. But we didn't find the command post and somebody said it was down farther on the other side of the overpass.

There was quite a bit of debris, quite a bit. We started walking south toward the overpass with Chief Cassano and we were a little bit north of the overpass when the North Tower came down. It sounded like a jet roar. You couldn't run far enough or fast enough. There was a fire truck there. I got down on my hands and knees and I crawled underneath the fire truck.

I didn't get hit with anything. The rig got hit with quite a bit of debris, but it didn't collapse. You saw the stuff raining down onto the sidewalk. And then it stopped, and it was once again deadly quiet. You couldn't see your hand in front of your face again. I crawled out and I could hear voices again trying to regroup and everything. It was a good 10 minutes, I think, before I could really see anything clear what was going on. It was unbelievable, the devastation. West Street didn't exist anymore. It was just covered with debris. The overpass that we were just standing by was completely collapsed and destroyed. Everything was completely down.

We went back to the tactical channel and there was a lot of radio traffic, all kinds of calls for help and Maydays, but nothing specific, not general locations. I went over to West and Liberty and I started working from that sector. Chief Cassano stayed up by West and Vesey. I came down around West and Vesey and I met up with Charlie Blaich, who was already working over there. Charlie and I worked with Chief Mosier, who also showed up.

We had a good fire in the building at 90 West. We had the equivalent of a fourth-alarm fire in there. We had fire in 50 and 7 World Trade Center. We had a smaller fire in one of the apartments in Battery Park City that we dispatched companies up there to put out.

We had a water supply problem because I remember the water main was broken. To get water over in our sector over there at West and Liberty, we got one of the fireboats to draft for us. It turned out it was the retired *John J. Harvey* that started drafting for us. When somebody told me the *Harvey* was pumping water, I said the *Harvey*? Thank God it was there because it pumped for us for about three to five days.

Chief Mosier took the operations in 90 West. I gave him X amount of companies. I said just hold it, keep her from jumping the street. The Marriott Hotel was across the street. I said just don't let it get out of the building here, just try to confine it, and he did a great job up there. They got some lines. They were able to hold it and contain it.

There were a lot of damaged apparatus there that were covered. We tried to get searches in those areas. By now, this is going on into the afternoon, and we were concerned about additional collapse, not only of the Marriott, because there was a good portion of the Marriott still standing, but also we were pretty sure that 7 World Trade Center would collapse. Early on, we saw a bulge in the southwest corner between floors 10 and 13, and we had put a transit on that and we were pretty sure she was going to collapse. You actually could see there was a visible bulge, it ran up about three floors. It came down about 5 o'clock in the afternoon, but by about 2 o'clock in the afternoon we realized this thing was going to collapse. Probably why it stood for so long was because it took a while for that fire to develop. It was a heavy body of fire in there and then we didn't make any attempt to fight it. That was just one of those wars we were just going to lose. We started to pull guys back because we were concerned for their safety.

I was standing on top of a truck that was covered in debris. I got on top of the rig only to establish a presence there. There was a lot of confusion, a lot of chaos. That was my command post in that sector. I stood on top of the rig and people could see who I was, that there was a chief in charge and that people could come to me and I'd give them assignments. It worked. I didn't realize it at the time, but it worked. People could point, there's the chief over there, rather than out of all this chaos and destruction, where was there a command post? You couldn't even make out West Street. So I saw the rig. I got on top of the rig and I stayed there. Eventually, we got a bullhorn, a radio, and we were able to get some type of order in the assignments and what we were doing.

We tried to get some type of accountability. I gathered everybody around me. There were hundreds of guys and there was a lot of confusion. I had everybody take their helmets off for a moment of silence, and it calmed everybody down. Then, I said please assist the chief officers in getting some accountability here. Whether you're on duty or off duty, give them your name, your unit. The chiefs made up a list and I had started getting a list of who I had working on the site there, also. It was just an attempt to gain some kind of control. Once I had the moment of silence, then I started giving out the orders to everybody about what we're going to do. After that, we had some type of organization. That's the only way I could have done it. I couldn't think – I needed help. It was a desperate measure.

We had to pull everybody back from Building 7. It was very difficult. We had to be very forceful in getting the guys out. They didn't want to come out. There were guys going into areas that I wasn't even really comfortable with, because of the possibility of secondary collapses. We didn't know how stable any of this area was. We pulled everybody back probably by 3 or 3:30 in the afternoon. We said, this building is going to come down, get back. It came down about 5 o'clock or so, but we had everybody backed away by then.

At that point in time, it seemed like a somewhat smaller event, but under any normal circumstances, that's a major event, a 47-story building collapsing. It seemed like a firecracker after the other ones came down, but I mean that's a big building, and when it came down, it was quite an event. But having gone through the other two, it didn't seem so bad. But that's what we were concerned about. We had said to the guys, we lost as many as 300 guys. We didn't want to lose any more people that day. And when those numbers start to set in among everybody.

My feeling early on was we weren't going to find any survivors. You either made it out or you didn't make it out. It was a cataclysmic event. The idea of somebody living in that thing to me would have been only short of a miracle.

I just couldn't believe it. Two 110-story buildings gone. I'm in lower Manhattan and I can't make out streets or anything. Then, when I was assigned to start cleaning up, I thought where do we even begin? We couldn't even find the streets. They're in there somewhere.

First Due

Firefighter John Morabito
Ladder 10, Lower Manhattan, World Trade Center

Ladder 10 is located just south of Tower 2. We respond there about 600 times a year, mostly false alarms for smoke detectors. We also respond to stuck elevators, minor fires and medical emergencies. We had a high-rise drill on the 95th floor about two years before 9/11. We had a full first-alarm assignment, the collapse rescue and a squad.

For a response to the South Tower, we would pull up directly across the street. For a run in the North Tower, we would pull into the semi-circle in an alcove. Units would report to the command station. We would gather information and went up every time. Sometimes, we would respond for the same alarm box in the same day. The Port Authority always had personnel on the floors – always. We used to go to Buildings 4 and 5 quite a bit.

I came in and relieved the firefighter driving the night tour. At 8:46 A.M., I heard the first plane. I didn't think much of it. It sounded like a truck hitting a pothole. Covering Lieutenant Harrell asked if that sound was normal. The house watch yelled out, a plane just hit the Trade Center. Two firefighters jumped up from the table and ran outside. It was pitch black, debris was falling. We are really going to see some bad stuff.

I didn't know it was a terrorist attack or a commercial airliner. We saw people in front of quarters crouched down, looking up in shock. We physically yanked them into the firehouse.

As first-due Ladder 10 responded, a civilian ran out of the North Tower on fire. Two firefighters remove the injured man to an ambulance minutes after the first plane hit.

David Handschuh

I peeked outside without getting hit by debris. There was smoke blowing past the top of the South Tower. Flying past were papers, some were on fire. The debris was hitting harder. There were body parts in the street.

We got on the rig and responded west on Liberty Street. There was a woman halfway in a car. She couldn't get it in gear. A police officer tried to move it but it wouldn't move. I pushed the car out of the way and onto the sidewalk with the apparatus. I turned the corner towards the North Tower. You could feel the body parts under the tires.

Just short of the vestibule, a man comes running out of the building on fire. His eyes were black. He had no expression. A security guard with a jacket knocked him down to the ground. All the members went into the building.

I grabbed Terry Rivera, who rode with us. He asked what do I do, I don't have a mask. I said don't go into the building. Help me with this guy. I grabbed a burn blanket and an ambulance pulled up. The ambulance took him away. He suffered 85% burns. I think he survived.

I went into the foyer of the North Tower. Two elderly people were completely burned. Their clothes were burned off. She died. A firefighter used a water extinguisher to wet them down. An ambulance removed the bodies.

I heard the officer of Ladder 1 say check the perimeter. There wasn't much panic. I went to the command center in the lobby. They said the fire was on the 80th floor and above. I could see people still waiting on line for coffee near the South Tower. I told them to evacuate.

On the ground were wallets, plane tickets, purses and luggage. I went back into the North Tower to help people calm down and get away from the building. I heard someone say prepare for impact, there is another plane approaching. I said to another firefighter we are under attack. He said no kidding.

The second plane hit. I was near a revolving door. The lights inside the building flickered. I said we need to do this quickly, we don't know how many planes are coming in. I certainly didn't want to be in the tallest building in New York in a terrorist attack while people were aiming planes at it.

At that point, debris and jumpers were hitting people evacuating to the exterior. I took the first person in line and told them to go through the red doors. Two fire patrolmen and four cops were there. I told them to walk through the shopping plaza to Building 5 and then walk in the subway to Barclay and Chambers Street. Some people went down the escalators and some down the stairs. Some had been in the elevators when they stopped and some were burned or bleeding. It was organized chaos. They were following orders.

The lobby was filled with broken glass. One woman took off her shoes in the lobby. Now, there was blood and water in the lobby. People who worked in the building helped each other. I saw a man with a seeing eye-dog walking in circles. His regular routine was upset. I told two men to take him to the subway. I didn't know at any given point if there was going to be another attack or a collapse. I thought it would take 10 planes to bring down the building.

I saw Fire Commissioner (Thomas) Von Essen, a police chief and others conferring near the command post. That put me at ease. I saw Father Mychal Judge come into the North Tower. After awhile people stopped coming down from upstairs. I didn't know if I should go or stay. I heard Lieutenant Harrell call from the 17th floor. They were working their way up to 44. Apparently a man who came down from the upper floors reported he saw Lieutenant Atlas from Engine 10 on the 78th floor.

A woman went into the plaza. The lights went out. I heard her screaming. The South Tower came down. I felt the air rush at me. In total darkness I was hit by hot ash and debris. I got down on my hands and knees and was lifted off the ground. I was thrown through the air like a rag doll by the wind. I was in the air for two seconds. I crawled to a doorway and prayed to stay alive. After 11 seconds I could still see something there. I thought a train in the station with a nuclear explosion had blown up under me. I remember the air rushing past me and the percussion of beams falling down outside.

In complete darkness, I was unable to breath because of the dust in my mouth, nose and eyes. I quickly turned on my air cylinder after cleaning my facepiece. It was all filled up with stuff. I shook it out. Panicking I thought I was going to choke to death. Walking west to get out of the building, I passed security gates that were filled with debris. Turning right I saw bodies in front of the elevators. There had been 40 firefighters staging there for instructions. I couldn't find anybody in the darkness. I worked my way north.

I saw a 10-by-10-foot patch that was actually a window. Smoke was going out. The window was located near an escalator that was holding up debris. The lobby was four stories high. There might have been two stories' worth of debris in the North Tower. The South Tower basically fell west and south.

Following my flashlight, a lieutenant from Engine 5 came up the basement stairs with five people and ran out the window. I walked out to West Street and saw Engine 10 all covered by debris. I looked around for chauffeur, Danny Peritore of Engine 10. I didn't see him. I ran north to Vesey Street near the Verizon Building. An ambulance was rinsing out the eyes of firefighters. I was waiting my turn when the North Tower collapsed. The building tilted to the north and then the west. It then came down on itself.

The dust completely enveloped you. You couldn't see two feet in front of yourself. I layed down on the ground. Quickly the dust lifted. After that I thought I was the last person on Earth. There was complete silence. As the dust lifted you saw gray images. I was relieved to see people. I was about to give up. I looked for my brother who was working in Engine 228 from Brooklyn. They responded following Engine 205 over one of the bridges. Members from Engine 205 were all killed.

I walked to the site asking for Engine 228. I was told my brother's name was on the list of missing. If they couldn't account for you, your name went on the list. I was at Cedar Street and West Albany when I was getting a drink and saw my brother. We decided to stay together. My car was destroyed. It was parked at the corner of Greenwich and Liberty streets. The car was lifted up on a pile of debris 15 feet in the air. It was facing upward with the lights on. Other firefighters cars were pushed 60 feet down the street. I saw the windows in the rear of the firehouse were pushed out despite the fact they were wire enforced. They cracked, but didn't fall out.

There was a woman covered by a sheet lying in the firehouse. She apparently worked on the 105th floor and she fell from the building into the firehouse. Doctors were inside the firehouse cleaning eyes. The firehouse hallways were filthy. The two companies were going to be relocated, but that was stopped. Engine 10 and Ladder 10 were given the assignment to be trained in GPS operations. When a body part was found, the unit would be dispatched to the site, mark the coordinates, place the body part in a red bag and transport it to the temporary morgue. It became very traumatic.

Visitors to the city would come by quarters and ask questions since it was the closest firehouse to the site. I felt it a duty to the firefighters killed to speak to the visitors. Sometimes I spoke to 50-60 at a time. Dignitaries visited the firehouse. We hosted the President, kings and monarchs. Many of the members of Engine 10 and Ladder 10 now suffer respiratory illness. Most all are off the job. I am getting checked now.

Take Cover

Firefighter Mike Cancel
Ladder 10, Lower Manhattan, World Trade Center
now retired

The second hijacked jet approaches the South Tower at over 540 mph.

AP Photo/Carmen Taylor

Ladder 10/Engine 10 are located on the south side of Liberty Street across from Tower 2. Before the 1993 bombing, we would respond 15-20 times a day to the World Trade Center. After the bombing it dropped to four or five runs a day. Each building has an individual fire command station. I was working 24 hours. I went upstairs to wash up. I heard a boom. It sounded like a steel plate shifting in the street. John Schroeder yelled out that a plane just went into the World Trade Center.

People were already running into the firehouse. The overhead doors were open. I put on my gear. It was raining like snow, but it was flesh. The streets were covered. The housewatch called the dispatcher and said 10-60, major incident. We followed the engine. I noticed a burned civilian in the street.

As we arrived I looked up. I had the roof position. I saw 10 to 15 floors of fire. It was the most fire I ever saw. We walked into the lobby. I was the last one in. There were two people – a man and a woman – on fire, still alive. We used the water extinguisher and a CO_2 extinguisher to put them out. I told the chauffeur, John Morabito, to get EMS.

We took the B stairs and headed up. Hundreds of people were coming down. They were calm. We asked some of the civilians to help the injured downstairs. As we walked past, they wished us well and tapped us on our shoulders. We went 10 floors and took a break. We found some water.

When we made it to the 31st floor, the OV, Serge Pilipczuk, had chest pains. EMS had come up behind us, so they gave him oxygen. He gave his radio to the can man, Sean Tallon. The officer, Lieutenant Steven Harrell, Jeffrey Olsen, irons, and the can man, Sean Tallon, kept going upstairs. The radio repeater wasn't working. An FBI agent came by and said a second plane is coming, brace for impact. Over the handie-talkie radio, there is another plane, he's coming around, take cover. There was still a good volume of people traveling down the stairs. We went into the hallway and braced against a wall. We were aware that something hit. The other members of Ladder 10 made it to the 40th floor.

I was trying to reach the lobby to notify them of the member with chest pains when the building started to shake. We were being tossed around. I thought the building was going to come down. Someone said the South Tower came down. I said what do you mean it came down? There were frequent Maydays. Firefighters were down and trapped. After 10 minutes, the lights in the North Tower, which had gone out, had come back on. From the lobby we heard Mayday, Mayday, evacuate!

We could feel the building starting to twist above us. I called Ladder 10 three times. There was no answer. I said we have to evacuate, the building's coming down. Again, there was no response.

Peter Matthews

Division 6 from the Bronx was relocating to Division 3 in Manhattan when the South Tower collapsed. They were sent to the scene to re-establish radio communications. They set up a command post on Broadway near Park Row.

EMS went above us. Firefighters were still walking up the stairs. I said, didn't you hear the order to evacuate? Nobody heard the order. They looked at me like I was crazy. I said we have to go down. I got as many firefighters turned around as I could. I was pushing them down. I tried to call the lieutenant. The last time I heard him on the radio he said he was on the 40th floor.

I started to walk down with the OV. When we reached the third floor, there was a group of civilians who said it was flooded below, we can't get out. I went down to check. The door to the lobby was closed. There was some water. The lobby was dark. I called back up to the remaining members to come down. I said the first floor is clear. There were 8-9 workers that were lost in the lobby. The lobby was all blown out. Nobody else was in the lobby.

A group of 20 or 30 firefighters and civilians came down the B stairs. We met with building personnel. We looked south and saw all the rubble. All the glass was out in the lobby. I took them out through the windows to West Street. I didn't want anybody to get hit, so I said, look up, make sure you don't get hit. I had them stick to the side of the building. Ten feet away a jumper landed. I had heard that earlier a jumper struck a firefighter.

I took the Serge to Vesey Street to be treated by EMS. I found the chauffeur of Ladder 10. I said we have to find the rest of the company. John Morabito said he needed to find his brother who was a firefighter. I saw firefighters from Engine 10. I said we have to look for our guys. They were in shock. I said I'm going back to the building. Then it started to come down. I tuned around and started running towards the water front. A big cloud came towards me. I prayed to God, don't let it come to us. The wind changed and it blew the other way. I thought about putting Serge in an ambulance, now I think he is dead. It was snowing ash and dust. I saw Serge walking towards me like a ghost. He was not a ghost. I put him on a boat at the river to New Jersey.

We used to go to the Trade Center complex two to three times a day. We not only responded to the North and South Tower, but to all the other buildings, hotel and the subways. We used to respond to the mechanical rooms and the floor below the antenna, where radio stations were located.

A week or two before 9/11, we responded about 20 times during the week. Many of these runs wound up to be false phone alarms. I think we were being tested. There was a fruit vendor that used to sell fruit in front of the firehouse every day, every single day. On 9/11 he wasn't around. A few years later, when I was a fire marshal, I had to go to court one day. I had to run in for something. As I entered the building who did I see but the fruit vendor. I said to him, remember me? He was shocked that I knew him. I said wait here, I will be right back. A few minutes later when I returned outside, he was gone.

It Just Kept Coming

Firefighter John McGinty Special Operations Command, Roosevelt Island, East River

now Decon Operations

McGinty, get out here! I was in the locker room. They said a plane hit the towers, you've got to drive (Battalion) Chief (Ray) Downey. I grabbed my gear. Chief Downey said wait for (Battalion) Chief (John) Moran. We waited for him to load his gear into the sedan and headed out.

We took the Queens Midtown Tunnel, the FDR Drive and just as we got to the Brooklyn Bridge, the second jet flew overhead, hung a hard left turn heading west back towards the towers...I know I screamed. Chief Downey turned to Chief Moran, he said did you see that? And that's when he said, and I'm going to quote, "John, this is it, this is the big one." Now I believe that John was for John Moran, Chief Moran, but I'll take credit anyway.

I heard the second jet hit the South Tower, but between the radios and the cell phones ringing in the car, both chiefs didn't hear it. So I said Chief, they just hit that tower. That's when over the dispatch radio they said another jet had crashed into the south tower. Chief Downey said Car 40 Adam (radio designation for Doney's car), I suggest you transmit a fifth alarm for both towers. And I think he told me to slow down and calm down at that point because I was quite excited. It was pretty scary.

We proceeded southbound down the FDR through Battery City, Battery Park. Now we're heading northbound on the West Side. And as we got to about the midway point of the two towers on West Street, we saw the members of the command post heading southbound on foot. I pulled the vehicle to the side right by the island, stopped there and Chief Downey said I'll be over with Chief (of Department Peter) Ganci, get my gear out of the trunk and we're going to set up a command post over here, it looks like. It was on the west side of West Street, just south of the North Pedestrian Bridge. The police commissioner was there. The mayor was there. The fire commissioner was there. The chief of the department, Chief Downey and companies are starting to assemble there. They started to put together teams, lining the truck companies up, lining the engine companies up, just the manpower, no apparatus, to prepare them for some form of attack.

As they would show up, they'd say get on the back of this line with your officer in two rows; the truck guys were on the left side and the engine guys were on the right side. And it was pretty much everybody had that look in their face of, what do we do? I mean, there were a lot of people looking for advice there.

They were concerned that we had nothing going on in the South Tower and Chief Moran just said all right, I hope to see you later and headed off to the South Tower. About 10 minutes, 15 minutes into it, (Battalion) Chief (Charles) Kasper appears at the command post without any bunker gear or any radio or equipment. He came from home. He commandeered my handie-talkie, much to my chagrin. And he said that the SOC box truck would have gear for him, bunker gear, on Vesey and West. He said go get the gear and meet me in the South Tower, we got to set up a command post in the lobby of the South Tower. I went to the box truck, got it and proceeded to go south back to Liberty. I got to the South Pedestrian Bridge and debris was raining off that South Tower pretty fierce, balls of flame, people, concrete, papers, plane parts. Not a minute or two went by that someone didn't come out hitting the ground.

Incoming officers receive assignments at command post at Broadway and Park Row, east of the WTC site.

Peter Matthews

Peter Matthews

Firefighters attempt to maneuver through the debris field.

I got him a helmet and some bunker gear and I was going to go into the South Tower. I guess I would have been his aide, but I had no access to the South Tower because of the debris coming down off the south end of that building.

I made a choice to go through the Vista Marriott, which is at the southwest corner of the South Tower. I figured I would go through the bar on the corner, Tall Ships Bar, into the hotel lobby into a stairwell. If I get up a stairwell, get out on a fire exit, I can get onto the promenade level of the World Trade and I might have a shot of getting into it because I didn't feel I had a chance of making it in without getting hit by something from any other approach.

I decided I was going to go up the stairwell. I made it to about the third story and I heard what I thought was dynamite or C-4 or whatever. In reality, it was pancaking. The building was collapsing. But, because I'm inside the hotel, it sounded to me like they were detonating bombs. So I said it's time to get out of here.

I turned around. I started running back down the stairs. I got down to the lobby and. I was buried in debris somewhere in that hotel. Nothing too serious, duct work, tiles, Sheetrock. And it was pitch black, as black as you could possibly get, and a lot of dust. I had no mask, so it was all in my mouth, my nose. It was in my eyes and it was scary because not being able to breathe or see is usually pretty scary.

I got hit on the head pretty good. Actually, the first few times I stood up after the initial collapse, I fell down and I didn't know why, but it was just that my equilibrium was rocked and I just couldn't stand up. It was like walking on the side of a wall.

I got out from underneath the debris and there were some voices in the room and some guys had flashlights, so I knew I was with other firemen and I would guesstimate maybe about 14 other people in this area who survived. About six, seven firemen and maybe six or seven or eight civilians with them. And after a little while of searching around, someone found we were pretty much entombed. There was nowhere to go.

We all started banging and feeling around, and one of the firemen found a roll-down gate. He pushed it up and there was just a hint of light, and he says I think I found a way out. But we all single filed through a little narrow opening, like a cave almost, and it started lightening up. You still couldn't see. It was a white-out from all the dust blowing around.

We just kept following the light. We had to climb over this 30-foot pile of steel and rebar and beams and concrete and junk. I couldn't even make out anything other than pulverized stuff. And it got bright, like daylight bright, but white-out. We just continued moving and I ended out on Liberty Street. There was some open steel beams that we were walking over and you couldn't see into them. I would guess it was probably a garage down there, but everybody was, whoa, don't fall in between these beams. To survive that and then fall through them.

I got outside finally and I hear this PASS alarm. I kind of thumbed around and couldn't move any steel beams or anything like that. I couldn't find it and I walked away from a PASS alarm. That's something that's been haunting me quite a bit.

When I got to Vesey Street, it was by North End Avenue and I ran into Joel Kanasky over in Rescue 1. He was off duty, but he was in bunker gear. He was with a couple of other rescue guys and I said to them I drove Chief Downey, I'm his aide, have you seen him? And they said yeah, we saw him up on West and Vesey. And I said before or after the collapse? And they said no, we saw him after. I said are you sure it was after? Yeah. So I said all right, I'm going to go find him.

I found an abandoned mask. Someone dropped their mask and I picked up an axe and a six-foot hook and I headed eastbound on Vesey looking for Chief Downey. I wasn't even thinking of Chief Moran at that point, regretfully. That was kind of weird. You go on automatic, I guess. So I got to West and Vesey and I looked south and I saw the destruction. I saw the debris.

I took a quick look south, a quick look north, and the North Tower started coming down. You could hear the roaring of it. So this one I had a visual on unlike the south one, so I turned and I started running back towards the Hudson westbound on Vesey again and the debris started catching up to me. I had dropped the axe, dropped the hook, couldn't get the mask off because I had the hip belt on. The debris, like I said, was starting to pass me, it would fly by.

Over by North End Avenue on Vesey is a big office building with big, recessed glass windows down on the ground level, and I just jumped in and hid behind a cement column. I was hoping that it was not going to collapse too. I was trying to keep an eye out and a cop went flying by and I just reached out and grabbed hold of him, pulled him in. Now we're face to face and it was sheer terror to see his fear. It was like when things are happening, you just don't see it as much, but when you see someone else's eyes, it really explains to you, yeah, this is the end of the world. So once again my life passes before me. That was the second time. The first time it was when I was in the hotel when I heard the collapsing, which I thought was dynamite and my life passed before me. Now I said, oh, I'm not going to survive this one.

Then the debris turned into just wind and paper and dust. The two of us took a quick vote and said let's run for it and we did. We made it around to the west side of that building and I tried just to regroup.

All that stuff was just like a cloud. It was like a science-fiction movie, where this creeping, living, moving thing just kept coming and coming and coming. It was tough breathing. And then it was eerily quiet. It was weird. It was either the loudest thing in the world or it was weird quiet.

I wasn't sure what to do at that point, so I tried to get my eyes cleaned out. We assembled down by the river between Vesey and Murray, right on the river, right on the promenade. There were a couple of officers and they started taking names of anyone who was working. I guess they were going to attempt some sort of plan of attack.

After about 20 minutes, I decided to head back south right to the towers, to possibly help or find anybody. I found a radio in a crushed Suburban, so now at least I had a handie-talkie. There was a lot of screaming and yelling on the radio. I think it was about 6 Truck when they were stuck and how helpless I felt. But there was very little else from someone saying come get me or here I am – there was nothing. You stand there and you say oh, my God, everybody's dead. We gave up a lot of great guys there.

By now, 7 World Trade Center had been free burning for hours and hours. I was pretty aware that eventually it's got to come down. Nothing was going to withstand that. It was like the whole city was going to collapse.

You Could Hear The Roar

Citywide Tour Commander Sal Cassano Headquarters, Downtown Brooklyn

now Fire Commissioner

That morning, I was in headquarters in the command center. I was listening to the department radio, doing some administrative duties with Chief (Gerard) Barbara and Chief (Donald) Burns. And we heard on the radio transmit a second alarm, a plane had hit the World Trade Center. I was assuming different things, a propane explosion, anything, but the radio was blaring. Gerry and Donald both got up and started to move and I continued to listen to the radio, tried to get some more information.

Things started to perk up, so I decided I'd better head on over there. So I came in looking for (Chief of Department) Pete (Ganci) and they were already gone. I looked out the window. I could see smoke, heavy black smoke. And I just remember commenting to one of the chiefs who works here, Chief (Mike) Canty, I said, that's not an accident. On a beautiful day like today, a plane's not going to hit that building by accident.

Then I responded. I took a couple of EMTs who were responding from here with us and we got right to West Broadway and Vesey, right by 7, when I heard another explosion. I looked up and I thought it was a secondary explosion in the North Tower, but things started to rain down, so we dove into a garage until things calmed down. I didn't realize it was a second plane until I got back into my car and I said I'd better get out of here, this isn't a good spot, and I headed back north, went down Chambers to West and drove down a couple of blocks and parked my car. And then I got to the command post and Pete and Dan (Chief Nigro, Chief of Operations) were maybe inside the building. I didn't see them.

I got to the command post and then all of a sudden everybody started to come back to the command post. People were going to different spots and I was helping get the frequencies up working with Chief Galvin. We had sent them into the Marriott and communications were poor at that time. So I took a walk into the lobby of the Marriott to get phone numbers from the lobby command post and the lobby desk. I remember talking to the companies that were there and assigning the command post companies, to help Chief Galvin. Things were hectic.

I remember getting all the numbers and walking out of the Marriott, but on the Liberty Street side because there were some people jumping and some debris falling. I walked along Liberty back up to West and I met Commissioner (Bill) Feehan and Commissioner (Lynn) Tierney there. They didn't know what was going on. I directed them to the command post. I told them to walk across the street because there was a lot of stuff raining down.

Then we got back to the command post and there were still plenty of companies at the command post, but some of the companies that were there originally before I left were sent into the Marriott. I don't remember which companies they were, but I remember the roar of the South Tower and we all dove into that garage that we had planned on as our safe area right from the beginning. We stayed in there for a few minutes until it cleared up and then came outside again, and that's where I met Chief Ganci and Commissioner Feehan and I got the order to send everybody north and set up another command post. We were moving people north and Pete and Bill started to go south. They had heard people were trapped, so they went south. I started to move people north, telling them of the orders that the chief of department gave us, move people north, go up north.

Then I realized that we still had plenty of people left in the North Tower. We were trying to get Chief Ganci on the handie-talkie and I started making my way south to meet up with him, to go down there and help him command some of the operations down there. We had plenty of commanders going up north, so I said I'll walk south and meet up with him and maybe we can help out. I was just north of the north bridge and the north tower. And then I looked up and you didn't have to see it, you could hear the roar. It almost sounded like another plane was coming over. That's the kind of deafening roar it was.

I looked up and started running up north and I looked up again and I said well, I'm not outrunning this building. There was a rig somewhere on West

Steve Spak

Debris and damaged apparatus are parked north of the North Tower looking to the bridge at Chambers Street (white bridge), where a new command post was established after the second collapse. Chief Cassano dove under Rescue 3 (arrow) when the North Tower collapsed, saving his life.

Street and I dove under this rig. I just hoped that that one made it. I was lucky there. I got hit with some debris underneath the rig and I was just hoping that this dust and dirt would stop because we didn't have much breath left, anybody that was there. Once the dust and debris stopped, I tried to get up. I couldn't get up. My back was banged up real good.

I believe it was Rescue 3's rig, maybe Rescue 3's collapse rig and Rescue 3. I'm still not sure. Then they carted me off to St. Vincent's Hospital. I stayed up there for a couple of hours, got x-rays and then I came back to work, came back to headquarters and stayed here and helped out here.

Early on, Chief Nigro was still down at the scene, and when I came back from the hospital, we had a meeting, I'd probably say around 6 o'clock that night. We had a meeting with (Deputy) Commissioner (Thomas) Fitzpatrick, (Assistant) Commissioner (Thomas) McDonald, (Assistant) Commissioner (Stephen) Rush and we started working on tools and equipment and apparatus right at that point. We had put in calls for Seagrave and different manufacturers of apparatus and started to put them on alert that we would probably need some rush orders on apparatus and the same with tools. Not much later than 6 o'clock we were doing that. We knew we had lost a lot of equipment and that we had lost rigs, but it took us a couple of days to get a handle on which rigs we had missing.

FACT

OVER 400 FIREFIGHTERS were initially listed as MISSING; 606 CHILDREN of firefighters were left FATHERLESS

Start Getting Out Of Here

Firefighter Peter Blaich Ladder 123, Chinatown, Manhattan (was in Engine 9 on 9/11)

now Lieutenant, Ladder 2

I came in for the day tour, so I got there about 8 o'clock and relieved the guy on the backup on the engine. A fireman, Ray Hayden, was actually standing in front of quarters and he saw what he thought was a small plane and then an explosion right into the North Tower. You could just make out the tips of the towers from the firehouse on Canal Street, so he got everybody in the house on standby and we were waiting to be dispatched. Then, at that moment, it flashed on the news that the North Tower was on fire. We weren't dispatched yet, but Hayden turned everybody out. We took the satellite because we had the satellite with us. 6 Truck went. 9 Engine went and Satellite 1 went.

You could see the top of the North Tower still, a lot of fire and a lot of smoke. As we got closer towards the towers, I lost the view I had from the cab of the engine. It was blocked out by the other buildings. Engine 9 pulled up on Vesey and West Street, and the satellite was behind Engine 9 and in front of 9 Engine was 6 Truck.

As soon as we pulled up, I remember getting off the rig and Lieutenant Foti from the engine said everybody grab an extra bottle along with our rollups. He's a captain now, he was promoted after 9/11. Then he told me to take the life-saving rope and try to keep that with me as long as I could because we had jumpers at that point.

So I had the rollup, I had an extra bottle, I had the life-saving rope and then I remember looking up and seeing the first body hit one of the lower towers in the complex. And then I saw another body land not too far in front of us, right on the hood of a car. I had never imagined seeing anything like that, ever.

We proceeded into the North Tower. All the windows were blown out, and there were one or two burning cars outside. And there were burn victims on the street. We walked through this giant blown-out window into the lobby. There was a lady screaming that she didn't know how she got burnt. She was just in the lobby and then next thing she knew she was on fire. She was burnt bad. And somebody came over with a fire extinguisher and was putting water on her.

In front of one of the big elevator banks in the lobby was a desk with the corpse of a security guard. The elevator bank was melted, so I imagine the jet fuel must have blown right down the elevator shaft and I guess caught the security guard at a table.

Chief Pfiefer was just setting up the command post. It was us, 1 Truck, 7 Engine, 6 Engine and 55 Engine. Chief Pfiefer told us and 6 Truck to stay

A firefighter from Ladder 113 looks for falling debris as mobile emergency room vehicle burns after the South Tower collapses.

Todd Maisel

together and to start making our way up the B stairway, which was the attack stairway. As we got to the third floor of the B stairway, we forced open an elevator door which was burnt on all three sides. The only thing that was remaining was the hoistway door. I didn't recognize them initially, but a guy from 1 Truck said, oh, my God, those are people. They were pretty incinerated. I remember the overpowering smell of the jet fuel.

We figured the South Tower got hit as we got to the fifth or sixth floor. I remember the whole North Tower literally vibrated. The only way I can explain it is if you were at the edge of a subway platform and the train was coming in, you felt that wind and the sound, but with an added effect like the floor vibrated. Everybody just cringed and really was not sure what was going on. I just assumed that it was something above us. I had no idea that the South Tower was hit.

At one point in the B stairway, there were still civilians coming down and we were going up. and I couldn't believe how small the stairways were. I thought in the Trade Center, you'd have these huge stairways that you could fit a truck up. Every time a civilian came down, with the rollups and whatever extra tools you were carrying, you always had to turn to the side so they could pass you, and a lot of them needed help down so you would put your stuff down and help them down to a floor or two to another fireman, and then you'd go back, try to catch up with your company and make the walk back up.

When we stopped on the 12th floor and moved, there was like a mass of civilians coming down. When we moved them over to the A stairway out of the B stairway, that definitely helped because after that point it flowed for us going up because there were no more civilians at that point coming down. And it had to definitely help the civilians get out of the building faster.

We proceeded up to as far as the 25th floor. When we got there, it was that same effect, like being on the subway platform, but you could tell like that something was really wrong because we heard windows blowing out on our floor. I remember looking at the top of the door, it crimped in. I was thinking that can't be structurally good. It was almost like at that moment the door wanted to get sucked out of the building.

That was the first time also that we encountered a smoke condition. We had to force open the door on the 25th floor from the B staircase. Captain Jonas came running back and told us the South Tower was down. I don't know how he did it. He was as cool as a cucumber, but he was saying we've got to start getting out of here now. He went up a couple of floors and made sure that he notified whoever was above him. He transmitted over the radio what he observed and that we were getting out, and at that point we started our descent. I heard Maydays after the collapse, there were Maydays all over the place.

As we were going down, we were trying to stop and double-check the floors that we got to. We did still encounter some civilians on the 20th floor on the way down. There was one guy downloading stuff off his computer and we just told him to go now. He really didn't want to leave, but we basically forced him out of the building. I would say most of the civilians were out at that point.

We tried to check the floors as quickly as we could. Some floors had smoke conditions on them and some floors didn't. It was weird. Maybe debris from the tower only landed in certain floors and lit them on fire. I don't know. But there was definitely heavy smoke on one floor and then the next floor you'd go to there would be no smoke.

The lights were out. The emergency lights were on in the North Tower at that point. The alarm was going off the whole time we were there. It was a deafening alarm sound.

We got down to the third floor. It was us, it was 9 Engine, 6 Truck and there were about six civilians at that point and one lady, Josephine, who was not ambulatory. She couldn't walk. We were staying with 6 Truck to help them and a chief told 9 Engine, I want you to take these people and get them out. I'll stay with 6 Truck. We didn't want to leave, but that's what we were told, so we did it.

When we did encounter Josephine and the six other people... our first thought was why the hell are you still in the building? And one of the women told me we can't go down there, there's smoke and we can't get out. When we got to the lobby, it was nothing but debris, heavy smoke and fire.

I masked up. Lieutenant Foti told me and Sean O'Sullivan to see if we could find the way we came in. We went over one pile of debris and we found one fireman that was definitely deceased. We tried to drag him back with us, but Lieutenant Foti said listen, we can't do anything for this guy now and we got to get out of here. We didn't want to, but we had to leave him. We had the other people to try to get out who were still alive.

Lieutenant Foti knew that if we dropped down into the loading dock area, we could get across and come up on Vesey Street. He didn't want to take these people through this thick smoke condition and sheared steel and rubble.We dropped down and the smoke went from bad to tolerable and we were able to take the people across the loading dock out towards Vesey Street.

We were out now on Vesey Street and we were going to head back in and make sure that 6 Truck knew that they could come out this way because we knew that they had Josephine. And we turned to walk back down the loading dock and the whole thing just started coming down, the whole North Tower. There wasn't even time to run. I got hit with a huge piece of debris in the back of my air cylinder, which took the wind out of me and knocked me flat on the ground.

A firefighter, Michael Price in 9 Engine, pulled me under a Port Authority tow truck and it just went black as night. My helmet came blowing right off my head and the next thing I knew there was nothing but debris and dirt and that plume of crushed concrete all around us. You could hardly breathe. I remember sticking my head in my coat and trying to conserve as much air as I could, figuring I'm probably going to suffocate because I know this whole thing came down around us and I have no idea if anybody's going to get us out of here.

Mike and I stayed in there. We talked to each other for what seemed like an eternity. Eventually, it did clear enough that we could see each other. We couldn't come out of the truck the same way we came in. We had to back ourselves up out of the truck. I remember the whole top of the tow truck looked like somebody took a can opener and just peeled it right off. Maybe 10 feet from the truck was the biggest piece of steel I-beam I've every seen, and there was a dead Port Authority cop right there. We tried to get his body, but we weren't moving the steel beam.

Maybe 30 minutes went by before the company found each other. Lieutenant Foti said let's just try to find all our guys first and let people know where 6 Truck is. We knew we probably couldn't get to them by ourselves. We had no tools or anything.

Then we heard a Mayday from 6 Truck – we couldn't believe they were still alive and we knew that we had a shot to go back in and get them at this point. We got back to where Engine 9, the satellite and 6 Truck were. Off-duty members from 6 Truck and 9 Engine were there now.

I remember my father was on the radio trying to locate me because he came with my uncle on the relocation. One of the lieutenants, Lieutenant Chin from 9 Engine, told me your father's over by the subway, just go tell him that you're alive. The first thing he said to me was, do you remember how you got out? We need to get back in.

We could still hear 6 Truck talking, but I thought there's no way we can get anything to get up there. It was completely sealed. It was like they were entombed. We stayed in there trying to figure things out. Other supervisors came at that point, other chiefs, and we knew that they were right above us, but we just could not reach them.

We stayed in there as long as we could and then there were other collapses starting. That's when my father said, that's it, we got to get out of here now! So we backed out. Thank God, that's when 6 Truck radioed that they found a way out. They were basically entombed. I couldn't believe that they walked out of there.

William Johnson from 6 Engine was assigned to 276 Engine and was on rotation to 6 Engine. We were going up the floors together. We were in the same probie company together. When we got there, he said, oh, man, we're going to have a good story to tell when we go back to Brooklyn! He didn't make it.

Evacuate

Lieutenant Gregg Hansson
Engine 24, SoHo, Manhattan

now Captain, Engine 276

The alarm came in and we rode out with one extra firefighter. On the rig were Firefighters Richard Billy, Dan Sterling, Robert Byrne, John Ottotrando and Marcel Claes. We responded down Varick Street – it was a straight run.

There was a good-sized hole in the North Tower. It didn't look nearly as bad. I thought it was a small plane. I was confident that we could go up and operate. We parked at West and Vesey streets. This was the same position as in 1993. We took our three 50-foot sections (roll-ups) of hose into the lobby. Deputy Chief Hayden was there, and we heard him tell one of the Port Authority people he wanted both towers evacuated.

There were no elevators working. All the glass on the west side of the lobby was broken out. We were standing next to the crew of Ladder 20. We followed them to the southeast corner and entered the A stairs. There were a lot of people self-evacuating. We got the people to come down single file just so we could go up the stairs. We interviewed people as they past us – what floor were you coming from? What were the conditions? Most people said they were coming from the 20s, 30s and 40s.

Civilians evacuate the World Trade Center. Both towers were burning. The majority of those working below the fires managed to escape.

David Handschuh

Around the 20th floor, a person said he had come from the 90th floor. He saw fire. A girl with him had blood on her shirt. She was asthmatic and was having an anxiety attack. We also heard urgent messages with firefighters reporting chest pains. I realized our own guys were having chest pains. I saw a woman who had suffered burns to her arms.

We continued up to floor 27. I left a firefighter with a man in a wheelchair. I told the firefighter to stay with him. If you get help, take him out. Three other firefighters remained with me. We heard Captain Pat Brown from Ladder 3 giving a message about a collapse in the 60s. We heard other firefighters calling Ladder 3.

At the 35th floor we caught up with Ladder 20. We stopped for a break. On this floor was Engine 24, 33, Ladder 20 and 5 and the 11th Battalion. We were waiting to proceed up. We decided to take half of the roll-ups. There was a person getting oxygen from two EMS workers. Over the chief's radio, which was on the command channel, we heard the order to evacuate. The chief had a megaphone. We saw Ladder 5 go to the B stairs.

Suddenly, the building started to shake. The chief was screaming to get into the stairwell. Lieutenant John Fischer of Ladder 20 went to get his guys, who were one or two floors above. We went down and found the firefighter we left with the person in the wheelchair. One of the firefighters said he left his mask on the 35th floor. I said, leave it, just get out!

Captain Burke from Engine 21 was with his company. They said they were going to take the handicapped person and another civilian down with them. There were no elevators. We stopped at the 19th floor. There were 10 firefighters and eight civilians. I told them, you have to get out!

At the third floor, we were stopped by Firefighter Pat Kelly from Squad 18, who needed help getting a civilian out. The stairway was blocked. We transferred to another stairway. We finally made it outside. There was 10 to 15 feet of visibility. We were standing under the overhang of Building 6, the Customs House, when we heard a thunderous roar. Next, it got pitch black. Everybody scattered. I didn't know it was the tower coming down.

I was hit by a lot of debris and concrete. I had dropped my mask when I left the building. I was trying to crawl on my belly. A police officer was shining his light, which way to go. I found Firefighter Byrne. Firefighter Billy was giving a Mayday. I tried to call, there was no response. There wasn't anybody around. I tried to use a truck radio. I met a safety chief in an ambulance and told him both towers had come down. Finally, we made it to Engine 7/Ladder 1, which was being used as a triage area.

In A Ticking Time Bomb

Lieutenant Jim McGlynn Engine 39, East Side, Manhattan

now Battalion Chief

I had worked Monday night and was in the office. The housewatch reported a plane hit the World Trade Center. I could see the outline of the plane in the North Tower on television. There was speculation by the news media as to whether it was an accident. It was a crystal clear day with a blue sky. I said this is a commercial aircraft and this is an act of terrorism.

I pretty much knew we would respond because we have a High-Rise Unit in quarters with us. In the first five minutes, we received a ticket for the third alarm. This was about 10 minutes before the second plane hit. As we left our quarters on East 67th Street and headed down Second Avenue, I was amazed at how light the traffic was. Usually there are a lot of cabs; I didn't see one.

At Houston Street, we headed west. A huge ball of fire was visible near the North Tower. That was the second plane hitting the South Tower. A minute or two later, we arrived at the WTC. I met with Chief Ganci. The chiefs always know what is going on, but he had a look of concern. This incident was out of the ordinary. His aide told me that people were jumping. He said try to watch out. We went under the North Pedestrian Bridge, about 20 feet away. We had to look up to avoid getting hit by the jumpers.

We made it in the front door and were assigned by Chief (Joseph) Pfiefer. We were teamed with Engine 65 to go up the B stairway and see what we could do. Walk up as far as you can and put out the fire, were the orders. As the firefighters carried their roll-ups we stopped every 10 floors. We regrouped every once in a while. We made it to 31 and stopped.

The building started to shake so violently that you couldn't stand up, you just hit the floor. I thought it was a collapse of the North Tower, but it was the South Tower collapsing. A man popped out of an office. He was Middle Eastern. I wondered what he was doing here. The police put him in handcuffs and took him from the building.

Chief (John) Paolillo of the rescue battalion was standing next to me. I said it's time to go. He said he needed to confirm. The building was shaking. He talked to somebody and and then yelled, everybody out! Leave the equipment, hose and standpipe kit.

As we walked down, I saw Captain Fred Ill of Ladder 2. He was searching a floor. I told him it was time to go. He said, let me get my guys first. We proceeded down the stairs. We passed Ladder 6 with Josephine. I asked if they needed help, but they said no, they had it.

In the lobby, we saw Chief (Richard) Prunty directing people out with his flashlight. Talk of heroism, here was a man standing in a building directing traffic in a ticking time bomb. Everything was a complete whiteout from the South Tower collapse. We did a roll call. We were missing one man. We thought he might have been with Ladder 6. I walked back into the stairwell. The other three firefighters followed me up. If they stayed where they were, they would have been killed. The missing firefighter had exited the building without our knowledge. All four of us walked up several floors looking for him.

As we walked back down, the building started to shake. You could hear the floors collapse on each other...boom, boom, boom. You knew what was coming. I said a couple of prayers and took shelter in a corner. It lasted 10 seconds. Pieces of the building were coming down the stairway. Finally it stopped. I dusted myself off and checked myself out. I was alive.

The collapse caused a vacuum, pushing the air out. Like a wind you were being sucked up. I was able to reach the three other firefighters. Bacon was next to me, lying on a handrail. Coniligio and Effimades were on the floor below. They couldn't get out from where they were. They said we can't move! We're trapped!

Chief Prunty issued several Maydays. He was pinned and couldn't move. I asked the two firefighters below me if they could help him out. They said they had no way out from where they were. I walked up a few steps and saw a door. I didn't know the entire building had collapsed. I thought if we forced the door we might find a way around. A firefighter from Ladder 6 forced the door and crawled in. It didn't go anywhere. I told Chief Prunty to hang in there, that we were going to get to him. He was losing consciousness. He said tell my wife and kids I love them.

I was trying to determine our situation. How much building came down? I thought the upper 20-30 floors collapsed. We are still alive in the stairway, so I didn't think the entire building came down. I tried the radio, but I couldn't reach anybody. Above me, (Ladder 6 Captain Jay) Jonas had more luck on the radio. You could hear him talk with Chief Nick Visconti. Jonas would say North Tower, B stairway, 2-3-4th floors. Nick answered, where are you? I now realized the whole building came down. I was thinking plan A, B and C. Is there anything that we were not doing? Is there another way out of here?

When the dust cleared, you could see light. Here we were in the middle of a black stairway, how could you get sunlight in here? Chief Picciotto was sounding the siren of a bullhorn. Eventually, firefighters found us and threw ropes down. There were still two of my firefighters below me. I had to get them out.

When Lieutenant Glenn Rohan from Ladder 43 came down inside the stairway, I asked if he had rescue or squad with him. He said he had two guys. I told him I had two of my guys trapped below. I told the two below that there was a crack in the floor on the half landing I was standing on. If we enlarge that crack and throw a rope down, they might get out. Lou, the heaviest man on the job, was not going to climb through that hole. It was something that he still jokes about.

We finally got outside around 3:30 P.M. It was one of those moments in life...it was block after block of devastation. It reminded me of Hiroshima.

Now that we were out, we had to walk. I let Glenn know Chief Prunty's location to get his body out. Then I was by myself. You had to travel a couple of hundred yards. I was exhausted, mentally and physically. Building 7 was well involved. There were 30 floors of fire within 100 yards of you. I said if these two came down, that will too.

About 7 P.M., I went back to the firehouse.

In the staircase it was like a cocoon. The walls and staircase were mangled, twisted and contorted. To come of out an area that was pretty hazardous, this had been our safe area. I heard the noise of both towers coming down, but it was a shock to see it. To think we were in the middle of this and survived. The odds of that happening were ridiculous.

Drop Everything

Firefighter Marcel Claes
Engine 24, SoHo, Manhattan

Civilians were helping each other out as we walked up the stairs in the North Tower. We stopped to take a break on the 35th floor. We heard a rumble. We thought the upper floors might have collapsed. There was a chief with us and he said drop everything and get out. On the way down, I saw the Second Battalion aide, Faustino Apostel Jr., on the 10th floor. Below that there was a woman walking one step at a time. She was being helped by Ladder 6.

I finally made it to the lobby. I was surprised to see so much debris. Someone said go out the way we came in. A building employee was looking up. We ran outside. I remember seeing Ladder 8 or Ladder 18 on the corner. We went out to the middle of West Street and saw the debris on the ground. We watched three people jump. The north and west sides of Tower 1 were totally involved. I was confused. I said is this really happening? The building started to come down. We ran north on West Street. The dust was passing us. I ran behind an engine. It was total darkness. Something hot went down my shirt. I was gagging on the dust. No one from the company was with me. I went back down the street to an engine that was still running. This engine was being supplied by another engine.

Firefighters started to take lines off. There were many rigs on fire. Lines were stretched to the Customs House. They were searching in there. They used the booster tank water from one engine, and then Engine 239 re-supplied that unit. Lines were hooked up to Tower Ladder 12. Someone was using a stang nozzle, but they didn't have much pressure.

We were kept away from Building 7 because of the potential of collapse. I felt sick. I had my eyes flushed out. I saw firefighters who told me Engine 24 made it out, but Ladder 5 was missing. I walked back to the firehouse of Engine 24/Ladder 5.

We're In The North Tower

Captain Jay Jonas
Ladder 6, Chinatown, Manhattan

now Deputy Chief

It was a quiet, routine morning, a beautiful morning. Guys were checking the saws. The apparatus doors were open. My house watchman was standing in front. He sees the plane coming across Canal Street. I was in the kitchen and I heard a loud explosion. It sounded like a truck driving off the Manhattan Bridge.

He started banging on the intercom. He said a plane just crashed into the World Trade Center. We ran out and all we could see was a plume of black smoke. We couldn't see the World Trade Center from quarters. He said turn both companies out. We're a second-alarm company, so I knew we were going. I went in to put my bunker pants on in the office and I heard the radio. Engine 10 transmitted an immediate third alarm and a 10-60 (major emergency), so I knew we were going. Whether it took a minute, a minute and a half, by the time we made the crest by the Manhattan Bridge heading down toward the Bowery, there were easily 20 floors of fire in the World Trade Center. It was the most incredible sight I ever saw.

We pulled onto West Street just on the north side by the pedestrian bridge. We pulled right in front of Ladder 20 and Ladder 1 was in front of us. We were using that bridge for cover because debris was still falling down, coming off the building. We were treating it as a high-rise building fire.

We gathered up all our equipment and made sure everybody was ready to make a sprint to the building. We just kept looking up for an open spot that we can make a dash for the building without getting hit. I gave the order, I said run and we started running to the building. And once we got to the entrance door, there were two badly burned people right there. I'm assuming that they were in the elevators and the

Andrea Booher/FEMA News Photo

The remains of the North Tower are on the right of the picture.

vapors must have traveled down the shaft. EMS had just gotten there to give them attention. You know, your first impulse is to stop there and help them, but there's two people here, there's a thousand people up there.

There was a lot of activity in the lobby. There was some loose debris on the floor. I saw (Captain) Patty Brown from Ladder 3 heading up. They got in before us. They were at a box, so they actually beat us into the box. (Battalion Chief) Joe Pfeifer and (Deputy Chief) Pete Hayden were at the command post.

There were two officers in front of me. I was waiting to get orders and that's when we heard another loud explosion and we weren't sure what it was, if it was something exploding on the upper floor of our building. Somebody came running in and said a second plane had just hit the second tower.

Then it was my turn to get my assignment. I looked at Chief Hayden. I said a second plane just hit the second tower. He said yeah, I know, I heard. He said just go upstairs, do the best you can.

Engine 55 was in front of us. I had Rescue 1 with me because I was talking to Jerry Nevins from Rescue 1 when the other plane hit. We just looked at each other and said they're trying to kill us. All of a sudden, it was almost incomprehensible what was happening to us.

I hit the first stairway. I didn't want the guys to take any elevator. I wasn't sure if there was a low-rise bank of elevators that was working. We had seen the people burned at the entrance lobby. I said elevators aren't the best thing right now. It's going to be tough and it's going to take a long time, but we'd better start thinking about taking the stairs. So the B stairway is the first stairway that I saw. That stairway is no wider than the staircase going up a firehouse.

There was a stream of people coming down as we were going up. They were very orderly. Every once in a while somebody would try to pass somebody, but we'd say stay to your side, we'll stay to our side, because if they jumped out of line, then we couldn't move. So they had to stay on their side.

Every floor had a vending machine, and they were breaking into them and giving us bottles of water, which was great because we were working like crazy just to get to the upper floors. Before we even went up, I told the guys, look, we're going to take breaks every 10 floors, just so we can approach this intelligently, so we'll have something when we get up to the fire.

So we stopped at 10. We stopped at 20. We stopped at 27 because I was missing two guys. I said all right, wait here, and I went down and looked for my two guys and we all got back up together. I said all right, take a break right now and take some water. I had Andy Fredericks with me from the squad and Billy Burke, the captain of 21 Engine. And we were all on that floor, taking a knee, catching a breath.

All of a sudden, we felt the earthquake of the other building coming down. It was a loud rumble earthquake sound and like a loud rush. Billy Burke and I looked at each other and he ran to the south side. I ran to the north side to see what I could see. I couldn't see anything. We both came back to the stairway and I asked him is that what I thought it was? He says yeah, the other building just collapsed. I said all right, all right, we're all going home. I said it's time for us to get out of here. So we all started evacuating at that point.

We didn't see anybody else going down. We ran into more civilians on our way down. That's where we picked up this woman, Josephine Harris, somewhere between the 15th and 20th floors. There was a floor that had a lot of incapacitated people on it.

So we saw her and I said all right, you know, one of my guys said Cap, what do you want to do with her? And I said bring her with us. Let's make the most of a bad situation here. Everybody was coming down with us. And I think maybe Andy must have spotted Billy McGinn, the officer of Squad 18, on the way down, so he must have peeled off. Billy Burke, I don't know, he must have peeled off and tried to tell guys to evacuate or something.

Once we picked up Josephine, it was very slow. She wasn't walking well at all. It was both feet on the same step kind of a thing. So it took a long time. A couple of times, we stepped to the side to let other companies pass us, like 28 Engine passed us, and then other groups of firemen. They got out, which made me feel good that we made the right decision.

It took a little while to get confirmation that our evacuation was the right thing to do. I was a little nervous about it, and justifiably so. (Battalion) Chief (Rich) Picciotto was ordering his own evacuation. He had a bullhorn with him and he was telling people to evacuate. I heard Patty Brown come out with a Mayday message that there was a collapse on the upper floor, this had to be while we were walking down.

We hooked up with Rich Picciotto, probably around the 15th floor. We're friends, so I said hey, Rich, how you doing and we're cordial and then I knew he was in front of us. And then when the collapse started, he was one of the guys in my mind when I gave a roll call after the collapse stopped, Rich Picciotto, are you there? He said yeah. He's a floor away from me, so we tried to figure out who was still with us, who wasn't.

Let me backtrack a little bit. You know, on the way down we came across 5 Truck with Lieutenant Mike Warchola and John Santore. They were working on a guy in the stairway who was having chest pains. I said Mike, it's time to go, let's go. And he says that's all right, Jay, you got your civilian and we got ours, we'll be right behind you. Like maybe a floor away from that on the upper floors, I saw the aide to the 2nd Battalion, Faustino Apostol Jr. I said Faust, it's time to go, come on. He said it's OK, Cap, I'm waiting for the chief.

So then we get to the fourth floor and Josephine falls to the floor and she says she can't walk anymore. And we're pretty much carrying her all the way anyway. I broke into the fourth floor to look for a sturdy chair that we could use to put her on and run out with her. It turns out this was a mechanical equipment room floor, it wasn't an office floor. There were a couple of overstuffed couches, nothing that was suitable to carry her in. I'm running around this floor looking for something and I'm not finding it.

I'm heading back to the stairway door and I'm about from the office door away from the stairway door when the collapse starts. And I hear this extremely loud rumble, like boom, boom, boom, boom, boom. It was like a train off the tracks and it's hitting railroad ties, so much of it that you're bouncing and the floor was moving. I couldn't get the door open initially and then a strong wind gust came. It must have helped me and I was able to open the door. I dove for the floor in the stairway and I just rode it out. Everybody who was in that stairway was just lying there waiting for the big beam to come and it never came.

Two or three minutes after the collapse, I got a Mayday from Mike Warchola that he was in the B stairway on the 12th floor, he was pinned and hurt bad. At the time, we were still buried with loose debris. I'm the highest one in that group on the stairway, so I get up and I start climbing the stairway, moving stuff, climbing. We were all encased in dust. It had to be six inches of dust. You scraping it out of your eyes, you were coughing, gagging. The visibility was about three feet.

So I get to the fifth floor and all of a sudden, I can't move the debris anymore. It's too big and too heavy. Mike continues his Maydays and I can't help him. I felt really bad the whole time I'm in there, but then once I got out, I looked at the stairway. He said he was on the 12th floor. The 12th floor didn't exist anymore. The 12th floor was in the debris pile someplace. And we were getting Maydays from a chief that he's in a long corridor between the lobby and the stairway, but we couldn't get to him. There were two guys from Engine 39 that were entombed. I believe they got out, but we couldn't get to them.

It took a while for a command to get re-established. Because I felt it was painfully obvious, I didn't want to give a Mayday when the collapse occurred. I thought it was redundant. Initially, we tried to continue our evacuation down. That was our first impulse. I had one of my guys, Billy Butler, take out his tubular webbing and put a full-body harness on Josephine to carry her down the stairs, so him and Tommy Falco carried her down the stairs. They got to the third floor and they couldn't traverse the stairs anymore and they couldn't go down anyway, so that kind of scuttled that idea.

Right about that point, I said look, we're in a bad spot, but we're alive. I'm talking to Richie Picciotto and he says we should turn off our radios, we'll keep one radio on. So I told my guys all right, turn off your radios.

The stairwell was like the worst vacant building

Micheal Rieger/FEMA News Photo

Captain Jonas and 12 others were trapped in the remains of the stairway at the far left. Building 7 was burning on several floors at the near right.

stairwell you could ever see. One landing was all twisted and warped and littered with debris. But we were alive. We could see out one side or the other, the side where the doorway was. I went to the fourth floor, there was a masonry block wall. The other sides were double Sheetrock, so parts of that were blown open and I could see mountains of twisted steel in front of us.

Our timelines are a little fuzzy, but we're thinking it was at least 3½ hours, maybe more, until the smoke and dust cleared enough where we started figuring out OK, that's our way out. As a matter of fact, about the 3½-hour point, a beam of light started shining through and I said guys, I see sunshine. There used to be 106 floors over our heads and I see sunshine.

And that's when Rich Picciotto came up. He said that's it, Jay, that's our way out. I said Rich, it probably is, but let's wait, the guys are coming for us. I said I don't know what's dangling over our heads, I just want to make sure. I said if you fall right now, I got no way of getting you out. So he held off. And then once we saw the guy from 43 Truck about 10 minutes later, that was confirmation enough for us that it was good for us to venture out that way.

There were holes in the stairway and they yelled down to Matt Comaraski, who was the lowest guy, they said Matt, can we keep going down? He said no, don't come down here, there's no way out. So they stopped at that point.

To backtrack, after Rich said everybody turn off your radios, I had everybody turn off their radios and I started thinking to myself well, he's on the command channel, I'll keep my radio on the tactical channel. He's giving out Maydays on the command, and he didn't know what I was doing up above. He didn't know until about three days later that I was giving out Maydays on the tactical channel. I told him that's why I wasn't very anxious for us to leave the stairway, because I was in contact with so many people. I knew guys were coming for us.

It took about a half hour, 40 minutes. The first guy I spoke to was (Deputy Chief) Tom Haring. I gave him a complete Mayday message, our location and unit, where we were. I said Mayday,

Mayday, Mayday, this is Ladder 6 to command post, Mayday. We are in Tower Number 1, which is the North Tower. We are in stairway B between the fourth and the second floor, we're trapped. And he says Ladder 6, I got it, I got it reported, I got your location.

And then guys really started coming on. I was speaking to (Battalion Chief) John Salka. I was talking to Cliff Stabner from Rescue 3. I was talking to (Battalion Chief) Bill Blaich from Battalion 1. I was talking to (Lieutenant) Gerry Murtha (Rescue 3). I could hear (Captain) Ralph Tiso (Rescue 3) on the air. I knew there were competent people on the way.

Then I started to talk to (Deputy Chief) Nick Visconti and Nick was very helpful. Nick's got a very distinctive voice. I knew exactly who it was. He was talking to me, all right, they're having trouble finding you, what's your exact location, how did you get there, so we had good communications going. And Rich didn't even know that all this was happening until three days later in my kitchen and I told him, yeah, I was talking to the world. He was talking to (Battalion) Chief Mark Ferran, who was with 43 Truck, so he thought he had the only communications out of our hole. And I said no, I was talking to everybody else.

There were explosions happening, the secondary explosions. We could hear the rubble shifting. Adjacent to us was the Customs House and 7 World Trade Center. They were on fire. We could hear those fires. It was tense for a little while.

Once in a while you get a whiff of jet fuel, so we're not sure exactly what's above us, how much of the building is intact above us, so we started searching for different ways out. We found a warped elevator shaft door. We could see into the shaft and we said there's a possibility we can rappel down the elevator shaft and go out a loft wall, but there was no guarantee we would be able to get in on a lower floor, so we postponed that idea for a later time, maybe a couple of days, if we were in a little tighter spot.

We started going into survival mode. We were conserving batteries, not only our handie-talkies, but our flashlights. We found a sprinkler room and they broke into that and they found sprinkler pipes. We thought maybe they could get water out of the sprinkler pipes.

There were 11 of us. Six from the truck. We had David Lynn, a Port Authority cop, Josephine Harris, the woman that we were rescuing, Chief Picciotto, Lieutenant Mickey Cross from Engine 16 and a Fireman Bacon from Engine 39.

Billy Butler was with the police officer, who had a phone. First, I told him, call the Manhattan dispatch and tell them where we are, but they couldn't get through. So he tried somebody's house in Staten Island, and he couldn't get through. So I told him, try his house because he lives up by me up in Orange County, and he got through. He told his wife to call Ladder 6 and tell them where we are and then to call the other wives. We knew they'd be watching on TV.

We have our life-saving rope with us. We spot this guy off in the distance and we sent Rich Picciotto out. We tie him off with the life-saving rope. I have Billy Butler in the stairway with a multi hitch on his personal harness, so if he falls, at least we have a way to retrieve him, because there was a big drop and there's all kinds of holes and everything. And visibility is still not great.

We send him out on the life-saving rope and I told him once you got out, tie off your end and we'll tie off this end, at least we'll have something to hold onto getting out of the stairway. So Richie went out about 100 feet and he tied off, and that's where he met the guy from 43 Truck – 43 Truck came in through 7 World Trade Center, and by the time they got through there, you couldn't go back that way because of the fire.

I sent out a couple of more guys, so we got about four or five people out of the stairway before 43 Truck made it into the stairway. We sent out David Lynn, Matt Comaraski was out. Lieutenant Cross was out. Fireman Bacon was out, and then I kind of held back. I was the last one out of our group. The only person we couldn't take out with us was Josephine Harris because she wasn't walking before the collapse. She certainly wasn't walking afterwards. So I had to wait for 43 Truck to get there and I kind of briefed them I said you need a Stokes basket for her.

I told them about the Mayday from Mike Warchola. I didn't realize the 12th floor wasn't there. I told them about the other chief, and Engine 39 was at the base of the stairway. And so I basically turned the operation over to them at that point.

We worked our way down, there was a ledge. You had to climb down and basically we had to start heading toward West Street. We were told don't go that way because you had craters and everything else. As soon as we exited the building, the Customs House, the ammunition depot for the Secret Service, starts blowing up. So we had all that to deal with at the same time.

We just kept making our way across and down. This crater had to be two stories deep that we had to shimmy down and then climb up the other side. Mind you now, everybody's pretty well beat up. One of my guys has a separated shoulder, one guy's got a concussion, one guy's got bruised ribs, so everybody's not doing really well, plus they climbed 27 stories with heavy gear just before that, so they're pretty well shot. They needed some encouragement to keep moving, you know. Every once in a while they'd stop. I said no, don't stop, you don't have to move fast, but you got to keep moving, just keep going, keep heading west, keep heading towards the river.

Eventually we could see. Once we got out of that crater, then we could see west. It was starting to clear out by the time we exited, the dust was starting to settle out, so we had decent visibility. Once we got past 7 World Trade, then the smoke cleared up, you know.

All the dust made like a fine powder. It was like trying to crawl on a slew of beams that are coated with talcum powder, so it was slippery. You had to be very deliberate in whatever you were doing. I kept my search rope because I thought that maybe we would need it making our trek across, and I kept my officer's tool. I think everybody else jettisoned everything else.

It had to take us a half hour by the time we left the stairway to reach a point of safety. You know, it was – it was a long trip. We had to actually go through the World Financial Center. They had ambulances staged on the other side of that. The first thing I wanted to do was go to the command post and report in, but when I was out, I knew I was talking to eight guys on the radio. I wanted the command post to know that I'm out. If you got a search party looking for me, stop them, get them to a point of safety.

Chief Hayden was on top of a fire truck running the show and I just yelled up from down below. I said Chief Hayden, Chief Hayden. And then somebody gets his attention. He looks down and his eyes are full of tears. It's good to see you, Jay. I just stuck my hand up and I was happy to see him, too. He did one heck of a job there. He was there standing on the roof, him and Deputy Chief Jim Di Domenico.

We all got treated for eye injuries right away. Some guys, like Matt Comaraski, he was swept away right away. So was Bill Butler. They were taken by ferry to Jersey City immediately for medical attention. I think Rich Picciotto too.

Once we finally made it out, once we finally exited the stairway, I couldn't believe what I was seeing, you know. The first thing I saw was the corner, the facade, that's still left standing. What an eerie sight that was. There were two times that I felt that I was like oh, my God, I can't believe I survived it, which was right after the collapse stopped. When we were coughing and gagging, I was like, oh, man I can't believe I just survived that.

Basically, that stairway was our life raft. And don't be so quick to jump out of the life raft. If you see an island five miles away, don't be so quick to jump out, float a little closer to the island, make sure that that's good.

We were very conscious. We were making incredibly lucid decisions about what we should do, what we shouldn't do. We didn't want to make a move just to make a move. We wanted to make sure it was going to be the right move. We didn't want to backtrack anything or have to rescue somebody from making a bad decision. We were closely evaluating everything that we did.

But once 43 Truck came, basically we were no longer their mission because we could get ourselves out, but we told them you got to get her out, she needs a Stokes basket. We're shot, we can't do it. And we told them about the chief and the guys from 39 Engine. We gave them a new mission, so they felt very useful and they did a heck of a job.

Safer Inside

Firefighter Steve Modica Special Operations Command, Roosevelt Island, East River

now retired

I was working as the SOC battalion aide. Chief John Paolillo and I were going to Squad 252 for a drill when we received the alarm for the World Trade Center. We had heard it was a plane, so upon receiving the alarm, a second alarm for a plane crash, we thought it must be a light plane or a helicopter. As we were responding, somebody said 10-60, so at that point we realized that it must be a pretty intense situation. As we got closer, we realized that it was a hole. You could actually see that it was a hole in that North Tower.

We started to put our gear on and that's exactly when the second plane hit. The radios just went completely wild. Guys were yelling, another plane! My God, another plane hit! Somebody said it was an airliner, it was a big plane. Somebody yelled out it was a military aircraft. It was inconceivable that this could be happening, so we really didn't believe it.

On the way down we noticed very large plane parts on Vesey Street, and you could tell at that point that this was not a small aircraft. There was a lot of stuff falling.

We actually saw bodies, but they weren't landing on Vesey Street. They were landing up in the plaza level. That's where mostly you could see them coming down, but we didn't see any fall directly in front of us. We heard a lot of crashing sounds, which I assume was the jumpers. The frequency was very rapid.

We went in through a window in the northwest corner of the building. There's a little command post there and we went right over to a chief who was stationed there. John went over to speak to that chief and he barely spoke. He was there for like a second or so. He turned around and I looked at him and I said well, what do we do? He said start up and wherever we could find ourselves useful, we'll help. So we started to go in toward the elevator bank area and just about every elevator bank had its doors blown off. They were just empty shafts, a lot of glass around, a lot of marble, a lot of granite off the walls, Sheetrock down, some traction cable, scorch marks in a few elevator banks. No doors, no doors. They were all blown off. Some of them were in the shafts, some of them were in the lobby. You had to walk over them.

When I first got there, I couldn't wait to get in the building because I thought it was totally unsafe to be outside anywhere around these buildings because there was so much stuff coming down. We immediately entered the B stairwell.

On the way up, we would ask people where they were coming from and what were the conditions? And people would give their floor. They'd say it was fine. We'd ask if anybody was stuck up there. They'd say no, we got everybody out of that floor.

I got up to the 24th floor. The chief at this point was out of sight and one of the last people that I saw coming down said he was from the 89th floor and there was a light smoke condition.

You had a lot of stuff in the hallway. You had life-saving ropes, spare cylinders. Guys were just jettisoning things when they realized how far they had to go. But basically that was it until I got to the 30th floor and I had to stop. I was with two other firemen from Squad 18 and we stopped and we took our turnout coats off and our helmets and our masks.

A few seconds after we got all our gear off, the building shook violently – damn near knocked you off your feet. You could hear a faint sound of a rumble. It wasn't loud, it was just a very faint rumbling sound. It lasted maybe about four seconds and then it got quiet and the lighting went out and the emergency lighting came on. The radios were completely quiet.

Then we heard this sound, this boom, boom, boom, boom. I'm like what the hell is that? It was four ESU cops coming down the stairs and they weren't even touching the tread. They were going from landing to landing. We had to put our backs up against the wall to get out of the way. Then there was a transmission on my radio. I was on Channel 1. Somebody said there was a collapse on the 65th floor. Then somebody came back and very calm, didn't identify himself or his company, and said we're on the 65th floor and everything's fine.

At the time of the rumbling and the shaking,

Todd Maisel

Firefighter Dan Suhr of Engine 216 was hit by a jumper near the South Tower (background). Suhr is removed to a safer location. Visible near the South Tower is Ladder 4. The rear of the hotel can be seen at the far left.

immediately right after, Rescue 1, Pattie O'Keefe, gave a Mayday, which was answered by, I believe, Terry Hatton, captain of Rescue 1. Hatton answered him and said Pattie, are you OK? He says yeah, I'm OK, I'm OK, what was that? And then they said a few other things, but I don't really remember because he said I'm OK and I was very freaked out personally after those cops went by. They didn't say a word. They just went by.

And then here comes a captain, he went by, then a bunch of firemen and I think a chief. It was quite a lot of guys and they went by going down rather quickly yelling, get out! Evacuate! They want everybody out of the building. I didn't hear any of that. The first time I'm hearing it is now from these guys that are going down, this captain, and they're yelling evacuate, evacuate! Everybody out, get out of the building! And they kept going.

I was starting to get really bad vibes. The 31st, something like that, was the highest I got. Then my instincts were to get the hell out of there. I thought about those cops, they must have heard something. They're flying. Big buildings don't shake like that, so I'm like let's get out of here. I made my decision.

I started to go down and then I ran into Squad 252 on the 17th floor and I ran into Lieutenant Higgins and they were coming in off of a floor coming into the stairwell.

So I kept going. I saw Captain Freddy Ill from 2 Truck. I saw him down around the 17th floor. I think he was getting ready to get his guys together and start heading down. Then I ran into 6 Truck and that woman Josephine around the 10th floor.

When I get to the sixth floor, there was nobody around and I remember I had this urge to get out of the building so fast. And all of a sudden, this feeling – you know when your hair just stands up on edge? I wanted to get out of that building so bad that I started flying down those stairs. From the sixth floor down to the ground level, it must have taken me a few seconds because I was moving and I wanted to get out of that building. When I got down to the lobby and opened the door, it looked like a snowstorm in February. The whole lobby was white. You look outside and you couldn't see – it was a gorgeous day, but the sun was completely obscured. It was dark.

There were only a couple of guys from 18 Truck and they were by the corner of the building, just standing by that little command area. When I first got there, I had that urgency to get in the building. Now, I had this complete urgency to get the hell out of the building, but we were just afraid to make the move. We saw an engine man, and he was under the North Pedestrian Bridge. He was looking up at the building. We yelled at him to let us know when it would be OK to run, so he kept looking and a few seconds later, he started to yell, all right, run, run, run! So we all took off and got underneath that North Pedestrian Bridge.

At that point, I turned around to look up at the building and that's when I realized that all that stuff coming down, that was people. It wasn't debris. It was people. I turned away and put my back to the building.

Then you couldn't see the top of the building anymore, it looked like it was as if each floor was exploding. As each floor came down, you could actually see the windows and everything blow out. Things were blowing out the sides. I really believe that if you weren't watching the building, when you heard it, it was too late, too late to move. We looked up and we saw it and you didn't hear a sound.

I couldn't get myself to move right away and I was just stuck. And then I turned back facing north and I almost dove under 20 Truck, which was parked under the North Pedestrian Bridge. I started to dive and then at the last minute, I decided not to and decided to just run. You could see guys just running. I was looking down and I could remember looking at their feet because I wasn't looking up. I threw my tools and I started running. I think the building was down in about 10 seconds and you started to hear it at this point.

Now I'm running and you could hear this thing. It sounded like about four or five 747s taking off at full throttle. It just got unbelievably loud. And as I ran, out of the corner of my eye, I could see that avalanche come like right there and it's coming.

I literally did a flying dive onto the street. I covered up and this big rush of wind and everything went completely dark and it got quiet. Now I have my eyes closed. At one point, I thought I was dead because it was just so eerie and quiet. I realized I wasn't dead when I started to choke and I couldn't breathe.

I opened my eyes. That was a big mistake. They just got shut with the dust. I can't breathe. I have my mask on my back, but I'm afraid to stand up. My thought was, well, I guess I survived the collapse. Now I was thinking about all that metal sheeting, that light aluminum and stainless steel that's floating around. I thought that'll cut you in half, so I said let me just stay down. So I remember reaching behind me. I turned my tank on and I fumbled around for my facepiece. I get that on my face and I didn't even think that it could be full of stuff. I took a breath and I got some hit. I couldn't even swallow. I threw up. I put the facepiece back on and I laid there for a while.

I was on my knee. I couldn't breathe and I was descended upon by EMS people and they ripped my jacket off. I was basically fine, but I just was trying to catch my breath. They threw me on the stretcher. They're starting to wheel me over to this triage center and I finally got composed and I said listen, I'm all right, you're going to have bigger fish to fry than me, I'm fine.

I get off the stretcher and I go back to get my equipment. Everything's gone. My helmet's gone. My coat's gone. My radio, I have some guy holding my radio. I grab my radio and we all started walking north. I mean everybody was just walking north – no rhyme or reason, just a complete look of disbelief, horror.

We all sat on the divider, and I washed out my eyes. Somebody had a hydrant on. We sat there for about an hour and a half and then went back when you could see. I was just completely amazed at what had happened. That North Pedestrian Bridge was completely down, crushed right down to the street. 20 Truck was collapsed. I couldn't see anybody under the rig, but I only imagine that the guys that dove under that rig were dead because the rig was completely squashed. I mean it was flattened to the ground.

You know what? If guys would have stayed close to the bridge on the building side, they would have been fine. The way the bridge came down, it got crushed in the middle up against the building. It was a big area where they would have been perfectly fine. Guys who ran west or south or even northwest, they were dead.

We went underneath the bridge and then climbed up on top of the debris. It was like a two-story climb. And then you could stand up and survey the whole area. It was unbelievable.

We searched around for a little while, and I remember the first person I saw was Captain Ruvolo in Rescue 2 and I immediately broke down when I saw him. And he hugged me and he says it's OK, take it easy and I was just absolutely destroyed. He asked me where the command center was. I said I think it was here, but I'm not 100% sure.So we started to look for guys and we went down. There weren't even a lot of voids. I mean it was just like a completely flattened area. And the radio, no communication, no PASS alarms, no nothing.

Some stuff was burning. Buildings were burning, 7 World Trade was burning from the ground to the top fully involved. It was unbelievable. And I remember remarking to a guy who was with me that there's nothing here. This is a 110-story office building. You couldn't find a file cabinet. You'd think there would be rubble. You couldn't find a piece of wood, a piece of carpet, a computer. There was nothing. It was just dust and big, big pieces of steel. That was it. There wasn't even a lot of concrete. Everything was pulverized.

At that point, I just felt completely disgusted. I said this is impossible. I remember saying to myself, nobody could ever live through this. And I turned around and I felt my hip. My hip was bothering me and my shoulder was bothering me. I got off the pile and I went to an EMS bus and they took me to Bellevue.

Don't Tell Me Any More

Captain Al Fuentes Acting Battalion Chief, Marine Division, Brooklyn Navy Yard

now retired

I started work at 7 A.M. The secretary came running in screaming that a plane hit the World Trade Center. From the Brooklyn Navy Yard I could see both towers. I couldn't believe my eyes. I thought we should surround the Battery with fireboats, because that would be the best way to get the injured out...via water. We could use the boats to move companies into the area.

I took the super radio. When I was a lieutenant in Rescue 2, I constantly drilled with the members that there is no time to rely on messages in an emergency, call the dispatcher.

I traveled on Marine 6 across the harbor. We pulled up to Vesey Street. I looked up and saw the second jet slam into the South Tower. I knew we were under attack. Proceeding to the command post, I reported to Chief of Department Peter Ganci. Chief Ray Downey was there. He said Al, stay here with me. Marine 1 and 6 were on scene with a spare boat, the *Smoke*. Marine 9 was standing ready at their berth. Companies were getting assignments. People were jumping from the South Tower. Chief Downey said we better give Tower 2 more attention. It was hit lower and there are more people inside. I saw the four corners of the South Tower and knew it was going to come down. It started to collapse. I ran into the garage doors of the World Financial Center, located directly behind the command post. I made it in about 10 feet. I crouched down, put my head between my legs and said a Hail Mary.

The wind blew through. Debris was hitting me. It was pitch black. I tried to breathe through my coat. I found my way out through the interior. I emerged and couldn't believe my eyes. There was six feet of debris, gray dust all over. We better start searching West Street. Deputy Commissioner William Feehan walked by and asked if I was all right. I said I wanted to start searching. Two firefighters stopped and I told them to get tools. Chief Ganci walked by and gave me a look and shook his head. Chief Ray Downey said we just lost a lot of guys. Where are the fighter pilots? He thought there might be further attacks.

Six firefighters appeared across the street near the Marriott Hotel lobby. Debris was still falling from the North Tower. Chief Downey said I'm going over there, let me know when it is safe to come back out. Several of the firefighters came out, including Chief Brian O'Flaherty.

Then the North Tower came down. I was trapped from the neck down for 90 minutes. Several firefighters dug me out and carried me. I was covered by a piece of silver facade. (Firefighter Jack Flatley heard the radio Fuentes was carrying and located him.) I was removed via boat to New Jersey. They did a tracheotomy on me. I was in a drug-induced coma for a week, on a respirator, intubated. I had six broken ribs, a collapsed lung, skull fracture and needed a couple hundred stitches on my scalp, a broken wrist and fingers.

I was in the surgical ICU and then moved to a hospital in New York. I was placed in pulmonary ICU. I woke up one night at 4 A.M. I was having nightmares. I told my wife I need to talk with the fire department chaplain, Father Mychal Judge. She was quiet for awhile. "Is Father Judge dead?" I asked. Yes. "Ganci?" Yes, "Downey?" Yes. "That's enough, don't tell me any more."

I realized the second tower came down and got me. (Several weeks after the incident, Fuentes learned about the 343 firefighters who were killed.) I saw six doctors a week. I just want to be the same guy I was on Sept. 10. People have been so nice to me. I am humbled.

FACT

FDNY AS OF JULY 2009:

11,086	Firefighters
3,122	EMTs and Paramedics
120	Fire Marshals
301	Fire Inspectors
462	Dispatchers (Fire-183, EMS-279)
505	Trades People (Buildings, Fleet, Communications, Radio Repair)
315	Administrative, Management & Support Personnel

As the South Tower collapses, individual pieces of steel are visible in a wide area as they fall to the street.

AP Photo/Richard Drew

A Tremendous Explosion

Firefighter Robert Chyriwski Engine 3, Chelsea, Manhattan

I responded with Engine 3 and the high-rise unit. Two firefighters rode on the second piece. Near Canal Street, we were told to stage on West Street. There was chaos as to where to position the high-rise unit. I drove the engine further south on West Street near the South Tower to turn around.

As I made my turn, I heard a tremendous explosion. That is when the second jet crashed into the South Tower. Chief Ganci then said clear a lane for ambulances. The high-rise unit was positioned under the North Pedestrian Bridge. They hooked up with High-Rise 2 and Engine 39.

As we removed the ramp from the unit, we were going to position the 100 spare air cylinders on the street. The mayor and fire commissioner walked by to the new command post by the World Financial Center. I looked up and said we can't do anything. Who knows what is going to happen? A few minutes later, the first tower came down. We heard the roar and we tried to outrun the dust cloud. We helped injured firefighters and civilians onto ferryboats to be taken to New Jersey for treatment.

A piece of the first plane's fuselage lies in the street south of the South Tower on Liberty Street.

Todd Maisel

Dust and debris fill an apartment after the collapse of the exterior wall of the building.

Todd Maisel

Relocated

Captain Chris Rearer Tower Ladder 17, Mott Haven, South Bronx

now Battalion Chief

We came back from a run and the battalion chief said a plane hit the Trade Center. I thought it was a small plane. We relocated to Ladder 15 on South Street, the southern-most firehouse in Manhattan. It is a tremendous distance to respond, but I wasn't that surprised, we relocate a lot.

Many Bronx ladder companies relocated to Manhattan. Ladder 48 went to Ladder 12. Ladder 58 went to Ladder 20. Ladder 59 went to Ladder 10. Ladder 42 went to Ladder 25. Ladder 31 went also. When the second plane hit, I wasn't going to be surprised that we might not even make it to Ladder 15. We took in a few boxes. We had a report of people trapped at 44 Beaver Street. That was false.

The second tower collapsed. A captain was talking to the building's fire safety director. People were running in the street. You couldn't see anything. Two firefighters had to walk in front of the rig, which had to drive real slow as not to hit anybody. We had a report of people trapped in the City Hall subway station. We checked the station and no one was trapped. A firefighter came running up to us as we were leaving the subway and said Deputy Chief Esposito needs a tower ladder, can you get into the street?

We backed in and removed some obstructions. Tower Ladder 7 was in position. They were worried about Building 7 coming down. There was fire in two office buildings on multiple floors. We were supplied first by Engine 41, then Engine 278. Water was relayed from Broadway. We had good water pressure.

We shut down our large-caliber stream so they could search the rubble. Squad 288, searching the voids, found a victim. We handed them tools, a Stokes basket, a Honda generator and a Hurst tool with metal cutting blade. They found a civilian with two broken legs. Some of our guys relieved us at the pile. We had a rear-mount aerial in our original quarters that the crews manned as well, as we were sent to Ladder 5 for three days responding on their boxes.

An injured worker is given oxygen and taken to be checked by EMS.

Peter Matthews

Feet & Inches

Firefighter Rad Ocasio Special Operations Command, Roosevelt Island, East River

now retired

I was assigned to OAD, also decon, the dewatering unit, working a 24-hour tour on September 11. A firefighter came running into the office about 8:50 A.M., right after the first plane hit, and a couple of guys were screaming. One of them was Firefighter John McGinty. The first thing out of his mouth was, "A plane just ran into the World Trade Center."

At that point, Chief Ray Downey walked into the office. He said I'm taking John to drive me down to the World Trade Center. He then backed out of the office and he got his chiefs together. I would say approximately anywhere from seven to 10 minutes later, the second plane hit.

Then Lieutenant McQuade asked me to grab Chief Charlie Kasper's bunker gear, his turnout gear, and take it down to the World Trade Center because he was going to respond with Rescue 5 to the site. My orders were specifically to respond to Liberty and West. That will be forever imprinted in my mind. He said, you will take your bunker gear, you will go down there, you will find Chief Kasper and Chief Downey, you will hand them their bunker gear and then I need you back here.

I could not find Chief Kasper's equipment, so I ended up grabbing some of Chief Segal's equipment to take to Chief Kasper. I think that delay of about anywhere from three to five minutes saved my life.

I jumped on one of the responding rigs we have here along with Firefighter Jack Rooney from Rescue 3 and we proceeded down 57th Street, at which time we made a left on Fifth Avenue. We went with full sirens and lights going down Fifth Avenue to get everybody out of the way. Traffic was chaotic, but we did the best we could getting down there. We parked on Vesey and West. We could go no further for the simple reason that there was just too many rigs parked. They were blocking the street.

I knew we had to go to Liberty and West, that was where the command post was set up. There was so much radio transmission and chaos going on. We finally got a transmission that told us stay right there. John McGinty found his way back to us and he grabbed all of Chief Kasper's equipment and he headed back to the building. I asked John where were rendezvousing. He said the South Tower, everybody's in the South Tower. The command post is right by the firehouse.

I found a helmet, some extra equipment, some bunker gear and proceeded to Liberty and West, running down the street. I kept hearing this explosion sound. As I looked to my right, there was a police officer standing there. He looked totally startled and he kept staring up and looking down, staring up. And I said to him are you all right? He said you'd better move away from that wall. People are jumping from that building. I said you've got to be kidding. He said you'd better move, here comes another one. And as I looked up, here came a body flying down. I heard this explosion sound. It pops — Pow! — when it hit the floor.

I was standing on West Street with the cop, right past Vesey facing the North Tower. They were hitting the sidewalk as they came down. And I remember watching a lady come down and she just exploded.

I told the cop I'm going to move the fire truck up, you just watch and make sure nobody lands on the cab. You see somebody coming down, tell me. I remember jumping in the rig and moving that truck over.

I looked out the side of the truck and counted 19 bodies. Nineteen bodies and they were still coming down. I told that cop there are 19 bodies. He said there are going to be a lot more, here come two now.

I kept walking to Liberty with the equipment. As I got there to the South Tower, I put the equipment down in the lobby and told the firemen here's the equipment we needed.

I started to come back down because I remembered I had to get back to SOC. As I made it to Liberty and West, the South Tower started to come down. I heard a vicious cracking noise and then as I looked up, the building was already coming down. There was massive screaming and pandemonium.

I turned right on West and started running, trying to outrun the building. No sooner did I look to my right and back, that black gushing sound just started rushing at me – all that junk, whatever, was hitting the floor and rushing at me. I knew at that point that I could not outrun it.

As I kept running, there was a young fireman on my left-hand side. He was running parallel to me and he was totally frantic. I reached to my side, grabbed him by the right arm with my left arm and I specifically told him get under that fire truck, jump under that fire truck. He looked at me. He screamed and he said let me go and he pulled his hand away. I dove under the fire truck. I crawled behind the second set of wheels of that truck company, near the curb, and I got in a fetal position. The last thing that went through my mind was simply, I'll be dead in 30 seconds.

I remember hearing a vicious whooshing sound. I remember hearing steel bending, massive steel, and things hitting the floor and cracking and smashing sound and just a roar, a deafening roar. Then you had this storm-like effect of wind blowing so much dust through you. And then a dead silence set upon us. I mean you couldn't hear anything at all. I crawled out from under the truck. It was the very truck I moved. The truck saved my life. The front of the truck at that cab was smashed, totally smashed, and it stopped being smashed in front of

Bolivar Arellano

Two firefighters stand in front of the World Financial Center after the South Tower collapse. The spare Field Communications unit is to the left of the firefighter standing on the left. Units staging at the command post were standing to the right. Hose and airpacks are visible to the extreme bottom right.

the tires that I was laying down behind. It was incredible.

As I start to come out, I had trouble breathing. I was choking. My air passage was clogged, so I stuck my fingers in my mouth and forced myself to throw up all the dust and stuff. I collapsed on the floor. Then I got up and I couldn't feel myself walking. And I knew I was walking north on West. As I'm walking, I tripped on something. I felt my way around and I got up again, started walking. And then I tripped again, and I realized I was weak.

I started crawling and I heard somebody screaming. It was an EMS worker, and he told me keep coming, keep coming! He happened to be a block away. When I finally made to it to him, I collapsed and he grabbed me and picked me up. He says you're one lucky guy. I asked him why. He says have you looked behind you? As I stared back, I realized there was no one behind me. I was the only one who walked out of there, but the North Tower was still up.

They took my vitals. They checked me out. They put water on my head and rinsed out my eyes. I remember that EMS worker said to a lady who was also an EMS worker, this guy goes to St. Vincent's, take him to St. Vincent's. I said why do I have to go to St. Vincent's? I'm fine. I stood up. He said no, you're going to St.Vincent's, you've got to go to the trauma center. I said I ain't going nowhere, I'm going to go back and look for my buddies. A lot of my guys are hurt and trapped back there.

I found my way back to the truck, which I had left on Vesey, got the rest of the equipment we had there, and started to head to where I knew Liberty was, Liberty and West, and the South Tower. As I was walking, I realized that what I had tripped over was the fireman who had pulled away from me. He didn't make it.

I didn't quite get back to Liberty and West. There was an opening between the building that collapsed. I was able to find my way up through that way and head through the North Tower. I must have gotten about 15 feet from West Street as I was crawling up going towards the North Tower and I remember spotting Ray Downey in this huge spiral. He was walking back toward the North Tower.

Once again, I heard this massive cracking sound. And as I looked up, there was the North Tower coming down. Chief Downey simply glanced to his left. As he looked, our eyes met. He looked at me from a distance and just simply gave me a scramble sign, he just waved his hand. I turned. I wasn't going to question him. I know exactly what that signal meant and then figured he's going into the building, that's where he'll seek safe haven. I turned and I ran left on West and I could only go as far as about maybe 50 feet and there just happened to be a car there. I'll never forget the color of that car. It was white.

I crawled under that car. I heard that building come down, the horrific sound of cracking steel, metal breaking. I was very peaceful. I thought that the car would just crush me and that's it. I felt less safe under that car than I did under the fire truck. Anyway, I was there. I remember it had to be anywhere from three to five minutes.

When I finally found my way out of there, I moved all that dust or dirt, whatever it was that came out of that building. I pushed it all out of the way. I found my way out from under that car. I remember I was drenched in this white, dusty powder.

I started to walk, and there was this massive darkness again. As I was walking, I couldn't feel the ground at all, but I had a sense of peace. I couldn't hear anybody. All I heard was a deafening silence. And I just started walking. I had trouble breathing and I saw a small light in the distance.

I started walking toward that light thinking it was my way out. At that point, I'm going to admit I thought I crossed the line. I thought I was dead and I didn't feel death. I thought I was actually dead and that was the eternal light that people spoke about because the closer I got to that light, the more at ease I felt. And it was just a sense of peace.

I start approaching the light, and all of

a sudden I hear PASS alarms going off from everybody, the masks that were on the ground, that people had dropped. Maybe they came off of some of the members. I started hearing PASS alarms and I started hearing screaming, moving. And that's when I realized I was still alive. I said I'm in reality here. And all my instincts snapped back in, but at that point, I knew that no one could be helped.

You couldn't see. If you walked west, which is what I did, you went through the Winter Garden. There was massive glass. That's the only glass I saw. I got to the other side of that. Now I could see because the buildings blocked a lot of that dust.

All you did was feel and trip. Your instincts as a firefighter would kick in and I'm going to admit even then, no firefighter has ever been trained for anything like that. I thought I was entombed because all you had was a total darkness and from dark you went to a dark, dark gray and it wasn't getting better. It didn't get better until it actually started lifting.

Later, I found Chief Segal on top of a rig. I asked him if he would just take a minute to hear me out, that I knew exactly where I last saw Ray Downey. He said you saw Ray? I said yes. He turned to a guy from Rescue 4 who just happened to be walking by and said grab four firemen and go with this man. He's going to show you where you might find Chief Downey.

I showed the guys from Rescue 4 where the area was. They said OK, we'll take it from here. I simply looked at them and I said these guys will be looking to work a miracle because there was no way they were going to move that rubble to get to that man. It's just impossible. You need a lot more manpower and a lot more machinery to get it done.

At about 5 o'clock in the afternoon, I was finally able to get back in contact with the SOC command and they told me Ray Phillips was OK. Then word came back that John McGinty was fine. He was a nervous wreck. I found John and said you are one lucky guy to be alive. He said to me, no, you're one lucky guy to be alive because I know you were in a worse position than I was. I said John, you were in the building, how did you get out?

He got out of the building and ran west after coming out. He lifted some gate. He just survived. He was lucky. He was shaken up very badly.

We don't ask why or whatever. We just simply do it. That day, we all showed up, not to help each other, but to help anybody who needed help. We just kept coming and coming in droves. That was my instinct. I need to help where I can help.

Incoming members travel down Liberty toward Church Street as dust clouds lift.

Peter Matthews

So Happy To See Me

Firefighter Greg Macagnone
Engine 34, Hells Kitchen, West Side, Manhattan

now Lieutenant covering

I came in that morning, and was watching the television news in the kitchen. Over the voice alarm, we were dispatched on the fifth alarm to West and Vesey streets. We are a backup unit for Field Communications.

The apparatus was first parked near the command post located on the west side of West Street in front of the World Financial Center. There were two garage doors behind us leading into an underground garage. Field Communications was using a spare rig and was parked close to the building. There were one or two companies at the command post and nine or 10 chiefs waiting for assignments. I was handed a clipboard to list all the engines that were arriving at the command post. Another firefighter did the same

with the ladder companies.

Every few minutes we gave the list to the chiefs. There were 10-12 engines standing by. The engine companies were ordered to bring their masks, spare cylinders and tools with them. I was settling in for a long day. Bodies were dropping from the upper floors.

I was standing the farthest of anybody out by the curb on West Street. I heard this God-awful noise. I never looked up. I ran straight into the garage. Within 10 seconds the garage was filling up with the debris as high as the top of the garage doors. I could smell burning. The lights never went out. It was clear to me that we were trapped in the garage.

There had to be 30-40 firefighters inside. Two members from my company went back out through the debris by the garage doors. A lieutenant said listen up. There is a door at the top of this stairwell. If it is clear, we will go out this way.

At the entrance to the garage, there were about 45 spare air cylinders piled high. We found out eventually a lot of the cylinders were destroyed or exploded when the steel fell. The door was opened and they could see that the windows in back of the building had been blown out. It looked like a blizzard. It was dusty and dark and the sounds were muffled. Visibility was only about 10-15 feet.

I stumbled out by the marina. As you got closer to the water it became clearer. You could not see the top of the towers or the World Financial Center. I was trying to get in touch with my officer, Lieutenant Rice. I tried different radio channels. For the next 15-20 minutes, I worked my way up to the West Side Highway. I told the command post I was missing several members of my company. At Vesey and West streets, I was with two firefighters trying to contact everyone else. Everyone started to run north as the North Tower collapsed. I lost the other two firefighters I was with.

I finally found one group of guys I was missing near an outdoor parking lot close to Stuyvesant High School. This was across from the staging area. I made a phone call along with about 15 civilians. I was in shock for a while. We finally met the lieutenant and firefighter we were missing behind the World Financial Center. They had been extinguishing car fires. Lieutenant Rice was so happy to see me he gave me a hug that almost broke my ribs.

We heard over the radio to stay away from Building 7. We were several blocks away with about 600 firefighters when Building 7 came down. After it collapsed, then the companies were allowed to go back into the pile. After 6 P.M., we were ordered into the Verizon Building. We operated a hoseline out a ninth-floor window onto the rubble that once was Building 7. About six hoselines operated from our building. We could smell burning wires from the basement of the Verizon Building.

We were relieved at 11:30 P.M. to report back in the morning. A Queens ladder company gave me a ride uptown. I got home at 2:30 A.M. I shook in bed for about four hours. I drove back to the firehouse at 6:30 A.M. There wasn't any traffic. A lot of the family members started to show up. All the members of Ladder 21 were missing. (I had seen a captain and a firefighter run to take cover under a rig. They were caught under the apparatus.) Our apparatus, which had been moved farther north earlier, had been destroyed in the second collapse. Two days later we received a spare rig. Eventually we were given a rig that was donated.

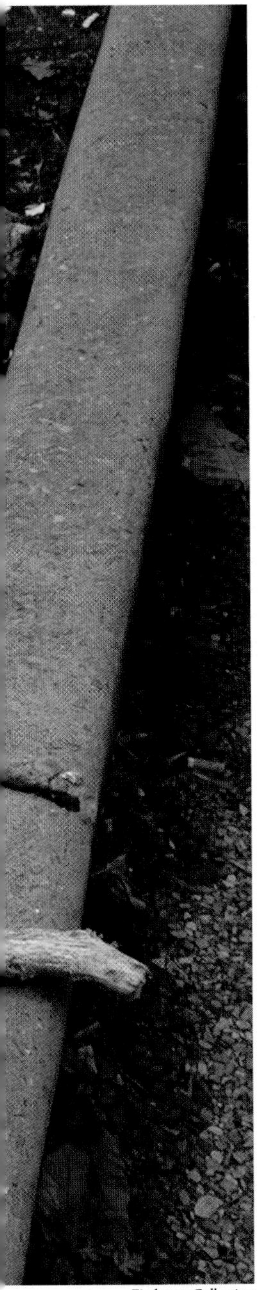

Firehouse Collection

Pile of recovered spare air cylinders. Some have been damaged or destroyed. Halligan tools and axes were also collected from the pile.

Catching A Ride

Firefighter Mike Shepherd Ladder 120, Columbus Circle, Midtown Manhattan

now Squad 41

I was in midtown and heard about a plane hitting the World Trade Center. I thought it was a small plane, but after the second plane hit I knew it was terrorism. I turned on the radio and heard that both towers were on fire. As Engine 23 slowed for traffic at Seventh Avenue and 57th Street, I flagged them down. They were responding to the towers. I told the officer I was off-duty and asked if I could ride down there with them. They had an extra seat, so I hopped on.

I sat with my back to the chauffeur. I gave the firefighter sitting across from me my name and badge number. He asked why and I told him this was going to be the worst job he ever had. He kind of looked surprised. The chauffeur had just come out of chauffeur school and the lieutenant was covering on overtime. The dispatcher assigned Engine 23 to the second fifth alarm at the North Tower at West and Vesey streets. I told the chauffeur to go south to 42nd Street and make a right. At the water, head south all the way down. Police were blocking the traffic. We saw Engine 37 go by. We got down there in no time.

At 23rd Street, I could see the Lieutenant's eyes wide open when he saw the black smoke and the gaping hole. Someone said there was too much structural damage, but I didn't think it was going to pancake. Just below Chambers Street we started running over debris in the street.

There was an extra turnout coat, helmet, gloves and a SCBA. There were no pants or boots. I got dressed and I took a length of standpipe hose. The Lieutenant looked at me and said where are you going? You're on vacation. Take the gear off and go help a chief.

I saw the chauffeur of Engine 9 hooking up to the standpipe connection. All the members of Engine 23 walked into the lobby of the North Tower. People were jumping. As I walked south, more people were jumping. I walked past the command post and saw Chief Ganci and Deputy Commissioner Feehan. I told them I was off duty and asked if I could help. Feehan said stand fast.

There were cars burning at the corner of Liberty and West streets. I asked Feehan if he wanted me to stretch a line and put out the car fires. He said no. He told everybody to stay back, nobody near the building. Tables and glass were coming down. I counted over 30 people that jumped. Feehan sent me to the exit of the Brooklyn-Battery Tunnel. He told me to direct any units from Brooklyn to him. I ran and when I got to the tunnel, I told Ladder 113 what Feehan said. Engine 240 came and then another Engine. I told them the same. I waited until no more units came through.

I asked the chauffeur of Engine 240 if I could borrow his helmet. He said he might need it. Chief Burns, Nigro and a police chief came up. There was a report of an unaccounted plane in the air. We walked to the command post in front of the World Financial Center. There was a helicopter that was so close to the building we thought it was going to hit it. A cameraman was filming the jumpers. Feehan said don't you have any human decency? Turn the camera off.

Suddenly, the South Tower listed…one hundred feet in each way. A ball of fire pushing black smoke erupted. I saw beams that looked like toothpicks tumbling in the air. I did an about-face and yelled at the top of my lungs, run!

I ran southwest. The noise was deafening. I was just north of the South Pedestrian Bridge when the building started to collapse. As soon as I hit Albany Street, I turned west to a parking garage. I tried to shut the garage door by hitting the button. The gates were open mesh. The dust was unbearable. There were 10 people inside. The garage filled with dust. I stretched the house hose line and I told a guy to turn on the valve. I started to wash the dust. It was like a tsunami of dust.

I was afraid of biological chemicals, etc. The wind was blowing towards Brooklyn. I sat down in the garage and said a few "Our Fathers." Several explosions were audible. I went outside and made a right turn. I saw (Chief Medical Officer) Dr. (Kerry) Kelly with a captain. I told her I was going to look for survivors and she said she was going to go with me.

We saw beams all laid out in the street. A big steel beam had fallen over two trees. Two other

Todd Maisel

trees were ripped right out of the ground 100-150 feet from the garage. That was the path I had run. We ran into a firefighter covered with blood. We asked if he was OK and he said yes, but there was another firefighter who was worse than him.

Kevin Shea from Ladder 35 had received numerous severe injuries. Dr. Kelly wanted to triage him right there in the street. I said let's bring him back to the parking garage. We can clean him up and we'll have water and shelter. We brought him back to the garage. I took off my shirt, wet it and cleaned up another firefighter. Now I have no shirt. I look at Shea, he is full of dust. I went to probie school with him years ago and I don't really recognize him.

We went to look for an IV. All the ambulances we could find were locked or flattened. It took 10 minutes but we couldn't locate an IV. I looked up and saw the North Tower burning. I said we have to get out of here. The doctor asked why. I said the tower is going to come down.

When the North Tower started to collapse, I grabbed Dr. Kelly and it was off to the races. We ran into the first building we saw in Battery Park City. Other people followed us inside. I asked anybody if they had any ice for the injured firefighter we were attempting to stabilize. They said there was ice on the fourth floor. I walked upstairs because there was no power. The black dust was swirling again. I threw up again. I asked someone if they

Kevin Shea from Ladder 35 received numerous severe injuries. Ironically, a different Kevin Shea (from Rescue 1) was injured in the 1993 WTC bomb attack.

Todd Maisel

Kevin Shea was eventually treated and shipped off on a boat to Jersey City for medical treatment.

Engine 23, the rig that Shepherd rode to the scene. All of the firefighters from Engine 23 were killed.

Thomas P. Buchta

had a shirt I could use and I was handed a woman's medium. I put it on. I came down with frozen water bottles.

Dr. Kelly and I got separated. When I got back to the garage, they were loading Shea into an ambulance. They put him on a boat and took him to Jersey City. I looked at the entire scene and just held my head. I walked towards Broadway. I saw Dr. Kelly later that evening. She gave me a paper mask and a hug. She said you saved my life. I said Lieutenant Gabarini of Engine 23 saved my life. He didn't let me in the building. All the members of Engine 23 were killed. They never found any of them that I know of. Not even the riding list. My stepdaughter was supposed to go on a class trip from public school to the World Trade Center Observation Deck that day. (Luckily) the trip had been canceled.

Wrong Turn

Lieutenant Bill Wall
Engine 47, Morningside Heights, Manhattan

Throughout the site, many pieces of steel hung precariously.

Andrea Booher/FEMA News Photo

We were additional units on the fifth alarm for the South Tower. We went down West End Avenue and we ran into West Street and just went straight down West Street. We parked about a block up from Vesey.

We saw a lot of smoke and flames in the upper floors. You really couldn't see the South Tower from where we were. We walked down the west side of West Street and we were keeping close to the buildings. And when we got to the Customs House, there was a policeman behind one of the pillars. He jumped out and said we got to get in because they're tracking another inbound, meaning another plane, but we ignored him. We kept going.

We went under the North Pedestrian Bridge to the west side of West Street and made our way down to the South Pedestrian Bridge, crossed under that and made our way into the Marriott Hotel. Chief Galvin was behind the desk and forming companies into groups. We event-ually hooked up with 22 Engine, 13 Truck and, I believe, 21 Engine. Chief Galvin told us to go to the 40th floor of the South Tower because that's the lowest report they had a fire. We were supposed to follow this guy who worked in the buildings. He was going to lead us to an elevator that still worked. But luckily, the guy who took us to the working elevator took us to the wrong tower. We went to the North Tower. Saved our lives. Wrong place at the right time. We never got into the South Tower. He took us right to the North Tower.

We get into the lobby of the North Tower to the first elevator bank. There was one elevator out of the six that still had the lights on, but they couldn't get it to work. Meanwhile, all the other elevators were blown off their doors. So we tried the next elevator bank of six and they finally got one that worked to the 24th floor. I think it was captain of 21 he went up to check. He went up and he came back down. He went up with his guys and someone from the truck took the elevator. And then the other engine went up in the next load, 22, and on the load after that, the truck was going up. They wanted one of our guys to run the elevators since there was only one truck, so I gave the control radio to Fireman Louie Cacchioli.

It seemed like just as soon as the doors closed, the panel went out. But he had actually gotten to the top floor and the rest of the truck got off. The last guy getting off was the irons guy, and Louie grabbed him back and says you got to stay with me because I need the tools. And as soon as the doors closed, the power went out and they were stuck in the elevator still on the 24th floor. They were able to force their way out pretty easy. They just popped the doors open because the elevator didn't move yet.

The guy from the truck thought his company went to the right and Louie went to the left.

View from gym in World Financial Center looks out to West Street. Damage in the street matches that of the gym.

Andrea Booher/FEMA News Photo

Louie found the staircase and I think he said he got down about six floors, but the staircase was blocked, so he crossed over and found another staircase and he made it to the lobby. He had to force the door open at the lobby because it was jammed. He made his way out into the street and he hooked up with the chauffeur just before the North Tower came down.

Meanwhile, in the lobby, it seemed like just as soon as the elevator doors closed, the power went out. It turned black and then it started rumbling and the wind and dirt was unbelievable. It was just like a hurricane. It threw me against the wall.

After everything stopped, I looked down and I says count off, you're supposed to take a roll call. Everyone shouted out their name and said they were all right. We locked arms together and started walking out. There was a building worker there that was going to stay, but Tommy Terilli convinced him to come with us. He was worried about his job. Tommy Terilli says they don't pay you enough, come on. When we got out of the elevator lobby, we made the right past the turnstiles and there were also people at the bottom of the escalator coming down. They were looking for a way out, so they grabbed on the line too. The visibility was zero.

On the way in, I noticed that all the windows in the lobby were blown out, and that it would be a good way out if we needed to – and it was. We had to make a right out of the elevator corridor and then another right. But it was so dark that I bumped into a wall. That's how bad the visibility was.

We started walking that way and it gradually got lighter, lighter and lighter to where we could see the windows. We went out the windows. We went straight across West Street straight out and then we got across the street and we went up north.

Debris was still falling. You couldn't see the sky. Maybe you could see like 30 or 40 feet up. And the weirdest thing, you could hear these booms above you. It sounded like bombs going off, but it was actually the military jets flying overhead. It was like an eerie feeling. You couldn't see anything, but you could hear these things going back and forth.

You could hear Mayday, Mayday and they were giving locations. So Tommy Terilli and I got some tools. We put our masks on and we headed back down, and we made it to Vesey and West Street. There was a chief directing everybody north saying they were going to regroup and go back in.

I went over to him and kind of stressed the Maydays were here and now, and we were talking and that's when the North Tower came down. You heard it, a big snap and a crack. And we looked up and it looked like the whole top just exploded.

Everyone just started heading north. Everyone just ran. We got hit by the wind and the dust and I was running with Jack Ginty. He was running. I caught up to him and we were talking as we were running, what the hell are we doing here, Jack?

The dust cloud overtook us and there was a big white Suburban. There was about seven of us behind it, huddled. Jerry Riley was there from 22 Truck, me, Jack and a couple of other guys. It was getting tough to breathe. I had my mask, so we were passing the mask around.

You couldn't see, so whoever was yelling for it, I would like feel their face and just like slap it on their face for a little while. Then feel the next guy's face and then pass it to him and then take some for myself.

After like the wind and stuff subsided and we realized, all right, there's nothing to do here, we just got to walk out of it. So we started walking north on West Street and walking and walking and we bumped into something and it turned out to be an apparatus. If you stick your face real close to it, you could see the light flashing. There was just no visibility.

Never Exchanged A Single Cylinder

Firefighter Dick Ward
Mask Service Unit, Fire Academy, Randall's Island, East River

now retired

I started at 8 A.M. and made phone calls to air cylinder depots to see who needed full cylinders. First stop was Rescue 4/Engine 292. The companies were already out. There were several people at the housewatch and I stopped to see what was going on. I saw on television that the North Tower had been hit.

Responding to the scene I parked at West Street and Vesey Street and reported in to the command post. I positioned the apparatus near the North Tower to exchange air cylinders when the South Tower came down. It sounded like a train running over you. I thought I was going to die.

I was hit by dust. I put my hands over my head. I lost the hearing in my left ear. I jumped into the truck and was buried. The windshield was blown in, the mirrors were ripped off. The doors became jammed. Lying over the motor, I put my hands over my head. I had to climb out the passenger window. My foot was injured and I thought I broke my wrist.

Moving north, I tried to get away from the smoke. I was placed in an ambulance about 300 yards north of the North Tower. My eyes were screwed up. The North Tower collapsed. The EMS worker in front of the ambulance ran away and the EMS worker in the back with me ran away leaving me in the ambulance.

I was covered in dust again. Eventually I was taken to St. Vincent's Hospital. They washed out my eyes and took care of my wrist. The Mask Service Unit carries 125 full air cylinders. I didn't get to exchange one cylinder. In the next few days I worked at the scene to recover air cylinders that were left all over the site. I have bad lungs, lost the hearing in one ear and have post-traumatic stress disorder.

The Mask Service Unit (left) was damaged in the first collapse. It was flattened in the second collapse.

Todd Maisel

The Chief's Plan

Safety Chief Al Turi
Safety Battalion, Headquarters, Downtown Brooklyn

now retired

When the attack occurred, I was working in the command center in Brooklyn with (Citywide Tour Commander) Joe Callan and (Assistant Chief) Gerry Barbara. We heard a loud thud. I thought possibly somebody dropped a case of books on the floor above. I made a joke about it and said that I'd better go up there to take a look.

Then we heard a transmission that one entire side of the World Trade Center was on fire, and that it was thought to be a propane explosion. Joe Callan immediately left the office to respond over there, and Gerry Barbara and I headed for Chief (of Department Peter) Ganci's office. He was already on his way down to his car. (Assistant Chief) Donald Burns was coming down the hallway telling us that a plane had just hit the World Trade Center.

My regular aide was on vacation, so I had a lieutenant who was assigned to Safety working days with me, Joe Trafari. I told him, Joe, I think you'd better come with me, I'm going to need help over there. We went down to the garage and started responding. Joe was driving and 1 was listening to the radio. When we reached the Brooklyn Bridge, we had a pretty good view of Tower 1 and I could see a large column of smoke. I counted approximately eight floors on fire. I said to Joe, this is no accident, look at this day, you could see a hundred miles, this is no accident. I also said to him, we can't put this out, there's no way in the world we could put out eight floors of a high-rise that's fully involved.

Chiefs Richard Blatus, Al Turi and Nick Visconti, along with firefighters, observe a moment of silence after the body of Chief of Department Peter Ganci was found.

Ricky Flores/The Journal News

When we arrived on the scene, we parked on the east end of the complex, on the corner of Church and Fulton, right near a little cemetery. When we got out of the car, I started donning my bunker gear, but as soon as I pulled my pants out of the trunk, I heard an enormous roar, what I thought was a jet just about to land on Church Street. That's when the second tower was hit.

I looked up. At first, I thought it might have been a missile, but Joe said no, I saw it as clear as day, it was a jet aircraft. The fireball was so enormous that standing where I was I could feel the radiant heat on my face. Of course, people were running in panic. My initial thoughts were that it wasn't quite as bad as it looked, that most of the fuel was expended on the exterior of the building. Those were my thoughts. I knew it was bad, but I just thought it looked worse than it would be.

The debris was of such magnitude that I couldn't stay at the back of my car. I had to run east with the rest of the crowd along with Joe or we probably would have been killed by debris right there. We ran about 100 feet. When we saw the debris coming at us, we turned and ran. It's just a natural instinct. You're not going to stand there and study it. We ran toward Broadway.

When I heard everything stop hitting the ground, I turned around and looked back to the car. There was what I believed to be part of a turbine from the jet about 20 feet away from the car, probably about the size of a cubic yard, burning merrily. Debris was everywhere. (The very next morning, I saw aircraft wheels and landing gear. I said my God, look how far away this is, it's unbelievable. And surprisingly enough, the tires were still intact. When I finally recovered my car, it had a broken windshield and I saw that something obviously heavy had landed on one of the fenders and put a big dent in it.)

I looked up to try and assess the damage, but mostly I was focused on the people who were

AP Photo/Ed Betz

jumping from both towers, more from Tower 1. At that point, maybe I saw eight from Tower 1, maybe only two from Tower 2. But I couldn't get a clear view of how much damage was done to the buildings. I was too far away, and I didn't have binoculars with me. Most of my view was obscured by the smoke.

We put on our bunker gear and went a little bit north to Vesey Street and took Vesey down to West, then we went into the lobby of Tower 1. I was trying to avoid jumpers at that time, just being careful that we weren't killed by somebody leaping. They were coming out of all sides.

Inside the tower, I think the first person I saw was (Fire Commissioner) Tom Von Essen and (First Deputy Fire Commissioner) Bill Feehan. I remember saying to them do you realize this is a terrorist attack? And they said yes, we realize that. I mentioned to them that they had better start thinking about a full recall of people and get hold of OEM (the city Office of Emergency Management) and start setting up staging areas at places where the guys could go to get public transportation down to the site.

Then I spoke with Chiefs Callan and Hayden, who were together. I told them, there's no possible way you're going to extinguish this fire, let's just get as many people out as quickly as we can, then we'll get out of the building and let it burn its way out. They said that's exactly what they had planned to do. We were talking about setting up a command post outside. I told Chiefs Hayden and Callan and the commissioner, who was standing with us at that point, that I would go across West Street and try to establish a command post to coordinate the rescue effort in both towers.

Joe and I left the lobby of Tower 1 and we found Chief Ganci, Chief (of Operations Daniel) Nigro and (Citywide Tour Commander Sal) Cassano right on the median on West Street. I said to them, this is not a good place, you're going to get hit by flying glass, this is a very poor place. We moved all the way to the west side, in front of the Merrill Lynch building, and I wasn't happy even with that location. I told them to move a little bit farther north in the vicinity of a parking garage that ran under there because if the glass or any debris became a problem, we could at least duck in there for an area of refuge. The command post was then moved again adjacent to a driveway that gave access to a parking garage.

From there, our biggest problem was communications. Field Comm was right in that area. We started setting up command channels and tactical channels for both Tower 1 and Tower 2, trying to get all that information to the commanders in each tower. We knew the command structure in Tower 1 and we knew the command structure in

The body of Chief Ganci is escorted from church.

When the North Tower collapsed, the antenna support structure lossened and began to wave. The antenna then came down, followed by the rest of the tower.

Tower 2.

The original staging area was supposed to be at West and Vesey. That was announced by (Battalion) Chief (Joseph) Pfeifer right from the beginning, but most people were drifting over to where we were. We told them to wait in the garage and that we would call them as we needed them. That little thing alone probably saved about 50 lives, just keeping them in there.

From then on, it was just mostly sketchy communications, trying to get reports from each tower. Every once in a while we would hear some reports. I recall hearing reports there was a heavy smell of jet fuel in the 50s and we were trying to find out who was up that high. There would be no acknowledgment.

Probably the worst report that we heard came verbally from an EMS lieutenant who had been in the lobby of building 7 with OEM people. He came over and told Chief Ganci's aide, Steve Massiello, that they were getting reports that the buildings were becoming unstable. Of course, that got our attention immediately. Pete asked Steve where we were getting this information from. He said a lieutenant from EMS just came running over. We got hold of the lieutenant and asked where are you getting this information? His words were there was an engineer-type guy in the lobby of 7.

Within 10 seconds to 15 seconds after that, I was looking at my clipboard, where I was writing all the communications and the location of commanders, and I heard Chief Ganci say what is this? As my eyes traveled up Tower 2, I saw a ring of fire I guess three-quarters of the way up. It almost looked like a shape charge, an explosion when they're going to bring a building down. Everybody was then running for that garage and I followed it up a little higher with my eyes and then realized the entire building was collapsing.

I remember thinking that I might have waited too long, I didn't know if I was going to make the garage in time, but I did. I got maybe 10 feet into the garage. I was still on the ramp because I didn't hit level ground, and the debris and the dust and the blackness blew in there like a hurricane. My thought was did this building pancake? Is it falling over on top of this other structure? I had no idea what damage was going to be done to the building that we were seeking refuge in.

The dust became so thick it was completely black. You couldn't see your hand in front of your face. More disturbingly, it was choking. Then I thought to myself, 33 years on the job and I'm going to suffocate in a basement. When I stopped hearing things falling outside, which probably was only 10, 15 seconds, I could hear a lot of voices around me, but I couldn't see a thing. Being that I was still on the ramp, I decided to exit the same way I entered, thinking that if it's blocked out there, then I'll have to turn around and find another way out.

There were two or three people around me, and we had some verbal communications between us. I said, just head up the ramp the same way we came in, if it's not blocked, we'll get out of here. The next thing I recall was that I walked into a tree, a small tree that was still standing when I got to the top of the ramp. I had climbed over some steel beams and walked into this tree – I could actually see it was a tree, so at least I knew I was now outside, that I wasn't trapped in that cellar. We stood there for three or four minutes, then the dust started to lift very, very slowly and I could see that the entire building had collapsed.

Chief Ganci had gone out the rear of the garage, found a stairwell and had come up on the side street, over to where I was. I remember saying to him Pete, get everybody out of Tower 1, that's coming next. I heard him on his handie-talkie. My handie-talkie was dead for some reason. I heard Pete issue the order to evacuate, evacuate Tower 1 more than three or four times. That's when I started to hear some Maydays on Pete's radio, but I was more concerned with the hundred or so people who were milling around on West Street in a daze right in front of Tower 1. Pete was trying to answer the Maydays and call for people. I told him that our main objective was to get everybody to move north, we have to get another command post set up, we've got to get organized because everything is gone right now.

I remember screaming at the people on West Street to move north, move north, Tower 1 is going to come down. And I wasn't very effective. I saw an ESU (police Emergency Service Unit) truck. I started toward it when I ran into (Chief Fire Marshal) Louie Garcia and I asked Louie, look in that truck, see if you can get me a bullhorn. I went back a little bit south again to start screaming at the people and Louie brought me over a bullhorn. I continued on the bullhorn to scream at people to move north, to move toward Chambers Street, where we could set up a command post. I did that for 15 minutes or so. As people were coming out, I was screaming at them, move, move.

I think I was a little bit north of Vesey when Tower 1 collapsed. About five or 10 minutes before Tower 1 collapsed, I had been with Chief Ganci. He was heading to where I was and out of the corner of my eye I saw him turn around and head south again. That was about five minutes before it collapsed. I'm sure he heard something on the handie-talkie and he was going to attend to it. When Tower 1 collapsed, I started running north on West. There was a young firefighter with me in a dust cloud down on the ground. I just told him put your coat over your head, you'll be fine. He said no, I think we're going to die here. I said I was just through the first one, so I didn't die in that one, you're not going to die in this one, just take it easy, the stuff will lift in 10 minutes, we'll be fine.

I could hear stuff landing around us, but nothing really close. I could hear steel hitting the ground 20, 30 feet away. We stayed on the ground for five minutes or so and then got up. We could breathe a little bit and I started heading toward Chambers Street.

I was outside when we heard reports that a third plane was coming in. The discussion was OK, there's a report of a third plane, there's nothing we can do about it. The decision was made to terminate operations at that point, but it was not going to happen, there were just too many people that were in need of rescue and help. When you're standing out there and you see 10, 15 people jumping, you start to wonder if there are people trapped below, people who managed to get below and now they're trapped. It's something we couldn't abandon.

When I got up toward Chambers, I ran into (Battalion Chief) Joe Nardone, who had come in from home, I believe (Battalion Chief) Jay Fischler and a whole bunch of other chiefs and I tried to organize them.

I asked them to get anybody coming out of the area on one side and to get the fresh troops on the other side, to start setting up staging. Then I think the shock of what happened actually hit me.

When there were enough chiefs overseeing the staging area up on Chambers, I walked back down to Vesey and I met up with somebody, it might have been Steve Massiello, who was still looking for Pete. I remembered where I had last seen Pete, so I took two companies with me and went over to search that area. We were searching for about five minutes before I walked back about 50 feet and looked up at the American Express Building. Up around the 15th floor there was a large piece of facade that was swaying in the breeze, so I ordered the men to abandon the search of that area because it was too dangerous.

At that point, Chief Nigro came back from his survey of the area – (Citywide Tour Commander) Chief (Frank) Cruthers was actually running the operation.

I reported back to Vesey and West and I asked Frank Cruthers what I could do. He said to me, why don't you go back over that way and supervise there? I was so mentally shot by then. I went back over that way and then I found (Deputy) Chief (Nick) Visconti. He was pretty much organizing whatever recovery efforts could be done in that sector. I said to Nick, just keep doing what you're doing, just let me know what's happening. About 10 minutes later, a firefighter indicated that he had found somebody and about 10 other firefighters were in the same area digging.

I went over there and I realized they had found Chief Ganci, whom I've known for 33 years, was in his wedding party, knew him before his wife knew him, was present at the birth of his children. My wife and I baby-sat his children and we were good friends for many, many years. We were able to extract his body from the rubble, put him on a Stokes and we walked him through the Merrill Lynch Building and the American Express Building to an ambulance over on Vesey, on the west side of West Street. I met Steve Massiello shortly after. I told him that's Pete's body, and he went over to the ambulance.

Then I reported back to Vesey and West and there was some heated discussion between some of the commanders about 7 World Trade, whether or not we could put people in there to try and fight the fires. There were some reports that some of our people had been in there and had been trapped. I

Michael Coppola

CHIEF GANCI'S 9/11 OPERATIONAL PLAN AS TOLD TO CHIEF TURI

1. No extinguishment efforts. The fire conditions and location were beyond the capabilities of any fire department. The fire would have to take its course and consume all fuel.

2. Rescue and evacuation procedures only, any hoselines would be used only to protect members during rescue operations. No operations would be conducted higher than the 60th floor, since local interior collapse on the upper floors would be expected. This would also ensure members could be evacuated in a reasonable amount of time.

3. Interior local collapse was expected on the upper floors within three to four hours.

4. To the best of Chief Ganci's knowledge there would be a 12-hour minimum time span before any possibility of total collapse.

5. Evacuation time of all members in both towers was to be implemented after two hours of operations.

6. A captain was sent to notify both tower commanders to report to the exterior command post for a strategy meeting.

7. Premature collapse occurred within five minutes of the captain's departure.

"It has been almost 10 years since September 11. Not a day goes by that I do not think about the horrors of that day. The bravery of the firefighters entering those buildings astonishes me; I will never forget the look on their faces. Each and every man, from the newest probie to the seasoned veteran, knew how serious that situation was. Yet they obeyed their orders just as if they were responding to a routine fire." – Al Turi

remember asking how old those reports were, and they said it was over an hour. I said if it was over an hour ago and you've haven't heard anything else, they're dead, and I strongly recommended we do not put any further people in 7, that we establish a collapse zone. Chief Nigro agreed with me and that's exactly what we did.

Shortly after that, it was probably about 2 or 3 o'clock in the afternoon, I went with Steve Massiello in a police car to Massapequa (Long Island) to tell Cathy Ganci that her husband was dead. I spent a couple of hours there, then I got a ride home from a New York City police officer in a squad car. I took a shower and I called Fire Operations. I had no way of getting back there. I thought maybe I could get a messenger or somebody to bring me back, but they told me that Chief Nigro had also gone home for a minute, so I called Dan up at his house and he was there. He only lives about half a mile from me. He said that he could pick me up in about half an hour, and we went right back to the scene. We stayed there until I think about 3 or 4 in the morning, then we went back to headquarters. I laid down for an hour or two, but couldn't get any sleep, of course.

At 6 o'clock in the morning, we started making plans of what we were going to do. I was given the job by Chief Nigro to coordinate all the activities in Operations, to keep the rest of the city operating and to provide firefighters. Most of that morning I was meeting with staff chiefs and trying to figure out just how we would maintain coverage in the remainder of the city while still having to deal with the largest terror attack on United States soil in our history. We started drawing up some plans, especially for manning, with some different solutions. Of course, the easiest thing was to go on a 24-on and 24-off immediately, then as each day went by, we refined it until we had something that was workable. We had set up staging areas at Flushing Marina (in Queens) to ferry workers over to the site, then figured out how to get them clothed, how to get them fed, how to get transportation. The problem was we didn't have enough staff chiefs to do all this. 1 think most of us were probably working around 18 hours a day at that point.

When the first tower collapsed, I thought to myself, my God, we just lost 200, which probably wasn't too far from being right. After the collapse of the North Tower, some of our people did get out, but not the South Tower. When I reflect back on the whole thing, I think what's really important to bring out is that the courage and the bravery of the men was more outstanding than I thought it possibly could have been. You could look in their faces and you could see the fear. They knew what they were going to. They knew they were going to have the worst fire fight of their lives, yet they all went, without question. You could almost see the relief on some of the people that we didn't send in, put in the staging area. All we had to do was say you're up next, you're on your way, and then they would have went.

There's been such tremendous talk about how many people came there on their own (and there were quite a number of people) and did they contribute to our fatalities because they became fatalities. The answer is, yes, it's a shame and it's unfortunate that we didn't have better discipline within the department, where we would have been assured they would have reported to a staging area or a central location, but when you think about it, it's part of our culture as firefighters to do exactly what they did. That's why they did it. It's that mental attitude that enables a normal person, which is what a firefighter is, just a normal person, male or female, to go into a burning building. That's what keeps the fire department running, that mental attitude. The same thing that caused those people to leave what they were doing when they were off and report to that site, that's the attitude that enables them to enter burning buildings on an everyday basis. Obviously, in the future, the department is going to have to demand more discipline from people, but somehow not stifle that attitude that enables them to enter burning buildings.

I pray that it is a once-in-a-lifetime thing, but there's no guarantee that it is, and the fire service has to be ready for that again. I don't care what the cost is, the professional firefighter will tell you we need the training. We need the resources to deal with that incident should it happen again. It's that simple.

Having Their Hands Full

Firefighter Bill Spade
Rescue 5
Concord, Staten Island

now retired

I'd been in Rescue 5 since April of '91 and been working the last three years in Tactical Support 2. (Tactical Support Unit 2 is in quarters with Rescue 5 on Staten Island.)

That morning, I started work at 7 o'clock. The TAC starts at 7 A.M. Usually at that time it's kind of quiet in the firehouse, but everybody seemed to be up that morning around the kitchen table. There were about 12 or 13 guys around the firehouse table.

At about 8:40, the alarm went off in the firehouse, for the engine and rescue to respond to a steam leak at Bailey Seton Hospital, which is nearby. I was left back in quarters by myself and I assumed the house watch. I was out there maybe two or three minutes, straightening up the house watch area, when the phone rang. It was an off-duty fireman, Anthony Rocco from Rescue 5. He was on his way home on the BQE (Brooklyn-Queens Expressway) and he told me he saw a plane hit the World Trade Center.

I called the Staten Island dispatcher and said I was going to head for the city for the box that just came in, so they said OK, we'll put you on it. It's a one-man unit, the TAC. I grabbed my gear, it's all in one bag. I threw it in the rig and took off for the Trade Center.

As I was approaching the toll plaza to the Verrazano (Narrows Bridge, which connects Staten Island and Brooklyn), to my left I could see smoke coming from the tower.

I was driving along in the HOV lane. The cops already had it shut down. I was making great time. I seemed to be the first emergency vehicle in the express lane, and as I got toward the Gowanus (Expressway), the road went up the hill and down to the Brooklyn-Battery Tunnel.

I continued down the hill to the tunnel. I was not too far from the entrance and I saw the second plane come through and hit the tower, and there was a great big ball of fire. Then I thought wow, the chiefs are going to have their hands full with this one.

As I was going by one of the streets, there was a traffic light. A car was parked there with a jet motor through the back of the car. It seemed to be a small or midsized car and the jet motor went

After the collapses of the North and South Towers, a three-story section (at the bottom of the photo) is all that is left of the hotel.

Bri Rodriguez/FEMA News Photo

through the trunk of the car, the back seat of the car. And it seemed that whoever was waiting for the light, this motor came down and it looked like they opened the door and walked away. And I thought, wow, somebody got lucky, maybe this is going to turn out to be a good day, fortunate for some people.

I proceeded to the corner of Liberty and West streets. As I pulled up, I looked up and reminded myself that I can't park in a collapse zone, but then I thought, well, everywhere around here is a collapse zone.

I got into the lobby of the Marriott Hotel, where I saw Chief (of Operations Sal) Cassano. He was ordering some companies to go to the 70th floor.

Cassano was the only chief I saw at the Marriott. I said, chief, TAC 2 is here, what can I do for you? He said to me go to the North Tower, report to the command post there and operate there.

I started to leave the Marriott and that's when I ran into (Ladder 9 Lieutenant) Bobby La Rocca. We've known each other from Rescue. He had just entered and I was about to leave. He said I'll team up with you, I'm off duty. There was a small overhang on the outside, it seemed to be 15 or 18 inches, so we were able to hug the wall of the Marriott underneath it. All the way to the North Tower we hugged the wall. People were dropping right at our feet from above.

We walked inside the North Tower right there and the only person that we saw there was Reverend Judge (Father Mychal Judge, an FDNY chaplain). I'd known him for a while and he wasn't himself. He was saying his prayers nervously and a lot of things seemed to be bothering him.

People were milling around up there and they didn't seem to know how to get down and out of the building. I said to Bobby why don't we go upstairs and find a way to evacuate these people in an orderly fashion, and he said it seemed like a good idea.

I stayed there at the promenade level and told people to go to their right and walk, don't run, don't look up and they would almost be out. Bobby said he was going to go to the third floor and tell people there to stay to their right because firemen had started going up the stairs and it would make it easier for them to go up. I remember seeing Ladder 2. I knew two guys on Ladder 2, Carl Molinaro and Mike Clark. They had been in Engine 160. Both did details there.

Soon after that, Bobby asked me to go to the third floor to help him carry a woman down the stairs. I went back to the staircase to assist the people coming down when all of a sudden I heard a loud, loud screeching, twisting of metal. It seemed to me like six or seven trains pulling into a subway station at the same time. I was only a couple of feet from the metal door where the staircase was. I pulled the door shut and I got in the corner of the staircase.

I had my flashlight on. Everything went black. The air starting filling up with debris right away. A minute or so went by, and the noise stopped. We were still alive. It was tough breathing and my eyes, I remember, got scratchy right away from the glass particles that were flying around in the air. I could hear people screaming on the outside of the door.

I went out into the hallway area, but I couldn't see. It seemed like when you shined your light, it was like you're in one of those snow globes and the glass was just shining all over almost like a snowstorm.

I could see a couple of people approaching my light. I said I'm a fireman, if you can see me, come to my light, I can't see, you come to my light. They came to my light and I put their left hands up against the wall and I said follow this back to the door and go in the staircase, there will be somebody in there with a flashlight. I'd say 10 or 15 people came to me and went back to the staircase.

Everybody joined hands. I remember grabbing the first woman's hand, a Chinese woman. I grabbed her hand and we started walking out of there. I got them to the doorway with the cops and I said, here you go. Then I went back halfway through the line where they were going and I started lighting up the area where they were walking. The people just kept filing past. Again, no panic and everything.

Michael Rieger/FEMA News Photo

Firefighter takes a break while contemplating the damage and the toll it has taken on civilians and firefighters.

Now, the flow of people seemed to stop. It really slowed down, so he said, I guess we'll go back to the staircase. There were eight of us left in the staircase. It was me, three firemen, a civilian and three cops. The sergeant said to me I think it's time we get out of here. I closed the door to the staircase and asked everyone to count off.

We started leaving the North Tower. We got to what I now know to be 6 World Trade Center and there was an alleyway in between.

We started walking in between the tower and 6 World Trade Center. I looked to my left as we were walking in this alleyway underneath the overhang and I was checking out windows already blown out. I said if anything happens, that's where I'm going. We hadn't been out of the Trade Center maybe more than a minute or so when I heard that same noise again of the twisting steel.

I didn't look back. I took two steps toward that window and I was blown into the bottom of the window. The force just blew me right into the window. I remember smacking up against it.

I was down on my knees. My hand was reaching up and I was at the window sill. I tried twice to get up in the window, but I couldn't pull myself up into it. I was just thinking I don't want to get pinned here with my legs bent behind me, with something coming down on my legs, I've got to give it one more good shot. I gave it a good effort and I got into the window and I tumbled in.

I stood up in the room and I started getting hit by things, and I realized that I had lost my helmet. I went down to my knees and covered my head. At this point, I said good-bye to my wife. I said good-bye to my 6-year-old and I said good-bye to my 2-month-old son and I thought he'll never know his dad. But I said I'm not going to give up like this, so I just stayed in a ball. Then, more debris fell and everything covered me. It seemed like a minute or so, then everything stopped and I was still alive. It was just light debris that was on me, maybe ceiling tiles, grids, panel grids and some duct work.

I cleared off the debris and looked around the room. I saw the three other firemen. My mouth was full of debris, so I reached in my mouth and was pulling it out to get an airway, then I thought of that bottled water. I reached in my pockets, but my water was gone. I realized that I had lost my water, my flashlight, my helmet, my halligan. I had nothing. I stood up and saw that the windows we had come in through were all filled up with debris and things were on fire. Everything was smoking on that side.

The lieutenant who was there had a probie with him. He was clutching his probie pretty tight, keeping good track of him, and there was another young kid (firefighter) in the room say 25, 26 years old. The lieutenant asked me, do you think I should call Mayday? I said to him, Mayday? We're beyond Mayday. Nobody's coming for us in here, we've got to get out ourselves, we've got to breach the wall and try to get farther away.

Then, the young kid, who was kind of by himself, said to me I think I found a way out. I said I can't see, so he grabbed my hand and put it on the wall. I followed the wall along, and up at the top of the window there was a way out. He helped me get up there. We climbed up to the top of the debris over the window. It was the last window and jumped out 10 or 15 feet into a debris pile.

The other guys followed, so four us were now outside. The lieutenant asked, what are we going to do now? I had no helmet, and I felt very vulnerable to anything hitting me, so I said we'll just stay here underneath the overhang until the smoke and everything clears up, then maybe we'll be able to find a way out. There were explosions to our left. There seemed to be cars or whatever else, things exploding, and it really looked like a scene from a war movie. Then the young kid said I think I see a lamp post. He ran about 60 feet straight ahead. We were up on the concourse level, about 30 to 40 feet above the street. He ran to the edge. I guess there used to be a railing there, but it was gone. He saw the lamp post. It was one of these that run out both ways over the sidewalk, and we were about 10 feet or so from it. It would have to be a 10-foot jump just to get to the lamp post. I asked him, what are you going to do? He said, I'm going to jump to the lamp post and slide down it. It was a pretty good jump, but before I could even say that, the kid jumped. He seemed to land in some soft metal, it kind of gave a little. He fell flat down and I was wondering if he was going to get up. He got up. He never looked back.

I'm at the edge now. The lieutenant's there with his probie and me. He asked me what I was going to do. I said I'm not jumping. I remember telling him I'm 42 years old, this body isn't going to make it like that kid did. I'm not going to kill myself, we made it this far. I said we've got this webbing, we can slide with it a little and take 10 feet off our fall and then drop down. I said stay here, let things clear, if we hear that noise, we jump. Twice I had one foot over the edge with the webbing wrapped around me, thinking I was going to give it a shot, but I really didn't feel like jumping at that point.

I was walking up the street and there wasn't a person around. It was just burnt-out vehicles, things on fire, fire trucks and police, everything just desolate.

Up that way we saw (Deputy) Chief (Tom) Haring. I had known Chief Haring from the 8th Division and also from the 1st Battalion. I had no helmet. My eye was swollen at this point and I had bruises and cuts. I just went up to him. I remember saluting him and I said Chief, there's been a collapse, I was with eight guys and I think we lost four of them back there between the buildings. He said, get in an ambulance. I got in an ambulance and they took me to Metropolitan Hospital. I remember being interviewed by the PD and a bunch of other people.

While I was in the emergency room, I was able to get in touch with my wife. They gave me a cell phone which got through. I just told her I'm alive, I'll probably be in the hospital a couple of days, but I'm alive, don't worry. She was happy to hear that. I tore my ACL on my right knee, my breathing was affected, the whole right side of my body was injured. On my face I had abrasions and contusions and black eyes.

It wasn't until that night that my brother-in-law Tommy Aiken, who's a fireman in Rescue 5, called me and he told me that everybody was missing. And I said what do you mean everybody? He says everybody. I started naming guys from the kitchen table that morning and he said Bill, they're all missing. I just couldn't believe that – every guy. As it turns out, we lost 11 guys and I was the only guy that came back alive.

The next morning, I was able to get in touch with my wife again and she said to me I've got bad news. And I said I already know, I spoke to your brother last night and he told me everybody's missing. She said, no, I've got bad news. Joe Driscoll was a good family friend, and we called him Uncle Joe. She said Uncle Joe was on Flight 93; she said Uncle Joe died.

I remember telling her give me all the bad news now because I can take it, I'm at an all-time low. I hung up with her and that was it. I just sat in my hospital room for three days by myself and I guess I took it in little by little.

I remember hearing Reverend Mychal Judge lost his life and then I saw the sun shine through that morning. It was almost like it was him shining through to show me the way to get out. Looking back, maybe I saw 30 or 40 guys that day, and only two are alive that I knew.

But I remember when I called my wife that afternoon in the hospital, the first thing I said is you've got to call Rescue 2 and tell them I was with Bobby La Rocca. He was with me. He was off duty. Nobody knows he was there. That was my main concern when I was in the hospital. I think I found out a couple of days later that he was alive. I spoke to him a couple of nights after I got out of the hospital. He assisted the woman Olivia out. I believe he took her all the way to the ambulance and that's when the South Tower came down.

Flying Girders

Firefighter Robert Reeg
Engine 44, Lenox Hill, East Side of Manhattan

now retired

I was working the night before and was working for someone else for the day tour. The dispatcher came over the voice alarm and was pretty excited announcing box 8087 for the World Trade Center.

Normally we relocate to the area of the fire and cover an empty firehouse. When the second plane hit, we were assigned as the second engine on the first alarm. (Normally, there are four engines assigned on each alarm.) We made good time responding to the scene. Sometimes it takes five minutes to go around the block because of the traffic. The burning tower was visible as we arrived.

Parking a few blocks away, we took extra air cylinders and tools. Large crowds were watching from West Street as we made our way south. We were told to stick together. NYPD and FBI officers told us to be careful; the Pentagon was just hit by a third plane. We kept hearing explosions.

Reporting in to the command post, I saw Tommy Sabella from Ladder 13 leaning on his hook looking up at the jumpers. At the ramp to the garage, located behind the command post, engine companies lined up on one side and ladder companies lined up on the other side. The rolled up lengths of hose were placed in one area and the extra air cylinders were stacked in another location.

The jumpers kept falling. One of the young guys put his hands over his eyes and just said, No, no, no! Lieutenant Dan Williams from Ladder 16 turned around and said lads, don't watch them, we have to focus. It was unpleasant to see. Some of the firefighters were probies; it was their first fire.

A chief ordered 44 to go to Liberty and West Street to make sure the apparatus didn't block the street. Walking south on West Street I saw Father Delendeck. How about a general absolution for the lads? I asked. Then I looked up and saw another jumper. Make that for everybody.

At Liberty and West streets, there were 30 cars on fire. All the smoke was heading toward the pedestrian bridge across West Street. A chief there said see what you can do about the car fires. A company from Brooklyn was stretching a hoseline. I went to get a dry chemical extinguisher out of an apparatus. There was a lot of debris falling, it looked like confetti but would cut you in half.

At Squad 41's apparatus, I opened a compartment. Looking straight up at the South Tower I could see the top of the building starting to mushroom. Girders were flying past me like they were shot out of cannon. A great gust of wind picked me up and I got hit in the head real hard. I got hit in the back by a piece of steel. I lost my breath and was knocked down covered by light debris. I couldn't see or breathe. It was like talcum powder. It was like a tornado. I was waiting to be hit by something else. I was covered over by dust.

It was quiet, like a snowstorm. I felt heat and pushed debris off of me. I broke several ribs, which were pushed into my lungs. Crawling headfirst, I ran into a police van. I banged my head real hard and reached up to open the handle of the door. The air inside was clear. I hit the horn and stayed inside for about 10 minutes. Some emergency service cops came by and gave me water and I rinsed out my mouth. They then helped me toward the river. They were all dazed. The cops didn't realize the building had collapsed. One of the cops was a childhood friend. They left me sitting by the side of the river.

I had been a paramedic. I unbuckled my coat and I felt as if there was something wrong. My chest felt like bubble wrap. I knew that pressure was building up. I told EMS to get me out of here. They packed me with sandbags and were going to give me an IV. I asked how my vitals were. They

AP Photo/Gulnara Samollova

Steel from the towers flies through the air as the building collapses in less than 11 seconds.

said OK. I said let's get out of here.

As we were in the ambulance traveling one block north of the North Tower, it collapsed. The ambulance was hit by debris. The windshield caved in, the front was damaged. We hit a city bus at an intersection. They took me to St. Vincent's Hospital. Lying next to me was a man who was burned by jet fuel. He was screaming. He later died. They put a chest tube in and stabilized me. I was there for three days and was getting worse. They transferred me to the intensive care unit of Montefiore Hospital.

I had smoke inhalation and a staph infection. My lung was filled with bone fragments and several other things that were wrong. I had been on the critical list for a week. I had surgery and had to remain in the hospital because they were afraid of infection. I recovered in three weeks. The other members of my company were pretty banged up as well. Matt Shannon suffered a broken leg after being hit by a piece of steel. He was taken to New Jersey and eventually the leg was not set right and had to be rebroken. Rich Boeri had a laceration on his head. Ed Kennedy dove under a car.

FACT

40 FERRIES
used to move civilians

204 FDNY UNITS
responded

1 DISPATCHER
took 5 calls from one man

How Bad Were We Hit?

Deputy Chief Tom Galvin Third Division, Upper West Side of Manhattan

now Assistant Chief, Chief of Training

When the second plane hit, Division 3 was assigned to the South Tower. Battalion Chief Dennis Devlin, who coordinated special events in Division 3, and Firefighter Carl Asaro got in the car with my aide and me. We parked at West and Vesey streets. I told them to take the command board and I would meet them inside the South Tower.

At the command post, I ran into Chief of Department Peter Ganci. I asked him what handie-talkie frequencies we were going to use in the South Tower. The main command post was being moved to the World Financial Center. I made a mad dash into the Marriott Hotel. I wasn't familiar with the complex. I asked hotel security if everyone was out. He couldn't tell me.

I was near the main desk on the south side of the hotel. I asked where the South Tower was. How do I get there? I walked into the North Tower by mistake. Walking back inside the hotel, companies were reporting in. I told them to switch radio channels.

Engine 23 was assigned to run the elevators. Engines and Trucks were assigned to check three to five floors each. At that time, no more units were reporting in. I said I need to get into the South Tower. The South Tower collapsed.

I ran into an area where a portion of the hotel had been reinforced after the 1993 explosion. We made it to a solid roll-down gate that had dropped when the collapse occurred. We lifted the gate between the restaurant and the bar. I ran into two firefighters from Engine 58. They were missing their lieutenant. We tried to figure a way around.

I went outside past Engine 65 and ran into Lieutenant Ray Brown from Ladder 113. You couldn't really see anything. Cars were on fire and rigs overturned. I thought only the hotel had collapsed. I found firefighter Tom Gaby, Chief Cassano's aide. Then I ran into City Wide Tour Commander Frank Cruthers who had just arrived. It was like a minefield. Everywhere you walked there were problems.

The South Pedestrian Bridge was still up. That's when I noticed the North Tower was separating. I grabbed my helmet and went stumbling down the street. I thought I was going to suffocate. I saw people from Rescue 3, a safety chief and a person from training. I asked if they could get a few engines together so we could get water on Greenwich Street. I asked a police chief to see if he could get a DMORT Team. We also asked for the FEMA team cache by orders of Chief Cruthers.

For the next few hours I was sent to be a liaison to the police. Chief Kilduff relieved me. I returned to the scene about 30 minutes before Building 7 collapsed. I returned to Division Headquarters. It took over two days to see how bad the Third Division was hit.

I had to replace the officers who were killed. We asked firefighters to take details into the division. Firefighters who had been on rotation through Third Division units were also asked to spend time in the units they were familiar with. We had to determine how many apparatus were damaged or destroyed. Missing handie-talkies and hand tools had to be calculated. We had to operate with personnel at the WTC and in the neighborhoods. Every firehouse in the Division was talked to. "Who are we missing? Who responded on their own?" We worked for 40 hours at a time. Units in the First, Third, Eleventh and Special Operations Command were decimated.

Many firefighters stepped up to the plate. A lot of retired personnel came in to help. They gave up their time and did whatever was asked of them. You didn't have to ask. If I said I needed a guy here to do something, they did it. Battalion Chief Jeff Lever was assigned to the Family Assistance unit located on a pier. The families were taken care of in a few hours. These people who helped them were the first ones they saw besides the firefighters in the firehouse.

Many of the off-duty firefighters responding on the department recall assembled at Broadway and Park Row to get further orders.

Steve Spak

Waiting For Tools

Firefighter Dan Potter
Ladder 31 (was detailed to Ladder 10 on 9/11), World Trade Center, Manhattan

now retired

I took a detail to Ladder 10, as they were looking for senior people to work in lower Manhattan. I live only a few blocks from the World Trade Center. I was in a promotional class on Staten Island with Lieutenant Harvey Harrell of Rescue 5. Someone came into class and said that a jet hit the World Trade Center. You could see smoke. My wife works in one of the towers.

I left class and got in the HOV lane on the highway. As I approached Albany and West streets, body parts were all over the area. An ambulance was nearby that had been hit by pieces of the aircraft. I saw Ladder 4 across the street near the South Tower. I met Captain Mallory of Ladder 10, and asked him to get some spare tools out of the equipment locker. Firefighter Pete Bielfeld of Ladder 42 came in and borrowed some gear. Pete wanted to go. I said wait, I'm going to get some tools. He left and was killed minutes later in the South Tower collapse.

A civilian was injured and I helped him inside the apparatus floor. The South Tower collapsed. The wind and dust blew through the open doors of the firehouse. I covered the man as best as I could, but I could hardly breathe. I was able to get the man into the kitchen in the rear. The force of the wind blew out the kitchen windows. I left the man for EMS.

I went out the back door of the firehouse and into the bank in a high-rise across the street. I knew there was a day-care center there. There was a lot of damage to the lobby. I met Fire Marshal Mel Hazel inside. A cop came by and said the other tower is going to go. We braced up against an interior wall.

We made it out into the street. It was pitch black. There were cars on fire. I saw Ladder 113 and several ambulances on fire. My wife was on the 40th floor of the North Tower when the South Tower got hit. She had cleared the area before the first tower collapsed.

I found Ladder 10's rig, and the aerial ladder was flayed. Some of the aluminum ladders had melted and dripped. The entire rig was five feet high. There were heavy steel beams on the rig. The diamond plate was on the ground. We used a search cam to check if anybody was under the rig.

Inside the 10 & 10, a triage center was set up. EMS supplies were stocked. A lot of debris hit the roof of the firehouse. That was cleaned and the roof was used as an observation post. The glass on the windows in the pole hole doors was blown inward.

Steel and debris has already been removed from the front of Engine 10/Ladder 10's firehouse.

(arrow) Current location of 911 Family Tribute Center.

Firehouse Collection

Following Orders

Firefighter Anthony Castagna Hazardous Materials Company 1, Maspeth, Queens

now Lieutenant, Hazmat Ops

When I saw Harvey after 9/11, I never expected him to ask me for my story. I said you don't want my story I did nothing heroic. I was never trapped nor did I save anyone. With that said, Harvey told me he wanted all stories and to think about it and he will get back to me. Well, I never thought about it again until Harvey came by for a second time. Still apprehensive about it, Harvey said we can start talking and if you want to stop, we will. Since I knew Harvey from when I was assigned to Ladder 48 in the Bronx, I felt comfortable talking to him, so we began.

I was coming off a 24 and scheduled to wait relief; the detail was from Squad 41. Four members of Haz-Mat were detailed to Headquarters for company medicals. The firefighters working that day were hired on overtime to cover the open positions. Firefighter Kevin Smith was the senior man as well as my 24 partner and he asked me to relieve Firefighter Hack, which also meant that I now had the watch and resource. Kevin assumed my entry position, which he would get anyway at the change of tours.

Firefighter Smith was standing on the apron, smoking a cigarette, when he yelled to me sitting in the housewatch hey, Tony, a plane just hit the Trade Center. I said yeah right. He said no, take a look (our firehouse had a perfect view of Manhattan skyline). After I took a look and confirmed what he saw, I called the Queens dispatcher on the department phone. I gave him a verbal alarm for a plane into the World Trade Center. The dispatcher said we don't have anything on that. I said no, I'm not asking you, I'm telling you, we can see it. He said something which I could not make out, but as I hung up, the Box came in – Third Alarm and Hazmat was assigned.

Hazmat Co. 1 is an eight-member unit and responds with a first and second piece. That morning, since it was so close to the change of tours, we ended up riding heavy with Lieutenant Crisci, Firefighter Tim Welty from Squad 288 and a visiting probationary firefighter, Phil Larimore from Engine 280.

Since I had resource, I had communications and called the Midtown Tunnel as soon as we left quarters. I requested that we enter the eastbound plaza from Borden Avenue. Since it was rush hour, this would allow us to bypass the usual westbound delays coming down from the elevated LIE into the toll plaza. They assured me they will be ready for us, and ready they were. The plaza was shut down and the eastbound tube had one lane cleared for us. Near the toll plaza, we saw Rescue 4 trying to make its way through the westbound traffic jam.

As we entered the tunnel, all communications were lost so as soon as we got out of the tunnel, I called Manhattan Dispatch for an update and where they wanted us to report. Manhattan acknowledged with a "stand by" but they never got back to us. Firefighter Scauso was the chauffeur of the first piece and decided to go east on 34th Street to the FDR Drive South.

There was not much talk on the rig; I was sitting in resource, Lieutenant Crisi was to my right, Firefighter Hohmann was behind me in the jump seat, Smith was standing in the well by the side door as he usually does, smoking a cigarette. Firefighters Gardner, Welty and Larimore were in the back. We were listening to the department radio for any information we could get.

As we got near NYU I remembered to call my fiancée (she worked at Cornell) to tell her I was on a late run. She knew more than I thought cause she asked me to get off the rig. I remember saying jokingly OK, I will tell them to stop so I can get off, and then the call was dropped.

We decided to get off at South Street because that gave us more options, since we did not know where the command post was as of yet. Also, at this time we did not know the South Tower had been hit until we turned right onto Frankfort Street. That's when Welty, who was looking out the top hatch, yelled out to us all. He jumped down and couldn't believe what he saw, nor could anyone else. At that time it was apparent to us that it was a terrorist attack.

We took note of the wind direction and decided to proceed to the northwest side of the North Tower so we would be upwind in case there

View of West Street from the North Pedestrian Bridge to Vesey Street after the second collapse. Various apparatus are covered by dust and debris. Rescue 3 is in the middle of the picture and Rescue Collapse 3 is on the bottom, right. Hazmat was close to the scene, but repositioned farther away.

were chemicals and/or radiation involved. We wound up on the West Side Highway, just south of Vesey Street, not far behind Rescue 1. We all got off the apparatus when Lieutenant Crisci turned to me and said to stay here with the probie, and he would call me when he gets to the command post because we don't know if we're here for Hazmat or Rescue. Until then he wanted me to get the rest of the equipment ready.

I went around to the chauffeur side of the first piece and saw Firefighter Scauso struggling with where he left the apparatus and the need to don his bunker gear. I told him I will take care of the apparatus and you get dressed. He asked if I was sure and I told him I was ordered to stay behind, so I got it. He thanked me and donned his bunker gear.

I turned and was surprised to see Firefighter John Giordano, (he was the only one I did not know was working) I said John, what are you doing here? He shrugged his shoulders as he walked past me, all geared up and ready to go. As the members walked through some sort of temporary fencing, I saw a white flash, and that was the last I've seen or heard from them again.

Both apparatus were located in a bad spot and I had Larimore guide me as I backed them up to the left lane of the northbound West Side Highway just north of Vesey Street across from the Verizon Building. I chose this spot because it was still in line of sight of where we were first positioned (so if anyone came back they would see us) and would not get us blocked in. This move had nothing to do with me thinking the towers were coming down.

Now that the apparatus were in position, equipment ready to go, I stepped outside with binoculars in hand to see papers flying down and people jumping from above the fire floor. Radio communications were pretty poor, and even though I had the portable 800 megahertz, department radio and handi-talkie on, I was not able to make out radio transmissions too well. I was thinking, if we only had the radios we were experimenting with prior to this incident. They worked everywhere we tested them: Javits Center, *Intrepid*, Grand Central Station and, ironically, the World Trade Center.

By this time Larimore told me that his boss from Engine 280 ordered him to go with his company. Firefighter Ceriello came by and asked about SCBA or spare cylinders, I forget which, but I convinced him to change to a 60-minute air cylinder instead of the 30-minute that was already attached. He later tells me, at Firefighter Eric Allen's funeral mass, that if he did not take the time to change the cylinder to a 60-minute one, he would have most likely been caught in the first collapse.

I was out in front of the rig when I thought another plane was coming in. There was such a loud roar that I ducked and looked overhead. Instead of a plane, there was a plume coming my way. I ran to the back step door of the first piece and as I was jumping up I heard a Port Authority cop asking to follow me into the fire truck and I yelled back yeah, there is room in here. As I got in, I had to jump up to shut the rear-most hatch, then the side door window and also the hatch in the resource area. I did not get them all as the plume engulfed us.

Breathing was difficult so I handed out PAPRs (power air-purified respirators) to the PA cops and gave them instructions on how to get them operational. Some got it working; some did not. I remember crawling past them to get to my SCBA (the only one left on the rig). When the dust settled, they all disappeared, leaving behind the PAPRs and a few gun belts. No weapons, just bullets.

I went outside and turned on the on-board generator for lighting. I remember somebody telling me that the plume wasn't from a plane, it was from the South Tower collapsing. As I walked toward the corner of Vesey Street, I kept staring at what was now the collapsed South Tower, trying to figure out if that was really what I was seeing.

I ended up at the back of the first piece when Firefighter Joe Angelini Sr. came to me and said I need help...I think there are people trapped over there, pointing to the area of the Winter Garden within the World Financial Center. (I knew it was Joe because we had met earlier that year when we had a Hazmat job with Rescue 1). Just as Joe finished talking, EMS asked me if I had an O_2 cylinder, somebody was having a heart attack. I said yes and told Joe I would be right with him.

After I tested the cylinder to make sure it had O_2, I walked toward the Verizon Building, gave EMS the O_2 and looked toward the Winter Garden for Joe, but he was gone. Before I could follow him, my HT chirped, so I went to change out the battery.

Something made me look out the side resource window and that is when I saw the top of the North Tower and the antenna tilt, and start to come down. I felt I was in the collapse zone and looked for the best place in the apparatus that would give structural support.

As I heard the debris hitting the apparatus, I just stood there frozen, waiting for a large crushing piece of the tower to land on me. The truck shook and when I looked out the window, it seemed like I was in a snow blizzard at night. It was dark and all I could see was clouds of white powder and debris rolling against the windows, under pressure with nowhere to go. The dust inside the rig was worse this time. The pressure blew out the window separating the cab and box of the apparatus allowing dust and

Peter Matthews

Smoke and dust clear as papers cover the street and fallen steel sticks into the street and subway.

debris to come in. As daylight reappeared, I stepped out and thought I was in a war zone from another part of the world.

Hazmat Co. 1 off-duty firefighter members McArdle, Borkowski, Bob Hunter and Koroghlian all met up with me at the first piece. I believe Firefighter Hunter told me when he saw the spotlights he knew it was Hazmat 1. (I was notorious for turning on the lights all the time.) The decision was made to drive the apparatus north toward Canal Street where we regrouped. Hunter was able to get a call to his wife and had his wife call our families to let them know we were ok. I saw a familiar face in Jimmy Guidice from Engine 94.

Once our families were contacted we regrouped, picked up other members walking down the West Side Highway and headed back to the Trade Center – this time we parked on Barclay Street. Since I was junior, I was told don't give up any tools and make sure nobody takes anything, we will be back in an hour to relieve you. As I waited, I put out a few spot rubbish fires with a can and, before the hour was up, I was ordered to move the apparatus to Vesey and North End Avenue.

Other members from Hazmat Co. 1 were now there (Firefighters Hack and Schramm), so I proceeded off to the area of the Winter Garden. While searching in that area I picked up a wig and when I turned it over I realized it was not a wig, but somebody's scalp. Stunned, I dropped it. As I turned around I saw that the North Pedestrian Bridge crushed Rescue 1's rig. (We were originally parked next to that location.) I realized I dropped the scalp and when I went back, I was not able to locate it.

Back at the "base camp" North End and Vesey, I was ordered to take a van to Staten Island to drop off Lieutenant Connolly and pick up supplies at Rescue 5. On the return trip, a Highway Patrol officer wouldn't let me across the Verrazano Bridge, even though I was in a department van, my uniform was covered in white powder and I had my P-95 mask on. He told me to remove my mask and asked me a few questions, maybe he was just seeking information. Soon after he let me proceed and told me to be careful.

I was there to witness the collapse of WTC 7. This time I was not as close and we were well warned before it came down. On September 12th around 1800 hours Hazmat Co.1 was 10-8 from the World Trade Center. As I drove up the West Side Highway, there were hundreds of people cheering us on and waving flags.

After 9/11 the company was down to 14 members. We worked 24 hours on, 24 hours off until October, and then went to an ABC chart well into 2002. The memorial inside Haz-Mat and Squad 288 lists 19 members killed in the line of duty on 9/11, including members working in other companies for the tour and the Chief of Haz-Mat Operations, Jack Fanning.

Get Out

Battalion Chief Rich Picciotto
Battalion 11, Manhattan Valley, Manhattan

now retired

I came into work for a day tour. I saw on TV that the North Tower was in flames. It was horrendous. I knew it was terrorism. I telephoned the dispatcher and said this is the 11th Battalion. I was there in 1993, in charge of evacuation in the North Tower. We were discussing what to do when the second plane hit.

There was a request for a double assignment. I told the dispatcher that I was going to the North Tower. He said go. I saw Pete Hayden, Division 1, in the lobby. I was teamed with Ladder 110. The SOC chief, John Paolillo, was near the elevators. I asked how we were going to get upstairs. With that, an elevator opened. A building employee was ferrying people down from floor 16. Ladder 110 and I got on the elevator. Chief Paolillo took the stairs.

We got off on the 16th floor, but there was no one there. I checked the C stairwell and went up. At 21 there was no re-entry. I told 110 to put something in the door so it doesn't lock behind us in case we need to get back on the floor. I told them we have to go up, take your time and take breaks.

As I continued up, people were coming down. They stopped coming down steady after the 21st floor. Up at the 35th floor, it was like a staging area with numerous companies. Then the building started to shake. Something was crashing. The noise was getting louder and seemed like it was coming at you. It seemed to last forever. Everybody froze. The noise stopped and it was deadly silent. There were no transmissions on the radio. No one talked. Somebody said what was that? I said something major just happened.

Was there a collapse? There was silence on the radio. Does anyone know what just happened? The tower came down, was the response. What tower? I was thinking it was the radio tower. Then they told me that the whole building came down. The whole South Tower!

I tried to contact the command post, but I was getting nothing. I made the hardest decision I ever had to make. I said we're evacuating. I was then going to make sure that everybody was going down. I had a megaphone, and yelled into the three stairways to get down. A sweep of every floor was done. I went from C stairway to the A stairway then back to B.

We kept using the C stairway until floor 20. Firefighters were clogging it. Someone said the C stairway was clogged with debris. They said there were people clogging A. The B stairway was moving. There were numerous handicapped people in an office off of the C stairway on the 12th floor. The B stairway was still open. Lieutenant Mickey Kross from Engine 16 and another company were switching off as they carried a patient. I said we have to go faster.

I looked out a window on the 12th floor that faced west. Dust and debris were visible. As we made it to the sixth floor all hell broke lose. The North Tower had collapsed. Lieutenant McGlynn from Engine 39, Lieutenant Kross, a firefighter from Engine 16, Captain Jay Jonas and the entire crew from Ladder 6 were there. Josephine, the woman Ladder 6 was assisting, and a Port Authority police officer were all together. I said don't move. I don't want a secondary collapse.

A door was visible between the second and third floors, with debris against it. A tool was handed down and when the door was opened, you could only move a little bit. It was full of compacted debris. I radioed Maydays nonstop. There wasn't any answer. After quite some time I was finally able to talk with Battalion Chief Mark Ferran from the 12th Battalion. I told him we had 20 people in the B stairway on the third floor of the North Tower. Some of the people were counted twice. He said, where is the North Tower?

What I thought was there may have been 60-100 feet of rubble covering us. No one will ever find us. There was another chief who was trapped below us. We could hear him calling. Then he didn't call anymore. The lower section of the stairs was missing. It was dusty and smoky. You were able to breathe. Soon it was getting lighter and brighter. Jay said he thought he could see sunlight.

The firefighters coming to rescue us were nowhere near us. I climbed up and down on a ledge and was able to see the rubble field. There was a 40-foot drop. Out in the open was utter devastation. There was no sign of life, just smoke, twisted steel and a burning building. My megaphone had a siren. I radioed Chief Ferran that I was going to turn on

Greg Semendinger

The towers measured 209 feet by 209 feet. Fire burns on several floors early on. The first aircraft made the hole on the north side of the tower.

the siren every five minutes. He said we can't get there from here, we have to retrace our steps. It took another hour.

I saw one firefighter making it through the smoke. I wanted to climb down. Apparently Ladder 43 was exhausted by the trip to find us. The troops still didn't know how they were going to get to us. They were zigzagging, shimmying down steel loaded with six to eight inches of powder. Chiefs wanted the rescue team to leave the area because several buildings had floors burning.

After we were helped from our entrapment, it still took a long time to get off the pile. I had my eyes washed out and was bandaged on the scene. My lungs felt burnt from the smoke. There were a lot of EMS workers standing by with not many to treat.

Another One Just Hit The Towers

Lieutenant Dan Williams Ladder 16, Lenox Hill, Manhattan

now retired

One of the guys put the TV on and the housewatch said a plane flew into the tower. Everybody was thinking it was a small plane. Then I went out and took a look and said oh, this isn't good. It's something big! So, I told the day crew that was coming in to go change because we're going to be going.

I was taking a look at the rig, doing my own visual inspection to make sure we had everything, when the guy on the watch yells that another one just hit the towers! Now, you know for a fact that it's a terrorist thing.

At approximately 9:10 A.M., we got the response as an additional unit on the fifth alarm. Four guys tried to get on the rig prior to us leaving, but I told them to get off. I was only taking the day crew, the guys on the riding list. We convoyed down with the 10th Battalion and 13 Truck. When we cleared the midtown high-rises, you could see both towers. I never saw anything like that in my life. Listening to the radio traffic, you got the number of occupants trapped and everything else.

We parked approximately two blocks north of the north walkway and proceeded to the command post. They were breaking the engines and the trucks – engines to the right, trucks to the left. We were the last truck left at the command post. A lot of debris was coming down off the towers...jumpers, too.

I told my members to get back into the loading dock area and stay under cover, while I stood at the command post. I was keeping an eyeball on the towers when I noticed that the South Tower was starting to collapse. The only thing I remember is yelling, run! Everybody got into the loading dock area, and that dust cloud chased us right in. There was zero visibility in there for a short period of time.

I did a roll call. We were missing one of our members. He didn't answer. So, I got the rest of the guys together and proceeded back up the ramp to find our member. We started seeing a number of walking wounded, both firefighters and civilians. They were bleeding and had minor injuries. I told the members to start evacuating the injured through the back of the Financial Center toward the river.

We saw the North Tower directly across from us, burning. We started fanning out to look for our member. We found an EMS worker who had broken his leg, a heavy-set fellow, and tried to evacuate him by carrying him out. We put one guy under each shoulder, but the pain was too intense for him. One of the brothers found a gurney and we put him on that. I start wheeling him into the loading dock area. A member from 6 Truck was saying that he couldn't find his company, so I said stay with us until I can get radio contact and let them know we got you.

We got the EMS worker up on the loading dock and we're wheeling him through. I told my OV man and the man from 6 Truck to put the gentleman in an elevator to get up to the level to get out the rear of the Financial Center. When it was reported to me on the radio that the elevator went down into the sub-basement and the lights were flickering, I told them to get out of the elevator. I said I'll go get help. Get this guy up the stairs.

As I was on my way up to get the rest of the members in Ladder 16, I heard a deep rumbling. I thought it was the Financial Center, the building that we were in, collapsing. We just balled up behind the stairs. The door flew open, and a lot of dust and debris came down the hallway.

Once it calmed down, I headed up and found the three members, but we were still missing the one. I found the other members plus a couple of other members, one from 53 Engine. We proceeded down into the sub-basement. We all got a handle on the gurney, got the gentleman up and out of the stairwell and wheeled him across to the marina, where he was loaded onto a police boat and taken to parts unknown.

We walked along the promenade down to what I believe was Liberty Street, where we had three fireboats tied up to the bulkhead. Assistant Commissioner Gregory said he was running the command post and to help the guys stretch a

3½-inch hose down to Liberty.

Now we could view the whole devastation of the area. We were still looking for one of our members. Everything was in disarray. We headed back north and that's when we ran into the member near the marina. We ran into our fifth man from Ladder 16. A very happy moment to see him. We proceeded back through the loading dock area and started searching the debris field in front of the loading dock area and outward. A couple of the members did a quick sweep of the Financial Center to see if everybody was out. It's hard to say how long we operated there.

On Vesey Street, we found an open restaurant. Nobody was in there. We just got ourselves rehydrated, drinking a lot of water. We found a phone that was working, so I had the brothers call home to tell somebody that we were all OK. This is when I first got word that 39 Engine was trapped in the North Tower.

We proceeded over to the north command post. The chief there said just stand fast, they have companies in there looking for 39. We did run into two of the members earlier from 39 Engine. I guess it was approximately 4 o'clock in the afternoon. We were told to head north, check in at the command post up at the Stuyvesant High School. As I was checking in, Building 7 collapsed. I guess it was about 5, 5:30 at night.

About an hour and a half later, we met up with the guys from the company that were there on recall. We were told by the command post to take the rig home. That was about it.

Initial operations looking south on West Street. Smoke rises from car fires on Liberty Street. The command post was at the bottom right of this photo.

FDNY

The Worst Day Of Our Lives

Chief of Operations Daniel Nigro Headquarters, Downtown Brooklyn

(became Chief of Department after 9/11) now retired

We were having an informal meeting in Pete's (Chief of Department Peter Ganci) office that morning. The next thing I heard was Pete yelling look out your window, a plane just hit the World Trade Center. I stood up and there was a very clear view of the North Tower and I could see a large volume of black smoke coming out of the north side.

Pete and I responded together in his car, so we could talk about what we were going to be doing. Pete transmitted a fifth alarm, probably at the Manhattan side of the Brooklyn Bridge. We had a larger body of fire in a high-rise building than I had ever seen before. I know I told him that this would be the worst day of our lives. It appeared to me like we had some amount of fire or smoke on 10 floors. That would have been just a ballpark guess.

When the second plane hit, I don't know if we had moved yet or we were in the process of moving. We might have still been in the middle of West Street and heard the roar of another plane, which immediately made you look up. And all I saw was a blur, a crash. I didn't know what hit the building.

(Assistant Chief) Gerry Barbara was concerned that the plane we saw had hit the building. At that point, anybody who didn't know yet that it was a terrorist attack – almost everyone had the same feeling that I had, that these two planes hit the towers on purpose, and what else is going to happen?

We called in a second fifth alarm. I think we knew this was a terrorist attack. There were two fifth alarms, which we knew were only going to be a start. We thought let's get everybody back to work and then we'll see where we're going to go from here. There's a combination of factors – if it were just the fires and even not the collapse and the two planes hitting the tower, my feeling is we would need a recall.

There was one command post already in the lobby of the North Tower. We had quite a number of firefighters behind us at the command post and we sent a group of them to the South Tower to start the evacuation.

Chief (Donald) Burns (citywide tour commander) originally went into the North Tower, then he walked over to the South Tower. Chief Barbara went to the South Tower also. So we had Chief (Joe) Callan (citywide tour commander) and Chief (Peter) Hayden (Division 1) in the North Tower and we had Chief (Tom) Galvin from Division 3 in the hotel. For the South Tower, the order was let's get this place evacuated as fast as we can.

There was a staging area set up on West and Albany where the companies were reporting to. There was another one set up north of Vesey Street. It appeared that maybe some companies went to the staging area and the staging chief directed them based on their assignment to the tower.

The plan was once we had everybody in place, I told Chief Ganci, let me walk around the building quickly and see how badly damaged they were because we couldn't see over from West Street. The extent of the damage that occurred to the South Tower was much more clearly visible from north and east than it was from west. I did not get as serious a picture from that side.

I could see that parts of the plane actually came through. I knew it hit the South Tower from the south. I could see a hole in the north side of the building, so we realized at that point that part of the plane went straight through the building. There were a number of sections of the building missing on the east side, which was not apparent from West Street.

I heard someone say something about a plane crash at the Pentagon. There are 10 more planes or some numbers, another plane heading for us. There were a few stories, but I do recall the "third-plane-is-heading-for-us" story. And I think an F-15 came by at one point and a lot of people had thought that to be the third plane.

I heard a noise that I immediately identified as a collapse. I looked up and saw a large section of that outside wall coming off the building with the rest of the building. I didn't think we would get out of the way in time, but we tried anyway and we were successful.

A lot of big pieces fell, crushed a car that was next to us, took out a couple of windows around us. And we were in a safe haven from that. We thought we would choke on the dust, we started breathing the dust, which I think everybody on the scene felt at one point or another there – they escaped being hit by the

David Handschuh

building, but now they were going to suffocate.

We walked down to West Street and found a large Field Comm truck with a tractor-trailer. Two Field Comm members were in there, two communications guys, (Chief Medical Officer) Dr. Kerry Kelly and (Deputy Chief Medical Officer) Dr. David Prezant were there with an officer from either Engine 10 or Ladder 10. It ended up there were six of us and I asked the people in the Field Comm truck, OK, what's going on, what do you hear on the radio, where's the command post?

They told me the command post was on Broadway and Park Row, at the foot of City Hall Park. (Deputy) Chief (Tom) Haring (Division 6) was in charge and that's where the command post was. I immediately felt, again, that everyone had been killed because Chief Haring wasn't even there when I left the command post, so who was in charge?

We walked over and there was a large number of members and Chief Haring. There were fires all over on the side streets and there were vehicles on fire. They said the other command post, the larger one, is on West and Chambers. Joe Callan was there. They said Chief Cassano was hurt, that he had to go to the hospital. Chief Ganci was missing. I got the rundown of who made it and who didn't. Commissioner (Thomas) Von Essen survived. (First Deputy) Commissioner (William) Feehan was missing. I took over and Chief (Frank) Cruthers and Chief Michael Butler were with me. Chief Frank Fellini was running the operation back down at Vesey. (Butler and Fellini were assistant chiefs and citywide tour commanders.) Chief Haring was running the operation on the east side.

There was a tremendous amount of fire burning in 7 World Trade Center. It was determined that a large amount of damage had been done to the structure by the collapse and that even though there were some rescue operations or search operations in the area, the building was in such danger of collapse that we suspended all operations. Then we determined a collapse zone around 7 to move everybody back about two or three blocks in each direction. We were able to continue searching in one area because people had seen where Chief Ganci and Chief Feehan were and we continued to search that area and located them. Finally, around 5:30, the building collapsed.

It took hours and hours and hours to get the fires under control, simultaneous with doing a search, with doing an assessment of how many of the buildings were seriously structurally damaged and were in danger of collapse themselves.

I remember hearing that we had companies from Westchester staffing Bronx firehouses and Nassau and Suffolk companies in Brooklyn and Queens.

The request for FEMA teams was done pretty soon after the collapse through OEM. I'm sure it's the largest number of FEMA teams that have ever been used anywhere.

Engine companies reported in with the rollups – 50-foot sections of hose in preparation of fighting fire, as one firefighter said, "like we always do."

Nobody Was Answering

Firefighter Ray Phillips Special Operations Command, Roosevelt Island, East River

now retired

At approximately a quarter to 9, I was making my way to the TAC rig to put my gear on and the voice alarm went off. He was saying a second alarm was being transmitted for the World Trade Center, all units assigned start out, particulars to follow. Guys came out of the kitchen yelling that there was a plane crash.

We came down the east side of Manhattan. Somewhere around the Brooklyn Bridge, we saw the second plane come in. We saw it dip its wings to the left like it was turning to the left. We didn't see it hit, but I said to (Firefighter) Joe Angelini, who was riding with me, Joe, that plane's awfully low.

We came north on West Street, came down from the lower part of Battery Park and ended up going to Liberty Street. There was a lot of debris coming off the building. One of the silver coverings had come flying down like a missile and just missed us. I told Joe to walk up to 10 Engine and 10 Truck and at least grab a helmet.

I got dressed and proceeded to look for Joe. A member of OEM came over and froze everybody in the street underneath the overpass and said that a third plane was coming in, he wanted everybody back. 25 Truck was standing next to me. Dr. Kelly was standing next to me. We stood there maybe five to 10 minutes waiting for this guy to make a decision.

Actually, where he stopped us, we were under a covering. Then we just stood there and watched some people jump. I actually went back to the rig at one time and got binoculars just to get a better of view of what was going on because the rig was right there. Finally, I got a little antsy and I proceeded to cross the street, watching the debris come down.

I went to go look for Joe. There was a place for parking cars, a park-and-ride, on the corner of Liberty Street. There were a couple of cars on fire. People were saying that they thought there might have been people in the cars, so I made my way over there. Joe was coming down. We started checking cars.

The debris coming down was tremendous, more so off Tower 2 than Tower 1. Building debris,

A firefighter assists a person across Liberty Street. Note debris in street falling from building.

David Handschuh

plane parts, paper, a lot of coverings over the exterior. Some stuff was sailing. Some of the covers floated down. So actually if one was coming at you, you had some time to act. But then for the most part, some of them came down like dive bombers. I guess maybe the wind just caught them.

One car in particular was really roaring. It looked like the door was open, like somebody had been driving it and that was the car we were trying to make our way over to. It was right by the South Pedestrian Bridge that went across West Street. There was a concrete wall there. You couldn't climb over, you had to go around. Then some kid yelled to me. He said we need an ambulance! We need an ambulance! We got somebody down!

I walked back to Albany and grabbed the first EMS ambulance. The guy shot passed me. He stopped just before Cedar in front of 90 West. As I was walking back down, the guy says we had a fireman down and it turned out to be a guy from an engine company. Two or three guys had him and they were dragging him. It looked like something out of Vietnam, where you're looking for a sniper or something that's picking guys off.

We went over to the building at 90 West, which was under renovation. They had the scaffolding around all four sides of the building. We started CPR. The backboard came. We really weren't in too much of harm's way as far as debris coming down because we had the scaffolding over us protecting us, but we didn't know what else was happening.

They put him on a gurney and they got him in the ambulance. I got a paramedic off one of the private ambulances to jump in there with him. Then they took off for Bellevue Hospital.

Our gear was all over the place – masks, helmets, turnout coats. We tried to regroup. There were about five or six people in the lobby. They had come out and asked if everybody was all right. I think they saw the look on our faces. Now we realized that we had lost a guy, so some of us were kind of out of it. So they said can we get you a drink of water, can we do anything?

We went in the lobby to start getting dressed. I just was going to throw some water on my face and a guy says come on, I got a bathroom over here. It turns out we're on the second floor. When he got me in the elevator, he went up to the 13 floor, of all numbers to pick. I was like, the heck with this, maybe just go down. I said let me just throw some water on my face.

Something was wrong. I wasn't having a heart attack or anything, I just didn't feel right. All of a sudden, there was like a rush of air. All the air left the building. You heard this explosion. There was a rumbling noise and the building we were in shook. All the ceiling tiles fell off. The lights went out. I thought the building collapsed. I thought the building had been hit by something. We proceeded to get out of the building.

When we got down toward the lobby, it was on fire. They had made sort of a triage center right in front of 90 West, with all ambulances. It wasn't until maybe 10, 15 minutes later when I finally made my way out of the building that I realized that every ambulance they had parked there was destroyed, was on fire. Some were flipped over or on top of each other. There were at least a dozen of them. Any rig that was in the street was gone.

I never made it to the lobby. It was too dark and I didn't have a flashlight. I couldn't see. It was getting a little hot. And I went back up. All the floors were locked. I said here I am, I'm stuck in the staircase. I had no tool with me.

I made my way back up and finally on the fifth or sixth floor, I got in and then found all the people that had been in the lobby had fled to that floor. We opened some windows. I think the most ironic part was that by myself, I opened the window up, thought I was looking at exposure 2 between two buildings. I didn't realize until Wednesday that I actually was looking at West Street, but it was so dark and the dust had filled this netting that was protecting the building that it made it look like there was another building there.

We made our way to the street. Another fireman came from somewhere and he tapped me on the shoulder and says, come on. We were just standing there in shock. The whole street – the South Tower was down. It was an unbelievable sight. I knew something had happened, but I didn't realize the whole tower had come down. They had given the transmission of a major collapse, but I figured maybe from whatever floor that plane had hit had fallen off, never expecting to see that.

From debris or rigs, the whole street was on fire. Oxygen bottles were exploding in the ambulances. Relief valves were letting go. I think it was Chief Kasper we heard on the radio calling for all the rescues and squads to the command center. I was trying to make my way to the command center, trying to figure out where it was. You couldn't go north. You had to walk across the street. We hadn't gone about a block and we heard this loud, rumbling noise. It was the North Tower coming down.

We stepped into a building, but it was closed. There was a gate and we got in, there was a column. I got under a column, covered my face. As the noise started to subside, we tried to make a run for it. We made the turn and as we were running, you could hear this loud noise coming – it was the dust cloud coming down and within two seconds, it had passed us and the whole block filled up.

If I was a step slower, it probably would have gotten me. I was getting ready to dive under a car. I saw an entrance to a building and a woman saw me from inside the glass. She's screaming open the door! Here comes a fireman! Open the door. The guy, without hesitating, opened the door. One, two, I stepped in, and three, he closed it and then it was like the end of the world. It was just like you looked out, it was pitch black. If there was anybody out there, you couldn't see them. You saw paper flying by.

Then, within like 10, 20 minutes, you started hearing Maydays. The loudest one we could hear was 65 Engine. And then the one with (Captain Al) Fuentes trapped in his car.

Fuentes was the tough one. They were trying to figure out where he was, where he was in the car. I talked to Jack Flatley in Rescue 1. He found Fuentes. He wasn't in a car, he was under debris. He had the super radio with him. That's how he was; everybody else thought it was a car. Flatley actually found him more toward the middle of the street. He was under one of those pieces of flashing we saw coming down. Flatley didn't have a radio. He said Fuentes had a tremendous gash and was semiconscious. He says can you help me get you out? He really couldn't. Then the Marine Company guys came and they helped him get Fuentes out.

And then we just proceeded to walk. An off-duty firefighter from 4 Truck, Danny Manning, found me and he guided me along. I was covered in dust. I was filthy. My hair was like cement. You felt so helpless. There was nothing you could do.

Someone came to me and said something about they were looking for a transit to monitor this building. So me and Kevin O'Brien, who was off duty, made our way all the way back through there, got the transit, headed back and we set a transit up under 7 World Trade Center. And that was really it.

I saw TAC 2 cut in half, all the rigs just basically crushed, big aerial tower ladders. There was one point in time I was sitting on, I think it was, a mask service truck and it was like as flat as a pancake. Someone finally said to someone who was sitting next to us, do you realize that's a mask service unit?

The destruction was just total – I mean when we first got there, we knew we were there for the day. I didn't expect the tower to collapse like it did. I expected, especially with the South Tower, Tower 2, that the upper part of the tower would have tumbled over like it started to do, not realizing that it was constructed to pancake on itself. It wasn't a long, drawn-out collapse. It came down real fast. All my years of going to building collapses and seeing buildings with Rescue 3 at the Collapse Unit, and studying building collapses, this is just phenomenal, both of them. I could see if one came down, but both of them coming down is mind boggling.

We're sitting there trying to figure out how many guys didn't make it. Everybody was throwing numbers around like we're probably missing 100 guys, maybe more. And then hearing it was over 300 guys. And then while you're there, you're finding out that they pulled out Ganci's body. They pulled out Feehan's body. We heard right off the bat that the chaplain, Father Mychal Judge, had had a heart attack and died.

Lucky

Firefighter Jimmy Guidice Engine 94, Hunts Point, Bronx

I worked the night before and saw the coverage on television. We were dispatched to Engine 35 in Manhattan as a staging area with Engine 50, 64 and 83. Inside the firehouse we heard the Pentagon had been attacked. The engines were on East 124th Street. We refueled the rig. We were part of five engines dispatched. We all called our wives on the way downtown. We parked on West Street. We were carrying our rollups and our standpipe kit.

We were about one or two blocks away when the tower came down. We ran – the dust was 12 stories high – and we ducked into a storefront. It was totally dark. We were covered in debris. I was throwing up; so was Dominick Carrone. The probie jumped into a van that was going by and headed north. The next time we saw him he was clean and we were filthy.

You could only hear PASS devices activating, there were no conversations. Everyone was stunned. I thanked God that I was all right. People started coming out who needed our help. A firefighter who was bleeding was carried past us. We helped Pat Carey from Engine 74 and a civilian who had a broken leg into an ambulance. We saw Chief Telesca being carried by two firefighters.

You could hear other collapses. There was no command post, and there was an absence of communications. Someone called the firehouse and told them to write on the blackboard that we had survived the collapse and we're all accounted for.

We were near Building 7 when it collapsed. We had just seen a civilian carrying fire tools and clothing and placing them in a van. He had apparently stolen the items off apparatus. We just grabbed him when Building 7 collapsed. We ran to safety, and the last we saw the police had him in custody after the collapse.

When we arrived, we had no hesitation. We were going to walk in and do what we had to do when the building came down. I had worked on the rotation in Engine 40 and Ladder 35 – 11 members were killed in that house.

Picture taken from under the North Pedestrian Bridge facing north. Engine 94 and several companies parked several blocks north and were walking south when the North Tower collapsed.

Firehouse Collection

Superman

Firefighter Joe Falco Engine 1, Garment District, Manhattan

now retired

I received a call to come in and work overtime on Monday morning. When I arrived I was told they found several firefighters to work and I wasn't working the day tour. They said I could work driving the engine Monday night. I hung around and worked Monday night. I had been out for a while and my first tour back was September 6. I was supposed to get early relief Tuesday morning. I was the only one going off duty.

At about 8:30 A.M. we had an EMS run to Penn Station a block away. I heard Battalion 1 radio in that he had a plane into the Trade Center. I drove around the block back to the firehouse. Within seconds of me backing into the firehouse, the tones went off for a run for the engine. I said I'm supposed to go home. The incoming chauffeur was there. I asked him do you want to drive? He said you take it.

I worked my way to the West Side Highway. We parked on the south side of the North Pedestrian Bridge. The guys got off the rig. I was getting dressed. The mask for the chauffeur was out of service. I met the officer inside. He said no mask, go outside and get water. It was hard to leave the building. People were jumping. I saw the chauffeur of Engine 65. I helped him hook up. An engine pulled up and parked right in front of the North Tower. As soon as the engine pulled up, someone jumped from above and landed on the roof of the engine. The rig took off.

I helped put the suction hose on a hydrant at Liberty and West Street. There was a walkway to where the standpipe connection was located. It offered a little bit of protection. We were next to the parking lot at the southeast corner of the complex. A couple of cars were on fire. There was plane debris everywhere. We hooked up to another hydrant and tried to put out a van that was close to the apparatus.

Stuff was falling off the building. People were trying to get out of the hotel. Cops were yelling that there were about 20 people in wheelchairs and they needed stretchers. EMS directed the civilians.

Firefighter Kevin Shea was an extra man on Ladder 35, and had gotten separated from his unit. He asked if we needed help with the car fires. He was on the nozzle with me backing him up. The chauffeur of Engine 65 was looking out. Kevin was trying to put out the car fires when I yelled run. The South Tower was collapsing.

I ran west. This wind comes and knocks my helmet off. My hands go out in front of me like I'm Superman. I'm flying through the air. I said I'm not dying like this. I heard my daughter's name. I go head over heels rolling into the center divider of the West Side Highway. I go up and over the divider completely into the southbound traffic lanes. I wake up. Everything is black. There is no light, no sound. There is debris everywhere except where I landed. They say you see light when you die. I said, I'm in trouble, because there is no light. I was getting pounded on my back, like you were getting punched by small pebbles that were landing on me. I had about 30 lumps on the top of my head.

I thought I had heard Firefighter Muldowney while I was lying on the ground. "Hey Boy" is what we used to say to each other over the handie-talkie. He was working and was killed. The dust started to clear. I thought I was buried. I reached around me and found I wasn't buried. Lights from an ambulance were visible in the distance. I thought a piece of the building came down, not the entire building.

I was still sitting near the debris when a firefighter yelled out, anybody here. I yelled back. He asked if I was OK. They came over to see if I was OK. I heard a firefighter yell out that he was trapped in front of an ambulance about 20 feet from me. My leg was hurting me so I couldn't go. The other firefighters that had left me came back. The firefighter was only wearing a turnout coat. He was bleeding from his head. The debris that was blocking the front of the ambulance was moved and the bleeding firefighter walked away.

Two firefighters assigned to Ladder 24 in my firehouse had just escaped the partial collapse of the hotel when the South Tower collapsed. They each grabbed one of my arms. There was so much debris, it hurt more as they pulled me. We made it in front of the North Tower when the North Tower

Thomas P. Buchta

Engine 1 was one of the 18 engine companies severely damaged or destroyed after the collapse.

collapsed. I went from not being able to walk to sprinting towards the Hudson River.

The wind and the dust started again. I put my head inside my coat and said, whatever happens. I walked in a straight line down some stairs to the bulkhead. I walked north until I was out of the dust cloud. I saw one of the firefighters, Grillo, who I had been with. I said where is Tyrone? I was going to go back into the dust until I saw a shadow and it was Tyrone. Grillo had injured his arm and his nose was bleeding. I sat on a park bench. I was in so much pain.

A sightseeing boat pulled into the bulkhead. I get on the boat. I couldn't walk down the stairs; I had to slide a ladder. They took me to Jersey City with several firefighters. They put me on a bench. There was no one around, so a lady called my wife.

Finally they took me to the Jersey City Medical Center. They triaged everybody in the lobby. Hundreds of people were in the lobby. There was a lot of damage to my legs. They stitched me up. They put the cops, firefighters and EMS in one room. I was fully covered in dust.

I said I wished I could talk with Father Mike, (Mychal Judge, fire department chaplain) I didn't know what happened to him. A lieutenant said don't you know, Father Mike got killed. I was so close to him, it was heartbreaking to hear. (Father Judge worked in the church across the street from Engine 1 and Ladder 24. He parked his fire department vehicle inside the firehouse and he ate every meal with the firefighters). It took the wind right out of my sails to hear that. He was such a nice man. He made everybody feel that you were important to him.

They were sending guys two at a time to take a shower. I had scrubs on and was on crutches. Do you want to take a shower? They kept asking me over and over. I said let someone else go. I was the last one to take a shower. I saw what I looked like in the mirror. I was the dirtiest one there. I was transported back to New York. Two friends drove in to take me home. That was my last day at work. I suffered injuries to my left side, left knee, broken knee cap, torn ACL, torn PCL, broken tibia, joint and bone crushed, left eye injury and left shoulder replacement. I had a right torn ACL and a bone/ knee crushed.

Redirected

Lieutenant Scott Maxwell Covering in Division 11, Working in Engine 219, Times Plaza, Brooklyn

now Rescue 3

I was working my second tour of 24 hours covering a vacation. The night tour was quiet. When the first plane hit I was in the office. You could see the Trade Center from the firehouse.

Captain Tim Stackpole had worked the night before. He went to Tillary Street where Division 11 headquarters was located. He apparently responded to the Trade Center with Acting Deputy Chief Dennis Cross.

Engine 219 responded to a few runs after the tower was hit. After the second plane hit, numerous Brooklyn units were sent on a ticket to the Brooklyn-Battery Tunnel. As we were responding on the same alarm, we were redirected to the Williamsburgh Bank Building. This building was 37 stories in height and was the tallest building in Brooklyn for numerous years. The chauffeur turned around on Fourth Avenue and arrived at the bank. I ran in and security met me in the lobby and said it was a false alarm. He said it was smoke from Manhattan.

Continuing on to our assignment, I told the other firefighters on the rig that this was the biggest job of our lives. The police had closed the tunnel. We were almost out of the tunnel when everything turned black. The chauffeur hit the brakes. You couldn't see out of the rig. Now I thought they hit the tunnel. You couldn't hear the Manhattan radio. There wasn't any handie-talkie traffic. It took four or five minutes for the smoke and dust to lighten up. I was waiting for the water to hit us. I had no idea the South Tower had collapsed. I had to guide the chauffeur the remaining distance out of the tunnel.

Once outside, people were running towards me. They were running every which way you could imagine. Some people were bleeding, they were grabbing me. About 100 yards south of the South Pedestrian Bridge we could see Ladder 113 on fire. Ahead of us, debris was everywhere. The South Tower had fallen. You could still see people jumping from the North Tower. I could hear the handie-talkie chiming up with Maydays. Gathering our tools and spare air cylinders, we saw the North Tower start to peel away. We dove under a rig. It took five seconds for the debris to hit. You could feel the debris hitting the rig. Everybody was quiet. I had a feeling I was going to die under the rig. I thought, is this how I'm going to go? It was a strange feeling. The chauffeur said, pray.

I tried to grab my facemask, but someone was laying on it. It took about five minutes for the dust to settle. That five minutes we spent responding to the Williamsburgh Bank Building saved our lives. Ladder 105, in quarters with us, went directly to Manhattan when we were redirected to the other alarm. Their apparatus was parked in front of the Marriott Hotel. The rig was destroyed and all who responded were killed. Looking at the perimeter, where we parked was the first group of apparatus not to get buried. I said I have all of my members, now I have to keep them alive. The radio was dead silent.

When we got up to the South Pedestrian Bridge, we thought we couldn't get under it. We were going to find another way around because of the steel and debris.

Ladder 105's cab was hit by a box beam and caught fire, which spread to the entire rig.

Firehouse Collection

Greg Semendinger

Engine 219 was enroute to the Brooklyn-Battery Tunnel when they were redirected to the 37-story Williamsburgh Bank Building near their quarters. That stop saved their lives.

I didn't know what we were going to do, even stay alive.

We made our way under the bridge. An engine company was hooked up to a hydrant and was flattened. Steel was sticking out of the Bankers Trust Building and the American Express Building. The scaffolding around 90 West Street was on fire. So was Building 7. It was such a big area of destruction. There were piles of burning debris. Hose was stretched from an engine to the river where the fireboats were located. Someone jumped up on top of a rig and was operating a deck gun. Everything was pretty much buried. Nothing was recognizable. Everything was white.

We had a report of a third plane coming in, but it was American jet fighters. Water started flowing from the fireboats. There were things exploding all around us. The chauffeur of Engine 65 was located in the debris. There were fires all around him. I remember seeing him being lifted out of the debris. He was all white and was missing some teeth.

We spent the rest of the day with a hoseline trying to do what we could do with it. Everybody who was killed, died right away. We didn't find any survivors. All of the firefighters who were working initially looked like zombies. My eyes were cleaned out in the World Financial Center. I finally got through to where my wife worked. I told the secretary to tell her that I was still alive and don't know when I will be home.

When Building 7 collapsed, everybody ran away. Another dust cloud appeared. I said here it comes, here it comes! Everything turned black again. Then the dust settled. It was strange to see people react. You were a collapse veteran trudging along doing your thing. I spent the whole night there. We were sent on missions all night. I finally gave my radio to a regular officer from Engine 219.

The members of Ladder 105 found their apparatus. They worked to uncover the rig through the night. They did an unbelievable job cleaning around the rig. I finally got back to the firehouse at 11 A.M. I spent an hour and then went back to the WTC. I stayed until dusk, then back to the firehouse where I collapsed. I finally made it home. It was hard to see.

I put an American flag outside the house and then went to the hospital. A psychologist told me I was done, that I could not go back to the site. I grabbed the doctor by the tie and said clear my eyes! I have to go back! Clear my eyes!

When I returned, the entire neighborhood had flags out. A volunteer rig was now in the firehouse. They were teamed with Ladder 105 who had a spare rig. They responded to a few incidents.

Wait For Me

Firefighter Patrick O'Keefe Engine 94, Hunts Point, Bronx

now retired

I worked Monday night and was going to work Tuesday. I heard the Bronx announce the second alarm in Manhattan. The fifth alarm was announced a few minutes later. Someone mentioned a plane hit one of the trade towers. I saw the television news reports.

After the second crash, we were sent to Engine 35 in Manhattan. They are located at East 124th Street and Third Avenue in East Harlem. Units were assigned to a staging area in case other units were needed right away. This way they were closer to the scene than responding from their original firehouse. Assigned were Engines 35, 50, 64, 68, 83, 84 and 94. Ladder 48 was sent later.

When we were dispatched, I drove down Second Avenue to 23rd Street. I went west to the West Side Highway and went south. Over the radio we heard a report of a major collapse of the South Tower. The dust was settling as we arrived.

We had to park quite a few blocks away, north of Stuyvesant High School. They all suited up. The covering officer took off. The members took the rollups, and I said wait for me. They stopped. I got dressed and radioed the officer, telling him that he forgot the standpipe kit. Someone returned to get it.

Once again, I radioed the officer asking if the firefighters really needed to carry rollups. I said the hose would already be upstairs. We stopped for the third time while we decided what to do.

The firefighters were walking south adjacent to the Verizon Building when the North Tower collapsed. Everybody ran north. I made the sign of the cross. When the antenna on top of the tower got to eye level, I took off.

The dust cloud was coming for us. I said I'm not going to make it. I was enveloped in dust, got knocked down and the wind pushed me into a van. After the dust cleared, it took an hour to meet up with the rest of the company. The officer said thanks for stopping me, if you didn't I would have been killed.

We helped a few people. One man had a broken leg. We helped Pat Carey from Engine 74. He had been on rotation with Engine 73 who had been relocated to our quarters for a year. They had their firehouse renovated. The dedication ceremony was on Monday, September 10. All the top officials were there.

Lieutenant Crespin, who was our officer, said there should be a roll call to see who is missing and who is not. I opened a hydrant and washed my eyes out. I remember seeing a multi-story-high pile of rubble. Several of the rigs were crushed like pancakes. Early on they found a life ring with Ladder 10 stenciled on it. Five levels down, the apparatus of Ladder 4 was discovered.

Companies from all over the city took turns operating at the site. This South Bronx engine company operates on Church Street.

Andrea Booher/FEMA News Photo

Last Truck At The Command Post

Firefighter Rich Rattazzi Ladder 16, Lenox Hill, Manhattan

I worked the night tour and got off in the morning. Engine 39 responded with High-Rise 2. Ladder 16 was assigned and the lieutenant wouldn't let anyone who was not working get on the rig. A few minutes later, the recall was announced.

I responded in the back of a police car with two other members. We had found two spare mask brackets, but no cylinders. We arrived and found Ladder 16. We took two spare cylinders to make complete masks. Another complete mask was found on another rig. We passed under the North Pedestrian Bridge. The South Tower collapsed and hit the center of the Marriott. We dove under rigs. We couldn't breathe or see. I heard someone yelling for help. I located a civilian and brought the person out to Vesey Street. I walked into the back of a rig, that's how dark it was. The dust started to lift. How was I going to meet up with the two firefighters I came with?

I saw the chauffeur of Engine 39, he had a broken shoulder. I walked him to EMS and came back. I looked at the rigs and heard PASS devices going off. I saw a lot of firefighters, but none from Ladder 16. Apparently, Ladder 16 was the last truck at the command post and was held there when the collapse occurred. Someone said Ladder 16 was in the subcellar helping remove an injured person. I saw a man throw a chair through a window on the floor below the top. People were yelling don't jump, we'll get someone to help you.

I was near a parking lot at West and Vesey when the second tower collapsed. I ran up to the street and was blown five feet off my feet. I was near the atrium area of a building. The glass doors were open and I ducked inside. I shut the doors behind me. A wall of black came down the street like a twister. Ten civilians came running through looking for a way out.

I met two firefighters from Queens. I told them I was missing two guys. I saw a cameraman who had a broken leg. He was going in and out of consciousness. I went up Vesey Street to get a backboard and grabbed two EMS workers. It took about 20 minutes to travel a half block because of the debris. I finally went to the Hudson River to get some assistance. I drank something, was given oxygen and had my eyes flushed.

Firefighter Steven Wright Ladder 16, Lenox Hill, Manhattan

We responded behind Engine 22, Ladder 13 and Battalion 10. We parked on West Street and reported to the command post. Walking down the street we could see people jumping. There was talk of a third jet. There were a bunch of companies at the command post. They asked the engines to stand on one side and the trucks on the other. Spare cylinders were in the middle. Ladder 13 was assigned. They were assigning a different channel for each tower.

I heard a noise and looked up and saw the building crumbling. We ran into the garage doors of the loading dock located directly behind the command post. Dust and smoke came in. We were able to come right back out.

There was an EMS worker down. He was a real heavy guy, over 400 pounds. We lifted him on a gurney and were going to bring him through the building and out the rear. We placed him in an elevator and the other members walked upstairs. The elevator went down. The building started to shake. The lights went out. The officer said get out of the elevator. We took him out of the elevator and had to climb three levels to get to the street. The North Tower was down. There were two or three inches of dust and papers all over.

We placed the EMS worker on a boat so he could receive medical treatment in New Jersey. We then helped stretch 3½-inch hose off a fireboat for two blocks. We had lots of help from other firefighters. The hose ran from the marina at the rear of the World Financial Center to Liberty and West streets. There were steel beams six or seven feet high where the command post had been. At one point, we could hear church bells.

Best Water I've Ever Had

Lieutenant Robert LaRocco Ladder 9, East Village, Manhattan

now Special Operations Command

I was off duty in lower Manhattan. I heard a low-flying aircraft. A few seconds later, I heard a loud noise, then people talking about a plane flying into the Trade Center. I went to my firehouse and changed into my uniform. I grabbed a ride in a police car and was let off on Broadway and Dey Street. Waves of people were running north. It looked like a movie. I walked west on Liberty Street, and could see about 12 floors of fire in each tower.

Standing in front of Engine 10 and Ladder 10's firehouse I said I have to get into the tower. There was a lot of debris and body parts in the street. I went to go into the South Tower when a man and woman jumped from an upper floor and landed right in front of the entrance. I had to step over the remains.

Inside, I went through the lobby and saw Assistant Chief Donald Burns, citywide tour commander, and his aide near an escalator. I reported in and asked the chief how I could help. He said I need a company right away. I went back to the entrance. Not wanting to get hit, I made myself a smaller target crawling over debris near a column. I saw Lieutenant Kevin Dowdell of Rescue 4 followed by the rest of the company walking west on Liberty Street. I said Chief Burns needs a company. Dowdell said we have orders to report to the command post on West Street. I reentered the lobby of the South Tower and Chief Burns was already talking with several companies. The South Tower collapsed.

I felt the treaded steps of an escalator, and went down the escalator backwards. I got to the bottom and crawled to an exterior wall. I turned right and felt for the floor. There were steps. I went down several steps and found an exterior door with a push bar.

I pushed the bar twice. Nothing happened. With all my force I pushed the door and it only opened a few inches. There was debris piled against the door. I lied down on the floor and pushed as hard as I could. I thought I was going to break my legs. I was able to get the door open enough to squeeze through. There was debris all around. I had a lot of stuff in my eyes.

I stopped for a second and heard a fire engine with the pumps engaged. I was walking to the sound when a voice yelled, are you hurt? It was Firefighter Phil Scarfi from Engine 235. He grabbed hold of me and, running, brought me to Engine 235's apparatus. He took off my helmet and he had a bent-tip nozzle we use as a water fountain after a fire. I took water in my mouth and gargled. The water was brown like coffee. It was the best water I ever had.

I reported to the command post. I thought we were missing a lot of firefighters. I was north of the North Tower when it collapsed. I started to run, but couldn't outrun the cloud. I decided to get behind a piece of fire apparatus. I wound up behind the tiller section of Ladder 118, holding on. We got hit really hard in that area.

Damage to a section of the World Financial Center.

Todd Maisel

Andrea Booher/FEMA News Photo

I wondered if I was still alive. I took a breath and took in concrete. I took a few more breaths. There was zero visibility.

I could hear guys whimpering, crying. I took a deep breath and yelled out if you can hear my voice, you're still alive. I said put your shirts over your head. Put your faces under your shirt. You want to see your families again. I took five or six breaths. I tried to talk to the guys to avoid panic. I felt something between my legs – a cop was under where I was crouching behind the tiller rig.

Six or seven guys gathered around after hearing my voice. We headed north on West Street. There was two feet of visibility. The cloud stopped at Chambers Street. I saw an open hydrant, took my shirt off and washed the debris off of me. The material had gone down my back and was irritating.

Making my way south on West Street, I saw a firefighter all covered in dust. I couldn't even tell who he was. He said he was Warren Smith, the on-duty lieutenant of Ladder 9. He said he was missing several members. I said maybe they are around in all the confusion. Let me go back and see if I can locate them. Three members were killed.

I heard jets overhead. With all the smoke and dust, you couldn't see where they were. We started to take cover. Finally I could see that they were our military jets. They were full of ordnance and had belly tanks. I stood there at that time and was proud to be an American.

Lieutenant Mike Warcola from Ladder 5 was working a mutual exchange of tours for the captain. The captain's birthday was on Tuesday. Mike said he would work 24 hours on Tuesday so the captain could be off. This was to be his last tour working in the firehouse. He was retiring Saturday morning. Mike and all the firefighters who responded from Ladder 5 were killed.

Firefighter Billy Lake insisted on working on Monday night 9/10 to celebrate his 20th anniversary. The firefighters in his probationary class were hired on September 5, 1986. Someone dropped out of the class and he was hired to replace him on September 10. He was bringing in the meal for the night tour Monday. Billy was killed along with the other responding members of Rescue 2. About 10 other members of his probationary class died.

After each collapse, a dust cloud covered most of lower Manhattan. Lieutenant LaRocco told firefighters around him what to do to survive.

I Just Called Your House

Lieutenant Keith Ruby
Operations, Headquarters, Downtown Brooklyn

now retired

I was working on the seventh floor of Headquarters. Someone said a plane crashed into the World Trade Center. There was a clear shot to view the Trade Center from Headquarters. Someone said another plane was approaching. I knew it was terrorism.

I wondered how many had died already from the planes and inside the Trade Center. I asked the deputy chief I was working for if I could go down to the command post. I ran to Flatbush Avenue and jumped into a fire department suburban. There must have been two dozen firefighters inside.

We went over the Manhattan Bridge and south on Broadway. I told the driver to park it on the sidewalk so we didn't block any apparatus. The guys exited the van and scattered. On my way to the scene, I checked every piece of apparatus. I was looking for gear. I figured I could get a set of gear at Engine 10 and Ladder 10.

I met Captain Paul Mallery of Ladder 10, who was off duty. I said I wanted to borrow some gear. There were injured civilians lying on the apparatus floor. He said he needed help first. Go upstairs to the truck office and call all the members of Ladder 10 for recall. I called the list. Most of the calls resulted in leaving messages to report to your command. I grabbed a helmet, pants and coat off the rack.

Lieutenant Jeff Guja worked at the Medical Office in Headquarters. We walked west on the south side of Liberty Street. There was debris falling. I told Jeff there was no need to get hurt, put your collar up and your earflaps down. We were trying to get to the command post that was possibly located on the West Side Highway. Jeff was five yards in front of me.

I heard an explosion on my right side. I turned to my left to take cover. The debris field came under my feet and picked me up. I flew about 50 feet over the sidewalk and through the glass window of a vacant coffee shop located on the first floor of Bankers

Lieutenant Ruby just left 10 & 10 when the South Tower collapsed. The arrow shows where Ruby was found.

Firehouse Collection

Trust (Deutsche Bank). This was directly across the street from the firehouse I had just left. I was in a complete black hole. I was thinking I was burned. I had no radio or tools. I must have been unconscious. I tried to move, but my legs were not coming with me. I apparently had a broken arm and a broken leg. I thought I was going to bleed out of my femoral artery.

The black ceiling started to turn gray. Light was visible. I yelled out for help. A red EMS bag that a fire company carries is the first thing I saw. The firefighters in the firehouse heard me yelling. They had to climb up over 20 feet of steel before they could climb into the coffee shop. I told them my name and where I was assigned. I gave them several phone numbers to make notifications. I thought it was over.

They placed an oxygen mask on my face. Another noise was audible. It sounded like bombs going off. You could hear the rumbling noise. A firefighter layed over the top of me. Someone yelled out to those firefighters who had been operating in my area, is everybody OK?

Down at my feet I saw a Ladder 10 helmet. I asked the firefighter his name. He told me. I said I just called your house for the recall. They stabilized me onto a backboard. They carried me up and over the steel back to street level. I was put on the tailgate of a pickup truck. We were driving in reverse. I said what am I doing on a tailgate driving in reverse?

They placed me into the back of an ambulance jammed with 20 people. It was utter chaos. People were screaming and yelling. Inside the emergency room they were cutting my gear off. I asked where we are. They said Beekman Downtown Hospital. I said we are too close, we have to evacuate. There was chaos and screaming in the emergency room. I was told I was to be transferred to another hospital.

I had surgery on 9/11 and 9/12. I woke up one evening and a retired captain came to see me. I told him my story. He said it was incredible. He told me it wasn't an explosion, it was the South Tower collapsing. I said that's impossible. I was right across from the South Tower. He told me that both towers were gone. He told me I was the only one they found alive. The lieutenant I was with was killed. He was blown into a stairway and buried in debris. His body was recovered three days later.

Andrea Booher/FEMA News Photo

Damage to Bankers Trust Building next to 10 & 10. The name later changed to Deutsche Bank. Two firefighters were killed in August 2007 when the building was under demolition and caught fire.

FACT

170 UNITS
damaged

$8 MILLION
in tools & equipment replaced

Write Down Every Serial Number

Lieutenant Dan Buckheit
Ladder 154, SoHo, Manhattan

now retired

I was assigned to a unit in Ladder 20's firehouse on Lafayette Street in lower Manhattan. An EMS deputy chief came in and said a plane had flown into the World Trade Center. About 50 firefighters went up to the roof of the firehouse. Most of the personnel were off-line.

A few minutes later, we saw another plane come down the Hudson River, turn and fly into the South Tower. I went downstairs and started to gather equipment. I took flashlights and spare masks from Squad 18, who was quartered with Ladder 20 while their own quarters were being renovated. A roof rope and a training rope were also brought downstairs.

Ladder 58 from the Bronx was relocated to Ladder 20. I told the officer to put all the spare air cylinders on the rig. He said do you think so? I said I know so.

I went to the Division 1 office. I asked the aide who I went to probie school with how many radios and spare batteries I could have. He gave me six radios and 12 batteries. He told me I had to sign for everything. I had to write down every serial number on each radio and on each battery. Several off-duty members climbed aboard Ladder 58 and we responded on a box near the Trade Center.

As we responded south, we had to stop for all the civilians running north in the street looking behind them in the area of the Trade Center. There was an EMS ambulance parked on the corner. The two EMTs were wearing paint masks. I asked them if they had any more. They handed me two boxes of paper masks.

Ladder 124, Buckheit's former company, operates in front of Engine 10/Ladder 10 on Liberty Street.

Thomas P. Buchta

These would come in handy. I was the only one on the rig wearing an air pack.

The sky went from blue to midnight. We arrived at Church Street. The South Tower collapsed. The dust hit us. We stood in a circle and I handed the face mask around to each member. Everyone took two breaths and passed the mask. It was a 45-minute air cylinder, so it lasted for awhile. I took a snapshot in my eye of the area before the dust hit us. I said this is the way out of here and started walking west.

We ran into a few fatalities. One man was terminally injured. I asked him if there was anyone he wanted me to call. He died in my arms. He was hit by a stainless-steel sheet that almost cut him in half. I wrote the number he gave me on my hand. Another man had a broken arm and leg. He was thrown on top of a Stokes basket that we were carrying with all of our equipment. He was dragged into a building.

The lobby had clean air. There must have been 50-100 people inside. You could see that people on the outside were dragging their fingers on the outside windows trying to find a door into a building. The smartest maneuver was to go inside at this time. Right after the North Tower collapsed, it was the worst snowstorm you ever saw. You couldn't hear anything for two blocks. Car alarms and PASS devices were audible. It was the silence of the dead. We left the injured person inside the building. I told a man to see what you can do for him. We were going to walk south then over to the river and then walk back. It was horrific. You couldn't breathe. It was lucky we had masks.

Ladder 124 was evacuating firefighters from the Engine 10/Ladder 10 firehouse. A firefighter had a possible broken ankle. We made it to a grocery store. People were carrying out shopping carts of water. We were finally in clean air. I advised all the firefighters to take off their gear. They washed their eyes out and took some water.

We went back on Liberty Street. I met Lieutenant Scott Maxwell, who was in Engine 219. There was a firefighter who was trapped in the cab of an engine. Fire was burning close to the rig. Maxwell said he had no water. I asked if he tried the Financial Center across the street. We went across and opened the standpipe on the first floor. A 2½-inch handline was hooked up

Andrea Booher/FEMA News Photo

and stretched across the street.

We found out there was so much debris in the street that we were standing on top of Ladder 110. The rig was crushed by steel I-beams. The only way you could determine it was a rear mount aerial ladder was the portable ladders sticking out the back. Over the radio we heard (Captain) Jay Jonas of Ladder 6 calling a Mayday. I asked if anyone knew where the North Tower was located. I had been there numerous times, but always by subway. We kept walking.

We saw Ladder 105. The apparatus was just starting to burn where the tormentor controls were located in the middle of the rig. We tried to search inside and under the rig. All searches were negative. We watched it burn from one end to the other.

On the west side of West Street, an I-beam was sticking out of the World Financial Center. The beam had apparently bounced in the street and was sticking out of the high-rise building facing down towards the street. If it had fallen and landed in the building from above it would have been facing skyward. The beam was at a 45-degree angle facing down.

The reports from Jonas were coming in stronger. We came upon the collapsed entrance to a parking garage. I went down the ramp into the basement. I knew of the entrance when I had relocated to Ladder 10 in the past. Walking in about 150 feet, I met a wall of concrete rubble under the building. I then exited the garage. Back on the main pile, I heard another transmission from Jonas. He was not broadcasting on a regular basis; I thought he was conserving his radio battery. We made our way toward Building 7.

Into a valley, we went three floors down and then we had to climb up three floors. A rope was attached to a box beam so firefighters could get up and around. Eventually, we made it to the area where Jonas and his group were trapped. We had to go across a beam over several elevator shafts. There was about a six-floor drop into the shafts if someone fell. There was a haze down in the elevator shafts. When you got to the stairwell, it was leaning and unsupported. Other firefighters were trying to reach a chief who was trapped below. All the ambulatory personnel were removed.

We stayed with Josephine, the woman that Ladder 6 had been helping down the stairs before the collapse. Deputy Chief Visconti was talking to Battalion Chief Keenan of the 49 Battalion. Captain Fred La Femina was talking with me. I was being asked if I could remove the woman. I said I needed a Stokes basket. It took about one hour to get the Stokes basket. Building 7 was burning right across the street. We were operating on the north side of the North Tower. I said the building won't hold. We have to get her out of here!

The Stokes finally arrived. She was tied in. Two firefighters took a position on the other side of the elevator shaft. I had a roof rope on my side. With her between my legs we dragged her across the elevator shaft. It took another hour to go from the North Tower to Vesey Street. In the process we had to go down three floors then back up three floors. We were being asked to leave the area. We couldn't leave until we got her out to Vesey Street.

Back on West Street, Chief Jerry Tracy lined up the trucks on one side and the engines on the other side of the street. Because of the possibility of Building 7 coming down, all units were moved two blocks to the Hudson River. EMS irrigated my eyes for about 30 minutes. I got up and opened the doors to an ambulance. Who was inside but Josephine. She blew me a kiss and said thanks.

Back on Vesey Street I had two firefighters left. I heard the rumble. I ran north. I said to myself I'm not outrunning this. All of a sudden it was midnight. A big cloud of dust, debris and heat passed me. I was like the Pillsbury Doughboy again. You could only see my eyeballs. When the dust cleared, I went into a store for a pack of cigarettes. The store owner charged me $7.50. I think I had $8.00 in my pocket.

The piece of steel hanging down in the exterior wall reportedly hit the street and bounced up into that position.

Collapse

When the World Trade Center Twin Towers were first designed in the 1960s, they were built to withstand the crash of a 707 jetliner. The Empire State Building, built in 1931 and located a few miles north of the Trade Center site, withstood the crash of a U.S. Army B-25 bomber on July 28, 1945. The plane crashed into the building between the 78th and 79th floors. Traveling at 200 mph, the plane made a hole 18 by 20 feet. Most of the impact was absorbed by the exterior wall and there was little damage to the interior. Thirteen people were killed and 26 injured. In comparison, the two jets that flew into the Trade Center were traveling at more than twice that speed and weighed 15 times more.

The construction of the Trade Center was much different than that of the Empire State Building. The truss floors allowed for a large, open-floor area built around a central core (elevators, bathrooms, stairs and machinery rooms). The Empire State Building has a steel skeleton and masonry walls.

Pieces of the aircraft were found up to 1,500 feet south of the complex after the first crash. Following the second impact, pieces of the plane were located five blocks north of the Trade Center site.

The extensive damage to the south and east side of the South Tower (the second tower to get hit) caused the first collapse to occur 56 minutes after impact. The North Tower withstood the first crash until one hour and 42 minutes after impact. The lightweight trusses that held each floor assembly failed with a pancake collapse.

The picture on the opposite page catches the South Tower as it fell to the ground in 10 seconds.

The following three pages catch the collapse of the North Tower. As the North Tower collapsed, severe damage was done to Building 7, which was located directly north. Pieces of the exterior wall of Building 7 were ripped away, allowing fires to start on many floors. This 47-story high-rise building collapsed almost seven hours later. Units had been moved from the collapse zone in plenty of time, so no one else was injured.

The South Tower collapses. Individual wall sections are visible falling to the street.

SEISMIC ACTIVITY AT WTC ON SEPTEMBER 11, 2001 ON THE RICHTER SCALE

08:46:26 A.M. FIRST IMPACT	09:02:54 A.M. SECOND IMPACT	09:59:04 A.M. FIRST COLLAPSE	10:28:32 A.M. SECOND COLLAPSE	17:20:33 P.M. BUILDING 7 COLLAPSE
MAGNITUDE 0.9	MAGNITUDE 0.7	MAGNITUDE 2.1	MAGNITUDE 2.1	MAGNITUDE 0.6
DURATION: 12 SECONDS	DURATION: 6 SECONDS	DURATION: 10 SECONDS	DURATION: 8 SECONDS	DURATION: 18 SECONDS

AP Photo/Richard Drew

The North Tower collapses, ripping holes in the south side of Building 7 and sending an enormous dust cloud north in and around the surrounding buildings.

Collapse sequence photos by Greg Semendinger

Photo By
Det. Greg Semendinger
NYC Police Aviation Unit

Any firefighter near the North Tower had to run away when it collapsed. Almost all firefighters were covered with dust and debris that outran them as they fled. The dust cloud finally stopped at the white pedestrian bridge at Chambers Street.

Welcome Back

Lieutenant Steve Terulli
Rescue 1
(was an instructor at FDNY Training Academy, Randall's Island, East River on 9/11)

now retired

Lieutenant John Citarella
Squad 252
(was an instructor at FDNY Training Academy, Randall's Island, East River on 9/11)

now Rescue 3

We heard Marine 6 give an urgent message that a second plane hit the tower. We responded to Squad 41 to get gear. We arrived and met Chiefs Fred Sheffold and Joe Marchbanks, both from the 12th Battalion.

We saw six people jump from the north side of Tower 1. There were four or five cars on fire near the south side of Tower 2. We heard that a jumper hit a firefighter from Engine 216. All four of us ran into the lobby entrance of the hotel from Liberty and West streets. We met Deputy Chief Tom Galvin in the hotel lobby. Engine 58 was there with their rolled-up hoses.

We were ordered to the 90th floor in the South Tower. The deputy said take Engine 58 with you and start walking up. Chief Sheffold said did you say 90? Sheffold said, hold on. Just then, the South Tower collapsed onto the hotel. It sounded like a train noise.

I (Terulli) made a ball with my body, but when I got hit I flattened right out. I tried giving a Mayday three or four times. It took five minutes for me to get out from under the debris. I saw Chief Stack from the Safety Battalion. There was a pile of debris up to the ceiling of the lobby, reaching 20 feet high. I heard someone calling for help.

We took a roll call. Lieutenant Citarella was pinned under a large pile of debris. I started to tunnel in to remove him. Pipes, Sheetrock, insulation, wood and brickwork were passed out to Chief Stack and his aide. I asked the chief for a Sawzall and to transmit a Mayday. He said there wasn't anyone else around.

I backed out of the tunnel I had made to get my mask. I pushed the mask in front of me and gave the facepiece to John. He could now breathe easier. There was a six-by-six-foot I-beam on his leg. I was able to move the beam one-half inch. John was able to back out on his belly. He gave me a kiss, and I said welcome back.

The chief said let's get out of here. We walked out near a four-foot-high wall going towards the North Tower. Chiefs Peter Ganci and Ray Downey, Deputy Commissioner Feehan and Captain Al Fuentes were in the middle of West Street. Chief Brian O'Flaherty of Safety was injured. We helped him over the wall. Downey came over and told us to report to Chief Ganci now. Downey stayed with Stack. There was a civilian with a leg injury and both chiefs stayed with the man. We crossed what was left of the street. We fell down a few times.

When we reached Ganci, he said to me let me use your radio. Feehan couldn't believe his eyes that we made it out of the hotel. The radio didn't work. Ganci said go north. We ran north on West Street for about 25 yards and the North Tower started to collapse. We were maybe 15 yards past the North Pedestrian Bridge when the air knocked me down under a tow truck. Dust got into my eyes, ears and mouth.

After a while, the sun started to come through the dust and smoke because the tower was down. I saw a few fighter jets fly by. I could hear explosions and heard ammunition going off.

Ganci, Feehan, Downey and Stack all got killed in the second collapse.

Todd Maisel

Cars burn across the street from the South Tower. View of the rear of the hotel is shown.

I Hope It's Not True

Firefighter Heinz Kothe
Tower Ladder 12, Chelsea, Manhattan

I came in for the day tour at 7:30 A.M. I relieved the chauffeur from the night tour. Firefighter Derrick Wilson was there. He had relieved me and I went home right before the 1993 bombing; now I relieved him. I heard the commotion over the voice alarm. A few minutes later, Engine 3 responded with the high-rise unit. (Battalion) Chief (Orio) Palmer and aide Steve Belson in the 7th Battalion responded. I saw the second plane hit and I knew we were going.

We got dressed and were dispatched on the next box. The probie went as an extra roof man. We made the drive in record time straight down Seventh Avenue. The towers were in front of us. I could see black smoke billowing from the towers. I said this isn't going to be a regular fire, we're going to be there all day. The guys in the back were looking out the side windows, saying there goes another one (jumper). As we got close to the building you had to watch out for debris falling down.

We followed a chief into the Marriott Hotel. You had to watch out as you ran in so no one jumped on you. We received an order to evacuate the 16th floor and above. We entered the C stairs on the south end of the hotel. We walked up and saw other companies searching the lower floors. We made it up to 14 and took a breather. I looked out a window and could see people on the rooftops of surrounding buildings that had jumped. We walked all the way to the north end and up to 17 or 18. There was a rumbling and the building started to shake. The door blew open and blew the guys back. We crawled into a corner. The lights went out and the dust came in. I thought it might have been a bomb in the basement.

On the 18th floor, I shined my light down the hallway. About 20 or 40 feet north of the south stairs the hallway was covered in rubble from when the tower collapsed. It apparently split the Marriott in half. Down at the fifth or sixth floor I was able to look out a window and saw a fire truck upended and wrecked. At the third and fourth floors you couldn't go any further. The stairway was blocked. The roof rope was left on floor 17. Lieutenant Philip Petti and Firefighter Angel Juarbe went to get the search rope. They also received a Mayday from a member of a ladder company. He reported that he was trapped and couldn't get out.

At the fourth floor we ran into a civilian we had seen before. A firefighter had found a way through the debris blocking the stairs. They tried to shimmy down a beam. Looking down at the stairs, the ceiling was collapsed, there was a three-foot space where you were able to slide down. I radioed the lieutenant that we found a way out. The firefighter from Ladder 4 said he was losing consciousness, he had fallen several floors. I said turn on your PASS device. He said he couldn't reach it.

I heard another roar, a deafening roar. The building started to shake. There was a pillar in front of me. I pressed up against it. It took 10 seconds for the North Tower to collapse. I thought I was dead. Everything was rumbling and shaking around you. It tasted like you had 10 cotton balls in your mouth. I was trying to catch my breath. I lost my facepiece. I got my breath back. I fell forward and ping-ponged on other debris. I hurt my foot and ankle.

At a fire there is always someone outside to grab your arm and help you out. No one was there. I thought it might have been a nuclear bomb. I expected to see people tangled in debris. All that was visible was paper, rubble, steel and concrete. There weren't any people, computers or desks. Someone said we lost 150, 200 firefighters. I said I hope it's not true.

Ambulances parked close to the South Tower were damaged, destroyed, burned or overturned after its collapse.

Steve Spak

You Had To Run For Your Life

Battalion Chief Michael Telesca Battalion 19 (detailed to Safety Battalion on 9/11), Brooklyn Navy Yard

now retired

Somebody yelled into the office to look at the tower. I have a perfect view from my office, so I could see it. Now I start hearing the radio pick up and I hear Pat Brown saying, 3 Truck, we're available for that. He takes it in. I hear Orio Palmer talking about the crossband repeater. Joe Callan is asking what alarm's been transmitted?

With that, Larry Stack walked into the kitchen and said everybody get dressed! I called everybody in from Safety, left messages on everybody's machines to come into quarters. We loaded up the car with all our gear and it was Brian Meyers, who is Larry's aide, Larry Stack, Brian O'Flaherty and myself in the car. We drove across the Manhattan Bridge. We parked on Church and Vesey by the back of St. Paul's Church.

I got dressed first real fast. I sized up the building. I said to Larry I count a minimum of five completely involved floors in 1 World Trade Center, and there are two to three in the South Tower. That's what I could see, fully involved. Then I turned to him and said you got over a 50-minute burn time now on the steel.

At that point, we started heading over. I asked Larry what our game plan was. He said we have to get up to the command post. We have to get radios from Field Comm. We have to get some lights, some masks and the only thing we're concerned about is the structural stability.

We went into the lobby of the Marriott and then walked in maybe 50, 100 feet and all of a sudden we heard an explosion. We stopped dead in our tracks and Brian goes oh, that doesn't sound good. There was a second of nothing. Then you felt a heavy vibration like an earthquake, then you start hearing the pancaking collapse.

Brian said it's coming down, and we all just scattered. I just looked around the room and I thought I have to get next to something. I saw the biggest column and threw my arms around it. As soon as I did, I got whacked on the head. It laid me out. I lost my helmet. Then I just went to the fetal position and I'm thinking that I'm going to die here today. But, we rode it out. There was no visibility, it was completely black.

Visibility was still next to nil about a minute later. I thought for a while I was the only survivor and then I heard somebody yell out an eerie scream.Help me, I'm trapped! Then I heard Larry call out and Brian Meyers and I yelled out, Larry, who's that? It's Mike, I'm all right. I've got Brian here. We were all within four or five feet of each other.

In a few minutes, we saw a flashlight. We started looking for a way out. I remember running into Brian O'Flaherty coming out of a room. I said Brian, I already did that. Everything was a dead end, we weren't finding any way out.

Certain portions of the lobby had a lean-to collapse, but there was enough to walk around. I never found my helmet; that was weird. I ended up with another chief's helmet. I just found a helmet on the floor and threw it on my head.

I yelled out does anybody know this building? The floors were collapsed. I remember holding onto and sliding on a BX cable electrical line. I was hand over hand on a water pipe at one point.

We went over all of this stuff and I got to the stairs. And when I came out, it was into the garage area. There was debris down there, some parts were completely collapsed on cars. There were other parts that were rubble, but the cars were intact. I went through there maybe 50 feet, then I saw the ramp going up to the street and and I saw a little light, daylight at the top of it. The nicest thing I ever saw in my life was that daylight.

I said stay here, I'm going to go up. I went up to the top and said, come on, let's go. Brian and those guys were following. I must have taken about 10 or 12 civilians with me and they were just following me. I was moving fast. They followed me the whole way.

So I came up. I climbed on top of the four-foot ramp and I climbed up on the top of the debris pile. I yelled at them. They followed me up and I waited and I gave it 30 seconds. I saw some debris coming down and I just started heading out on West Street. I headed about halfway, 100 feet or so, and I turned around and I looked up and I see the tower's gone. I see the collapsed debris. I'm looking down at the roof of the Suburban to see the rigs. I looked down, there wasn't a soul there.

I saw no firemen, nobody. Everybody's gone out here too.

With that, I continued out and people started calling me – Fireman, fireman! Help me! I turned around and said come on, let's go. You're ambulatory, come on, you got to help yourself now. As I crossed over, I got to where the command post was. I ran into First Deputy Commissioner Bill Feehan and Chief of Department Pete Ganci standing there. They're both completely, completely gray ashen, there's soot in their eyes. And I turn to them and said Brian, Larry and our aide didn't follow me out.

Captain Al Fuentes comes over with Chief of Rescue Services Ray Downey. They were just looking up at the building. I tell Ray Downey and Ray goes right there. I'm showing him the thing. I start going with him. He said, no stay here, Mike. I said right there! You see the ramp right there where those people are? That's where I came out of. So Ray and Al start heading over there.

I was hobbling. My foot was killing me. I'm heading up West Street. I kept walking up, walking up, and then two firemen grabbed me under my arms and we were all heading up. I remember a news guy coming over trying to say something.

Then we heard the explosion of the second one, which was the same sound I heard when I was down in the lobby. I remember turning around and looking at the north bridge. I remember looking over my shoulder and thinking that I was on my own. The guys dropped me, and I don't blame them. You had to run for your life. The cloud was coming. And I kept heading up West Street. I kept going, kept going. Another guy helped me, a captain from Brooklyn. I kept going up to the first ambulance. A couple of people helped me and I jumped into the first ambulance. I went to Columbia Presbyterian.

Firehouse Collection

Ladder 5 was positioned adjacent to Building 6. The collapse of the North Tower caused extensive damage to the apparatus. The aerial ladder had to be cut off.

Most of the apparatus parked close to the tower were destroyed after the collapse.

Steve Spak

In For A Surprise

Firefighter Thomas Gaby aide to Citywide Tour Commander, Headquarters, Downtown Brooklyn

now retired

On 9/10, I worked as an aide to Chief Burns on an overtime tour. The morning of 9/11, I was having coffee right outside Chief Ganci's office. Chief Ganci came out of his office and yelled out that a plane had struck the World Trade Towers and that Chief Nigro should look out his window. With that Chief Burns, standing by the commissary kitchen, said come on, Tom, let's go, and we were off.

We went down the elevator with most of the staff chiefs: Chief Barbara, me, Chief Ganci, Chief Ingram and Chief Burns. We got in our cars and proceeded to the Brooklyn Bridge. I was the first staff car in line. Chief Ganci was driving with Chief Nigro. Steve Mosiello was driving both of them. As we approached the World Trade Center, we got there pretty fast. I don't think there were that many companies there at that time. I pulled up under the north bridge in front of 1 World Trade Center. I opened the trunk for Chief Burns. He proceeded to get his gear out and his last words to me were Tommy, I don't want to get stuck here. Park the car far away.

With that I took the car and made a U-turn and headed north on West Street. I parked the car on the corner of Chambers and West. Looking back towards the scene as I was leaving, I wanted to see if I could find Chief Cassano's car. My turnout gear was in his car because I normally drive him. I was walking back and Chief Ingram grabbed me and told me he wanted me to alert Field Communications to setup in front of the World Financial Center on West Street. That's where our command center was located. That's what I did for a few minutes, even before I went and got my gear. I proceeded to look for the car again and then, spotting it, I came upon Chief Callan's aide, James Migalia. He came up to me and said he had no gear in his car; could he use my gear. I told him here, take my gear. I would get something else. Chief Ganci was yelling at me to get the rigs cleared out of West Street and the area. I ran back and forth a few times doing that and then left to get gear.

I went back up to Chief Burns' car and took Kevin Glock's gear, he is Chief Burns' normal driver. His helmet doesn't fit me, but I had it. I got his turnout coat and just his helmet. I had the radio on, I also took the cell phone with me and headed back towards the command center. Somewhere in there the second plane had hit. I saw it coming in, I heard it and bang, it hit. I went back towards the command board.

I didn't know exactly where Chief Burns was, but watching all the outside activities going on, I was trying to get a feel for where he would be. At some point I was able to ascertain that Chief Burns was in 2 World Trade Center, the South Tower. I said, let me see if I can make my way down there. I walked along the buildings on the west side of West Street, because people were jumping and the stuff was falling out of all the buildings. I went under the North Pedestrian Bridge to cover myself and made a dash for the Marriott Hotel. When I got into the Marriott, I was looking to see if I could find somebody who knew where Chief Burns was.

I went up to Chief Galvin who was in the lobby of the Marriott. I asked if he had seen Chief Burns, and he said he did not see him, but he said that he might be in the South Tower. Having gone in through the side of the Marriott, I noticed that there was a restaurant and I felt this would be a good time for me to take a leak. I knew it was going to be a long time before I got a shot at it, and I was up since 7 o'clock, I figured let me go now, and then I can go see Chief Burns. I went to the bathroom and was just about ready to come out and I heard a rumbling sound. Having heard on the radio previously that there was a possibility that the elevators were letting go, I was hoping that that was what it was. As it proceeded, it seemed like a long time, but I'm sure it wasn't.

In my mind, I thought it was the North Tower; part of it was coming down. I said let me sit down, get low. I might be OK here. As it turned out, after the roar, I had absolutely no damage in that bathroom. There was no smoke, it just was black as night. I initially tried to get out and the door was jammed. I couldn't tell how or why it was jammed. I had no flashlight. I didn't have my turnout coat, so there was no flashlight in there. I proceeded to give Maydays on every channel. I had the mobile radio, so I had every channel. I heard absolutely

Bolivar Arellano

Steve Spak

nothing. It was completely dead. I started to think that maybe I'd be OK there for a while. I could breathe, there was no fire, and I didn't seem to be hurt in any way. At least I'm okay at this point.

But the silence, the eeriness of having no communication with anything made me feel a little uneasy. Maybe what I should do is try to get out of here. I eventually forced the door open. Just by banging it and pulling hard, it opened in. Not being able to see, I kind of just walked into a wall. That wasn't there when I came in. I gave Maydays again on all the radio channels and I heard nothing. I tried to use the cell phone that I had and there was no cell service. That was probably the only light I could see. I really couldn't see much.

I was a little bit nervous, but basically still not aware of the gravity of the situation. Let me sit down and calm myself, and then I thought, I'd be better off if I could get out of here. So I opened the door again and felt for a way I could get out and somehow, through whatever divine force there was, there was a void low in the left-hand corner. I wasn't able to get out with my helmet on or my turnout coat, but I could fit through that crack. I took the helmet and I pushed it ahead of me. There was all sorts of debris and stuff there, but it seemed to be moving. I said, I'll go as far as I can. Maybe I can just see a light or whatever or yell to someone, and luckily I was able to push it far enough that I could see that there was an opening all the way down. I got maybe six feet and I could see the entrance to the restaurant on my left was still in good shape.

I said I know I'm getting out of here. Now I could see daylight, and I just kept pushing ahead. It didn't take that long, maybe five or six minutes, and I was able to stand up in that area of the restaurant. I put my turnout gear back on and I proceeded to run outside, and I couldn't make heads or tails of what was going on because it was still smoky, kind of like a dense little fog. There was a guy from rescue out in the street yelling to people to keep running, and it was rubble all over the ground, a couple bodies lying there. I

The South Tower collapses, steel concrete and debris fall in about 10 seconds. Note the 44th and 78th floor sky lobbies, as indicated by the darkened windows on the left tower.

(inset) The hotel after the second collapse. Many members inside the lobby climbed up the steel to the right of the hotel and out to the street.

immediately tried to run. I tripped a little bit, he held me and I ran across the street. I was looking for everybody and it didn't seem like I could find anybody. It was kind of eerie. It was almost like I was the only person around.

I heard Chief Ganci on the radio talking to Steve asking for truck companies. I felt, oh, OK, I'm back in the game. There's somebody around. I still couldn't find anybody. I looked for Chief Ganci. I thought I headed north, but maybe I got turned around. Anyhow, I wound up talking to Chief Galvin again in the middle of West Street I said to Chief Galvin I don't know if anybody else is around, but I'll stay with you; this way I know I'm helping somebody. He yelled to me to get the guys from across the street. There were car fires all over the place. He said bring them over. I started getting guys who were trying to put out car fires to come across the street. Apparently Chief Galvin must have known about the other building. I had no idea that the first building was down. You still couldn't see it. I told the guys come across the street, and they were stretching lines. I was trying to help a couple of guys that were hooking up the hydrants, I was yelling to them, come on, the chief wants us over here. We got most of them across the street.

I heard a tremendous roar like I've never heard before and it sounded like I was on a runway with a jet engine just taking off over my head. I looked up in the air expecting to see a plane. I couldn't see anything, but I saw people running. This may be a good time to start running. I wasn't sure which way to run, but I watched them run and I went to my right and I started running, and then there was a complete blanket over me and I banged and fell down three or four times. Each time I got up, I got up with more stuff in my mouth and it was becoming increasingly difficult to breathe. I was trying to breathe through the jacket part of my coat to just try to filter some of the crap that was coming in my mouth. I heard somebody yell breathe through your nose and I was trying that, but it seemed like I wasn't getting enough air. I wasn't running anymore. I fell down three or four times. I said well, I can't even see. This is ridiculous to run. Maybe I'll just kind of walk and try to head in the direction of the sounds of people that I heard.

There was an Emergency Service Unit cop and he had some kind of water bottle on his back with a bite ball. He came up to me and said bite into this. Flush around your mouth and spit it out, and that's what I did. I was able to at that point clear out some of the crap in my mouth and I felt a little bit better. He had a towel and he said we'll share the towel and we'll start breathing. I started breathing through the towel with this guy. There were three of us on this towel. We got up to the west side by Albany Street and there was a hydrant open with very little water pressure and we cleaned off there.

I started heading back to where I thought maybe the command post would be. I saw regiments of guys coming down the highway, and even Training. I noticed a couple chiefs, Santangelo and Chief Idiart from Training who I've known. I saw them and they all started heading down towards the buildings. I ran into Steve Mosiello again and he was looking for Chief Ganci. I wasn't really aware of what was going on, but I was very lucky. It's bizarre, but through no real desire of my own, I was able to survive and it really was just a matter of where you were. I went with Steve. We looked for Chief Ganci. He was very upset. Then we heard the command post was up on Vesey Street. We got a ride with the commissioner's driver and we wound up with the mayor at 23rd Street. Steve wanted to tell the mayor that Chief Ganci was missing and that we lost a lot of firefighters. We hitched a ride back to Police Plaza to tell the police commissioner what was going on, and we wound up getting some clean clothes. They gave us police uniforms. Then they took us back towards the scene and we looked for Chief Ganci.

We were going back down the West Side Highway and saw Chief Cruthers and Chief Butler at the command board at Chambers and West. They said they found Ganci. Steve started running. He knew basically where Ganci was. Steve had an idea because when Ganci radioed to ask for truck companies, he must have told Steve that he was going to be south of where the command center was.

When I came out of the hotel, my first thing was to look for the command center. When I saw where I thought the command board was located, there was an airplane tire. My immediate thought was that another plane had hit. I guess being very lucky was in it for me that day. If it had taken one less minute in the bathroom, then I'm probably in 2 World Trade Center. The weird thing was, it wasn't like I had a pressing need to go, but I just thought that eventually I was going to have to go.

It's amazing to me how nothing happened in that bathroom. That bathroom was perfectly intact. I guess the only good thing I did out of this whole thing was being able to extricate myself. I could be here for a couple of days and that was an uneasy feeling. I was completely okay. There was no heat, no fire, no smoke, my body was OK. It was just that I felt uncomfortable being in this six-by-six-foot room.

What Fire?

Firefighter Matthew Castrogiovanni Ladder 131, Red Hook, Brooklyn

now Lieutenant, Ladder 135

I reported to work for the day tour. There were two other firefighters that were junior to me, but I went and checked the equipment on the rig. I took the two power saws outside and was running them. A man in a car stopped in front of the firehouse. I couldn't hear what he was saying so I stopped the saw. I thought he was going to ask directions. He said are you going to the fire? I said OK, I'll bite. What fire? He pointed to the Twin Towers. Smoke was visible, pouring out of the North Tower. A few seconds later the dispatch tone went off. Ladder 131 was directed to a staging area on the Brooklyn side of the Brooklyn-Battery Tunnel.

Our orders were to stand fast. While we were waiting, the second tower was hit by a plane. Units were directed to respond through the tunnel which had been closed only for fire apparatus. After we entered there was a delay in the tunnel, backing up numerous fire companies. There had been an accident or a stalled car. The Triborough Bridge and Tunnel Authority was pushing a vehicle out of the tunnel.

Almost as soon as we exited, there were car fires, fires burning everywhere, body parts on the street. We knew it was bad. The further we drove, the worse it got. The chauffeur parked next to the North Tower. I remember looking up at the North Tower. I asked the chauffeur if we were too close because of possible falling debris. The chauffeur moved the rig a block or two away.

The officer went to the command post. We were ordered to walk south to West and Liberty streets. From the hotel, we could enter either tower. People were jumping, so we walked on the west side of West Street. Information about a firefighter getting hit by a jumper was relayed to us. Someone said there were so many people jumping, they were falling out of the sky like rain. The chauffeur of Engine 279 was hooking up to supply the standpipe and sprinkler systems on West Street.

As we approached the Tall Ships Bar in the Marriott Hotel, civilians were still exiting. I saw a woman in a wheelchair being assisted. We timed our move and ran into the bar. We were told to take off our gear until we knew where we were headed.

Other companies were waiting in the lobby of the hotel. I made some calls, knowing my family knew I worked close to the towers. The officer thought we were going to be operating for a long time, searching and overhauling. Our orders were to go into the North Tower.

As we were gathering our gear to walk down the hallway it got very dark. People were running. I heard a noise. I thought it was another plane getting closer. Someone had mentioned about the possibility of another plane coming in. The chauffeur looked out the window that was behind me. He told everybody to get down. The sun disappeared. The collapse of the South Tower was occurring. We weathered the storm. I still thought another plane crashed.

After the collapse, it remained very dark. Debris had piled up over the windows. Walking through the hotel lobby we came upon a roll-down gate that had fallen. The gate was lifted and as I held it several civilians who worked in the hotel came out. Someone said they had seen Ladder 118 on the stairway. When the dust cleared we were able to walk out onto West Street. We had to transverse the steel. I remember a 30-foot drop from the debris at one point. I still didn't know the South Tower had collapsed.

I incurred injuries to my eyes. I couldn't keep my eyes open. Out in the street a firefighter came towards me. From what I had ingested and inhaled, I had trouble breathing. He helped me to a ferry and they took me to the Jersey City Medical Center. The second tower collapsed while I was on the ferry. I wound up with a detached retina and abrasions on both eyes.

Engine 204 (arrow) lies in the debris field after the second collapse. Many of the first units through the tunnel were killed.

Todd Maisel

We Were In A Hurricane

Firefighter John Breen Engine 74, Upper West Side, Manhattan

I came in for the day tour and heard the dispatch over the voice alarm. We were watching the television. Within a few minutes, we were dispatched on the second fifth alarm for the South Tower. Two firefighters remained behind. Responding were Lieutenant Nichols, Firefighter Mike Shagy (the chauffeur), Pat Carey, Jeff Johnson, Ruben Correa and myself. We took the West Side Highway and pulled up one-two blocks away at West and Vesey.

As I walked to the Marriott Hotel, I looked up wondered how we were going to fight this. The officer told us to walk as far away from the building as possible. One body was visible in the street. We entered the lobby of the hotel. Ruben was one of the senior guys and he said, stay close to me. Loosen your coat, don't overheat. Then he said, look, I'm scared too. We have to put that in the back of our minds.

We reported to Chief Tom Galvin of Division 3. Engines were on one side and trucks were on the other. I remember seeing Ladder 25, Engine 40, Ladder 35, Engine 54, Ladder 4, Ladder 11, Engine 23 and Ladder 12. Our orders were to search the top floor, there was a report of people trapped. We responded along with Engine 54, Ladder 11, Engine 23 and possibly one more company. We took the elevator by ourselves to the 18th floor and walked up to the pool, spa and gym. We searched the area with negative results. We could see where a piece of landing gear wound up in the Jacuzzi. The pool was intact.

We walked back down to the 21st floor and down the hallway to the elevator. We were waiting for the elevator when Lieutenant Nichols said that the elevator was running slow, and we should walk down the stairs to where we left the other elevator. We walked south to the south stairwell in single file. We heard the building starting to come down. The building started to sway like a ship. I could hear creaking. It felt like we were in a hurricane. I didn't think it was the whole tower, but just a section. Everybody froze in place. Somebody said, building collapse! I heard it getting louder and louder like an approaching train. You could hear the floors one on top of each other like dominoes, boom, boom, boom.

I stayed where I was and braced for it. I didn't think I was going to die. I thought I'd get stuck in a void and ride it out. I felt like I might get trapped, but I would be able to get myself out. I waited to go through the floor or wall. As it hit, a huge gust of wind pushed me flat on my face. It felt like a 260-pound linebacker hit me.

The debris started to blow over me. I started to cough. I wiped my mouth; it was like paste on my glove. I could hear other firefighters coughing, so I knew they were all right. The guys were yelling each other's names, putting on flashlights. I knew everybody in the front was OK. We started to yell for Ruben. Jeff was calling for Ruben. I turned around and it was about 10 feet away where there was just rubble from when the building collapsed. The hallway was intact. The electricity was knocked out. Sheetrock and metal were hanging.

I was in shock, I couldn't believe I was that close to being trapped. The officer gave a Mayday. Jeff went to the wall of debris and started to pull pieces off to see if there was a void. They couldn't find any. The officer asked what hotel room I was near. I said 2106-08. I noticed half the room was missing. I could see right out and down. I couldn't hear any response from down below. I thought maybe the radio wasn't working when we got no response. The only transmission was from a firefighter from a ladder company. Mayday, Mayday, I'm trapped and I don't know where I am, I'm running out of air.

We knew we had to get out and get help. We walked down the stairwell. We met Ladder 12 on a lower floor. At the sixth floor there was debris blocking the stairway and you couldn't go any further. I walked into one of the suites. One of the truckies breached the wall with a halligan tool. They decided they were going to tie off a hose with a substantial knot and slide down the hose out the window. That would be a six-floor drop. Somebody remembered seeing a rope on an upper floor. Two members of Ladder 12 went back upstairs to retrieve the rope.

Firehouse Collection

Lieutenant Nichols said we have to get around the rubble and make it to a lower floor. Jeff Johnson climbed down half a story and cleared the debris. On the fifth floor he found five civilians. Everyone started to follow the way down the stairs. I was the last one to make it to the third floor. On the third floor there was an opening in the stairwell. Jeff and Pat jumped out onto a patio. They took a lightweight beam and situated it so they could crawl out. They called out for the civilians to climb out. One by one they were assisted, held by curtains from a room. I felt like I was doing something to help. Ten firefighters and five civilians were making their way down slowly.

Two firefighters, two civilians and myself were left when the second building started to come down. I thought not again and braced for it. I said, please God, let me get through this one. As it came down it got dark right away. A cloud of dust hit us. One of the civilians was around 80 years old. I saw him moving. I grabbed his hand and told him to stay with me. As it came down I was thinking there is someone with you, you are not alone. I have some air and I'm near an opening and it won't be that bad if I am trapped.

After the noise, I started to hear voices from the outside. We're not trapped too badly. As the dust cleared I could see outside. My luck today is amazing. I looked out and everybody had scattered to get cover in other areas. In front of me was Lieutenant Nichols. Before the patio was open, now it was covered in debris like a bunker and foxhole.

Jeff was yelling. I'm thinking he's stuck somewhere impaled on debris over him. That's when Lieutenant Nichols said Jeff was yelling for Pat. I assumed Jeff was OK, now I was worried about Pat. The two of us were able to get the two civilians down. There was a lot of rubble and steel.

I made my way down an I-beam and down several stories of rubble. The first collapse took out the middle of the hotel. The second collapse took out everything else except the four stories at the south end. I was screaming for Pat, wondering where he might be. I thought he was gone.

It was a sunny day, but looked cloudy. It looked like a movie set. Ambulances and fire trucks were wrecked and burning. I saw a rescue firefighter and turned the old man with us over to him. I told him we had firefighters trapped. We met up with Jeff later on. He said he was able to get three civilians out and was trapped on a lower floor.

We made a phone call to the firehouse and found out Pat was in the hospital. He was trapped on the second floor, but made it out. Ruben is still missing. I was thankful for Ruben's help. I believe he helped me get out and was there for me the whole way through.

The front of the Marriott Hotel after the South Tower collapsed on it. Ladder 10 is parked on West Street in front of the hotel. The remains of the upper floors of the south side of the hotel can be seen at the top of the photo.

I Have A 22-Story Building

Firefighter Jeff Johnson Engine 74, Upper West Side, Manhattan

now retired

We were assigned to 2 World Trade Center. The rig was parked south of Vesey Street. People were jumping and debris was coming off the building. I was there in 1993. I knew standing in the street was not a good place to be. The lieutenant was discussing what equipment to bring inside. I said we have to get out of the street. We ran into the hotel and met Deputy Chief Galvin of the Third Division.

We were assigned to search the upper floors of the Marriott Hotel. The chief wanted each company with forcible entry tools. Someone ran outside and retrieved our tools. As we walked through the hotel, suddenly people were running through the revolving doors toward us. People were jumping from the upper floors from the tower. Assigned with us were Engines 54 and 23 and Ladder 1. In the elevator with us were a few truck company guys. We got off at floor 18.

As we walked past the gym, I saw a piece of the plane's steel shaft landing gear in the Jacuzzi. You could see where it came through the ceiling. There was a three- to four-foot-diameter hole in the top-floor ceiling. Looking out a window that faced southeast, we were facing the South Tower. You could see the sphere in the middle of the plaza. We didn't feel uncomfortable as the fire was in the North Tower.

We took the stairs to floor 21. Some companies were already searching further down the hallway. As we walked down the hallway, we were hit by what we found out later was the South Tower collapse. You couldn't breathe, you couldn't see. It was dark and dusty. I was lying on something soft. The dust started to settle. I could see stripes. I said, who is that? It was Lieutenant Nichols.

A quick roll call was taken. We asked each other if everybody was OK. Everyone answered, except Ruben Correa. As the dust settled some more, we all started screaming for Ruben. There was a wall of debris in front of us blocking the north end of the hallway. It was like taking a 40-yard container filled with debris and dumping it in the hallway from floor to ceiling and wall to wall. Ceiling tiles were falling on us. A call was made for Ruben over the radio. There was no response. The hotel rooms in front of us were 2106 and 2108. Maydays were given. There was no response. If we were able to respond, the firefighters did not know where they were located.

We thought there might have been a V or lean-to collapse. The thought was if we could get down to the next lowest floor we could go up the other stairway and search the north side of the 21st floor hallway. As soon as we got to 20, it was the same conditions as 21. We pounded on the remaining hotel room doors. There was only a small portion of hotel rooms left, so the searching went rapidly. We went down the stairway. Debris had to be cleared from the stairway so you could descend.

I took of my mask at the sixth floor so I could slide through the handrails. We entered the sixth floor. The floor layout was different. It was some type of suite with double doors. There were six or seven firefighters down there. We tried to report in using the fax lines, but the phones were not working. Some of the firefighters were discussing going out the window that faced 10 & 10. They were going to slide down a hoseline to get out. I didn't like that idea. The firefighters I was with were on an even decision-making level. We decided to keep trying the staircase. The other firefighters were going to go out the window.

There was an opening so you were able to look out toward West Street. Steel was sticking into the street. I didn't know the South Tower had collapsed. I thought only a portion of it collapsed, not all of it. I could hear voices down below me. Further down the stairway, there were four to five civilians who were trapped.

Once we got the stairwell cleared, we made it to the third floor. There was too much debris. You couldn't go any further. You could see the outside again. I took a piece of window frame and fashioned it like a kid's slide. Three of the civilians and firefighter Pat Carey came outside. We weren't close to ground level.

The hotel banquet manager was with us. He told us there was a big room with stairs near the Harvest Room. I walked in first, then the civilians

(opposite) The South Tower collapses. Within seconds the tower will crash onto the top of the hotel.

Mary Altaffer

and Pat Carey followed. The banquet manager told me where the stairs and the elevator were located. The elevator doors were cocked sideways on an angle. The stairway was blocked with debris. The Harvest room was pretty much intact. There were tables and chairs. The ceiling tiles had fallen.

I was looking for a way out of the room when the second tower hit us. I yelled out to get down near a column or a wall. I heard the roar, it got faster and louder. You felt it from the top of your head to the tip of your toes. As I leaned against a column I thought of my daughter. I was so mad. We had gotten so far. I said don't let me go like this.

I was outside and now I am back inside. Just the compression knocked you down on your face. I finally was able to say I was OK. Pat was missing. I was alone with the three civilians. There was no way out. I didn't know what happened to the rest of the firefighters. A PASS alarm was going off under some debris. As I grabbed the straps of the mask, I realized this was my mask which I had taken off to go through the stairway handrail on the sixth floor. I screamed for Pat, John and the lieutenant. The Lieutenant said he could hear me through the stairwell. He asked if I had Pat. I said no.

More of the ceiling tiles had come down. The column I had leaned against was cock-eyed. You were able to walk around the room, it was much more compromised. As the dust continued to settle, light was visible. Putting my head out a hole in the wall, over my right shoulder I thought was a piece of loose concrete. I thought if it shifted it would have been like a guillotine. Six to seven feet away there was a steel beam leaning against the hotel. It was not an easy reach. BX cable had fallen from the ceiling. I tried but I couldn't get it to free up.

I took another look at the hole in the wall. What I thought was concrete wound up to be rigid foam insulation covering the three-foot-diameter hole. There were some drapes close by. I had the civilians holding onto a cord and they went out back first and onto the beam and into the debris field and went on their own way. I was the last one out.

Lights on an apparatus were visible in the distance. Two firefighters became visible. I was trying to tell somebody what happened. Firefighter Paul Hashagen from Rescue 1 and Citywide Tour Commander Frank Cruthers were standing together. I told them we needed to report to the 21st floor. We had a firefighter missing. The chief was not responding. I'm trying to tell him when Paul told me to turn around. I was giving a report for a building that was not there anymore. All that was left was a small portion of the 300-foot long, 22-story hotel. I said, what do we do now?

I didn't know where the streets were. They said head to the water. I said which way. I could barely see. My eyes were full of debris. I walked around the Winter Garden toward the North Cove Marina. Someone had a garden hose.

A police officer said the Pentagon was hit. They also said all aircraft were grounded. All of a sudden we saw a vapor trail coming down the Hudson River. I said, what the hell is that? I thought another plane was coming. I ran until I couldn't run anymore.

EMS cleaned me up. I called on the radio and the Lieutenant answered. He told me that Breen had made it to Battery Park. We hooked up and walked to Broadway looking for a working phone. A call was made to Engine 74's firehouse. We told them we were OK and and asked them if that had heard from the other firefighters. They hadn't heard from the chauffeur or Ruben.

At the command post, we were trying to tell them about our missing men. They thought we were reporting in. I said, no, we were in the collapse! We told them everything we knew. When we found our rig, one firefighter was hitting the air filter with a halligan tool. The other firefighter was kicking out what was left of the windshield. We looked under the rig for the chauffeur.

Ruben Correa was killed in the initial collapse when the South Tower fell onto the hotel. Pat Carey dove off the veranda when the North Tower collapsed. He was found in the debris field. He was injured, but is still working. The chauffeur was hit by a law enforcement car. He was hospitalized and never came back.

USS New York

U.S. Navy

On Nov. 7, 2009, the *USS New York* was commissioned into U.S. Navy service with 7¾ tons of World Trade Center steel in her bow. The fifth San Antonio-class amphibious transport dock ship has a crew of 360 and can carry up to 700 Marines. Two sister ships, the *USS Arlington* and the *USS Somerset* were named for the places two of the planes used in the attacks came down.

THE LEADERSHIP VOID

After both towers collapsed, 186 firefighters were injured, 10 critically. Eventually, a list was established to tabulate the missing firefighters. This list grew to more than 400 the first day. Because of the change of tours, many fire companies responded to the scene with additional personnel. Some firefighters were off duty and responded to the scene on their own. Much of the upper leadership of the fire department was lost including First Deputy Fire Commissioner William M. Feehan, Chief of Department Peter J. Ganci Jr. and Assistant Chiefs Gerard A. Barbara and Donald J. Burns. In addition, 18 battalion chiefs were killed, including Raymond M. Downey, who was in charge of Special Operations.

SOUTH TOWER OPERATIONS

Battalion 7, Ladder 15 and Battalion 9 worked their way to the upper floors of 2 WTC, the South Tower. These units were the only ones to reach this high. This is a partial excerpt from their portable radio transmissions.

0918 *B7 on the 40th floor, one elevator working staffed by a lad 15 firefighter.*

0932 *B7 on the 55th floor.*

0934 *Dispatcher to Field Communications: 1 WTC, North Tower, check floors 68, 82, 83, 88, 92, 100, 103, 104, 105, 106 (for people trapped).*

Check 2 WTC South Tower, floors 47 and 73 (for people trapped).

0939 *Two fire marshals encounter a woman with burn injuries on the 51st floor. One removes her, the other continues up.*

0939 *Lad 15 to Lad 15 OV: Sending 10 to 15 injured civilians down.*

0942 *B9 to B7, on 40th floor walking up. B7 on floor 69.*

0945 *Lad 15 to B7, B7 on floor 74.*

0947 *B7 to B9, Stairway wall compromised on 73-74.*

0947 *Lad 15 to B7, B7 on 74th floor stairway B.*

0949 *Lad 15 to Lad 15 OV, elevator not working.*

0951 *Lad 15 to B7, B7 in 75th floor stairway.*

0952 *B7 to Lad 15, we have two to three pockets of fire, should be able to knock it down with two lines. 78th floor, numerous 10-45's (dead on arrival), numerous injured.*

0955 *Lad 15 OV to 15, trapped in B stairway, 78th floor.*

0956 *B7 to B9, need you above 79.*

0959 *WTC 2, South Tower collapses.*

How Many Did We Lose?

Firefighter Frank Ocello Ladder 24, Garment District, Manhattan

now Battalion 18

Most of the companies entered the hotel through the Tall Ships Bar next to the South Tower.

I worked 24 hours on Monday and was awaiting relief on Tuesday morning. The dispatcher said a plane hit the World Trade Center. Engine 1 was dispatched. I was at the housewatch watching the coverage on television. I saw the second plane hit and thought it was a replay. Ladder 24 was dispatched.

I was sitting behind the chauffeur and was looking at the towers. We pulled up on West Street, just north of the towers. We walked over to the staging area. I was assigned to the roof position. As we were standing by the driveway to the World Financial Center, we saw nearly 50 people jump.

Captain Brethel, who had traveled to the scene with Fire Department Chaplain Father Mychal Judge, who parks in our quarters, came up to me. He said a lot of firefighters are going to die today, don't be one of them. All of a sudden 10 people jumped in a row.

We were assigned to floors 70 to 90 of the South Tower. Several other truck companies were ordered into the South Tower as well. Our orders were to save as many people as we could. We walked down to the South Pedestrian Bridge, went under the bridge and ran into the Marriott Hotel lobby one at a time.

When you entered the Marriott, there was a bank of phones. None of the cell phones worked. The lieutenant said he had to make a call to his wife. He was gone for about five minutes. He returned and asked the members what they wanted to do. I said I'm the junior man with two years, why are you asking me? He told me this might be my last day. We decided to do what we can and then come back down. I respected him for asking me, even though the other members had 20 years.

Other companies walked past us. Someone said another plane was coming. We were standing right

David Handschuh

Bolivar Arellano

by the windows and heard a noise and started to run. I took two steps then covered up. My helmet came off. The first thing that came to mind was to say goodbye to my three kids as I waited to get hit.

It was smoky and I couldn't breathe. Workers were grabbing us. We pushed up two roll-down gates that had come down. Someone saw sunlight on top of a pile of beams. This one woman kept falling. There were other civilians coming down with another firefighter. I remember the officer asking me if we were out. Two of us went left and the others went right. I never saw them again that day.

We walked towards Battery Park. We heard a sound and saw the antenna on top of the North Tower coming down with the rest of the building. There were still a lot of civilians and children in the area. We directed them into a bar to escape the dust cloud. There was a gas leak in the bar. We could hear the hiss. We decided to evacuate.

Boats were coming into the Battery. Fifteen to 20 civilians and kids were loaded onto one of the boats. We were shocked to see civilians still in the area. Finally we found someone who had a cell phone. I called my mother. I said tell whoever that I am still alive.

Other firefighters were stretching a hoseline back to the Trade Center. We walked down several blocks. It was still a snowstorm of dust. Several firefighters from Engine 1 and Ladder 24 saw us at the end of the block. We were taken to a staging area at Engine 3 and Ladder 12's firehouse, which is at 7th Avenue and West 19th Street. There were several hundred firefighters waiting there.

We were the first firefighters who had operated at the scene that they had seen. We were covered in dust and were white. A chief came over and asked, How many firefighters did we lose? 50? I said, 50? How about 500! Whoever was there is dead! That was the last question the chief asked. No one could survive.

I returned to Ladder 24 at mid-afternoon. Father Judge, who ate every meal with Engine 1 and Ladder 24, died of a heart attack in the lobby of the North Tower when the South Tower collapsed. He was laid out in the rear of the firehouse. There were five to 10 friars all around him from his church across the street. He was all cleaned up and had on a new robe. A lot of guys cried when they heard the news. Lieutenant Andrew Desperito of Engine 1 died coming out of the North Tower.

Two truck companies use caution as they head towards the Marriott Hotel. All members in the picture were killed.

Can You Lend Me $20?

Battalion Chief Ed Henry
40 Battalion, Sunset Park Brooklyn

now retired

I came in to work Tuesday morning and someone asked if I was going into Manhattan because a small plane had hit the Trade Center. It was rare for us to respond to Manhattan. I thought it was nothing.

We were dispatched to the Brooklyn end of the Brooklyn-Battery Tunnel. We responded up Fourth Avenue. I turned on the radio and they were reporting an airliner hit the tower. As we reached the top of the Gowanus Expressway we could see the upper portion of the Trade Center was burning. Then the newscaster said oh, my God! Another airliner hit the tower! I knew it was terrorism.

We went through the tunnel and then north on West Street. About five blocks south of the Trade Center there was a sheet-covered body in the street missing a leg. I thought this was unbelievable.

We reported in to the command post and stood around awhile. I got tired of watching the people jump. If you saw it, you would never forget it. I went up to Chief Ganci and said you have anything for me? He said here are the radio frequencies we are utilizing, give them to Chief Galvin. He is in the hotel.

I went into the hotel and gave the list to Chief Galvin. He said I want you to go to the 70th floor of the South Tower. I had never been to the complex before, so he told me to go through the doors into the mezzanine. There were a lot of companies there. I walked up a stairway in front of the main desk of the hotel.

Suddenly, the South Tower collapsed. My mask from my airpack and my flashlight were ripped right out of my hand. I was burned across the top of my forehead and my hands. The worst part was the total darkness. The debris was piled high, right up to an inch away from my left shoulder. There was a 20-foot space open to our right side. Other than that space, everything else was covered and piled high with debris. If you were to my right or left, you were dead.

Civilians were yelling and screaming. Someone gave me another flashlight. There was no way out. Then I saw a light shining through a little hole. I said if we don't get out of here, I am going to climb up to the light. Chief Brian O'Flaherty came by the main desk and said we have to find a door. He finds a door. He yells over, I have a door.

A wide view of the Marriott Hotel from West Street. First-due Ladder 10 is parked in front. Numerous firefighters were killed in the hotel. Amazingly, many firefighters survived both collapses inside the hotel.

Firehouse Collection

I'm going down. It was a stairway going to like a cellar. I asked myself am I in worse shape going or staying? I calmed some people down. I went down the stairs. I can't walk fast. It is pitch black.

O'Flaherty said you stay by the top of the stairs. I'll go down and yell back. He yells back that he has a door to the outside. Bring anybody you have down slowly. The door was 100 to 150 feet away. Apparently, there was a wall. I said I would climb over the wall to another door and open it. There was rubble all over. It took me 15 minutes to move the boulders from in front of the door. When I opened the door, no one was there.

I called my aide on the radio. I asked him where he was. He was about 20-30 feet away. He said everybody had gotten out. I walked out into the street and ran into Chief Ganci, Chief of Rescue Services Ray Downey and Deputy Fire Commissioner Bill Feehan. Ganci told my aide that he wanted three engines and three ladders immediately.

I just started to walk away. Stuff was coming down. I said the best place to be is at the corner. It is usually safe. I was walking to the corner of the North Tower. I just got under a big substantial portico. I thought I'd be pretty safe here. I was exhausted. I needed to take a break. A buff was taking photographs. He was leaning out from under the portico taking pictures of the North Tower about 40 feet away from me. He started to run. I figured I'd better run, but I was pushed to the floor and the portico landed on top of me. It stopped about two to three feet over my head. The wind pushed me away. I was in total darkness. I didn't realize the entire North Tower came down.

My legs were pinned, but not crushed. Rubble was passing by. I pulled my helmet over my head. Finally the rubble stopped. I moved my legs around and I wasn't pinned anymore. I started to crawl where I could feel a cool breeze on my left cheek. I crawled for what seemed forever. It was 250 to 300 feet. I had to crawl over the rubble to the north to an opening where it was getting light. I crawled up to the photographer who was standing under the portico. He is completely white. He said I think I'm having a heart attack. I told him to just lay there. Something hit my back.

Later, I saw a firefighter. I told him that we were in bad shape and need two backboards. It took him 20 minutes to come back with EMTs. They helped us up. My back was all messed up. They walked to a place where it was level. Walking over the rubble seemed to take forever. It took them awhile to get us to an ambulance. The photographer apparently died sometime later in St. Vincent's Hospital.

In the ambulance was a businessman covered in white and a woman who was going nuts. The ambulance attendant said no one can go to a hospital in lower Manhattan, word was that Beekman Downtown Hospital (New York Downtown Hospital on Beekman Street) was bombed. I was taken to Columbia Presbyterian Hospital at 220th Street. My aide had to run close to the building all the way to the North Bridge to Vesey Street. He crossed under the bridge to the command post. He was halfway across the street when the second building came down. He stood behind a large truck. The rubble came by and killed everybody. He didn't even get a scratch. He went back to work the next day to Engine 278.

I was cleaned up and given a CAT scan. My brother, who was a captain in Ladder 149, had been working at the Training Academy. He told me that my son, who was a firefighter in Ladder 21 on the West side of Manhattan, was missing. They told me I was going to be admitted, but I said I have to go. I left the hospital with a hospital gown and my boots. We went back to the scene.

A cop told us no one else was to be let in. We got into a big argument. The cop said sorry. My brother then drove me home. I couldn't get out of the car. My neighbors helped me up into my house. My three other sons couldn't find their brother. One son was a Port Authority police officer. The other two sons were firefighters. One was a lieutenant in Engine 58 and the other was a lieutenant in Engine 276. They couldn't find their brother who was working a mutual exchange of tours with someone else from Ladder 21. I saw my son on Monday afternoon. He was working Monday night and Tuesday day. He said could I borrow $20 for the firehouse meals? I said I'd never see the $20. I continued, Maybe I'll see you at the big one. My son said Ladder 21 never goes to the big ones.

I've Never Seen Anything Like This

Lieutenant Ray Brown
Ladder 113, Flatbush, Brooklyn

now retired

I worked the night before, and I was supposed to work overtime in Ladder 111 and there was an officer coming here, to Ladder 113. I had called over to Ladder 111 and Lieutenant Chris Sullivan was working Engine 214. I said I'll work in Engine 214. The officer who was coming here called up and said oh, no, I'll go over there. Then he called up Chris and he was going to do the same switch. Chris got an EMS run before the hour and he stayed in 214, and he died.

They said, turn on the TV. You could see the flames coming out. All the guys were saying to me, you worked in Manhattan, you had high-rise fires. I remember telling them this fire's not going out. We don't put out high-rise fires that big. When the fuel level diminished, we went in and knocked down the fires.

I was in Rescue 1 for six years. We had a transformer one year. We had a fire in the elevator another year. We rarely had fires down there (at the World Trade Center). We're in the kitchen. We're watching it and everybody is thinking the same thing, oh my God, people are going to die. Firemen are going to be hurt. We didn't want to even think that. While we're watching it, the second plane hit, and we got called to respond. I ran upstairs and I got my cell phone and I was trying to call my father. He is a retired battalion chief in the FDNY and the first chief of Rescue Services. He works for the Port Authority.

We were responding to a staging area near the Brooklyn-Battery Tunnel. Almost the whole way there I was frantic. I was calling my father and I'm wondering where is he because I know he works in Jersey City. He goes to a lot of meetings at the Trade Center. I didn't get through. It was hairy driving over there because we had a view of it the whole time. We got to the Brooklyn-Battery Tunnel and we were there maybe five or 10 minutes and they sent us.

I had a great crew. I had Dennis Dowdican. He's been my chauffeur for 10 years. Willie Roberts, who's the other chauffeur in my 24 group, he's got over 20 years. Richie Nogan's got over 20 years. Bob Pino, another excellent fireman, he's got 12 years. Tom Fisa, 16 years. Bill Morris, 16 years. I had a very experienced crew.

I was telling the guys to sit down, relax, this is going to be a long day. We got called to respond to a staging area in Manhattan. Just as we're going into the tunnel, Tom Manley – he's the sergeant-at-arms of the firefighters union, and a member of this company – comes running up and he tells us they hit the Pentagon. He rode through the tunnel with us. We're driving through and I'm thinking oh, my God, this is war, maybe the tunnel is a target.

I tell my chauffeur go, just get through it, and we got through. We parked the rig at Liberty and West streets and I reported to the staging area and the chief. He said 113 report to Building 2 at the command post. I went back to the rig and I told everybody get an extra bottle. Everybody check your mask here, get search ropes. I hadn't even gotten my mask on yet.

All of a sudden, we hear these incredible explosions. I looked up and thought fire was breaking out on the upper floors. Then the debris starting hitting and I ran. The reason I ran was because I didn't have my mask on. All the guys had their masks on, they hid under the rig. I ran across the street. I was getting hit with debris and I got knocked down. That dust, I had it in my mouth. I couldn't breathe. All of a sudden, it went pitch black. I thought it was the end of the world. My exact words to myself were they dropped the bomb on us and I'm going to die. People talk about a near-death experience, but I was calm, I realized maybe I'm not going to die.

I got up again and I started running and then I got hit with a bunch of stuff. There were people to the left and right of me getting hit with debris. I wasn't able to stop, but I'm sure they were getting killed. And then I happened to look to my right and I saw a wall. I ducked behind the wall and I heard more debris coming down. It was so quiet. You didn't hear a sound. You didn't hear a thing. Then I heard help, fireman, help me, I can't breathe. And I remember telling people, you can breathe and I was telling the people to go to the river. It was like you were in a thick fog. There was

Todd Maisel

maybe two or three feet visibility. All of a sudden, people would start popping up and, you know, you could barely hear them. You couldn't even hear them until they were right on top of you.

I realized I had to get back to my rig and see if my guys were OK. The fire truck was burning. There was so many ambulances burning it was incredible. You really couldn't see more than 20 feet in front of you. At this point, I still didn't know what happened. I still thought that fire broke out on every floor or they dropped a bomb somewhere. I didn't realize that the tower had collapsed. I could see fires in upper floors in all the buildings. When I got to the rig and I saw my guys, I was relieved that they were all OK and then I felt a lot of pride that they were ready to go to work.

They got some equipment. I ran into Deputy Chief Tom Galvin, who had just come out of the Marriott Hotel. He came running up and he said 65 Engine and 58 Engine are trapped in the Marriott. They tied a search rope to a pillar where 58 Engine was trapped. When Chief Galvin told us about the guys in the Marriott, my chauffeur had an extinguisher and he was trying to put out the rig, and I told him forget about it. There were a couple of my guys who were trying to help civilians and I had to tell them to leave them, because in my mind, if you were walking or talking, you were OK. That was a hard thing to do.

I said we've got to get into the Marriott. I told the guys get the Sawzall. They already had the airbags. We went into the Marriott Hotel and I ran into a guy coming out who told me that there are firemen trapped in there. I grabbed him and told him to come with me. He took us back and when I got there, there were two guys from 58 Engine and one of them I knew. He said our lieutenant's trapped in here.

I was trying to assess the situation. The best way I've been able to describe it is if you took an accordion and you squished it completely, and then tried to cut a little piece out of it. The lieutenant was OK. He was talking to us. He told us there were two chiefs and there was another company behind them. I also heard a Mayday from a company on the first floor in the Marriott and I responded to them and I told them, we're going to get you out, then we were starting to cut with the saws.

One of Engine 58's firefighters, Mike Fitzpatrick, was there. We gave him the portable

Members of Engines 58 and 209 assist Lieutentant Ray Brown from the hotel after the second collapse. Brown had been working with others to free Lieutenant Bob Nagel of Engine 58, who was trapped.

Sawzall and I told another guy we're under a void. I told John Wilson from 58 to keep an eye on the void. Mike Fitzpatrick and I crawled in and he started cutting to remove debris so we could get the lieutenant out. The lieutenant had asked for a flashlight. He told us he was OK and he kept asking how are his guys, he kept telling us about the guys behind him. It looked like a lot of ducts, pipes, aluminum and shelves, just a tremendous amount of debris.

We were able to get about 10 feet in before we had to start cutting. We only had five to seven feet because we cut away about three or four feet. I sent Richie Nogan and Bob Pino out to get more equipment. I wanted a Hurst tool and I wanted the electric Sawzall. I knew we were going to be there a long time. I wanted cribbing. I thought the Hurst tool would be best to spread, crib, spread, crib.

Even the guy next to me asks me, you were in Rescue 1, weren't you? I said yeah, I was in Rescue 1, but I never saw anything like this. I don't care how many years on the job you had, how many years you spent in any rescue company, this was just beyond anybody's capability.

In a section of the lobby of the Marriott, the ceiling tiles were still intact – which is incredible. Basically, the rest of the building came down in the section where he was located. If you were inside that reinforced area, you lived because that's why I'm alive. While we're in the Marriott, we're cutting away and it just seemed like an impossible feat, but I figured given time we were going to get him out. I remember even telling him yeah, we're going to get you out. He kept saying I'm OK, I'm OK.

After the first collapse, there was nothing on the radio. I was trying to call my guys and they weren't answering. And then all of a sudden, when I was in the Marriott, then I started hearing Mayday, Mayday, Mayday. My guys kept saying there's a Mayday, but I had to tune it out because we had to take care of our own situation. One of my guys stayed with me and two other guys from 58 Engine came in with a Partner saw. This wasn't something that you could use a Partner saw on. I was afraid of the vibrations and so I told the one guy to keep an eye on that void on the overhang.

Mike Fitzpatrick and I went into the hole and after that I don't remember. They told me that I yelled, get out. They told me that they heard a rumble. The guys from 58 were in the Marriott when the first tower came down, so when they heard that rumble, they knew it was a major collapse. They found me in the lobby about 15 or 20 feet from where I had been. Apparently, I got hit with some stuff and thrown across the room. The reason they found me is they saw my flashlight.

One of the guys came up. He said are you OK, and I said no, I'm losing it. They got kind of worried and they ended up carrying me out up over 40 feet of rubble. When they got me to the top, one of the guys tried to throw me over his shoulder and that's when I woke up for a second. I had five fractured ribs. The next thing I remember is waking up in the hospital six hours later.

The guys did a great job. They got me to the fireboat and they took me to a Jersey City hospital. I think I was in the same boat as Al Fuentes. I worked with Al in Rescue 1. I had a concussion. I got stitches on my chin, about 25 stitches in the back of my head. I had five fractured ribs. I was bruised on my back from my hips all the way up to my neck. My lower back was hurt, my neck, my right shoulder was hurt, my hip. Both kneecaps were bruised. I was out almost four months.

The thing that was weird was being in the hospital and not knowing what went on. From what I understand, they had me listed as MIA. They actually listed me as DOA, I believe. There's an office at 113. My brother was there for 12 hours. He didn't know what happened. He just knew that my rig was burned. Now I have two cousins on the job also that went down there and all they knew was they saw my rig and they heard that I was the officer that day, but they didn't know where I was.

When I woke up in the hospital, the doctor said to me did you hear your men are OK, your father's OK? I didn't know for six hours. I knew my brother wasn't working, so I didn't have to worry about him. With any line-of-duty death, you know the names, the company, you know how long they've been on the job. That's why this is so mind boggling.

(below) Firefighters wait under a stairway away from jumpers and falling debris from the towers. Note the motorcycles.

(bottom) A firefighter is trapped by a motorcycle and is assisted by other firefighters under a burned-out stairway. It is unknown whether the same firefighters were trapped or others.

David Handschuh

David Handschuh

Todd Maisel

Todd Maisel

(top) Ladder 11 is parked on West Street behind EMS. Note the "Eleven Truck" sign on the aerial ladder.

(bottom right) After the collapse, Ladder 11 was flipped upside down and caught fire. Tires were burned off. Only the word "Truck" remains on the sign after the fire.

Slide Down A Beam

Firefighter Adam Mazy
Engine 3, Chelsea, Manhattan

now Tower Ladder 79

A firefighter and some civilians slid down a beam to escape the hotel.

I worked the night tour. I was scheduled for overtime in Engine 34 on the day tour. I was walking toward my car when the first plane hit. The announcement came over the voice alarm.

Engine 3 and the high-rise unit received a ticket to respond. The officer wouldn't let me ride. He told me to proceed to Engine 34. When I arrived, Engine 34 and Ladder 21 had already responded to the Trade Center. I jumped aboard Engine 26, who was sharing the firehouse because their station was under renovation.

When we arrived, I didn't have a mask, so I went looking for Engine 34. I took the chauffeur's mask from Engine 3. I couldn't find Engine 34, so I went into the lobby of the North Tower, then into the lobby of the hotel. Both lobbies were filled with firefighters.

In the hotel, I met Ladder 12, who shares the firehouse with Engine 3. The company was told to switch to channel 2, the channel for the South Tower, and search upstairs from the 14th floor. We walked upstairs started searching the 14th floor. We went into a room and took a break. I put some water on my face. I looked out a rear window and saw 10 or 15 bodies lying in the courtyard. Earlier, I had seen people jumping.

We searched floor 15, then we split into two teams. One team searched 16, and the other 17, then we regrouped. I opened the door to floor 19. The South Tower started to collapse. It sounded like a bowling ball. I thought it might have been a bomb under the building like in 1993. I felt the wind – it sounded like all the doors were slamming closed. The wind came from above us. It threw us down the C stairs at the southernmost end of the hotel.

We started to make our way down when we received a Mayday. A firefighter from a ladder

Damaged air cylinder among debris.

Firehouse Collection

A USAR team searches a void.

Michael Rieger/FEMA News Photo

company was separated from his unit. He didn't know where he was. He had fallen a distance and was losing consciousness. Debris was blocking all the floors in the hallway.

At the fifth floor, debris blocked the stairway. We came upon several civilians who were located on the fifth floor. Entering the southernmost room, all you could see was white. It was quiet. There were little pockets of fire visible outside. The windows were broken. We figured the only way out was the window. The lieutenant and one firefighter were going to go back up to 19 to get the roof rope that was dropped and check again for the Mayday.

We ran into a firefighter, possibly from Engine 65. He had 50 feet of 2½-inch hose from a standpipe pack. If we did use the hose to go out the window, it would only leave us at the third floor. Firefighters were able to clear the debris in the stairway and made it to the fourth floor.

Outside, the debris was so close to the hotel that you could just about walk out onto the debris. Another firefighter from Ladder 12 decided to go and assist the two members who went back upstairs. We heard over the radio that they did make it back upstairs.

Now the second tower collapsed. I tried to get back inside and dove in under a staircase with another firefighter from Ladder 12. The building shook, it was dark. We were buried underneath the stairs, trapped under Sheetrock and light sheet metal. I made a space large enough to crawl out.

The I-beams that were too far away after the first collapse were now propped up against the hotel. Before you would have had to jump to the beam, now you were able to slide down. The civilians were assisted down 30 or 40 feet. I fell off the beam. Something tore off my mask. I had to crawl hand over foot up and down over the debris. I traveled south and then west to the Hudson River.

I had wondered if I ever would go to a job where a firefighter died. That morning, I saw people jumping, I thought someone might die. Before 9/11, 13 firefighters died since I came on the job. Now...

Boilvar Araellano

Members of New York Presbyterian Cornell Medical Center transport equipment towards South Tower. Ladder 10 is parked next to hotel (rear). Ladder 105 is positioned to the left of photo. Note Building 7 in the rear of the North Tower.

Get Me Out

Firefighter John Wilson
Engine 58, Harlem, Manhattan

now retired

We entered the hotel through the Tall Ships Bar located at West and Liberty streets. Lieutenant Bob Nagel told us to wait in the lobby of the hotel. Deputy Chief (Thomas) Galvin of the Third Division and Battalion Chiefs (Joseph) Marchbanks and (Fred) Sheffold of the 12th Battalion were conferring.

I took my mask off because I didn't know what we would be doing. Within five minutes I heard a rumbling, then boom, boom, boom. The noise got louder and faster. I assumed the floors were collapsing. Chief Galvin and everybody ran the way they came in. The force of the collapse picked me up and blew me down onto the ground. Debris was thrown on top of me. It took 10 seconds, but it seemed to take longer than it really did.

As I was trying to crawl on the ground, I was pelted by debris. Then everything stopped. It was dark and dusty. I was trying to get up. I called to the other firefighters. I determined I could walk around a little. The first person I saw was a hotel worker. As I continued to walk around, I ran into two other firefighters from Engine 58.

I remembered that I was given Danny Suhr's radio from Engine 216. He had been hit by a jumper. I called to the remaining members. The lieutenant wasn't answering. There were seven firefighters and the lieutenant. I was able to contact the others. Most made it out of the lobby into the street. A couple of probies were with me and two others. We didn't know what to do. I don't remember how we found the lieutenant. He was behind a wall of debris near the elevator bank. He ran one way and we ran another.

Lieutenant Nagel was talking to us. He asked where everybody else was. We told him four were outside and three inside. We reassured him that we've got everybody. I was able to walk into the bar area. There were cases of water and stacks of glasses that were intact. I was able to pass a bottle of water under the debris by snaking my hand through the debris. The lieutenant was able to reach his hand underneath and grab the water. Then he said, Get me out of here. He seemed to be annoyed that he was stuck and couldn't do anything. He was in a real tight spot. You could almost see him through the small openings.

Chief Galvin had tied a rope to a pillar. He brought the end of the rope next to where the debris trapping Nagel ended. We were afraid to pull the debris, which consisted of aluminum studs and BX cables. If we yanked on the debris, it might fall on him. I sent Scott Paskewitz outside to find some tools. Lieutenant Ray Brown and members of Ladder 113 came inside to extricate Nagel. When Scott came back in, he said the building was gone. I didn't comprehend that. What do you mean the building's gone? I didn't know the South Tower fell.

They were using a Sawzall to cut some aluminum. We were talking to Nagel. Then we heard another rumble, like the one we heard a half hour before. I ran toward the way we entered. The same scenario followed. I was tossed around, rolled on the floor and hit a wall. I covered up. I thought that was the end of it. After a few seconds I was still there. I started screaming for Scott and Mike. One of them was right next to me.

We found the rope ended at the wall of debris. Mike Fitzpatrick had been buried and was hurting.

Water from broken water mains runs down West Street. Remains of the Marriott Hotel are visible in the background.

Todd Maisel

Now we were in a tizzy and were trying to figure out what to do. Following the rope into the pile, it just ended. We started digging and called out for Lieutenant Brown. Outside is where we wound up. We had to climb the debris to get back down to street level. Brown wasn't anywhere to be found.

Then I saw him staggering out all bloody. We helped get him out. The street looked like Beirut. There were cars burning and there was a white dust everywhere. It looked like a snowstorm. Nobody was outside.

Eventually, we started to see people. I saw a guy with a camera while we were walking. I saw a firefighter from Engine 74 in the shell of the hotel. We met EMS and placed Ray into a chair. Ray started to scream, he had broken ribs and other injuries. Back into the hotel we went. A chief was there. We told the chief our lieutenant was missing. The chief said we're missing a lot of guys.

Then I remembered where he was. We went back to the area and started to dig. Water from the bar was helpful as we worked. There were a lot of people coming inside at that time. Other firefighters from Engine 58 met us. They told us they thought we were dead. They heard members of Engine 58 were missing.

We followed the rope from the pillar to where it was originally placed. Now there was another 20 to 30 feet of debris, pushing us further away from where we were standing next to the lieutenant before the collapse.

I was in a daze most of the day. Our eyes were cleaned out. I called my wife and told her I was OK. We left the scene before 9 P.M. I showered and returned to the firehouse the next morning at 8:30 A.M. We returned to the same spot. I had a good idea where we were and that digging in that area we would find Nagel.

Finally, one day we were digging and removed all the debris and hit the floor. The floor just ended. The concrete was cracked off. Nagel was gone. He could have been 10 levels down. That was a bad day. We never found him. It was just pure luck and a miracle that we survived. If I had come in a different way to the hotel, I might have run another way.

Andrea Booher/FEMA News Photo

(top) Members of Engine 58 concentrated their search efforts on the lobby of the hotel for weeks.

(bottom) Building at top right of photo would have been a fourth alarm by itself.

Andrea Booher/FEMA News Photo

It's A Statue

Firefighter Jason Faso Squad 61, Westchester Village, Bronx

now Rescue 1

I was getting off duty Tuesday morning. I was supposed to have an interview with Captain Terry Hatton of Rescue 1 that morning. I was trying to go to Rescue 1 on an onion skin (detail pending transfer). I heard the Bronx announce a second alarm for Box 8087, 1 World Trade Center. I thought it was a rubbish fire on an upper floor. I walked into the office of Squad 61. The lieutenant said a plane hit the Trade Center, put your uniform on. I said I had to go for my interview. The lieutenant replied that they would not be there.

Someone called the dispatcher and asked if they were going to send Squad 61. The dispatcher said no. A few minutes later one of the firefighters walked in. My back was to the television set. This fellow is pretty animated. He had his hands on top of his head with an astonished look on his face. He said another plane just hit. I said they keep showing the same thing over and over. He said, no, this is a different plane.

We were dispatched after the South Tower

Steve Spak

Michael Coppola

Statue of man reading the paper, found in the low visibility. Other items now adorn the statue.

collapsed. We loaded extra air cylinders and additional medical equipment. Traveling down the Sheridan Expressway we could see one tower still standing on fire. As we were going across Manhattan, all the radios from the scene went dead. We looked downtown and there wasn't any tower. I said, what happened. The dispatcher came on and said we have lost all radio communication. Tell us what is happening.

We parked on the West Side Highway. Firefighters were lying all over the place. We came up to Citywide Tour Commander Chief Frank Fellini. He said see what you can do. We heard Maydays from Captain Jay Jonas of Ladder 6. We went into Building 5 and 6. We didn't know we were in the wrong building to find Jonas. We found a security guard and a cleaning person. The smoke condition in the building was like burning cars. We found out cars were burning beneath the building.

We were trying to save our air in our SCBA. You could hear stuff settling in the building. The ceilings had fallen down; there were lean-to and pancake collapses. A piece of ceiling was on top of an escalator. We had to check to see if anyone was trapped. The smoke was starting to get pretty bad. We came out to Vesey Street. They were setting up a tower ladder for an exterior attack. I said, is this what's left of the towers? I had never been down to the Trade Center.

Possibly on Fulton Street we saw flames coming out of every window of the cab of the apparatus of Squad 252. The engine was still running. Over on Church Street I thought I saw a man sitting on a park bench reading the newspaper off in the distance. Everything was gray. I thought the man had died right there. Another firefighter said it was a statue, but I didn't believe him. I had to physically reach up to touch the paper, the Thermos and his briefcase before I could determine it was a statue.

Inside the firehouse of Engine 10 and Ladder 10, the rear kitchen door was bowed outwards. We started climbing up the pile. Someone said we found someone over here. Alive? No. Move on, we have to look for live people. You could not take in the full scope of the tragedy, only what was right around you. We saw a pair of feet inside a pair of EMS boots intertwined with steel rebar. It took four hours to remove them. I had a hopeless feeling. What I had seen, there was no hope. On Friday we found some firefighters from Rescue 1. A high line was set up to move equipment across the deep valleys of debris. Nighttime was a better time to search. You could see the stripes on the gear in the rubble. We found Bill Henry of Rescue 1 intact in a stairway. His six-foot metal hook took the shape of the stairway. No one felt a thing.

One day we were digging in the area of the North Tower when we found pieces of chandeliers. We knew we were in the lobby area. Chief Riches buried his mother, nothing to do with the trade center. After the funeral he went to the site, they had found his firefighter son. We found only doorknobs. No phones, only the cords. No computers only the components. In a stairway we found air cylinders with webbing, firefighting tools. Some of the papers you found gave an indication of what floor they came from. We found elevator cables all over. I finally went to Rescue 1 in January 2002.

(opposite page) Four floors are well involved in Building 5, east of the North Tower. Companies inside searching could see and feel the building starting to crumble. When they exited, they were amazed to see so much visible fire.

We Will Give A Report

Lieutenant Glenn Rohan Ladder 43, Lower Harlem, Manhattan

now Captain, Ladder 31

I heard the attack. Engine 53 was dispatched on the fifth alarm to the second tower. I knew it was going to be a really tough job; the guys were going to get their butts kicked.

I had the company check their gear and the rig for equipment. We received a run to East 41st Street and Lexington Avenue for a person with their foot stuck in a revolving door. We were assigned with Engine 26. There are normally trucks closer than we are, but they were already sent to the World Trade Center. The response was over 60 blocks.

I asked the Manhattan dispatcher do you want me to go downtown? He told us to remain in service. That took the heart right out of everybody on the rig. The chauffeur just said, come on, let's go. I said there is nobody left on the East Side. Every other truck company in our area is already assigned to the WTC — 13, 16, 14 and 26. I instructed the chauffeur to head uptown, but go slowly.

At Third Avenue and East 50th Street, we heard a firefighter screaming for help. I told the chauffeur, something is wrong. I heard the Manhattan dispatcher calling Field Communications numerous times with no answer. Then the dispatcher was trying to get any unit operating at the scene. I called the dispatcher and said that Ladder 43 would proceed south and give them a report. The dispatcher sent us.

We could see smoke from the towers. We didn't hear any report of the building coming down. I thought only pieces of the building came down. We parked as close as we could, about four blocks north near Warren and West streets.

Walking south near Barclay Street we heard a noise loud enough to make you look up. We backed up and ran north. The smoke and dust were coming; the North Tower fell. I told everybody to mask up. We had two search ropes with us. After the smoke and dust started to clear, there were cars, trucks and apparatus burning. We walked near the North Pedestrian Bridge and checked in, around and under rigs for trapped firefighters. Engines were started and the 500 gallons of water in the booster tanks were used to extinguish some of the fires in the rigs.

While we were searching for civilians, we ran into Chief Mark Ferran, Battalion 12. He told me he had a report that Chief Richard Picciotto, Battalion 11, was trapped in one of the towers. He said the chief reported he was with a number of firefighters in Tower 1 in a stairway and he can't tell where they are. We started asking everybody and anybody if

Andrea Booher/FEMA News Photo

It took several hours for rescuers to locate where Captain Jay Jonas and others were located.

they knew where Tower 1 was.

We went out and around Building 6, down to the parking garage and to Vesey Street. We walked east. There was a 40-foot-high pile of steel in the street after Tower 1 collapsed. The fire had entered Building 7. Fire was visible in 30 windows spread across four of the lower floors. We found off-duty members from Engine 53/Ladder 43 operating an engine and aerial ladder at a building where people were trapped on the upper floors.

We were now traveling farther away from our objective, but still didn't know where Tower 1 was located. Before we had left Building 6, Chief Picciotto had a megaphone with a siren unit. He was asked to sound the siren. We couldn't hear it.

We asked Battalion 11 to hit the siren again. We were just barely able to hear it. You couldn't get through the hole in the crater. Three firefighters went with Chief Ferran and four others went around another way. In the crater you had to walk on steel with 40- to 50-foot drops. The siren noise was coming from the southwest, but you had to walk west to north to go to the southwest. It was very steep, very dangerous with fires burning underneath. If anyone falls, I'll have another operation. Portions of the surrounding buildings were collapsing.

Building 7 was starting to fall apart. There were five floors of fire inside. I knew we didn't have a lot of time. Picciotto said you're going to need rescue tools to get them out. We only had halligan tools and roof ropes. I said, let's take one problem at a time. Every 20 minutes we could hear the siren echoing.

There were eight of us now within two groups. Chief Ferran said we might have to pull out. The fire in Building 7 was causing concern that it would come down soon. Then, Picciotto said we could start seeing outside and see the blue sky. At this time, it was about one hour that we were inside the crater searching. Picciotto was asked if he could see a vertical steel-like stair-riser. Picciotto said, you yell out. We did and he said that's right outside where we are.

It was a real climb to get through this. Looking at where they were trapped it looked like a three-story-high section, 30 to 40 feet wide. You couldn't tell it was a stairway. I said a prayer a second time. Firefighter Jerry Suden was standing on an eight-inch piece of steel 50 feet in the air. He could see Picciotto and hooked up a roof rope to get the people inside out 12 or 14 feet from the stairwell.

Trapped in this area between the third and fourth floors were 12 people, including Chief Picciotto, Captain Jay Jonas and five members of Ladder 6, a lieutenant and two firefighters from two different engine companies, a Port Authority police officer and a female civilian. Suden was going to have to take the rescued firefighters back out the way we came. After the first group emerged, they went about 50 feet and the fires burning beneath the steel wouldn't allow them to go the way we came in.

I asked where the two other firefighters were trapped. They were maneuvering down the remains of the stairway to what was left of a landing. Tools were going to be needed. I could talk to the two firefighters from Engine 39. I asked if they were OK.

Firefighters Jimmy Lanza and Thomas Corrigan came with me. I got a roof rope. If another collapse occurred, I would know where they were located. I cleared some rubble and concrete with a halligan tool near the corner of the landing with the standpipe. I hit some sheetrock. I was able to remove two layers of sheetrock and opened a small void. That's going to be enough to get them out.

I told them crawl up to the next level. Take the halligan and remove some of the Sheetrock. Step on the halligan tool, put one hand on the rope and pull yourself up. The next firefighter was larger. The next firefighter, Jeffrey Coniglio, climbed up, we grabbed on and he just made it. If he needed another inch, it would have been tough.

Everybody was yelling to evacuate now. We said a prayer and had to leave. We retraced our steps. When we finally made it back outside, there was a line of firefighters as long as you could see. It took 40 minutes to walk off the pile. We made it to Liberty and West streets and were there for an hour when Building 7 collapsed.

When we received an assignment, it was a relief. We are trained to do this job. We focused on the task. The pressure was off thinking of something to do. Let's take care of this problem. It was so discouraging that more of that wasn't going on. I thought guys were being pulled out all over.

We Were Part Of A Team

Firefighter Chris Eysser Ladder 111, Bedford-Stuyvesant, Brooklyn

now Captain, Division 13 covering

I came in for a day tour. It was one of the first tours back from vacation. The morning was busy for Engine 214 located in quarters with us. I had not seen the firefighters for awhile. They had responded to several EMS and ERS boxes more than usual. Over the television came the report about the World Trade Center. Someone yelled out you have to see this fire. From the angle of the camera shot, it didn't look like the WTC. There was heavy fire blowing out of the windows. I didn't think it was terrorism.

When the second plane hit the South Tower, the dispatch tone went off. Engine 214 was assigned to the World Trade Center. We put extra equipment onto the apparatus knowing that we were one of the only truck companies left in the area. We watched both towers collapse.

Later in the morning there was a fire in Bushwick that we responded to. In the early afternoon, we relocated to the quarters of Ladder 131 in Red Hook, Brooklyn. We were there for a few hours.

Looking toward Manhattan, there was a big cloud coming from downtown. Building 7 had collapsed. The company was now relocated to Ladder 1 in Manhattan. Looking down the street from the corner where Ladder 1 was located, you could see steel backlit by emergency lights sticking up in all directions in the middle of Church Street.

We had a few runs, then we were dispatched to the Trade Center site. We walked around Church Street onto the large debris pile into the center where one of the collapses occurred. There was a bucket brigade going all the way to the top. We worked our way towards the top. There were people from all different agencies working there. As we made it close, they needed a fresh truck company. Apparently, there were numerous companies working, relieving each other.

Squad 41 and Rescue 1 had been working on a trapped Port Authority police officer. We went on down into the area taking turns just scraping away debris. Any type of small instrument was being used. He was trapped in the area below his knees to just above his ankles. He was given IVs and his vitals were being checked. There was a Nassau County ESU cop with him. We were filling buckets to pass out debris. There was an elevator shaft nearby. You could hear a PASS device going off on a mask that had fallen down the elevator shaft by accident. The officer was lying on his back. We worked all night. A piece of webbing was positioned around his legs. The guys on top of the pile pulled, to no avail.

The officer was screaming in pain. We dug some more. We were determined to get the officer out. On the second effort we were able to remove him. He was placed into a Stokes basket. As he was passed down the entire line of people working the bucket brigade, the sun came up. He was put into an ambulance. He survived.

We stood on top of the pile looking down at all the people who supported us. We were the last in a long line of companies who worked many hours to free the officer. Just part of the job.

In certain places, the debris pile was several stories high.

Bri Rodriguez/FEMA News Photo

Patriotism

Captain Mike Dugan Ladder 123, Fire Academy, Randalls Island, Manhattan

I was teaching at an annual education day at the Fire Academy. We usually have between six and eight companies that are out of service. Class starts at 9 A.M. I heard that a plane had hit the Trade Center, but I thought it was a small plane.

I heard the request for a 10-60, a major emergency. I couldn't believe my eyes. I was in Chief Nick Santangelo's office when the second jet hit. Someone said we are under attack, put all units back in service. The instructors from the chauffeurs school and regular instructors — anybody with gear — get ready. Find flashlights, masks, radios and split up into four groups of 10.

We boarded a bus and arrived just after the second tower had collapsed. Many rigs and ambulances were on fire. I saw a wheel from the jet and other parts lying in the street. I had four firefighters with me. We entered the PATH subway station. We found two people injured in the collapse who were injured and removed them with Engine 249. Exiting the subway, I saw Firefighter Matty James, the Uniformed Firefighters Association Brooklyn trustee, with a flag. I said Matty, what are you doing? He said we have to get this up. At Church Street we got a portable ladder off a tower ladder, tied the flag to a street light and came down.

I worked until 11 P.M. I was scheduled to do a 24-hour shift in the morning. I wound up at Engine 231 manning an engine from Livingston, NJ. Ladder 120 was in quarters with the 44th Battalion. I went back down to the site in the morning for 15 more hours. Digging through the rubble, we found some remains of civilians. They were decimated. It was horrific.

Captain Mike Dugan, who responded from the FDNY Fire Academy, with the help of other firefighters, raises the American flag on a street light on Church Street.

You're On The List

Firefighter Garrett Lindgren Rescue 3, Tremont, Bronx

These are brothers that I worked with during the 24 hours from 0900 on September 10 to 0840 on September 11 (all of whom died):

CAPTAIN JIM AMATO
Squad 1

FF PETE BRENNAN
Rescue 4

FF MIKE CAWLEY
Ladder 136
detailed to Engine 292

LT. KEVIN DOWDELL
Rescue 4

FF TERRY FARRELL
Rescue 4

FF TOM FOLEY
Rescue 3

CAPTAIN BRIAN HICKEY
Rescue 4

FF JONATHAN IELPI
Squad 288

FF BILL MAHONEY
Rescue 4

BC JOHN MORAN
SOC Battalion

FF BRONCO PEARSALL
Rescue 4

FF ALAN TARASIEWICZ
Rescue 5

I worked 24 hours on Monday. I worked overtime in Squad 288 in Queens during the day, and a mutual in Rescue 4 Monday night. I was getting off duty Tuesday morning. I had woken early at 7 A.M. Pete Brennan from Rescue 4 wanted to relieve me and I said I was going to stay and have coffee, let someone else go. Pete Rigano from Squad 61 was relieved. I was going to go back to the Bronx and have coffee with Captain Brian Hickey of Rescue 4, who was working his first tour back on overtime following the Father's Day fire. Brian was working overtime Tuesday day tour in Rescue 3 in the Bronx. Al Tarasiewicz (Taz) of Rescue 5 came in on a detail or overtime and wanted to relieve me. I finally gave in. I took my gear off the truck and told him I had the irons (forcible entry) position.

Traveling north on the Brooklyn Queens Expressway, I listened to the radio and they were talking about a fire in the Trade Center. I could see the fire, smoke and a giant hole in the building. There was no doubt in my mind that someone detonated something inside. Then the radio mentioned a plane had hit the building. I headed to Rescue 3. I was already committed to the Triborough Bridge. When I arrived at Rescue 3, the second plane had already hit the second tower. No one was there, the rigs had already responded on the initial alarm. I was going to get on the phone list to notify all off-duty members when the voice alarm from the dispatcher announced a recall by orders of Chief of Department Peter Ganci. Right after that, Firefighters Bob Knabbe, Stan Sussina and Captain Ralph Tiso, all of Rescue 3, entered quarters. They had been undergoing dive training and could see the towers from their location.

The plan was to go to Special Operations Command (SOC) and get another rig in case there was another attack we could cover anything within the city. We were in a traffic bottleneck. A man in an unmarked city vehicle with sirens and lights asked me to ride with him and he would escort us where we needed to go. When we arrived at SOC, we started to put gear and equipment together. We obtained a rescue-pumper and a van and started loading cargo. I was outside putting equipment in the van when I heard the South Tower had collapsed. Smoke was visible in lower Manhattan. I told the others the South Tower collapsed. They said no way. We were responding in the van and the rescue-pumper. In the Queens-Midtown Tunnel there was a logjam of traffic. We went down East River Drive. As we approached the scene, thousands of civilians were running northbound. It looked like a Godzilla movie, just a mass of people running up the highway.

I called my wife and told her we were on the way to the Trade Center. I said a lot of us are going to die there. I think it was because we got jammed up at the tunnel that we arrived shortly after the North Tower had collapsed. As we walked into the site, you couldn't see. Captain Tiso called Rescue 3. It was dead quiet. I expected the radio to be on communications overload. Somebody said everybody is dead. It was quiet like a snow storm at night, very muffled, no visibility. We started seeing police cars and fire trucks on fire, ambulances overturned. There was tremendous debris. The terrain was difficult to maneuver. It looked like a war zone. We dropped our air packs.

We thought that there would be survivors in lean-to or compartmentalized areas waiting for help. You could hear some Maydays. There was an engine chauffeur trapped under a rig. We had no clue where that was. We heard guys calling for help. It was difficult to see and communicate in such a large area to cover. I was in the dust cloud with firefighters from other units and Chief John Salka. We heard 6 Truck give calm transmissions of where they were trapped. The only problem was that building didn't exist anymore.

A search rope was set up into a parking garage. Two civilians were located alive. There was a civilian on the collapsed pile. Ground ladders and ropes were used and a Stokes basket was passed up into that area. When we heard about the female survivor in one of the towers, we got a little bit of hope. If they survived in the collapse, maybe there were others.

The first day we were walking on the exterior steel framework of the towers. We could see police vehicles underneath and also firefighters' bunker

Michael Rieger/FEMA News Photo

To make the trip to the top of the pile easier, firefighters were lifted by crane in a man basket, saving at least an hour's hike.

gear. We operated by the hotel and shopping mall. We were lifted by crane and basket to the top of the South Tower. It was a constantly changing environment. The pile burned for months. You could feel it drop under your feet. There were a lot of colors of smoke, green and orange. Sometimes it was too hot to stand on top of the pile because of the wind currents. In some areas the pile was at least six stories high. There was total destruction. No desk computers, only the electronic guts, no phones, only the wires.

Generally we found firefighters (brothers) in the stairwells. We recovered some firefighting tools like hooks, halligans and some masks. It was emotionally overwhelming to walk around the pile and find a firefighter lying there. It was a most out-of-the-ordinary event to deal with for me personally. On the day tour on Monday I worked with Jonathan Ielpi for the first time in Squad 288. I was glad I got to meet him. His father worked in Rescue 2. There was a major Hazardous Materials drill at the Training Academy on Monday. The drill was attended by a lot of SOC units. I was able to hang out with so many firefighters I don't always see at one place. Many were going to die the next day. I spent the night tour in Rescue 4 in Queens. At 11:30 P.M. I was talking with Firefighter Terry Farrell of Rescue 4. He was driving that night. He told me that Rescue 4 had brought back bricks from the building where the Father's Day fire occurred. They were going to build a memorial for all the two members of Rescue 4 who died in the line of duty, including those two who got killed a little over eight weeks prior. Now Terry's name is on the memorial he was planning to build.

After I came to the pile the first day, I saw Chris Ryan of Rescue 3. He gave me a hug. He said we thought you were dead. There is a list at the command post and your name is on it. I called my wife. She saw the number on the caller ID and thought someone had found my cell phone and thought I was killed. Thankfully that wasn't the case. My daughter heard that I was missing. My son knew I would be at the scene, working or not.

On Monday, September 10, 2001, I attended a Haz-Mat drill at the Training Academy. The following companies participated:

- HAZ-MAT 1
- SQUAD 1
- SQUAD 288
- RESCUE 3
- SOC BATTALION

Digging Like A Gopher

Firefighter Liam Flaherty Rescue 4, Winfield, Queens

now Captain, Rescue 2

I responded from home to Rescue 4. Tons of equipment were loaded up onto a city bus. We came south on West Street. Walking down the street we saw Father John Delendeck. He said Father Mychal Judge is gone. It was like a punch in the solar plexus to hear he was dead. The scene looked biblical, like the hand of God came down and smashed buildings to the ground. We hooked up with Lieutenant Gerry Murtha from Rescue 3. You could hear Captain Jay Jonas calling over the radio that he was trapped in a stairway. We didn't know what building Jonas was in when it came down. Ropes and ladders were used to get up the pile.

We got equipment in place to get Josephine, who Ladder 6 had been helping down the pile in a Stokes basket after they had been located. Six Truck walked past us on their way out with a dazed look in their eyes. We thought they had been trapped after responding to the scene, not when a tower came down. Firefighters from engines, ladders and the rescues got together as a team and passed down the Stokes basket. It took dozens and dozens of firefighters to remove the woman to safety. If you saw it from a birds-eye view, it was like looking at a bunch of ants. Survivors told us in the area where 6 Truck was located there was a chief who was trapped. They said to get to him they needed a lot more equipment.

Building 7 looked really bad. They said it was going to come down. Deputy Chief Nick Visconti ordered everybody away from the perimeter and wait for it to collapse. We backed away and watched Building 7 come down. Liberty and West streets is where we backed up to, as it came down. It was a 47-story office building. It was a non-event. Any other time in history it would have been a career event, a milestone in your career. It made no impact on me as it came down. I remember being angry that we had to stop work in the area. We thought we were going to find hundreds of survivors. After it came down they gave an all clear.

Working by the hotel, it was hard to pick a spot to work. Some of the members went back up to where 6 Truck had been trapped. Communication was tough. Not everybody had a radio. The guys we found were gone. We marked the spot and moved on. The bodies were so intertwined; it was going to take a lot of effort to remove them. We were looking for live victims. Additional rescue companies were being requested. USAR teams were being dispatched to New York. We stopped by the quarters of Engine 10/Ladder 10. You could see the rescue effort underway. About 150 firefighters were handling whatever needed to be transported in a chain gang up and down the pile. Buildings 3 and 4 were burning. They were built of steel. We weren't really worried about them coming down.

Three of us from Rescue 4 were sent to help relieve other units that had been working on removing a trapped Port Authority police officer. At the end of the chain gang of firefighters you went straight down into like a cave. When you went 15-20 feet inside the cave you made a hard left past a deceased Port Authority cop. It was so tight only one person could go in. We might have replaced Rescue 5. Emergency Service cops, engines and ladders had been working on the removal. It was one of the hairiest places I was ever in. You were unsure of a secondary collapse. Even if something settled, I am a big guy. It was all I could do to crawl in there.

I could just see his head sticking out. There was a cop behind me. You could not wear a mask. It was hot and smoky. You had to take off your mask and place it to the side and take hits off of it. You wouldn't fit with it, the space was that tight. Basically you were in a tube, concerned with carbon monoxide poisoning. I told the cop to keep taking air from the mask. The cop was moaning and groaning, going in and out of consciousness. We could operate without a facepiece on. There were big pieces of pipe, debris, steel, dirt and

FACT

128 of 343 FIREFIGHTERS remain unaccounted for as of WINTER 2011

rubble. You were digging like a gopher. You couldn't throw the dirt anywhere except in the face of the guy behind me. I dug for a while. We rotated. It was punishing, very smoky and hot. There was a hoseline down there. The fire was close. I couldn't see visible flame. Smoke was coming out of every crevice. I asked the cop his name, he kept moaning. I was trying to make small talk.

A medic came down and asked if he could get in to assess him. I backed up and talked with the medic. I told the medic that the cop was in a lot of pain. The medic asked what part of his body was exposed? I told him his neck. The rest of the body was covered. We rotated in and out. Probably 100 guys did what I did. It was exhausting, painstakingly slow. There was a lot of hand digging. I was using a scoop or a ladle-like device for a while. I wasn't sure he was going to live.

I could see the effort it was going to take to get him out. Any cop or firefighter that went in there to help, I take my hat off to them. We were there for hours. Rescue 1 relieved us. My eyes were closed. The people on the chain gang guided us off the pile. I heard the next day the cop was removed. I considered it a miracle. Conditions were very bad, very smoky. One person couldn't do it by themselves. It was a team effort. I thought the first night we were going to find a lot of people.

Andrea Booher/FEMA News Photo

Workers from various agencies worked together to support those attempting the rescue of trapped victims in the voids in the pile.

Last Call

Firefighter Bob Athanas Rescue 3, Tremont, Bronx

I was assigned to Rescue 3, but was on light duty taking care of SOC Logistics. I had worked the previous 24 hours and was getting relieved at 7 A.M. on Tuesday.

I had a meeting with SOC Chief Ray Downey about an upcoming drill at Stewart Air Force Base in October. I was carpooling with Nick Giordano and we left SOC at 8:10 A.M.

I stopped at Squad 18 on Monday and saw Captain Joe Downey. I spoke with Firefighter Andy Fredericks and with Lieutenant Pete Martin of Rescue 2 on the phone. He said any time you want to have dinner let me know. I also spoke to Ray Meisenheimer, Chris Blackwell and Don Regan of Rescue 3 and Lieutenant Mike Healy in Squad 41, a former member of Rescue 3. Chief Moran worked the Monday night. Firefighter Joe Angelini of Rescue 1 was at the kitchen table. Firefighter Hank Molle was waiting for Firefighter Steve Modica. Chief John Paolillo was the chief in the rescue battalion on Tuesday.

Nick and I were driving up Route 17 in New Jersey when we stopped for gasoline. I turned on the scanner. I heard Engine 10 say it's confirmed. I said to myself what is confirmed? I looked at my BNN (Breaking News Network) pager and the message said a plane into a tower of the Trade Center.

Firehouse Collection

AP Photo/William C. Lopez

(top) Firefighters Bob Athanas (left) and Johnny La Femina work in a tent with a FEMA cache near Chambers Street.
(left) Thirty days after the attack, smoke vents skyward from fire burning deep in the pile.

We were on a hill and you could look back and see all the high-rise buildings in Manhattan. I could see the smoke coming from the World Trade Center. Nick drove another 1-2 miles and we pulled over. I called my wife who was watching it on television. I called other firefighters. I said we'd better go back.

The USAR equipment was unloaded at West and Chambers streets. There was a schoolyard that was fenced in. Security of the equipment cache could be provided. Around 5 P.M. there was a concern about Building 7 collapsing. When it did collapse, the dust cloud stopped right before Chambers Street.

We took a hoseline off an engine to wash the dust down that was covering the entire area. We heard that several other USAR teams from around the country were on their way. Before they arrived I figured out what channels they should operate on. An SOC command post was also established at our location. We were a mobilization point.

We had USAR radios and handie-talkies. SOC units reported in to us. We had an accountability system with riding lists. We knew who was there. Companies were told to report in with their tools. Some units had two and three sections. Nick and others set up and ran a forward tool cache. Units were calling for batteries, rebar cutters, shovels and spades.

We had numerous people entering our tent. Out-of-town departments, USAR teams, the former governor of New Jersey, and the Chicago FD all checked in. Companies dropped off equipment to us. We had generators, light towers, chargers and security. Some fire marshals walked in 24-36 hours after the attack. They said here are lists of those firefighters we think are dead. Two of the names on the list were just here.

I went home on Friday night and returned Saturday morning. We went right back down to the pile. We were trying to think where our guys might be located. My firefighters were concerned about me. I said my guys are in there! I want to go!

Rescue 3 lost seven members and Rescue 4 lost Captain Brian Hickey. We spent a lot of time sifting and digging. All of the firefighters mentioned earlier that I had talked to on Monday, including Chief Ray Downey, were killed, with the exception his son, Captain Joe Downey.

A War Scene

Firefighter Van Johnson
Tower Ladder 124, Bushwick, Brooklyn

now retired

I was standing in front of the firehouse when the second and third alarms were transmitted. We watched the news helicopters showing the actual fire. They were sending Brooklyn companies.

When the second tower was hit, we relocated to Ladder 5 in Manhattan. We responded over the Manhattan Bridge. We arrived at Ladder 5. Off-duty members were grabbing their gear. Engine 231 relocated to Engine 24 in the same firehouse.

Within 10 or 15 minutes, we saw the smoke from the fire change drastically. The smoke went from jet black to light. That is when the first tower collapsed. We responded to the scene. We drove down Church Street the wrong way. It was chaos. People were running away. The chauffeur hit the brakes. The mayor and his entourage passed us going to the firehouse we just left to use as a temporary command post.

We couldn't respond any further. We were being hit by dust. We picked up a few firefighters along the way. Hundreds of people were running by the apparatus. We ended up near 10 Truck's firehouse. There was a man who was severely burned and on fire. We extinguished the fire. All his clothes were burned off. We left him with an EMS worker.

We heard screaming from the rear of the firehouse. Three civilians sought shelter after the first tower came down, forcing them into the rear of the firehouse. One person had a broken hip and another had a broken arm. The man with the broken hip apparently had a lot of money in the briefcase he was carrying. He wouldn't let it go.

A person fell from another building and struck a police officer. I helped carry him away with the aid of another police officer. We heard a tremendous roar. We thought it was another jet coming in. The North Tower collapsed. We were starting to be buried with debris. Everyone had dust go up his nose and down their throat. We ran into a building. The force of the wind, it took three of us to pull the doors shut. We proceeded down to Liberty Street. There were rigs on fire, ambulances burning. Seeing the rigs destroyed, you got a feeling that many companies were lost. It looked like midnight, dead calm.

I could hear the Mayday from Ladder 6. There was another report from a company trapped under a rig. We wound up looking for Chief Ganci in the debris with Ladder 111. He had worked in both companies. It was ironic that these are two of the companies who found him buried under three or four feet of debris in the middle of the street near the Winter Garden. In some areas the debris was eight feet high. Firefighters were using torches, hand tools and Sawzalls.

Buildings 4 and 5 were fully involved. Someone had moved our tower ladder and it was operating near Building 4. A tool depot was initiated at 10 & 10. There were hundreds of tools, shovels, hand tools, Stokes baskets.

I guess I was in shock. I couldn't comprehend what had happened. Almost getting killed. We didn't know where to look and there were fires everywhere. It looked like a war scene. The fires burned all day into the night. Because of the debris, we couldn't get the tower ladder into a better position.

It was my son's first day on the job. He was assigned to Ladder 36 in Manhattan. It was his first day and he heard that his father was lost. My son finally met up with me in the hospital later that night. I was shocked to see a rig from my volunteer fire department at the scene.

Among the steel and debris, an exhausted and dirty firefighter takes a break.

Todd Maisel

Something Terrible Had Happened

Battalion Chief Richard J. Blatus Covering Battalion Chief, West Farms, Bronx

now Special Operations Command

I was assigned to headquarters at the time, in Operations. The night before, my daughter had broken her arm, so I was with her in the doctor's office when it occurred. I was just leaving, it was about 8:50 A.M. It was odd because as soon as I heard it on the radio, (Battalion Chief) John Salka called me on the Nextel and asked me if I heard what was going on. We made arrangements to meet in the 18th Battalion, keeping each other posted all the way down.

The initial thing that struck me coming down on the Taconic Parkway was that everybody was going north. Everybody was leaving the city.

I met him in the 18th and we went up to the Seventh Division where they were having the muster site for the Bronx recall, to help get things organized. They decided to send John, myself and Deputy Chief Mike Rappe down to the site. We came in from the east side, the City Hall side.

A lot of guys were reporting in. They set up the command structure. We had them with their riding lists, trying to keep a count of what was going on. They commandeered a couple of buses on Webster Avenue (in the Bronx), sent two buses down immediately. It was almost like looked like a scene from one of the movies you see, like *Pearl Harbo*r with people running across Webster Avenue. Traffic was unbelievable, cars all over the place. So they ordered up two buses.

They sent us down in a car with the division messenger. We couldn't get any closer than maybe three blocks east of City Hall. We came in on Park Row and that's where we stopped. We couldn't go any farther. We were all shocked that even that far away there was six inches of silt on the ground. Everything was covered.

The site was just clogged with vehicles – everything, fire vehicles, ambulances, ESU vehicles, cop cars, civilian vehicles, but really not a lot of people.

We started walking down Park Row. I'm not even sure what street it was on, but they had an east command post set up. It was a big open area and there was a chief there. It was very chaotic and he was trying to get a handle and trying to organize. It was really odd because there was one group of officers right on the corner where he was standing, officers were around him, but all the firefighters were on the other side, kind of sitting around. It was odd, like half the guys were in a daze. Other guys were coming down not knowing where to go. So we stopped there for a bit and (Deputy) Chief (Tom) Haring told us to walk down to the site. He said there was a command post set up somewhere on the west side of the site.

We walked down Broadway. For a couple of blocks, we saw nothing, then we saw the first rig – its windows were blown out. And it really struck me that there was no radio traffic at all. There was nothing on the radio.

Guys were walking around kind of in a daze who obviously were down there when the collapse occurred. I guess we arrived there maybe 15 minutes after the second collapse. It was very dark, hard to breathe. It was surreal, almost like a glow.

We walked around and all of a sudden, we saw the remains of the facade of one of the towers. I couldn't believe it – it was 100 feet in the air. I really thought it almost looked like the world was coming to an end to me. It must have been the South Tower because we walked around and ended up coming upon 10 & 10. In fact, it struck me so much I called my wife on the Nextel. I said this is really bad. It almost looked like one of those movies. I'm sure everybody says that.

We could only see 50 to 75 yards and it was hard to breathe. We grabbed a couple of paper masks from an EMS ambulance and it helped a bit, but it didn't help that much. But it really struck me that there were very few firemen that you could see. The ones we saw were either sitting down trying to breathe or trying to recover themselves, or they were just walking around in a daze. And again, no radio traffic. I didn't hear radio traffic for a long time.

We got (extra handie-talkies) from the division. Then we started encountering debris. We came up upon 10 & 10 when we met a captain. We asked him for a way to get around to the west side of the building. There was very heavy debris in front of 10 & 10, so he took us through 10 & 10 and around the back to the west side.

Andrea Booher/FEMA News photo

Firefighter works atop a multi-ton box beam as it is prepared to be lifted out of the way in the cleanup process.

I remember the debris went right into the quarters. We ended up somewhere near West Street and it probably took us the better part of an hour to climb over and get to the command post at West and Vesey. And somewhere in that time when we were walking around 10 & 10 is when we heard the Mayday for guys trapped in the B stairway of the North Tower and John said that sounds like Jay (Jonas).

We stopped and listened for a while and he said that is Jay. And then John called Jay directly – is this Jay Jonas? And he said yes and all he would tell us is that he was in the North Tower in the B stairway. And John tried to get some communications through to make sure the Mayday was heard. They told us to report up to the west command post. We started climbing over that debris, and it took the better part of an hour to try to get up that way.

We were trying to go up West Street. It had to be 20 feet high, 30 feet high, up and down over the big beams. Somewhere in the middle of that trek up there, we came upon a rescue rig. There was a chief on top of the rescue rig. We approached him and asked him if he knew about Jay being trapped and he said yes. And there was really no kind of rescue that we knew of underway.

We heard later that 43 Truck was trying to come in from the north side, so he assigned John and I each five rescue guys who were there to try to ascertain where Jay was. We tried to stay together, but we ended up getting split up. I guess we walked around for an hour trying to climb into the site, trying to get around the fires that were there, and then we heard that Jay was out. He had self-extricated. That probably encompassed at least the first two hours that we were there.

I heard a couple of the Maydays, but nothing really solid. It would come and go. I don't know why that was. I remember there were times when the radio was blocked out. You could tell guys were climbing over something and buttons were getting pressed. After those couple of hours, when Jay was extricated, I finally got to the West and Vesey command post. Chief (Frank) Fellini (Citywide Tour Commander) was there and it was as well organized as you could be at that point. He initially directed me to go to the OEM command post to be a liaison, but when I got there (Deputy Commissioner) Tom Fitzpatrick was there and he had taken it over, so they didn't need me.

Andrea Booher/FEMA News Photo

Total devastation covers the entire street.

When I came back, I met up with (Chief of Safety) Al Turi. And he asked me to accompany him. He wanted to get around to the middle of the site; they were looking for (Chief of Department) Pete Ganci. We walked through the World Financial Center, came out just north of Liberty Street and started climbing over the debris, I would say south of the middle of the site. Al was my first lieutenant in 48 Engine. We stayed together and maybe 15 minutes after that, they called us and said they found Pete Ganci. We were only about 20 yards away, so we walked over. We helped them dig Pete out. Probably the next hour was spent bringing Pete through the Winter Garden and back out to Vesey Street.

After we completed that, I went back down to the command post and ran into (Deputy Chief) Nick Visconti. Nick said I don't know how to tell you this, we found (Ladder 24 Captain) Danny Brethel, who was a very good friend of mine. He said we found him 10 feet from where Pete Ganci was, underneath apparatus. I knew Danny was down there because somewhere in the chaos I had met (Captain) Jack McDonald (now a battalion chief) and Jack had told me he knew we were close, Danny and I. He told me Danny drove Father Judge (FDNY Chaplain Father Mychal Judge) down. He said he's here somewhere.

I tried to get back over to where they were to bring out my friend, but by the time I climbed over everything, they already brought him out. They brought him out the other side and he was taken away.

That was probably 4 or 5 o'clock in the afternoon. There was a big discussion about 7 World Trade Center. We had to keep everybody away on West Street, worried that it would collapse. By that time in the afternoon, it was pretty much fully involved. There was fire on 30 floors. It was amazing to see that much fire – 30 floors of fire.

That took a lot of time and in between, during the discussion, they were trying to get guys out of 7 World Trade Center. There were guys searching in there and they weren't sure if they were out. Nick Visconti was up on a kind of scaffolding and I went up there and helped him out. We successfully evacuated guys, and it was really pretty much a standoff operation until that building fell down, which was about 5:30. It came straight down, to the shock of everybody. I would have bet you a million dollars that that building wasn't going to come straight down. It didn't even move. It came straight down in a vertical.

Vesey Street became totally impassable. The debris was pretty bad before from the Trade Center, but now it filled Vesey Street. It was just all lumped on top of each other, a big pile of burning debris – instead of 47 stories high, now it's probably 12 stories high, some of it burning. Surprisingly, a lot of the fire went out.

Immediately after that, they had reports there was fire in the Verizon Building as a result of the collapse. Chief Fellini asked for three battalion chief volunteers to take three teams of seven guys each. One battalion chief I wasn't familiar with, myself and John Salka took these guys up into the Verizon Building. We went in the entrance on West Street.

We divided the floors. It was a 21-story building, so we took seven floors apiece. John took the upper seven. I took the middle seven and the other chief took the lower seven. We never found any fires. We didn't find anybody in the building. There was some evidence of structural damage, but nothing substantial. But for the first time that day, I went up on, I don't know, maybe the 12th- or 13th-floor setback, and I could see the whole site. It was just breathtaking. There was nothing you could say. I can't even describe it. Total devastation. I stood right there looking out south over this whole thing.

When we came back out, it was dark. There were all sorts of requests, all sorts of different information coming out. The Army was going to be there in a couple of hours to take care of the site and every once in a while, you heard a jet fly by. One of the fighter jets would fly around the tip of Manhattan, which was pretty amazing.

We went back and forth, and stood fast for a while. They were trying to send guys home at one point, but nobody would leave. Maybe it was 11 P.M., they sectored the west side and I was sent down to work in the middle of the West Side Highway with a couple of other chiefs.

We got lights in there that had come down and it was strange because you looked out and you saw orange cones sporadically about the debris. The guys told me that's where a member is that we can't get out. They used traffic cones or paint, whatever they could gets their hands on.

There was a company – I can't remember which, so much went on – but their officer was buried beneath the debris. When I relieved the battalion chief in my sector, he said they've been working there for three hours, they're trying to get him out, but they can't. And when I looked down, he was directly underneath – you know how the facade came down and it was all box beams? He was right under that and the guys were trying everything they could think of to get him out. Airbags, Hurst tools. Our job doesn't have a torch that's readily available. The rescues have the exothermic torch that could be used for that. In fact, they worked on him until I was relieved at about 4:30 in the morning. I found out later the next day that ironworkers had showed up just about daybreak and they were able to cut the beams away and get him out, but those guys stayed there all night long trying to get him out. It was an engine company. That's all I can remember.

In my experience on this job, we're never in buildings when they would collapse. We just get out. We know it's coming. But when I saw those guys walking around initially that morning, I knew that something really terrible had happened and we were in there.

Later on, when I got up to West Street, I saw Steve Mosiello (aide to chief of department) and he told me Pete Ganci was dead and he said Rich, we had hundreds of guys in there. That was when I knew that we had lost so many guys. You start thinking, who do you know, who's a friend of yours that's down in that area that would be there? Then you start hearing companies were coming from all over the city. Who thinks when you're responding from home that it's the change of tours and guys are going to hop on a rig? We all know it happens, but who thinks about those things?

Another thing that struck you is when you saw those cones that night and when we were going through the voids. Everybody was crawling through the voids, officers, chiefs, everybody. You think you're going to find guys all over the place. Although there are maybe a dozen or more cones out there and you're finding guys, it's not who you'd expect. They're telling you hundreds of guys are missing and you think, OK, we're going to crawl down this void and we're going to find six, eight guys, and there's nobody there, not even civilians. I think that was very hard on the guys too, that we expected to find our guys right away and we expected to find civilians, and we didn't.

Standing By

Battalion Chief Jack Calderone
Battalion 22, West New Brighton, Staten Island

I was home when the attack occurred. I had the scanner on, so I heard the second alarm go out. My aide, Kenny Pogan, called me to tell me to put on the Manhattan fire radio frequency, to listen to it, a plane hit the World Trade Center. I was watching it on TV.

When the recall was announced, we came in and got our gear together, then called Division for instructions. They said get everybody down to Division. We got everybody together and we car pooled down to the Division, where Transit Authority buses were waiting for us. I went inside and talked to the deputies. No one had directions, just go to the ferry terminal and go to Manhattan. While I was upstairs in Division, I grabbed a pad of riding lists. I went down to the buses and I gave each officer a riding list, and I told them to form companies of six to eight people each.

We got down to the ferry terminal. The bus ahead of us had arrived a few minutes earlier. They already disembarked and got on a ferry that was pulling out as we got there. We were told we would be on the next ferry, but before it came in, somebody from the ferry operator came out and told us we had a phone call. We went in and took the call, and were given instructions to set up a triage and staging area, that they were going to start bringing victims and bodies over.

Now, none of us had any radios. All we had was our own bunker gear. And more buses arrived after that. I guess the biggest group we had was about 400 firefighters and officers. One of biggest problems was that I had no radio to talk to the dispatcher. We had no radios to talk to each other. We were spread out across the ferry terminal. We wanted to set up. We had EMS people there, people we normally work with, and we were discussing how we were going to set up our triage area and staging area and where we were going to put things. It just got crazy, using runners back and forth.

I finally got someone from the Department of Ferries there to run a phone line out for us. I called the dispatcher. I knew at this point that they had manned the brush units and the reserve pumpers and I had the dispatcher send one of the brush units to whatever units were still in quarters in Staten Island and take a handie-talkie from each of those units. I managed to procure some tables from someplace. We set up a command post at the lower level of the ferry terminal. We worked with EMS and they set up their triage area. I had all the guys who were CFR (certified first responder) trained to assist EMS.

Our EMS personnel arranged a full operating room staff, doctors, nurses. We were probably as best prepared as we could possibly have been without any prior planning for this. We were ready for anything that was going to come our way. We sat there for approximately six hours and I think we had a total of 16 injuries, all of them were walking wounded. The most serious was a broken bone.

Ferries were running, bringing mostly walking survivors over. On the return trip, they were bringing over people who had been cleared, hospital personnel, EMS personnel, some firefighters. Although we were told to set up a staging area, I was ordered not to let any other firefighters go over to Manhattan.

We attempted to get a RAC (Recuperation and Care) unit and they were all committed. Our next stop was the Jersey City Gong Club and they were already committed to Liberty State Park. Kenny Pogan, my aide, suggested the Bayonne fire canteen. We were able to get the dispatcher to have them come and supply the people to rehydrate them. As the day wore on, we were able to get a local politician to get the Richmond county Vank Ballpark (home of the Staten Island Yankees) food stands open and they started cooking and supplied food to everybody that was there.

EMS command, through whatever mutual aid network they had, somehow mustered approximately 40 ambulances at the scene. We also had mutual aid companies reporting to the scene, so we set up a staging area in the parking lot of the ferry terminal. We had 25 to 35 pieces of apparatus from New Jersey. One of the more frustrating things was that we knew the towers had

Steve Spak

Engine 166 from Staten Island is parked across from Building 6 at West and Vesey streets. Numerous units from Staten Island and New Jersey waited in a staging area at the Staten Island Ferry Terminal.

collapsed, we were getting no information at all from Manhattan and I'm assuming that they had some type of a rescue operation going on, whether it was tunneling or trenching, and I had with me the Collapse Task Force from Elizabeth, NJ, which consisted of their heavy rescue, an engine, a truck, battalion and the collapse rig. And I couldn't get through to anybody who would comprehend that I had a trained unit who could do something worthwhile at the scene.

Speaking to people at the Emergency Operations Center that day, I couldn't get anybody higher than a firefighter to talk to and all I was getting back was, by orders of Chief (of Department Peter) Ganci, nobody is to go over there. Meanwhile, at this point Ganci was already dead. They were using his name and giving orders out. I couldn't get anybody to listen to the fact that I had a trained collapse task force there that could make a difference. It was well into the afternoon, before I finally got somebody from OEM who we worked with, Bobby Wilson. He was on his way over there and was able to relay to the command post at the scene that we had these personnel who were trained, that this wasn't a rinky-dink operation, it was a legitimate heavy rescue unit that could make a difference.

After about an hour and a half, we had everything set up to handle whatever was going to be thrown at us. Everything was running smoothly. It was just total frustration because we sat there and nothing happened. Then it got to the point where we started, I don't want to use the word revolt, but guys were getting impatient. They wanted to get over there and work. They wanted to do something. If we had victims coming at us, I wouldn't have had that problem because they would have been occupied. We had 400 people here now raring to go, ready to work with nothing to do. And basically that's what we did for the day. We sat there and waited and watched the towers burn and with the exception of those 16 or so victims that walked off the ferry, we did nothing.

After about six hours being at the ferry terminal, and after we had things running as smoothly as they could be and nothing at all happening, we got a phone call from Emergency Operations to start winding down at the ferry terminal and send the guys back to their units and reduce the number of people there. At that point, I felt that I should come back here to the battalion and ride and let (Battalion) Chief (Robert) Miuccio make his way up to the Trade Center, which he did. Chief Miuccio, who was working here, knew his brother had been in the one of the towers when it came down. In fact, he died.

Later that night, we were sent to Staten Island Hospital to check on some injured members, I think the number was two, maybe three members were injured. When we got there, I wound up having over 20 members in the hospital. As a matter of fact, I had most of 6 Truck in the hospital. After compiling a list of members there and sending that to Emergency Operations so we could account for those people, I spoke to Division and suggested that they assign a chief to the hospital because there were constantly more people coming in and most of them were members. One of the recall chiefs was put there with a firefighter and took over that function. We went back into service.

The 22 Battalion was in Staten Island the whole time. The 21 early on relocated to Brooklyn and then went to the fire. The 22 actually had a working fire a couple of blocks away with New Jersey units that afternoon. The following morning, they had one right around the corner from there with New Jersey units.

I did a borough status report before I left to go to Division and we were down to 30% availability on the island when I left. That was maybe 20 minutes after the second collapse.

I could see the smoke. I saw the fighter jets going over, a lot of military helicopters. The biggest thing was the frustration of being there prepared to do whatever had to be done and nothing happened, just looking out the ferry slip at that cloud of smoke coming up. For not having any kind of a formal disaster plan that we were involved with, things went real smoothly. The people there made things happen the way they should happen. Everybody worked well together, us, EMS, the police, the hospitals, the National Guard people.

Ferry people supplied us with tables and chairs. We were able to set up a command post. We were down there with nothing and we were able to have an operational command post with 400 people. The police captain from the 120th Precinct was there. We got him to assign us an officer, I believe it might have been a sergeant, with a radio so that we could at least hear what information they were being given.

Let me backtrack. I was listening to the radio tapes of units that were staging in Brooklyn. Two minutes after they were ordered to respond to the Brooklyn-Battery Tunnel and report to West and Albany streets, there was a bomb scare in the Brooklyn-Battery Tunnel.

When the brush unit arrived on the scene with the portable radios, we distributed them to each chief officer on the scene and I kept the brush unit there to have a radio contact with the dispatcher. A few minutes after I established that radio contact, we had a bomb scare at the ferry terminal and it just seemed in retrospect to be too much of a coincidence. It was almost like people were monitoring our frequencies and deliberately doing stuff. After we were there a while, it became obvious that we were going to have a logistics problem with the 400 personnel we had there, firefighters and EMS people, the cops, the hospital staff, nurses.

At one point, we had a female police officer come up to us with very specific information that a boat was coming over with injuries. Where was this information coming from? We had EMS right next to us and we were passing back and forth what we were getting. The only thing is we don't know where we were getting it from, all these sources that we were getting this information from and none of it was valid.

Don't Jump

FDNY Marine Company Operations on 9/11, Hudson River, Gansevoort Market

Two women had jumped into the water to escape. They had to be rescued. Many people jumped onto the boat. There were 200-250 people on board *Marine 1* including children, infants and handicapped people. Marine 1 went to New Jersey to seek medical help for many of these people. While they were in New Jersey unloading their passengers, the North Tower collapsed.

Lengths of 3½-inch hose were on hand and stretched to West Street. This size hose was stripped off every pumper at the scene. Additional older hose from the quarters of the Marine Battalion were obtained and personnel were able to utilize the old hose with different couplings by using adapters. Additional 3½-inch hose was delivered on pallets from technical services.

The East Orange and Paterson, NJ, fire department engine companies supplied five-inch hose to relay additional water to the site. It was estimated that 250 lengths of 3½-inch hose and 20 lengths of five-inch hose was utilized. Every fireboat responded to and operated at the scene.

People were so frantic to get away from the WTC that they jumped on deck, injuring themselves, or into the water near the boats.

Photos above by Greg Semendinger

(top) Marine 1, the Tender Smoke, and several engines are used to relay water from the Hudson River to the WTC site with 3½-inch hose, then five-inch hose.

(above) All of the large and small fireboats, including a retired boat, were used because of numerous ruptured water mains after the collapses.

Courtesy of Jersey City Fire Department

It Was A Neighborhood Collapse

Firefighter Paul Hashagen Rescue 1, Hells Kitchen, Manhattan

now retired

I was home on vacation. I was notified of the attack by phone from active and retired members of Rescue 1. I asked the volunteer chief if we could borrow an old chief's car to respond to the city.

We had three off-duty members of Rescue 1 and one retired member. We were in the car and listening to a scanner when the first tower collapsed. We could see the smoke and dust from the towers. I felt like a Thanksgiving balloon that lost air. We were allowed though the Queens Midtown Tunnel. We went across town to the firehouse of Rescue 1. We met another off-duty member.

We parked two blocks from the Trade Center. Heading south I heard a noise and saw a jet of flame come out of the tower. It started to fall. I turned around and yelled, run. We ran a few hundred feet. The dust and glass flew by. I tried to breathe through my shirt. The dust cloud looked like a rolling sea. In the cloud, there were pulverized pieces of paper. You couldn't see and could hardly breathe. When I thought it was safe to go out, I popped my head out and called the names of the people I was with. I got no answer. I walked one block south. I was actually 50 feet away from the other people I came with, but couldn't see them. We started to look for injured firefighters near the apparatus. I saw that the north walkway was collapsed.

I was absolutely amazed at how quiet it was. You could hear PASS devices, then guys calling out for help. I saw Lieutenant Ray Brown being carried out of the rubble. He was walking on top of eight feet of rubble, but being supported by other firefighters.

Firefighters from Engine 58 had a search rope where their lieutenant was trapped in the hotel. We followed the search rope across the floor of what was left of the lobby of the hotel. The rope disappeared under a huge pile of debris. The entire area was covered from floor to ceiling with debris. We had very limited tools, no extrication equipment. It really didn't matter because of the tremendous weights involved.

This was our first taste of what it was going to be like in the coming days. The weights made the area impenetrable. We continued to climb up and down the pile. We thought we were below grade, but were still at street level. We checked the voids. Even if we were able to get in one, there wasn't anybody there. We heard people calling for each other on the radio. We heard the Mayday from Ladder 6. Most of the people calling for help didn't know where they were, making it difficult for you to figure out where they were. You could hear the people giving directions, but the buildings didn't exist anymore. It wasn't a building collapse, it was a neighborhood collapse.

Chiefs were trying to organize units. I bumped into two of the firefighters I had initially responded with. We found the rig of Rescue 1. I almost didn't recognize it. I saw firefighters on top of the pile of latticework near the street. They had to go down 40 feet and then climb up several stories high. The steel seemed stable, but you never know at a building collapse. I saw a man come out of a staircase and down the debris. He had to be carried out in a Stokes basket, hand over hand, over the mountain of debris. Then a woman came out. It was exhausting, but exhilarating because now somebody was coming out alive. It didn't sink in the first few hours seeing we were in a collapse, but were in serious trouble.

I saw (Deputy) Chief (Peter) Hayden. He looked like a snowman; everything was white from the dust except his glasses. They were trying to gather the riding lists from each apparatus to determine who is missing. I told the chief to call for the FEMA teams. Hayden said talk to OEM. Someone said the FEMA tool cache was being brought to the site. Somebody said I think it's being done. They said don't think, make sure.

I eventually found something to drink. We found several firefighters who were deceased, but couldn't be moved. Realizing how bad it was it wasn't good for our company. We figured out our guys were dispatched on the initial alarm. Being three miles away, it was a straight run. They got there quickly. We thought they might have reached the fire floor. It was a long walk.

There was a tremendous amount of weight over the rescuers' heads. We found some flashlights,

Michael Rieger/FEMA News Photo

The aerial view shows all of the buildings that were destroyed and the remaining buildings that received some type of damage, from moderate to severe.

halligan tools. There were 45-ton box beams lying on the pile. The chiefs warned if anything came down, everybody would be wiped out.

I got my first 360-degree view of the site. It was staggering how large it was. We found some of the firefighters from Rescue 1. They were in a staircase close to the B stairs just east of the North Tower. It was just the way it fell. We worked with ironworkers for two days before anybody did any cutting. They were doing things I thought only firefighters could do, like lowering themselves into voids.

By the third day, we were working hand in hand with the ironworkers. They were cutting big sections of steel. We recovered a significant number of firefighters. You had to first cut, then lift the steel. In some areas, two or three floors were dumped together. After a few days, you got better acclimated to what was there. A few weeks later, digging in the South Tower, I came upon a watchband. You were almost like an archeologist and a forensic pathologist. Identifying bones and pieces of building. This was a defining moment of the fire service. No one had ever been confronted with such a situation. Eleven firefighters and officers from Rescue 1 responded to the incident on the rig and were lost. One of my best friends, Battalion Chief Ed Geraghty in the 9th Battalion, was killed. At least six probies were killed on their first day.

When I drive to work in Rescue 1, for over 19 years, I always look at the skyline. I've been to the Trade Center dozens of times with Rescue 1. You took it for granted that the Trade Center would always be there. It was part of the life of the city. I heard some of the names of those killed – (Chief of Department Peter) Ganci, (First Deputy Commissioner William) Feehan and (Battalion Chief Ray) Downey. When they said Downey, it was demoralizing and tragic. If there was one person that we needed to run this operation, it was Ray Downey. They got the best of us.

No Pressure

Captain Chris Boyle Engine 94, Hunts Point, South Bronx

now Battalion Chief, Battalion 7

I was at home and I didn't see the first one hit. I called Division 6 and asked if there was a recall. They said no, stay by the phone. The second one hit, and I just went in and got here about a quarter after 10. Just before the first tower came down, I had one of the probies calling, making sure that we were getting everybody on the recall in case they didn't see a TV. Right after the first tower came down, Division 6 said come to the Division, we're going to muster up there.

There were about 10 of us. When we got there, (Deputy) Chief (Tom) Fox said I need one officer and five firemen. Both Ladder 48 and I were one guy short. Everybody was looking to fill out their roster of five guys. There was only one bus at the time and everybody wanted to be on it, so we were scrambling around trying to get a guy. I picked up Chris Delisio, I think from 47 Truck. Collecting the riding lists was a captain who was just promoted, Jimmy Rogers.

We grabbed some radios and anything else that was lying around. We didn't think of goggles and stuff like that before we left, but we had oxygen bottles and blue gloves. Chief Fox got on the bus with Sal Gigante, he's an aide with the Sixth Division. We started getting on the bus just after the second tower came down. We were there at the Sixth Division when the second tower came down. We saw it on TV. It was just numbing. Everybody was just real quiet.

Probably after about five or 10 minutes, the bus was full. Chief Fox had said there's going to be another bus, don't worry, so guys weren't panicky to get on it, but it ended up that was the only bus that left that day. It was one of those double buses, the articulated ones.

We headed for I think it was the Third Avenue or Second Avenue Bridge and it was a total traffic jam because the bridge was closed. We were totally blocked. It ended up that a lot of the cars were firemen trying to get downtown, but Chief Fox and Gigante and another officer at the front of the bus moved a bunch of cars and we were on our way. As we got farther down south, everybody was heading north and we were in the one lane going down. We probably got down there about 11 o'clock because we left after the second tower came down.

We stopped at the Civic Center area there and we disembarked. And that's where the dust was heavy. We got off the bus and there were some people handing out paper masks. We went up Park Row toward City Hall and we were carrying our bunker gear because we figured that we would get as close as we could before putting the boots on and everything, because it was kind of tough to walk around in. As we got to Park Row, we suited up, and we started heading toward what looked like a group of firemen gathering.

After that, we headed to Vesey and Broadway. That's where Deputy Chief Tom Haring was. He was starting to put together a command post. I think he was the Sixth Division that day. He had an officer there collecting the riding lists and I noticed a face, (Battalion Chief) Butch Brandes. I said what are we doing. He said just wait and see. All the officers were making a line to get assignments. Haring, I guess he got some type of order from somebody, and all of a sudden I see him grab a guy from the 21 Battalion and this was the first assignment he was giving out. I rushed right into the small circle of guys and I ended up getting in on the assignment. It was four engines, three trucks to World Trade Center 7.

We're heading east on Vesey, we couldn't see much past Broadway. We couldn't see Church Street. We couldn't see what was down there. It was really smoky and dusty.

Before we took off, he said look, if you see any apparatus, strip the apparatus for hose, nozzles, masks, anything you can get. As we headed east, we reached Church and all of a sudden, we could see Building 5 come into view. It was fully involved. There was apparatus burning all over the place. Guys were scrambling around. There were a lot of firemen, and there was a lot of commotion, but you couldn't see much that was going on. I didn't see any lines in operation yet. But we found a battalion rig there. We got a couple of harnesses out of there. We had some bottles from another rig, so we put together a couple of masks.

Steve Spak

Captain Chris Boyle, Engine 94, on Dey Street as Building 5 burns on at least four floors. Water had to be relayed from the east side or from fireboats.

We went one block north over to Greenwich and then headed south. There was an engine company there, right at the corner. It was right underneath Building 7 and it was still burning at the time. They had a hose in operation, but you could tell there was no pressure. It was barely making it across the street. Building 6 was fully involved and it was hitting the sidewalk across the street. I told the guys to wait up.

A couple of the other officers and I were going to see what was going on. We were told to go to Greenwich and Vesey and see what's going on. On the north and east side of Building 7 it didn't look like there was any damage at all, but then you looked on the south side of 7 there had to be a hole 20 stories tall in the building, with fire on several floors. Debris was falling down on the building and it didn't look good.

But they had a hoseline operating. It was hitting the sidewalk across the street, but eventually they pulled back too. Then we received an order from Chief Frank Fellini, we're going to make a move on 7. That was the first time really my stomach tightened up because the building didn't look good. I was figuring probably the standpipe systems were shot. There was no hydrant pressure. I wasn't really keen on the idea. Then this other officer I'm standing next to said, that building doesn't look straight. So I'm standing there. I'm looking at the building. It didn't look right, but, well, we'll go in, we'll see.

So we gathered up rollups and most of us had masks at that time. We headed toward 7. And just around we were about a hundred yards away and Brandes came running up. He said forget it, nobody's going into 7, there's creaking, there are noises coming out of there, so we just stopped. And probably about 10 minutes after that, Deputy Chief Nick Visconti was on West Street, and I guess he had another report of further damage either in some basements and things like that, so Visconti said nobody goes into 7, so that was the final thing and that was abandoned.

So after Visconti came down and said nobody goes in 7, we said all right, we'll head back to the command post. We lost touch with him. I never saw him again that day.

We ended up getting back to the command post at Broadway and Vesey. By that time, there were probably 50 officers standing in a row, and I was not going to stand on another line like that. We found out that Fox was over at Cortlandt and Church. They were putting a tower ladder into operation, so we made our way over to there. We ended up helping.

They had no pressure at all off of any of the hydrants from Broadway. He was asking if there was any way that we could do anything at Broadway or West. From Broadway to West westward toward Church Street there was no pressure at all. We spotted one of the squads up on Cortlandt over by Broadway hooked up to a hydrant. We were just sitting there, so we stretched the line off of him. We relayed it to 274, who relayed it to another engine down the street and eventually we got more pressure. I think it was 22 Truck on Church and Cortlandt and they were operating to number 5.

We did that for a little while. It took a while to get the hose there because there was a White Plains company helping us and they had some different fittings. So we got water to 22, but then that's when they said all right, number 7 is coming down, shut everything down. I don't know what time that was. It was all just a blur.

Everything was left where it was. Just shut everything down, move everybody back. You got a half block away, you couldn't see it. All we heard was they were worried about it coming down, everybody back away. We were there about an hour or so until Building 7 came down and everything was black again.

It was like it was night again. First, we went to Liberty and Church and that was the big pile from the South Tower that came down. There was a pile there, had to be 15, 20 stories high with guys roaming around on the pile.

That was the first time I really saw one of the towers fully down. I had no idea. It was an amazing site, stunning, it was surreal. Guys were climbing around in the pile, but I figured we had to try to hook up with Chief Fox. We headed north on Church and we ran into Fox again. They were putting the tower ladders back into operation.

Then he had us do a search of the Millennium Hotel. There were some glass shards that were missing. We headed up into the hotel and after we were on the second floor, removing some shards, I was missing one of my guys, I couldn't find him. We started searching around the hotel. We figured maybe he fell down, collapsed, something like that. It ended up he never made it into the hotel. He had walked in and all of a sudden he just made a turn, went to the corner, sat on the corner and never came in. They found him out there. An ambulance was working on him.

That was pretty much the day right there. It was bizarre. You would figure that it would be Beirut, but it was Manhattan. You couldn't believe what was happening. You see it on TV everywhere else, but not here. This was the first time I ever thought anything was possible.

We heard the fighter jets overhead. You couldn't see them. My brother was in Vietnam. I remember walking down the street with him one day and he heard a backfire. He fell to the floor, this was soon after he came back from Vietnam. That was bizarre. Jet fighters shot overhead and you could see everybody, you saw the heads duck. The first time I ever felt like that.

There were probably about 30 guys involved in the hose stretch. The closest engine was about 100 feet east of Church, so we had to go across Church, across the courtyard, up those little steps in between, past 5 and 6 and then they went probably four or five flights into the pit after that. It was tremendous. They were in there for a while, but I don't think they found anybody at that time and we ended up leaving.

The side of the pit opened up and you could drop 30 feet, maybe even 40 feet because that whole courtyard was built on I don't know how many levels. It was all collapsed. It was like an old movie, like an old painting you see from the Middle Ages. It was weird.

There Was An Eerie Silence

Firefighter Tom Caruso
Ladder 48, Chelsea, Manhattan

now Lieutenant, Ladder 130

I was on a 90-day detail to Engine 3. On September 11, I was off duty. I was at Seventh Avenue and Grove Street when I heard the explosion, ran out into the street and saw that a jet hit the Trade Center. I made it back to Engine 3 to get my gear. I jumped on a Con Ed electric truck and was brought to the scene. I held my helmet out the window and the police let us through.

About three blocks away, I jumped out. At this time, both towers were burning. I took an airpack off a rig and found a halligan tool. I went into the North Tower with a makeshift group of firefighters with a captain. A woman jumper hit a man about 35 feet away from us. I saw eight or nine people jump. I was amazed.

People were coming down the escalators near West Street. We made it into a stairway. There were numerous people coming down. It was tough going. I heard a transmission about the South Tower suffering a partial collapse. We were still walking up. I think we were at the 11th floor. People were still coming down. In another minute or two we came down.

The lobby was pitch black. We were fumbling around. I tried a dozen times to get out. Finally outside I saw Ladder 12 with their bucket up. Then the North Tower came down. I was on the opposite side of West Street. I heard the rumbling, ran to a building and threw my halligan tool through the plate-glass window. A whole bunch of people ran inside. I could see the silhouette of a rig in flames.

We stayed in the store for a few minutes because of the dust. There was an eerie silence. Three or four engines were burning. Ladders 5 and 12 were smashed. Engine 3 was on the southbound side of the street and was all right. The high-rise unit was smashed under the North Pedestrian Bridge. We heard a Mayday given by a member of a ladder company.

When I ran into the scene, I never expected the towers would come down. My best friend, Firefighter Sergio Villanueva of Ladder 132, was killed.

Engine 214's damaged rig after a collapse. Note debris and dust in the area. All members of the company were killed except the chauffeur.

Peter Matthews

Let Me Find One Person

Lieutenant Jack Flatley (Rescue 1 firefighter on 9/11), Hells Kitchen, Manhattan

now Captain, Squad 1

Nobody was really saying anything. I asked a deputy chief what was going on, where do they need us, what was happening, were guys out? I had no idea what had happened.

I saw a guy who drove (Commissioner Thomas) Von Essen and thought oh, my–the whole upper echelon of the job is over here somewhere. I climbed up on top of a few things. You could just see there was nothing there. Everything was just piled up in the street. I was walking along the top. There was nobody there. It was just me. I was calling out if anybody could answer me or anything. I didn't know where to start to look.

After a couple of minutes, the whole thing just started to hit me. I didn't hear anybody. I felt like I was walking through a nuclear storm. All this debris and it's raining down this – this fuzzy white stuff. And I was looking around calling out and I just stopped for a second and I actually said to myself God, just let me find one person to make me being here worthwhile, because I was unsure of why am I here right now. Two minutes later, I would have been dead. Two minutes earlier, I might not have come.

With that, all of a sudden, I heard a radio. I was hearing a progress report or something. I couldn't really make it out. I just moved toward that direction. As I came over one pile of stuff, all of a sudden, I could make out a guy lying on his side. I could just see his head and his arm, and I could hear the radio. So, I took the first piece of metal off – that aluminum coating that was on the outsides of the building – that was on his upper part of the chest. I was able to lift that off by myself.

I didn't really realize what frequency he was on, but I started hearing progress reports about some things. And I don't remember if they said that they were looking for him or whatever. I said brother, what's going on? Who are you? He was unrecognizable, just with the powder and the stuff and he had a huge gash along the top of his head.

I really didn't know what was going on. I didn't have any tools, so I just got on the radio and I said that I had a trapped member and that I needed some help with some tools.

I asked him again who are you? He goes, Fuentes! He was wearing chief's brass because he was acting – he was the ABC! So I said on the radio it's Chief Fuentes! I need assistance! I need somebody with some tools! He's pinned under some steel! I put my helmet on top of his head because I was afraid his cut was going to get infected.

I gave an urgent. I told them what I got. It's Al Fuentes! I tried to see if he could help me, if he could pull his legs or something. I couldn't tell where he was stuck, because all this stuff he's under is pretty solid. It was lot of tin. It really wasn't any heavy steel.

I tried moving some stuff by myself. Then Neil Frederickson shows up and he's got a pry bar, so we kind of worked out something where I could trace his leg down to the other side of the stuff. I'm like all right, if we can push his leg out here and get him out of this, at least we'll be halfway there. Neil put his bar in, he lifted it up. Then with that, a bunch of other people started showing up and we just kind of worked him out. There was a bunch of people that were coming and it wound up being that it was a lot of the guys from the Marine unit. I don't know if they had heard that he was trapped because, mind you, I didn't hear any of these reports. I heard his radio and I just went in that direction.

There were two ambulances right there that were blown up and we got some EMS stuff out of there. And we got a backboard and a Stokes – I don't know where the Stokes came from, maybe the Marine guys brought it. So they loaded Fuentes into the Stokes and they took him off. I figured they had enough guys to carry him.

After that, I went down West Street. I walked maybe another 100 yards, went up closer toward the Trade Center, came back along that perimeter and still nothing. And it seemed like I was really getting tired and I was getting dehydrated. I wound up meeting up with Kevin Kroth and we went down the ramp that's in the West Street area. We did a quick search to see if there was a way to get through there, but we could only go so far because I don't know if Kevin had a mask. I had borrowed a mask.

Heavy smoke was ripping down there, but I knew that in those garages there was all sorts of stairwells and stuff like that that went into these buildings. But as soon as you got to the bottom of the thing, you could see the whole right side was blown out.

We went in for a little bit. There was heavy fire ahead of us. I said if we're going to do this, we're going to need a line. So we went back. The chief was up there. I said chief, I think that we can under pretty far in here, but we're going to need a line. It's not pancaked. We're going to need a search rope and stuff like that.

We went down under there. We took the rope with us and we went in another 100 feet and we got the line, but there was nothing you could do.

Later on, around a couple of weeks later, we actually found another way in through another void into that area. And I mean we never would have gotten into the Trade Center voids from that area.

West Street is searched as debris and an overturned ambulance is visible.

Todd Maisel

Bringing People Home

Firefighter Mickey Conboy
Rescue 3, Tremont, Bronx

now Lieutenant, Squad 41

I responded in a pickup truck with Lieutenant Gerry Murtha, Cliff Stabner, Doug Hantusch, Joe DiBernardo and Mike Davis. We had a police escort down the Grand Concourse. On the FDR Drive, people were walking north from the 50s and south in both lanes. The dust was like a blizzard. We found some extra masks and made it to the South Pedestrian Bridge. Lieutenant Murtha got a radio. We heard that the chauffeur from Engine 65 was trapped. He was located under two motorcycles, pinned with a broken leg. I cleared the dust from his mouth. He was complaining of pain and had hard time breathing. He was covered in dust. We put him on a backboard.

In the rear of 10 & 10's firehouse it was obvious that the dust blew through the place. A lot of debris and steel covered the street. We went out the back door of the firehouse and started up Church Street. We heard Captain Jay Jonas giving a Mayday. He told us exactly where he was located. As we passed Church and Liberty streets there was a wall of steel that fell and went right through the street and in some cases went into the subway. At Building 5, there was fire out 100 windows covering all floors.

All of a sudden, a firefighter appeared on the roof of Building 5. Firefighters had to jockey a rear-mount aerial into the plaza and remove the firefighter at the same time. Around the corner, Building 7 had a beam missing from the southwest corner of the building. Heavy black smoke was venting from the 47-story building.

We continued to West Street, almost making a circle. We found the Rescue 3 rig. We looked for more masks. It was already stripped of tools. We regrouped there. We thought our members might have been in the North Tower. The rig was closer to the North Tower. Everybody was pulled back from near Building 7. We found two firefighters crushed under the steel of the North Tower. Through the dust, the stripes on their coats were visible.

We started to work on them when we realized we needed torches. Someone marked the steel with paint and we notified the command post. We were wondering who was missing. Someone said Fire Commissioner Von Essen, then we saw him walk

Mickey Conboy, center, and other firefighters operate on Church Street.

Firehouse Collection

Firehouse Collection

Rescue 3's replacement rig is parked in front of the Millenium Hotel on Church Street. The lower portion of the high-rise hotel suffered damage.

by. Other names we heard were Ganci, Feehan and Judge. There was a report of a chief who went into the Customs House parking garage and didn't come out. A large portion of the Customs House collapsed.

Lieutenant Murtha and myself went down to the B-5 level. There were about 20 cars burning in the garage. We were standing in water. We left the area for the stairway to return to the street. Everything went black. The gasoline floating on the water ignited.

Back in the pile we found numerous dead-end voids that we could crawl into. On the second day we entered the PATH subway station. We searched the first four cars with negative results. The last several cars were crushed. To climb on the pile we slid down ropes and then climbed ladders. Eventually a high line was set up to bring guys across. I came across an I-beam that was molten metal, just bubbling away.

We made it into the B stairway in the North Tower. We located a chief. He was trapped in a closet. It took 5½ hours to get him out. Someone said it was like working in a phone booth with someone else in there. We felt it was the first thing we did to bring someone home to his or her family.

Someone had said they had seen Captain Brian Hickey in the South Tower lobby. They had been on their way to the 20th floor. They were right on the money. Surveying the scene in a basket suspended by a crane was Murtha, John O'Connell from Rescue 3, an ironworker and Firefighter Dan Foley. A team on the ground placed a search camera in a void and the camera melted.

There was much more heat and fire below the debris of the South Tower. Spotters from 10 & 10 used sight glasses. Someone spotted a helmet. We were directed to the spot. Then we found a mask harness and a Rescue 3 helmet. We found a pair of bunker pants and inside was Gerard Schrang's name. We put him in a Stokes basket and carried him to the morgue with Captain Tom Kelly from Ladder 33, Gerard's former company. Danny Foley dug and found Tommy Foley's remains. They found his arrowhead necklace.

With so much dust it was very hard to make out what was in the debris. We searched an area of the Marriott Hotel. We had to crawl in on a 45-degree angle to the hallway. Four rooms were in perfect shape. We were tearing out coats, shirts and pants. We had no respirators, only dust masks. What worked best was basic hand tools, collapsible shovels, battery-operated rebar cutters and Sawzalls. One of the ironworkers had to cut through three box beams weighing 20 to 25 tons each. He said he'd be here for hours. Some of the box beams, which were located on the corners of the towers, twisted like a bow or a pretzel. They were four inches thick.

There were no survivors, except for a woman the second day. Thousands were trapped. It was so hard to find them. In the below-grade area of B-4-5-6 you could see all the compaction of the floors. Most of the people we found were in the stairways and the bottom of the elevator shafts. The South Tower didn't stay intact like the North Tower.

Setting Up Shop

Firefighter Nick Giordano Rescue 3, SOC, Roosevelt Island, East River, Manhattan

now retired

We had just left here in a carpool. We were 20 minutes away. We had the scanner on and we turned around. We were making phone calls to see what was going on. And as we stood there, we saw the second plane hit the tower, the second tower. You could see the explosion. You could see the flash from as far away as we were. And with that I said, we're going back.

When I got down to the site, I hooked up with Rescue 3, with Firefighter Mickey Conboy and Lieutenant Gerry Murtha, and there was like seven or eight of us. We started searching. As time went by, we were searching through some of the heavy steel that was collapsed at the West Street, where the transverse went across West Street, by Liberty. The south bridge, all through in there.

The high-rise unit was crushed underneath the south transverse. Rescue l's rig was crushed almost beyond recognition. You knew it was a rescue because of the body configuration. There were rigs everywhere. You would have thought it was like a toy center; somebody came along and just stepped on them.

The building where we put the curtain wall up, that was going. The older building on the south side of the southeast corner, that was going. That fire burned about two days, but the building is still in good shape.

The dust and everything was still permeating the air down there. It was horrific. The magnitude of it was just indescribable. When you try and describe it to somebody who wasn't there, when you saw the pictures on TV and the still photos, it just didn't give it the true view.

We worked down there until dark. The second day, later in the day, we tried to get the FEMA cache. We got it set up at Chambers Street. That was done with the guys from hazmat ops and whatnot. They set up the FEMA cache at Chambers Street between West and the next one over, Washington. They got it going the first day and then the second day they got it going full tilt. And then the second day, I was working with Hazmat Chief Ingram at the command post trying to get a lot of things done. Then finally on the third day is when we wound up separating some of the cache from the Chambers Street site and we got it down to South End Avenue, the last street that's by the water going into the Financial Center there.

We wound up bringing from the cache a lot of the rescue tools like the Hurst tools, chain saws and a Stanley system. By the third day, we started getting a good influx of Sawzalls and Sawzall blades and hand tools, shovels, rakes, plus dust masks and the lot. FDNY Tech Services wound up setting up a spot on the corner of West with Partner saws and blades for the Partner saw, metal cutting and concrete cutting. There was no real concrete breaking or breaching that was involved. All the concrete was just pulverized into dust. It was more for cutting the rebar. It took like a good three days just to get some of the bigger cranes in there because they needed the boom cranes and they only had the hydraulic cranes for the first couple of days. By the fourth day, we started getting some of these outfits like the Wall and the Holmatro, Hurst and Milwaukee Tools were in there too. They started coming in with Sawzalls and batteries and chargers.

The magnitude of it all was just enormous. You had the FEMA teams coming in and they were self sufficient. But we had to start our own. We had to start a tool cache from what we could salvage from the shops because they would request equipment and the manufacturers started to get on the bandwagon and start funneling things in to us. We ran that. That was going 24 hours a day.

Coveralls were an issue, boots and gloves for the guys because we were kind of stymied because our guys are always in bunker gear and stuff and it wound up being more cumbersome. Hard hats rather than our fire helmets. There was always a big demand for the Partner saws and stuff. Hazmat Ops were on top of getting us respirators.

Once they got the pier set up on the West Side, the passenger terminal, anything that we were really in dire need for, we could get through our fire OEM representative and they were working 24 hours a day up there. So between Tech Services and contacting OEM direct, we were able to start

Michael Rieger/FEMA News Photo

some kind of ordering system in trying to get equipment down there.

We were dealing with such a large area and so much equipment was needed. It took us about two weeks to get a handle on getting stuff in there. And then once we had all that stuff in there, the magnitude of everything that was going on, we had to maintain it. We had to make sure we had gas because we had no electricity down there. We had portable lights that had to be brought in.

We started running generators. We wound up getting portable generators. We would run the portable generators, get the chargers going, hand lights, small hand lights. We had a minimum of anywhere between 50 and 75 different chargers, groups of 15 to 20 different various manufacturers and that was just that one location. At any given time, we had maybe 100 to 150 guys down there going. We were trying to supply them with stuff.

As guys would be working, if they were finding anything or anybody, they would get them out of there. They would get the bodies out of there. But then they would get relieved and a lot of the stuff was getting left out on the pile. Those guys were either tired or they thought the incoming crew would be taking them back. We were trying to get the stuff back so we could do maintenance on it.

The fact of the matter was a lot of the rigs that were there had equipment on them and guys were taking equipment off the rigs that were demolished just to try and have something to use. We had thousands of people down there trying to work. It took us a couple of days to get a handle on some kind of order.

We got rebar cutters, other cutters. There were masks and respirators and gloves and helmets. All the little things – trenching tools, knee pads, goggles, gloves to work in. These guys were coming out of the voids. They were filthy, so there was a big turnover of that stuff.

A lot of the ordering went through either Tech Services or up through the pier, but the majority of stuff, once things got rolling, we got the ironworkers in there to do the heavy steel cutting and we were basically doing everything by hand. Buckets, five-gallon buckets, we had thousands of them sent down there to remove the small debris. The first three or four days it was just insane because we had long chains of debris removal. I know the initial stages, the first three days, there was a lot of voids and whatnot that were being searched. Suitcases of orange and lime-colored paint so we could mark what we had done. And that really didn't get squared away until like the fourth or fifth day.

Firefighter Billy St. George got the search

The fire department was divided into two commands after 9/11, operations at WTC and regular firehouse operations.

cam. I think we wound up getting 10 sent in to be used. It was a manufacturer's hands-on field day, in reality. Any manufacturer that wanted to get some of their equipment out there for people to use, it was the opportune time. Holmatro had that pump spreader cutter. That worked out really well because you didn't have to use any batteries or anything to cut rebar. And you could use it for a spreader or to lift something. I think I saw at least 20 of them. Hurst sent in these battery-operated spreaders.

Water, gallons, cases and cases of water, pallets of water, water by the pallet. The Army Reserves came in with some wash stations and potable water and stuff like that. There was always an ongoing thing in the early days keeping the generators fueled up because the place was so devastated it was hard to get equipment around and organized.

We had to get gas brought in on a daily basis. After the third day, we wound up going for a 24-off/24-on, Firefighter Rick Duran and myself, so when we came back here to SOC, we would make sure that before we left in the morning when we were relieving the other guy, we would make sure if they needed gas or whatever. We would bring a Suburban over full of five-gallon gas cans, make sure we have fuel mix for it.

They were using the Partner saws like crazy, cutting a lot of the steel and going through metal cutting blades like you would throw Kleenex away, really wearing them out. This place was like a depot. A lot of the stuff would come in through here and then we would get it over to our location. We would try and inventory and get an idea what we had and it was just constant. We could have had on any given day two or three thousand guys working down there at the pile. And then out of SOC alone, we'd have a couple of hundred guys. Everybody was looking for everything under the sun. That doesn't even include the volunteers.

For the first five or six days, we were inundated with people from everywhere, which was a blessing in one respect, but it was hard in another because we had no control over anything that was going on. We didn't know who they were, where they were coming from. They were there to help, but the enormity of the whole situation – the fact that we lost such a big chunk of the hierarchy, trying to get things set up and situated. It was good that we got the FEMA teams in there because they had a good idea of how to respond and stuff. Plus there was no shoring. All these buildings were down, just in big piles.

Binoculars and spotter scopes, spotter glasses were another hot ticket. Portable lighting because you were talking about a 16-acre site. A theatrical company brought in those gigantic lights when they play those golf tournaments at night.

GPS started going really hot about two weeks into the operation, and then after that, everything was GPS. The other big thing was the lights on the helmets, helmet lights, stuff like that so when these guys were in the voids, they had their hands free. We got 400 of those sent in.

There were transits set up. We had all our transits out of here, which was about six of them. I think we had three or four transits set for the first couple of days. Then once the engineers got in, they started setting up their own.

I would be remiss if I didn't mention the fact that we had some retired guys, who were involved with us with the New York City FEMA team, who came in and with their help we moved the whole cache. They were instrumental in getting the cache set up down where we were at the 7 Financial Center. Mark Bowden, Billy McCarthy and Paul Yeager were instrumental in getting that going.

Phones were down, so we were using cell phones and handie-talkies. We were getting radios from the FEMA cache. That was one of the big things we used from FEMA. The radios that we had from the FEMA cache was instrumental. There were a couple of hundred of those.

We maintained an SOC tool van down there set up with battery chargers, Sawzalls and rebar cutters, gloves and hard hats. We've got battery chargers, Sawzalls, gas for the Partner saws, knee pads, gloves. We got a donation of boots. Instead of the guys having to wear leather long boots, we've gotten construction boots, welder's boots. We had jumpsuits brought in so these guys could work a little easier.

We Were Going To Leave But...

Captain Abe Haiman
Ladder 30, Harlem, Manhattan

now retired

I was off duty and heard that a plane had hit the World Trade Center. I saw it on the television and went to work. We had a reserve engine in our firehouse. It was numbered 511.

I called the dispatcher and said that I have a spare rig with manpower. I told him we were going down to the Trade Center. I expected to be canceled. To my surprise, without any hesitation, the dispatcher told us to take it in. I said send me a computer ticket to make it official.

Our battalion chief called and told us to go to Ladder 23 and pick up additional manpower. That may have saved us from the second collapse. By the time we arrived on scene, both towers had collapsed. I had heard word of collapses coming over the radio, but I didn't envision a total collapse. We weren't prepared for what we would see.

Approaching, we could see a big, brown cloud from the street to the sky. I was on the handie-talkie trying to talk to the command post. There was no answer from anybody. I don't know what street we were on. There was a tall fellow with a fire department windbreaker. He flagged us down and pointed to a street. He said go in there. I think they need your help. I asked who he was and he answered don't worry about me, I'm retired.

We wound up in front of Building 7. Every car and piece of fire apparatus there was fully involved. At the end of the street was a pedestrian overpass to the pedestrian plaza of the Trade Center. I told the chauffeur to put the rig on the hydrant. The firefighter started to hook up, but all the water mains in the area were destroyed.

A man on the seventh floor of Building 7 started yelling at us with a bullhorn. He said he couldn't get out, he needed help. The dozen cars on fire in the street and the big, brown cloud from the Trade Center hadn't dissipated. I couldn't see the man.

I found an entrance to the building. You could see big-time fire on numerous floors. A large portion of the exterior had been broken out. There was a smoke condition in the stairway. A security guard, who said he was evacuating the building when he was left behind, was located on the seventh floor. He said there were two other people on the eighth floor.

Three civilians were removed from the seventh and eighth floors of Building 7 by members who responded on the department recall.

Thomas P. Buchta

All three of these people were remote from the area where the fire was venting. We walked everybody down the stairs. We left the building and met a chief. He said should we go back in and do a secondary search of the building. I told him the security guard said the building had been evacuated.

An hour later, the wind shifted. It first became evident of what happened. The WTC didn't exist anymore. I didn't know it until then.

Climbing all over the debris, way down underneath us you could see a fire department engine. It was buried under layers of steel and concrete. It was squashed like a pancake. The body of a firefighter was near the rig. You could see his blue pants. We spent most of the day digging, not finding anyone alive. We were there until midnight.

We found the hydrant near Building 7 that we had hooked up to. The hydrant was there, but the apparatus was missing. We searched the area. No engine. Somebody probably needed the rig. Four days later, we found it parked on a sidewalk covered in dust blocks away. We cleaned it off and brought it back to the firehouse.

Creaking and Cracking

Battalion Chief Butch Brandes covering Division 15, Rockaway, Queens

now assigned to Battalion 41

The 47-story Building 7 burns on multiple floors after the North Tower collapsed into it.

Thomas P. Buchta

I was on the Boardwalk in Rockaway, Queens. I could see smoke from where I was located. Another firefighter saw the plane hit the Trade Center. I dropped my son off at home and went to the 42 Battalion where my gear was located. I had been covering a vacation there.

I met Battalion Chief Shawn Reen. We piled into a Suburban and took extra flashlights and spare radios. When we arrived at the Brooklyn-Battery Tunnel, the police wouldn't let us through. All the units were in a line. We detoured to the Brooklyn Bridge. After waiting a while, we finally made it to Manhattan.

At Broadway and Park Row we put on our gear. The second tower collapsed. Deputy Chief Tom Haring set up a command post on Broadway. You could hear Acting Battalion Chief Al Fuentes give a Mayday. We didn't know where he was located. Reen went to look for him. I never saw him again.

I became the staging officer and gave a couple of companies assignments. I was sent over to Building 7 with two chiefs and 10 companies to determine the structural stability and if we could fight the fire inside. We entered the building from the north.

Inside conditions were bad. We didn't have any masks. We had lights and a radio. The first floor was charged with smoke. On the eighth floor, half of the south wall was gone. We made it halfway across the floor. Smoke was coming up from below. We never saw any fire. We could hear the building was creaking. The floor was bellied in the middle.

The engineer with us said it was OK to bring the companies inside, but the three chiefs decided not to. We went downstairs via another stairway. The stairs were blocked at the second or third floor. We couldn't get out. Parts of the building had fallen. We were able to make it across to another stairway. All the units were ordered from the area. Debris was falling down. We told Chief Haring that the building was coming down. We wanted transits placed around the building to monitor any movement. Two hours later, the 47-story building collapsed.

Units were being requested for a fire in 90 West Street. Day turned into night. Building 5 had a good amount of fire burning inside. We tried to get a tower ladder set up. Eventually everybody was ordered away. Units were removed from the area of another hotel where a collapse was possible.

Firefighter Dan Suhr from Engine 216, the first firefighter killed in the morning, (he was hit by a jumper) lived right behind me. I spent some time inside Engine 10/Ladder 10 firehouse. There was so much debris. I didn't even recognize it to be a firehouse. On December 24, the firefighters found 10 bodies, eight of which were intact. We had the most amazing guys operating with ingenuity to think of the things like lifting steel beams with the ironworkers. The guys never quit!

Come And Get Us

Battalion Chief Mark Ferran Battalion 12, East Harlem, Manhattan

now Deputy Chief, 14 Division

I was watching TV at home. I saw Tower 1 burning. I called the 12th Battalion and was talking to the aide. In the background, Chiefs Fred Sheffold and Joe Marchbanks yelled out to stay home. I said I wish I were working. I'm never going to say that again.

I reported to work. Several companies were starting to stage at Engine 35. I grabbed a radio and responded with Engine 35 down the West Side Highway. We arrived at Chambers Street. The first building had already collapsed. I told the lieutenant from Engine 35 to remain at staging. I met Chief Mike Keenan from the 49 Battalion. I started down to the command post to see how I could help.

As I passed Murray Street, the North Tower started to sink. The antenna went straight down. I ran toward the Hudson River. The dust cloud passed right by. I could eventually see the lights on the rigs flickering on West Street. I reported to Deputy Chief (Pat) McNally, Division 14. He said switch to the command channel. (Battalion) Chief Rich Picciotto heard me on the radio, he said he's trapped in the B stairs in the north tower on the fifth floor. He said he was with Ladder 6, they're all right, but you have to come and get us. Don't leave this channel.

I found Ladder 43 and asked them if they were available to do something. They answered yes, so I radioed Picciotto that Ladder 43 was on the way. I also told Division 14 that Ladder 43 is looking for him. We were just north of the North Pedestrian Bridge. The bridge was partially collapsed, blocking the street.

We climbed a ladder up to the veranda of Building 6, the Customs House. A firefighter was lying dead in a stokes basket. The firefighters were in shock. We were looking for Tower 1. Someone said if we enter this building, through a window, you have to cross over a total collapse. It was like a mountain in front of you. Rich, I radioed, we are in a building on the corner. Picciotto had a bullhorn with a siren. I said blow your siren. Did you hear that? No. We thought about going through the parking garage. We couldn't see down the street.

There was a 10-story gash in the side of Building 7. The southwest corner was taken out when Tower 1 came down. We went back out to West and Vesey streets and into the Verizon Building. We exited the rear to Barclay Street and walked around the rear of Building 7. We walked to West Broadway and then to Buildings 5 and 6. We met a firefighter from Ladder 18 who said he knew the way. We went down an escalator. Into the concourse level 50 feet in, we had to make a right turn and then were able to see all the way to the next escalator.

At this location there was a total pancake collapse. I-beams and pieces of steel were through the ceiling of the concourse. We backed out and split up into two groups. We climbed up and across the debris field about 25 feet apart from each other. As we passed 40-foot-long I-beams lying sideways, the smoke and dust increased as the fires below intensified. I called Picciotto to blow the siren again. I thought I could faintly hear it in the distance. I said we're coming. Afterwards, he told me it was a big comfort knowing we were on the way.

We met a firefighter from Rescue 2 with a civilian looking for a way out of the plaza area. We had two firefighters lead them out. We finally made it to the east wall of Tower 1. I told Picciotto that we were up to the wall, yell out. We heard the yelling. Picciotto said yell out, I hear you. One minute later, they were united. Picciotto told me there were guys below them. There is a chief trapped downstairs, you're going to need extrication tools and more help.

The firefighters from Ladder 43 entered the stairway and worked on removing those still trapped. I wound up standing alone outside the wall. There were five floors of fire in one of the nearby buildings. I wasn't sure we were going to get back they way we came. It was getting bad. Debris was falling down all over. It was luck that Picciotto heard me on the radio. Ladder 43 did the best they could to save people's lives. They were fortunate to get an assignment to get the people out.

It Took A Lot Of Courage

Lieutenant Pete Lund Rescue 2, Brooklyn, Retired from FDNY

Died in the line of duty, June 14, 2005, Woodmere, NY

I came in on a recall and had stopped to pick up two guys along the way. At that point, it was pretty overwhelming. There's a point as you're driving towards Brooklyn, where you always could see the Twin Towers, but one tower was already down and it almost appeared as if the second one was leaning.

There were 19 or 20 of us. We commandeered a bus and the bus driver said I know where I'm going, this is my neighborhood. So she did some zigs and zags in downtown Brooklyn and got us over the Brooklyn Bridge to just south of City Hall. That's where they were stopping everybody. That was when you got the first effect of how big this thing really was because there were still papers floating in the air. The dust was so thick; I mean the dust in the street had to be six or seven inches deep.

We worked our way to Broadway and started heading south. We got about a block north of the Trade Center and then started to head west. We got to Church Street and headed south again. We grabbed whatever hand tools we had in the supply lockers. We got to Vesey and could see that both buildings were now gone. There was still debris floating in the air everywhere. You were choking on the dust.

It was amazing to see the immensity of this whole thing and what was pretty terrifying was that there was nothing left except for three or four sections that were like fingers sticking up. It was like a pencil that they had just dropped straight down into the ground.

We found our rig at West Street and Liberty, the cab was damaged pretty badly and there was debris covering both sides. We couldn't open the compartment doors. Some guy with a payloader came by and was able to scrape some of the debris away from the side of the rig so we could at least open up the compartment doors and get some of the equipment out, but the rig was pretty much stripped. There was not a hook, not a halligan, no masks…nothing on the rig at that point.

What was totally frustrating was that we knew

"It was overwhelming when we realized that, as we were climbing over debris that was well over eight feet high, there were rigs intact or crushed below us."

Andrea Booher/FEMA News Photo

AP Photo/Kathy Willens

Without the help of steel and construction workers using grapplers, the job of removing the steel and debris would have been impossible.

that when the tower came down, it had covered the command post. So, we had no idea at that point where our guys could be, where we could begin looking. It wasn't until much later that we ran into Commissioner Lynn Tierney and she told us that Rescue 2 had guided her into the lobby and they had been in the North Tower.

But it was beyond the veritable needle in the haystack. We've done collapses in brick-and-joist buildings. We've done collapses in wood-frame buildings. Just knowing the weight of the steel that was involved here, we knew that the chances were pretty slim that we were going to find anybody. It was overwhelming when we realized that as we worked our way along West Street, that we were climbing over debris that was well over eight feet high and that there were rigs intact below us, and rigs crushed below us.

What was scary was nothing was being said on the radio. Nobody was saying where they were, there was just nothing being said. The silence was deafening.

We tried to divide up and cover as many different areas as we could because we really didn't have any idea exactly where the guys were. We were hoping to find some witnesses that could at least guide us in the right direction. We worked in the area of (Buildings) 1 and 2 and in what was left of the hotel. That was pretty much where we worked for the next two months.

It was just overwhelming to think back to Oklahoma City and to see that that was a nine-story building and essentially the middle, maybe a third, of that building had sustained all that damage. Now, to think that this was two 110-story buildings, a 20-something-story hotel in between, and it had been literally leveled. The hotel was the only thing that had anything recognizable to me – and that only looked like about three floors above the lobby.

Two Inches a Day

Battalion Chief John Norman 16th Battalion, East New York, Brooklyn

now retired

I was home in bed and the battalion called and said I know you're on vacation, but there's a total recall because of what happened to the Trade Center. I'm still sound asleep. I said what happened to the Trade Center? He says you don't know? He says turn on the TV and he hung up. He had a million calls to make. I turned on the TV just in time to catch Tower 1 falling, so I jumped out of bed and ran downstairs.

I had all my FEMA gear packed, ready for a FEMA deployment, and I had a second set of bunker gear in my trunk. I just jumped in the car and I headed right to the city, heading for the Trade Center, but I stopped in Brooklyn at 175 Truck and 332 Engine's quarters, to see whether they had any word on the recall, what mustering sites there were or anything.

Chief Norman oversees operations in the pile. He was the Search and Rescue Manager after 9/11.

Andrea Booher/FEMA News Photo

They had commandeered a bus and loaded it up with all the spare Scott bottles they had in quarters, because they're a depot, and as many hand tools as they could find. About 25 of us went from there, drove to the 15th Division mustering site at 283's quarters. I checked in with the deputy chief there, Seamus McNella I believe was working. They had a bus that was leaving for the Trade Center right at that point, so I hopped on it and we drove to the Manhattan Bridge. (Deputy Chief) Dave Corcoran was in charge of maintaining control of the units, finding out what units he had available, so we switched over from the bus. There was a convoy of apparatus about to go over to Manhattan. (Lieutenant of Rescue 1) Mike Pena and I hooked up there with Ray Graywin and Al Schwartz from 4 Truck and we all piled onto the back, I think it was 264 Engine's rig, and headed over the bridge and came in on the Broadway side of City Hall Park.

Deputy Chief Tommy Haring had a command post set up at Broadway and I think it was Dey Street, so we got a radio off of one of the trucks that had arrived and we sent the team. We could hear (Squad 270 Captain) Freddy La Femina calling for assistance. He had trapped firefighters in, I believe it was the North Tower. We sent Mike and put a SOC team together. Squad 288's rig was right there. I went over and took everything we could get that might be of value in the technical operation off of 288's rig and headed over.

There were some companies stretching lines on Vesey Street, so I went over there to see if they needed a hand. They were saying no, no, the guys around on the West Street side really need the help. I started to go down Vesey toward West, but there was a lot of debris blocking the way and they were telling me no, you don't want to go down there – they're worried about that building collapsing. I looked at 7 World Trade Center. There was smoke showing, but not a lot and I'm saying that isn't going to fall. So I went up Church Street two more blocks and went across to West and went right down behind 7 and got a good look at three sides. Again, there were a lot of fires on the ground, some crushed mail trucks, some burned-

Andrea Booher/
FEMA News Photo

Markings describing searches are visible on steel beams in the pile at the WTC.

up engines. It was a scene out of a war zone.

I continued around to West and Vesey and reported into the command post. They were very concerned about fire extending into the telephone company building. They gave me a couple of companies and said get into the telephone company building and check on extension there. We had extension on the first and second floors, so we took some standpipe lines, put them in operation and knocked that down. From there, we looked out at 7 World Trade Center again. You could see smoke, but no visible fire, and some damage to the south face. You couldn't really see from where we were on the west face of the building, but at the edge of the south face you could see that it was very heavily damaged.

We knocked down any fire and checked for extension in the phone company building. We tied the lines off and left them flowing out onto the debris piles that were burning out in the street there between the phone company and 7. I came back outside and I forget who the incident commander was at that command post, but he says we're getting a lot of reports of firemen still trapped. They think they know the location of the original command post and why don't you get over there and see if you can get a hand, organize something over that way.

OK, where is it? And he says it's on the other side of that bridge right there. You had the North Pedestrian Bridge that was blocking the entire access. We had to go around, behind and through 3 World Financial Center and come back out onto West Street at Liberty. And again, an absolutely incredible amount of devastation. It was absolutely astounding. I really couldn't see how bad things were up to that point because of the smoke condition. I was still expecting to see large sections of buildings standing and everything. Once I get out onto West and Liberty and see that there's nothing left, the whole steel of that building is out covering the block, it's just incredible.

Now we're still worried about 7. We have guys trying to make their way up into the pile, and they're telling us that 7 is going to fall down – and that was one of the directions from the command post, to make sure we clear the collapse zone from 7 and this is a 600-foot-tall building, so we had to clear a 600-foot radius from that building.

Guys are looking at me when I'm telling them to move away, we're over by the North Tower and we got to get out of here. They said what building are you talking about? I said that building and they thought the phone company because through the smoke you couldn't see what I'm talking about. They said that building isn't going anywhere. I said no, not that building, the one next to it, the big one. It was tough getting them to understand what we're talking about because until you had done either a couple of 360s around this whole site or if you got an aerial view somehow, you really

Andrea Booher/
FEMA News Photo

FDNY and USAR team members apparently await orders via radio.

couldn't appreciate the scope of the damage.

But now we get out there and we could crawl through this mass of steel. There were window openings in the steel – what used to be the windows of the exterior walls. You'd look down every step and say that's an aerial ladder down there dropped down into the void. Guys are searching in all those areas. There's got to be people here.

Where are the engine chauffeurs as we come across rigs? Some of the engines you could get in underneath and some of them were just flat right to the ground, pancaked to the ground, so that even if the engine chauffeur dove under the rig, there was no void space. The guys are saying that we've got to have a lot of people under here.

Then, when they found (Chief of Department) Pete Ganci's body and (First Deputy Commissioner) Bill Feehan's body, we said there's the command post, everybody else has to be right here too. But to lift that stuff – these were the massive, three-finger sections of steel. They weigh 25 tons. There was just nothing we were doing to lift them. That's when we realized we needed heavy equipment in there, but with the access being blocked, that became a major problem.

I went back to the command post, reported what I saw and we tried to organize a plan. That's where I said you've got to get this north footbridge cleared out of the way. We've got to be able to get some big cranes in to start lifting that heavy steel.

They were bringing some cranes in. They had some mobile hydraulic cranes by nightfall and started working from the south end, but they were really very small capacity and they were 600 feet away from the North Tower. That's when they gave me the job of getting that north footbridge out of the way. I worked on that all night the first night.

By 10 o'clock in the morning, we had started to get some heavy equipment in. We got the excavators in, the grapplers, and started to make some headway on it. We peeled off all the facing. This is a tremendous bridge, it's a 300-foot-long bridge. It was a steel box, almost a truss, like a space frame. We started to make some headway through that and by about 1 o'clock that afternoon, I was just shot though. I said I've got the plan organized, we're getting the equipment in to do it and this is where we've just got to keep going. I left and went up to Rescue 1's quarters that afternoon. By that point, a lot of the families were there – Dennis Mojica's fiancee, Maria. Just trying to deal with them was very hard. Mike Geidel was there with his father, Paulie. And naturally, Paul having been a lieutenant in Rescue 1, we're trying to reassure him that, yeah, there are a lot of areas that we haven't gotten to yet. We haven't given up hope. We're going to get him. It was tough trying to explain that.

I went upstairs and laid down for about an hour and a half. I couldn't sleep. I picked up some dry clothes. I stole some clothes from Mike Pena, a new T-shirt and underwear, and went back down.

I worked on the north bridge that second night. First, Chief Frank Fellini sent me with the guys from Harlem, 35 Engine and 14 Truck down to check the 1 and 9 subway entrance into the concourse to see whether there was a way to come into the collapse area from underneath. We got as far as up as we could until we were stopped by solid rubble. We came up into the concourse level from underneath. We checked right up to the PATH escalators, started to go down them, got down to the first level and there were some signs that the area had already been searched. So we went back up.

I said let's go back to see if we find areas that nobody's gotten to yet. And we went down in the east side of the wall. On the east side of the concourse, it's only three sublevels. We got down into all of them, and there were some real protected areas, but anybody that was in them got out. Nobody trapped or anything in any of those areas. A lot of places where people survived or could have survived without being pinned.

The casualty differences were enormous. In a war event, usually you have one killed for every two or three or four wounded. Here, incredibly, it was almost the opposite. Look at our numbers – 343 dead and only a dozen serious injuries. If you were out of the collapse zone, you lived and were relatively unscathed. If you were in the collapse zone, there was no alternative.

There was heavy equipment already on the way. By the time I got to West and Vesey, it was already very clearly understood that there was nothing we were going to do until we got the big heavy construction equipment up in the way. I talked with Mike Pena early on while we were over at the Broadway side still when we first got into the scene and got a handle on the size of the devastation. One of the things that he took care of was making arrangements to get the New York City FEMA task force on the way and get the equipment coming. Mike actually handled most of those arrangements.

It's a big deal. It's basically three tractor-trailer loads worth of equipment. You got to get the tractors hooked up, they're not kept up where you jump in and drive away.

Real early, we said we've got to get at least four FEMA task forces on the way. Unfortunately, by the time the task forces arrived and deployed, there were no live victims to be recovered. The last five victims were recovered about 26 hours later, just after noon on the 12th, and most of task forces hadn't even deployed. Pennsylvania was in at that point already and Massachusetts, and I believe Ohio. They began working, but there were no more live victims for them to recover.

The Ohio task force was staged over in one of the residential buildings in Battery Park City. In the process of doing a primary search they did find a person, not unconscious, but unable to move, injured pretty badly, in one of residential buildings and that's a block and a half away from the towers.

At that point, we put many of the incoming task forces as well as our resources, teams of firefighters, police officers and the FEMA people into the job of performing a good primary and then a secondary search of all of those buildings. And remember, we're talking a lot of big buildings, 50 stories, 300-by-300-foot buildings with no elevators and no power inside them.

We told them take their time, if it takes you eight hours to do that, go ahead. You've got to walk up. We want everything searched. I want the roof searched for bodies that might have fallen onto the roof. I want every setback searched. I want every staircase, every office, every elevator searched. They did a great job. It was a very long, difficult, hot-weather task to do, but it was necessary.

We needed heavy equipment, those 25-ton grapplers, 1,000-ton cranes. We were getting into areas where we were finding firefighters or civilians in voids and people were wondering whether anybody could have survived in those voids. In some cases, it might have been possible that they weren't crushed in some of these areas, but given the high carbon monoxide levels from the fires, I didn't see them as survivable voids. It took us over three months to get to these areas using the heavy equipment at the most rapid pace possible and we were still looking for remains or victims.

Without the heavy equipment, we weren't making any headway. We were taking I figured about two inches a day off of those piles at the rate we were going with hand equipment. We would be there for a hundred years at that rate. Just had to go to the heavy equipment.

One of the things we talked about with the voids was how would we make the decision to go to a recovery from a rescue operation – a tremendous number of considerations. Certainly, the families were a big one, but then we had to deal with the injury or fatality possibilities to rescuers, and we had to honestly evaluate what the people's chances of survival would be in that structure.

At that point, it didn't look good at all. We hadn't uncovered any voids where we didn't find crushed people. We didn't have anybody lying there who looked like he could have survived if it weren't for the fact that he was just stuck there so long. We went beyond the outside window of survivability. We know we've had people trapped in earthquakes for 14, maybe 15 days survive. But that was without the carbon monoxide coming up from underneath them constantly. So we went to 18 days just to be certain that we could say that there would be no way that anybody could have survived.

We asked each other how we were going to handle our own consciences if we came across a pile of bodies and they had a diary, this is day one, we know you guys are coming to get us, day three, where are you, and, day five, we're out of air, we can't stand it anymore, we're dying here, come get us, help us.

The FEMA teams made a lot of void entries and did a lot of good reconnaissance, but the type of debris that we encountered here was unlike anything that had ever been encountered. Even earthquakes topple primarily concrete structures. Concrete is easy to breach. A hundred-foot-long I-beam that projects 90 feet into this pile that's got three-inch-thick members, it's a box that's five feet by three feet with three-inch-thick web members, you're not penetrating. Even with the heaviest torches that we had in all the FEMA caches it would take hours to burn a single hole through that beam. This was something we needed, the heaviest industrial-sized equipment available. The grapplers that could lift that.

We were cutting with the FEMA torches. We were cutting those box beam sections into eight-foot lengths because that was what was able to be moved. When we got the excavators in there, they could take the entire 40-foot-long section in three pieces out in one piece. We had to segment that into a dozen pieces, so we were really overwhelmed by the type of construction. It wasn't a question of punching holes with a pavement breaker or jackhammer and getting through anything.

Up to that point, we were burning up a lot of resources and it wasn't very productive. That was a little bit of controversy within some of the FEMA responders. They wanted to continue burning, but again at that point I made a decision that we were being ineffective. We were putting people in bad places, places that had been searched. We knew we didn't have any survivors in those areas and we were just burning up oxyacetylene. It was almost a feel-good effort, kind of like the bucket brigades.

The bucket brigades that a lot of the police officers and firefighters were manning were ineffective. They didn't do anything to get to anybody, but it was a feel-good effort. Everybody wanted to pitch in and help, but in reality and hindsight now, we were moving tiny, tiny fragments of debris. Actually, it was impeding the operation. We needed to get the big equipment in so we could start moving the big steel out of the way.

We had 10,000 firemen wanting to come to the site. The scene was overflowing with people. We sent them back to their firehouses. But the guys in the firehouses, they weren't going to rest, they weren't going to sleep knowing that there were all these guys missing and buried.

Then we had the problem with all the out-of-town units that came in unsolicited and out of control. We didn't have a good handle on who was where. They really created a major, major morale problem for us. We would have our people in their firehouses wanting to come dig out their brothers and then we'd tell them no, stay back there, protect the rest of the city. And they would turn on the TV and there would be coverage of a firefighter from out of town telling them how he just spent eight hours digging out New York City firemen.

The guys were in rebellion. They wanted to come to that pile. We had many, many reports that guys were saying if you don't let us go, we're going to leave the rigs here and go in our cars or we're going to take the rigs with us and go and you're not going to stop us. That was a real serious problem, especially the first week.

Once the guys saw the capabilities of the FEMA teams and that these were not just volunteers who drove in on their own, that they had expertise, that they had all this ability and that we had requested them, that solved some of the problems. It didn't stop it all because nobody could stop Joe Blow from giving an interview out in the street.

The FEMA personnel were very disciplined that way. They didn't give interviews off the cuff. They explained they were part of the system and so on. But anybody who put a turnout coat and a helmet on and walked down outside the fence in the perimeter area was interviewed by some news network. A lot of them never spent any time at all on the pile, but they showed up in fireman's gear and now they're telling guys what a great job they did. We had cases of people arrested as impostors. Absolute impostors that got their hands on some turnout gear.

Security was a major issue for us. We went through many, many types of IDs. Right away I requested a company of active-duty U.S. Marines for perimeter security and that was rejected. We ended up with police and National Guard. I wanted the Marines because I wanted some 19-year-old kid standing on the corner who, when his sergeant gives him an order, he stands to and nobody passes that point without the proper credentials. Instead, what we got was I got a friend of mine in there, or my brother's in there, and some of that was legit and people let them go. There were others who just didn't really care who showed up dressed as a fireman or a police officer, a mailman. If you had some kind of uniform on, they just waved you in.

It took a long time to get security under control. OEM was in charge of giving out the badges. To get badges, everybody had to personally report to the pier. Rescuers spent hours and hours and hours waiting on line to get their IDs so they could get down into the site. When they get there, they'd see other people walk right past them with no ID at all who weren't even part of the rescue teams.

Several times, we changed it because people were giving out ID badges to anybody who showed up. Now we had badges that basically became useless. Yes, you had a badge, but you didn't belong getting a badge or maybe your commitment has expired, the things that you could do were no longer needed. We don't need you coming into the site and gawking anymore.

Some of the FEMA teams, in uniform on buses with an escort, were stopped at some checkpoints. Other guys, if you just drove two blocks over to the next checkpoint, nobody was there to even guard the gate, so security was an ongoing issue. The threat of secondary issues going on at the site was a severe issue for us. We had no certainty that there wasn't going to be a secondary attack on all the rescuers working there. It was a challenge.

After a couple of weeks into the incident, the federal government brought in interagency incident management teams, basically wildland firefighting logistics teams. The first one was from the southwest region, New Mexico and Arizona, and they were terrific. These are people who have a lot of experience running campaign-type operations. This was very different for us. The incident management team took over our logistics operation, handling it, setting it up for us, maintaining inventory controls and tracking. They were an excellent resource.

I took a picture from the command post. We had (Citywide Tour Commander Frank) Cruthers and (Deputy Chief Peter) Hayden and (Deputy Chief) Charlie Blaich. Blaich is huddled up with the guy from the U.S. Park Service and another guy from the Incident Management Team from Albuquerque, New Mexico. If you had told anybody on September 10th that you would have people from the U.S. Park Service and the U.S. Forest Service helping us run an incident, everybody would have said you're out of your mind, it could never happen. And here they were and they did a great job.

It Was Personal

Firefighter Joseph Esposito
Rescue 5, Concord, Staten Island

I met up with other off duty members at the quarters of Rescue 5. The Staten Island Ferry took us to Manhattan. It was loaded with firefighters, a couple of ambulances, equipment and tools. At a rallying point we were given instructions.

As we were walking up West Street, one of the firefighters pointed out that there was heavy construction equipment parked down the block. Being a heavy equipment operator, I always carry my key. I drove the big excavator, designed to dig and move stuff, and cleared a large pile of debris from the side of the apparatus of Rescue 2. Firefighters could now open the compartments. The owner of the machine appeared and said I have the operator here. Do you mind? I said OK.

We started to search. We found helmets and bodies. It was chaotic. It was getting dark. Some guys asked if I wanted to go home. I said no, I am staying! My brother, Lieutenant Mike Esposito from Squad 1, and my cousin, Firefighter Frank Esposito assigned to Engine 235, were both missing.

We were dead tired and standing near the firehouse of Engine 10 and Ladder 10 when we heard they needed a rescue company on the pile. Four of us went past this conga line of responders passing up equipment. There was a Port Authority police officer trapped. Apparently, he was in the mezzanine before the collapse. Someone said call his wife, he is going to die.

Apparently, a Marine had heard a noise and located the cop. We had to climb up four stories and then back down the same to get to this area. You had to move steel and move debris to go back down to where the officer was pinned. Another officer was nearby, but he was dead.

There were open beams. You had to look for a place to put the debris we were removing from around him. One firefighter was able to kneel down and pass debris to the next firefighter. He then handed the debris to me. I found an elevator shaft nearby. I would dump the debris down the shaft. EMS had made it down there and given him an IV. He had been cleared down to his hips.

We operated for a few hours. Other companies relieved us. I was sitting in a chair by 10&10 at about 8 A.M. when someone came by and said did you hear, they got the cop out?

I was trying to find my brother. Trying to figure out where he might have been. Sometimes moving across the pile, you could feel it shift. Once I found a door and opened it. It was an open shaft that went down several floors. My brother was thought to be in the South Tower. They never found my cousin. I was always at the site. It was personal.

(bottom) Steel lays out across West Street from the South Tower.

(right) Early bucket brigade works in plaza area near sphere.

Andrea Booher/FEMA News Photo

Andrea Booher/FEMA News Photo

Front Page

Firefighter Billy Eisengrein
Rescue 2, Bedford Stuyvesant, Brooklyn

I was scheduled to work Tuesday night. Firefighter Billy Lake was my 24 partner. (*Editor's note: He worked Monday night because it was his 20th anniversary on the job and he was buying the meal.*) I reported to the firehouse and we took our gear and whatever spare equipment we had and took a bus across the street into the city.

We arrived 20-30 minutes after the second tower collapsed. We split into three groups so we could attack the site in three different ways. I didn't realize we were at West Street. There was absolute silence, which never occurs in Manhattan.

We made our way into the pile from the southwest corner. We paired up with another crew. We called out is anybody there? We got a response. We went up and over the pile towards the voice. We continued to go up and down and through the debris. It took 5 to 10 minutes to get to the voice. It turned out to be a firefighter. One of our guys had worked with his father.

Near the south facing wall of 4 WTC there was a firefighter and a Port Authority maintenance worker. There eyes were caked with soot. We helped get them off the steel. A battalion chief arrived from a different direction. The chief took them to safety. We assumed the firefighter found them as he came upon them somehow. We went back into the pile to search what we could.

We hooked up with some more SOC guys. After one or two hours, a call was put out to clear the whole site as they were worried about Building 7 coming down. I had a radio and talked with Captain Tiso of Rescue 3. I climbed to the top of the pile to see what I could see. One of the guys left the group and got separated. I made my way back through the pile to Rescue 2's rig. There wasn't any equipment left on the rig. It was completely stripped. They even

Several firefighters from Rescue 2 climbed over the pile, finding a firefighter and a Port Authority worker who were having trouble finding a way out.

Firehouse Collection

© 2001 The Record
(Bergen County, N.J.)
Thomas E. Franklin

took the SCUBA gear. Who would take the SCUBA gear? That was pretty amazing.

I was sitting on the back of the rig with Firefighter Bob Gallione. I saw Firefighter George Johnson, a lifelong friend, and another firefighter (Daniel McWilliams) who I had never met about 30 feet away. I saw them carrying an American flag on a short pole. I knew exactly what they were going to do. I asked if they needed any help. I hooked up with them. I asked them where they were going to put this.

At the northwest corner of Liberty and West was a construction trailer that had several flag poles sticking into the air. There was a green flag hanging on a pole. We put a piece of stainless steel, which had covered steel beams, and placed it up to the construction trailer and climbed up. We took the green flag down and took the American flag off the pole it was on. They tied a knot and taped it over with electrical tape. We raised the flag, stepped back and looked at it for as second. Another firefighter walking by gave us thumbs up. We came off the trailer and went our separate ways.

I stayed overnight Tuesday and returned on Thursday. I noticed it was gone on Friday. I was a little disappointed. At that time there were 10-20 flags flying around the site. My girlfriend called me Wednesday or Thursday to to say you're on the front page of the paper. I said no big deal. I had my picture in the paper before. We had a lot more important matters to deal with.

Then I received a call from *People Magazine*. They said you don't know how big this is, it's in Paris, Japan, around the world. The paper where the picture appeared wanted a release. I said only if we do it for the right reason.

George talked with his brother-in-law and we started a charity called the Bravest Fund. We had to split the money 50/50 with the paper and we received $1 million. To date we have given away nearly $1 million. People have to apply to the Bravest Fund. It is mainly used to pay unpaid medical bills for families who have someone with cancer. We started the fund to help firefighters, police, Port Authority and expanded it to anybody we wanted to give it to.

It was passed on by mostly word of mouth. If anyone of the three of us gets sick we cannot use the funds. We haven't received a dime from the fund. I still receive letters and phone calls from across the country. People tell me how proud they were to be Americans once they saw the picture; they knew we as a country would be OK.

The American flag is raised near the corner of Liberty and West Streets. It was gone in three days.

The Gates Of Hell

Captain John M. Sullivan Covering in 6th division (was in Fire Prevention Bureau on 9/11) Bronx

now Battalion Chief, Battalion 27

I was up in the Bronx working in Fire Prevention, so I had a fire department car. I heard on the radio that the towers had been hit and I started to respond. I picked up an unmarked police car with lights and sirens and I was able to weave in and out of traffic following him down there. We were going up one-way streets the wrong way, the whole nine yards.

I was going down Church Street against traffic and it looked like a movie scene. There were thousands of people running up the street. And just at about that point, when I was probably about maybe five blocks away from the Trade Center, the first tower collapsed. At that point, because of the volume of people, I had to pull over to the side of the road because I was going to hit somebody.

I got out of the car, put my bunker gear on and I was going to head down the street. I saw 124 Truck come in. They were going against traffic, but a rig could get through. So I flagged them down, jumped on the side of the rig. The whole width of the three or four blocks down on Church Street I was yelling to the captain on 124 do you know where the command post is? He didn't have any idea, so I went straight down Church.

We got off the rig and the thing that struck me was there were rigs, ESU, EMS, and fire trucks all over the place. There were was just no people there. I proceeded down Church to the corner of Church and Liberty, the scene of the South Tower collapse, and there I came upon a bunch of guys from I believe it was 10 Truck, that were helping a Lieutenant Ruby from Operations. He had sustained a compound fracture of, I believe, it was his left leg, and they were trying to get him packaged, so I jumped in with them to help them get him out of there.

While we were putting him on a board, all of a sudden, you heard this tremendous roar. I thought another plane was hitting. You didn't know what it was. It was just the loudest sound you ever heard in your life.

And then everything turned black and dead silent. The air was so thick you could literally chew or taste whatever was in the air. Then, eventually, it started to lift. I heard the cops yelling. The cops were missing a man. We were able to find him right away and then we got Lieutenant Ruby. He was on a board and we carried him around 10 & 10's quarters and then out to West Street, where we hooked with an ESU pickup truck, threw him in the back of that, and got him to an ambulance.

Then I ran into Lieutenant May from Operations and Lieutenant Pete Clifford. Lieutenant May was telling me that he came in with a bunch of people who were all on a line and they were strung out heading towards 10 & 10 to get some gear to try to help out. And he made it into 10 & 10, but he felt the rest of his guys must have been trapped someplace.

I reported in to a chief. We got a team together of five or six guys and circled back around onto Church Street. We couldn't find the guys right away, so we were trying to project where the command post might have been without any information. When we got into the concourse, it was partially collapsed.

Some stores were fairly intact. There were partial collapses everywhere. You're crawling over stuff, and a bunch of uncontrolled fires. I just didn't like the looks of the situation. To the south was completely collapsed and to the west, we went as far as we could and the center of the Trade Center was also collapsed. I was about to call the search off for safety reasons when Lieutenant May heard somebody screaming. We climbed over a couple of more piles of rubble, passed fires and we found a civilian. He was severely burned from one of the fires when Lieutenant May found him. We were able to get some water and put the fire out around him and then clear the rubble, but we needed something to cut with. So we had to get a truck in there. We stayed with him, kept the fire away and we talked to him for a while.

Eventually, someone came with a Sawzall and they were able to make the cut and get him out. And once he was out, they found a DOA below him in the same spot in the concourse level. He was trapped by rubble and there was a metal bar, I guess it was a pipe, that we couldn't move because it was probably 20, 30 feet long. It had to be cut. There was no way to get him out from underneath

Firehouse Collection

that. He was a very large man, over 300 pounds, so we couldn't maneuver him around it.

You could see where the South Tower had collapsed the concourse. And then as you went forward, there was the collapse in the center. The area where they had that huge, metal ball. That area was collapsed.

There were piles of rubble that you had to climb over. For a while you were just walking around. The first thing that was kind of shocking was the darkness and the smoke and everything. And it was really kind of scary because it looked like bodies. And then when you got a little closer, there were mannequins all over the place from the different stores that were partially collapsed.

I'll never forget that sound or when that black cloud came, the dead silence. I've never in my life seen or heard just like that eerie complete silence – the closest thing you could describe to it is like when it's snowing where you don't hear anything. And it was just black.

For a second you're thinking maybe I'm dead. You can't hear. You can't see. I'll also never forget when we were on West Street after we put Lieutenant Ruby in an ambulance, just the devastation when you're looking and you see all the fire trucks and police cars burning. That's where I saw Firefighter Ray Phillips. It was literally like if you can look into the gates of hell, that's what it was.

It's just like the World Trade Center, something that's been there your entire life almost, completely mangled and just everything burning and just the devastation. It was hard to appreciate the enormity of how bad it was. The first time you saw everything on West Street was something that I'll never forget either. And one weird thing — when I was on Broadway, I could have sworn I saw Father Mychal Judge. Then I was over on the other side when they pulled everybody back to wait for that collapse and Jack Wells tells me no, Father Judge is dead. It was strange.

One of the firefighters interviewed said his boots were destroyed due to the intense heat below the debris heating up the steel.

FACT

As of SEPTEMBER 11, 2001

2,156 FIREFIGHTERS per shift

and 30 DISPATCHERS per shift

A Needle In A Haystack

Battalion Chief John J. Salka Jr.
Battalion 18
West Farms, Bronx

I responded from home to the Battalion. And then from the Battalion, we went to the Division. Everybody was forming up there, breaking into teams, each with an officer and five firemen. We loaded a bus up and got going. We left an officer in charge of the firehouse to get the rest of the guys. We jumped in the spare chief's car. We had (Battalion) Chief (Richard J.) Blatus, myself, Deputy Chief Mike Rappe, two 18th Battalion aides, Steve Calcutti and Jack Shavon and a driver. We went down the East Side on the FDR Drive. It was desolate, just emergency vehicles going south, pedestrians running north.

We got off at the Brooklyn Bridge exit, right near City Hall, and that's when we encountered all the dust and the paper and the debris filling the streets. We stopped right outside City Hall, at City Hall Park. We got out of the car there. We sent the Division van back and we tried to stay together, then we started walking. We ended up getting some paper masks from an ambulance right there and put them on. We all had radios.

We ran into (Deputy) Chief (Tom) Haring, who had some kind of command post starting to be set up there. My brother-in-law was working in 10 Truck that morning, so I was trying to get down that way to see what was going on. I said to Blatus let's try and get down there. We walked south, I think down Broadway. Then we made a right and walked past 10 Truck and west on Liberty. We were encountering debris all over the place. It was unbelievable. There was fire, heavy fire. I remember walking past 10 Truck – 10 & 10. The doors were blown out. The windows were blown out. You couldn't even really tell it was a firehouse.

I heard somebody say Ladder 6 on the radio. I said Ladder 6, that's Jay's (Captain Jay Jonas) company, I wonder if he's working. I got on the radio. I said 18 Battalion to Ladder 6, is that you Jay? He said yeah, is that you John? I said yeah, so we started talking. And, of course, he was talking to a lot of people, but I got in there and said where are you? I'm in the North Tower, we're in the B Stairway, which didn't exist anymore, not in the configuration that we'd recognize it.

We called him a couple of times and said where's your rig, is your rig parked out on what street, were there any other rigs near your rig because we kept making our way closer and closer. Then I could actually see some rigs. There were a load of rigs there that were just either partially crushed or partially buried. We asked Jay did you walk straight in from your rig because we couldn't see his rig at all, but he didn't recall that.

He was really, really calm. I remember saying how's the smoke condition, how's the atmosphere in there, is it breathable? He said it's a lot of dust, it's a little tough to breathe, but we're doing all right. And there was no heat. I asked him about fire, is there any fire near there? He said he didn't think so. They could smell something burning, they knew there was a fire nearby, but it wasn't bothering them yet. So many things were happening at once. Anytime you saw anything that looked like it was like a rig or a helmet or something, guys would be digging in that area, so it was just like a million little operations going on there.

Guys were looking through rigs and looking through really everything. Debris was all over the place. We were trying to find our way to Jonas, to 6 Truck. Other guys would be talking to him, asking either similar or the same questions, but we were still trying to make our way over there. I remember at one point seeing (Deputy) Chief (Peter) Hayden and saying you guys hear 6 Truck, you know 6 Truck is trapped? And he said yeah, we're trying to get somebody over there. There was a lot of stuff going on. He was trying to do 10 things at once.

At one point, he told me to take a bunch of guys. There were some Rescue 1 guys there, Rescue 3, Firefighter Cliffie Stabner, a couple of other guys from Rescue 1, obviously off-duty guys that were down there with their gear. He said take a handful of guys and see if you can get in there and find Jonas, which was like finding a needle in a haystack. We were trying to talk to him. We were trying to search around for him. It was a lot of fire still burning too. There was a lot of smoke and heat.

We went around to Vesey and we went into

Michael Rieger/
FEMA News Photo

The upper floors of Bankers Trust were damaged. Mold took over the building and it was determined to take it down.

a garage level on the north side of that building. There was a rolldown door. It was down, but it had been cut. There was a triangle opening. We walked through that. By now, there were a pile of guys with us, maybe 15 or 20 guys. Now, that's right across the street from 7 World Trade Center, which was still burning very well, still intact, still standing, 40-something stories.

We went in there. Everybody was concerned about being near that, but we went in there anyway because we were still trying to get to Jonas and we thought that would be maybe a way to get down towards where he was into the rubble.

We went into Building 6, which was the Customs House. We got in there and it was pretty good downstairs, a lot of dust and debris and stuff, but it was all intact. We were thinking there was a connection in there where we would be able to get into a stairway or maybe that he even was in there. He was telling us he was in the North Tower, but we were thinking maybe we can get to him from there. So we did get in there. There was smoke in there. You could see where part of the North Tower had ripped right through 6 World Trade Center, which was a much smaller building. We could see where we were was a loading dock and the loading dock ended and then there was just a debris hole. It almost looked like the first one in 1993, when there was an internal collapse inside the building. You could look down.

I grabbed the riding list off every rig I went past. I jumped up into the cab. I must have had 10 or 12 of them. I handed those over to Chief (Frank) Fellini (Citywide Tour Commander) or one of the guys that was with him, one of the other chiefs or an aide. I was still trying to get to Jay. Every once in a while I had to remind either Hayden or Fellini or whoever it was I was talking to, is 6 Truck out yet? No, they're not out yet, we haven't got to them yet. You'd almost get sidetracked from trying to get to them because so many other things were happening. All of a sudden, you'd encounter hurt guys or guys saying here's something else happening over here. Somebody said there's a guy under this rig. It just never ended.

Somewhere along the way, (Battalion Chief Rich) Picciotto shows up. We're standing at Vesey and West. They had just towed Rescue 3's collapse rig out of the way and Picciotto comes out all disheveled, just his white shirt on and his bunker pants, no helmet, no coat, saying there are guys in here and this is the way to get to them. At that point, I did not know that he had been in with Jay Jonas. He is one of the first guys that made it out of there. So we got another group of guys together. Fellini told me to take these five or eight guys, go with him. We made our way down there. As we walked along, we picked up more guys.

We weaved our way and I said somebody tie off a search rope. Somebody else said I've got a life-saving rope. I said good, we'll tie her off to one

Michael Rieger/
FEMA News Photo

Amidst tons of rubble, the brass sculpture "The Sphere" survived the collapse of both 110-story towers with only moderate damage. Six months after the attack, the sculpture was temporarily relocated to Battery Park. An eternal flame joined the sculpture as part of a memorial to all those lost on 9/11.

of these beams here because we were going into this rubble, plus it was heavy, heavy smoke so we don't get lost in there if this fire extends. We started stretching that in there and we picked five or six guys to start walking through up these beams.

The footing was terrible. We had to make our way over all that debris and start working our way into what was a really big pile. I ended up working up there and that had to be 15 stories in the air after when we were working on the top of that B Stairway the next day. But, of course, this is the first day and we didn't know that at the time. It just looked like a gigantic pile of rubble. Somebody said on the radio we got them out now and they removed them from the scene. So all that work, as crucial as we thought it was going to be, we never actually got to them. But they did get them out. That consumed a lot of the time.

A lot of smoke was popping out of Building 7 and then almost like a typical job, if you can imagine, it was getting heavier and heavier and heavier. Then you could see fire here and there. It was just working its way up. Eventually, there was smoke coming out of every floor and somebody said there it goes. I remember hearing a rumble. I was on Vesey Street with a lot of other guys and that thing just started to go. It almost fell straight down. But it was down pretty quick and then that actually solved that whole problem. That opened that whole area up to people being able to go back in and work because it was down.

I was still trying to find out about my brother-in-law. Right along the way there now, anytime I saw a guy from 10 Truck or 10 Engine, I would ask was Mike Cancel around anywhere, did anybody see him? A couple of guys said no, I haven't seen him since the beginning. Finally one guy said oh yeah, I saw him, he's over there. I said he's alive, he got out? He said yeah, I definitely saw him a little while ago. I said you definitely saw him? He said yes. But I never actually saw him that day.

The 18th Battalion was relocated to the 4th Battalion. Now we were the acting 4th Battalion and we started taking runs in down there. There was smoke all over the place. There were a couple of relocated battalions from Brooklyn, but for the most part we had almost all the way down the Battery because we went on runs all the way down.

The second night we were up on the pile, right across from 10 & 10. We went to 10 &10 command. That's what it was that night, 10 & 10 command. There were two or three chiefs there and this was just nothing but a gigantic pile of rubble in front of us, right up to the edge of the firehouse practically.

We worked there all night long and that was the night where they had all those chains of guys handing stuff down one piece at a time, bucket brigades and stuff like that. There were firemen and cops from all over the place digging. I remember asking for saws and asking for torches and they were just trying to tunnel down and dig into the pile in a hundred different spots.

There was a hole in the ground like the Grand Canyon. Whether that was a wall that kicked up the dirt or something, it was cavernous. It was so deep it was unbelievable. I was trying to figure out how that happened, whether something dug in and kicked all the dirt out. I couldn't figure that out. I remember that was amazing to me, the size of the hole in the ground there between Liberty Street and the South Tower, a gigantic hole. You could put five Goodyear blimps in there, that's how big this hole in the ground was.

Just the terrain was amazing. All of sudden, these mountains of steel and then these big gigantic holes right next to them and guys just looked like little ants on these piles. You could just go up and go over the crest of a hill and all of a sudden, more appears to you, it looked like miles. Actually, it's only 16 acres, but when you're going in on one edge of it looking at it, it was just piles and piles of stuff. In the background you could see buildings still burning.

Later on that night, some urban search and rescue team showed up. They were from the Midwest. They had real search dogs. On that same pile where they were carrying those police dogs in and putting them down and then having to carry them out, they went in with these dogs, unleashed them and said search. And those dogs covered a 100-by-100-foot square in two minutes. Those dogs were running around, jumping up and down, jumping – going into holes and coming back out. Once I saw that, I said wow, those are the dogs that are really trained to do collapse rescue and void searches. These were really, really sharp dogs.

We started working up on that tower that second night, up on the North Tower, that high spot where you had to climb down. There was another one of those gullies along there, so it must have been something with the collapse that dug up the dirt because there was another one of those ravines, whatever you want to call it, along let's say the curb line between the North Tower and West Street and they had ladders set up. You'd go down the ladders and there was rope strung so you could hold onto the rope and climb on the ladder all the way down to the bottom of this pile, which ended up maybe a floor or two below grade. Then you'd come back up the other side, pull yourself back up, walk up the ladder, several ladders strung and hooked, all just attached together.

Then you'd would work your way up all the way up onto the pile onto the North Tower, which was a big irregular pile, but you'd work your way up and then around. They had ladders strung and across all these little voids. Eventually, they put plywood on them. There was rope tied from beam to beam to piece of debris so you could hold onto the rope as a handrail and walk on the ladders until we get to the top of that pile of the North Tower, and that's where there was like the top of a stairway. That's where they were all working.

When we were at the top of that large pile, there was always a SOC operation, although there were other guys up there helping occasionally too. West Central Command we were talking to, what we were doing, what we were finding, what we needed, more tools, more bottles, more of this, more of that. Another company was sending Rescue 4 down, sending Rescue 3 up, and they would all come up there.

They were digging by hand with these little garden spades, halligans and things like that. You could barely use shovels there. They were digging, digging, digging, and they would uncover a turnout coat and they would start digging around that. Eventually, that stuff got moved and the whole pile went down too, but most of the time you were digging in a hole. There was smoke coming up from everywhere so they were sticking lines in holes to keep the smoke from coming up right where we were working.

Anytime I showed up, I would say I've been working with rescue and they would let me go up there. And so that went on, on and off for a couple of different days I was there, but that operation just kept continuing right there. And then you'd come back and they'd be 20 feet lower, but still digging in the same spot. Then they'd take us all out of there. The cranes would lift three or four or five or 10 big pieces off. Then we'd go back up there again and now the whole pile was a little bit lower.

These other guys that were up there with us, these guys didn't have to be there. These guys were tradesmen, steamfitters, and they were up there doing it with us, which I thought was really super.

They were very decent guys, and we couldn't have done it without them. Rescue knows how to cut with torches, the machines and the stuff like that, but not like these guys. We had a crew of six guys up there and they could just cut stuff and move it really quickly. They facilitated the whole thing up there. They knew how things were going to move when you cut it, so it was really good having them up there. So we were working on that and that pile just kept getting lower and lower.

There were a couple of big beams 30, 40, 60, 80 feet long, those big 100-ton beams, that were just sort of like teetering up there. They were held down by wires and by other beams leaning on them, but I guess they could have just fallen, so we tried to stay away from that. We found a couple of helmets and frontpieces up there. I remember finding masks and cylinders. You'd see the top of a bottle. You'd go digging down to that.

Eventually, we didn't have to climb up and down anymore. They would bring a "man basket" up with the crane, and we'd all climb into the basket. Then, they'd hoist us and lower us back down, so it took us two minutes to get up and down rather 25 minutes to climb up there. We would bring all our tools up or back or if we were going to come right back, we'd leave everything up there and come down.

A couple of times, they tried to get me to leave there, but we were uncovering fireman after fireman. I said no, we've got firemen in our hands here that we've partially uncovered, we're not going to come down right now.

I took a detail to SOC because all the guys in SOC got killed so (SOC Chief) John Norman called me up, asking if I could come over there for a month or so. I said yeah. I went over there and every tour we spent half the day down there. Most of the other chiefs who were down there were in sectors because they were on the detail or they were on the task force, but the SOC chiefs, we had a little bit of leeway. We could almost go anywhere we wanted to go. Anytime we'd think we've got something or we've got somebody, I would zoom right over there.

Fellini was the boss. (Firefighter) Sammy Mellisi was there every day working with those grapplers, standing up on the machine, telling the guy what to do and what not to do. The guy knew how to operate the machine. They uncovered a guy and we pulled him out, then they uncovered another guy and we're digging in this hole. Every time he dug, something else would come up, a tool or a helmet or a Scott bottle, and sure enough it was another guy. I think we pulled nine guys out of there that night and we were there for 12 hours digging in that hole.

We were just uncovering these guys one after another after another. That's when they started using a fire helmet to carry the guy out because they wanted to make sure everything looked right and that we did everything the right way. We put them in a body bag and then we put them in a Stokes. Then we handed the Stokes up out of the hole to the top of the hole. They put it down and put the American flag on it up there somewhere. Then, when I had two or three of them out next to each other, they would carry them out and line everybody up. All the other guys who were standing around or helping would put all the buckets down and line up, and that's when we were still removing the guys on those little EMS golf carts, for lack of a better term. Eventually, they said let's bring ambulances in here, which is more professional and dignified.

One of our fire department chaplains was up there, standing by, waiting for us to pull guys out. As we did, he would absolve them and say a prayer in his official capacity as a chaplain. But he couldn't be up there 24 hours a day and certainly some of these older chaplains who were volunteers coming in from different places weren't going to be at the top of that pile. So a couple of times, I was the guy. I was the only chief up there and all of a sudden they'd get a guy out. I'd say all right, let's hold on, let's get him in the Stokes, lay him down. OK, brothers, everybody uncover and we'd say a little prayer, sometimes we just said the "Our Father." Sometimes I just said God, grant him peace and watch over his family and whatever, and then we would cover him back up and get him out of there and keep on digging.

Cheering Us On

Lieutenant Mike Scotto, Ladder 58, West Farms, Bronx

I was writing my morning roll call when the second plane hit the South Tower. Ladder 58 from the Bronx was relocated to Ladder 20 in Manhattan. We could see the smoke from the Bronx at the location of the Bruckner and the Sheridan expressways. There was heavy traffic on the southbound FDR Drive. The police closed the road below 23rd Street.

We traveled down to Houston Street and went west to Ladder 20. We were there for maybe 10 minutes when the South Tower collapsed. We did not get dispatched. A few minutes later, we received a run to a collapsed building with a person trapped at Cedar and Church streets. The recalled members of Ladder 20 climbed on the rig. We loaded extra equipment. As we responded down Broadway people evacuating the area and running north were cheering us on like it was a football game. They were also running north on Lafayette Street. We parked at Broadway and Cedar Street.

We saw papers flying, dust, dirt and debris. Then the second tower collapsed. The cloud of dust was coming our way. I made it from the officer's door to the driver's door when the cloud hit us. Several civilians came to the back of the rig and the firefighters laid on top of them. I reached into the cab and turned on my mask. I handed it to the civilians and to the members.

The sound was like after a snowfall. Dead silence. The rig radio was on the citywide channel and I could hear them say there was a major collapse. The cloud lifted in a few minutes. The first couple of minutes it was tough to breathe. We walked west on Liberty Street past the firehouse of Engine 10/Ladder 10. No one was around. Every building around was on fire. You couldn't walk past the bank building because large pieces of steel were hanging out of it. Once we got around the corner onto West Street we could see the pile of debris. We could see cars, police cars, ambulances and fire trucks that were destroyed and covered in debris. We saw an aerial ladder upside down.

Climbing on the pile, we started to look around the hotel and North Tower. Rigs were searched. We saw some firefighters' bodies that were covered. We worked on a hoseline going into the pile. We handed our masks to the firefighters who were working down in the pile. It took 20 firefighters to back out the hoseline.

(One story that Scotto related: There was a meeting in the 90s of the South Tower. After the first plane hit, the person running the meeting said is it OK to continue? Two men left the meeting. As they were exiting the South Tower, the second plane hit. All those who stayed in the meeting were killed.)

Ladder 84 from Staten Island is one of the many relief companies pouring water on the debris of the 47-story Building 7 that collapsed around 5 P.M. on September 11.

Thomas P. Buchta

It's Time To Go To Work

Lieutenant Joe Dimartino Engine 294, Richmond Hill, Queens

retired

We were dispatched to relocate to the quarters of Engine 261 in Long Island City. Just when we pulled up, we were redirected to the Trade Center. We entered the Queens Midtown Tunnel and were the only vehicle in the tunnel. As we exited the tunnel, we heard that a tower was down.

Crossing midtown, we drove south down the West Side Highway. We were able to park near the Pedestrian Bridge at Chambers Street. Spare air cylinders were taken along with some hand tools. As we walked south on West Street, the North Tower came down. We took cover behind a car. A couple of guys started running. The top 10 floors seemed to blow out in slow motion. The tower came down and a tidal wave of smoke came toward us. I took my chances right there. I was never going to outrun the cloud. Everything went black. Debris hit all around us. You could hear things banging. There was concrete, paper-like confetti and dust.

When the smoke cleared, I took out a cigarette. I gathered the members together and said it's time to go to work. Apparatus was flipped over and on fire. It was unbelievably quiet. It was silent, no sound at all. We proceeded past a rear-mount aerial on fire. A minute before, tons of people were around. Now, no one was around. A few people started to come out with a few stray firefighters.

At that time, no one was in charge. The rear-mount aerial on fire still had equipment on it. I told my firefighters to strip the rig of equipment before it was destroyed. They took the ladders, tools and air cylinders off. We found the apparatus of Ladder 101. That was the first company I was assigned to after I was promoted to lieutenant. We looked into the cab and there was no one there. We were trying to locate anybody who was on the surface of the debris. We saw six or seven police officers on the balcony of Building 6. Portable ladders were raised to the balcony and we brought them down.

Only the hosebed of an engine company is visible after steel and debris covered the apparatus following a tower collapse.

Larry Lynch

Michael Rieger/FEMA News Photo

The rear half of Building 6 was missing. It ended right in the middle of the stairway.

There was a steady stream of firefighters going up the ladders. The windows were broken to gain access to the nine-story building. We found a fire lieutenant who had been killed. We found the riding list of the members working that tour in his pocket. They brought a Stokes basket up to remove him. We said there was nothing we could do for him now, so let's see if we can help someone else.

Into the building, a few firefighters ascended one stairway, while the others went up the other stairway. We were forcing the doors and making a search. The rear of the building was missing. It had collapsed when the North Tower fell. The rear half of the building ended right in the middle of the stairway. Firefighters had to go hand over hand on the railing because most of the stair treads were missing.

One civilian was found on the top floor. Two firefighters from Ladder 14 escorted him down. The building started to fill with smoke. I went down a ladder to the street. There was no other good place to go because the debris and steel were piled so high. A roll-down gate located under the balcony blew out. We thought there was another bomb in there.

A search of the voids near the Marriott Hotel was attempted. I went under a 2-by-4-foot piece of steel. Another firefighter was going to go in behind me. I said, "You can't because if something happens to me, you have to go for help." As soon as you did one thing, there was something else that needed to be done.

We checked a parking garage. We went in for about 100 yards, then the floor just dropped off. There was smoke and heat inside as there were multiple cars on fire. As we were searching, we realized we were standing on top of the Mask Service Unit. It was flattened like a pancake. The entire height of the debris covered that rig. We thought we were walking on the street. I realized that we were not going to find anyone there.

We worked until about 3 A.M. I talked to a chief and when he heard we had been there all day, he released us. My brother is a police officer. He had been on the 50th floor trying to get people out. He made it out and took refuge in a fire truck. We were listed as dead or missing.

Searching For Survivors

Captain Hugh Mulligan
Engine 236, East New York, Brooklyn

now Battalion Chief, 48 Battalion

I was off duty and 11 members met at quarters. We left East New York for Manhattan in a pickup and a volunteer chief's car. We brought all the tools and equipment that we could carry. We had masks, hooks, and oxygen cylinders. We identified ourselves as firefighters and the police let us across the Williamsburg Bridge. We drove down side streets to West Broadway and parked north of Vesey Street. We walked to Broadway and Park Row where a command post was set up.

One of the plane's engines was on Vesey Street. There was a large amount of debris on fire. Paper was swirling around. I sent the members inside 225 Broadway while I waited for an assignment. High winds made it difficult to keep your eyes open because of the dust. It took 20-30 minutes to get an assignment. As I was receiving the assignment I told the senior man to get the members. We were assigned to work with Tower Ladder 124. Their bucket was up between Building 4 and 5. Portions of these buildings were well involved. We stretched a supply line to 124 so they could operate. There was a concern about a possible collapse of one of these buildings. They shut down and moved back. That was done several times. We finally decided that operation was not netting the results we had hoped for. Together, we decided to operate with units around Tower 1 and Tower 2.

When we reached Tower 2, we broke into teams of two so we could reach more area, staying in eye and voice contact of each other. We proceeded to see if there was any access to the below-grade areas of the buildings. In between searching the members would call out to see if anybody was trapped or if they were underneath us. Firefighter Brian Harvey called out and made contact with a male. Brian, Pete Strahl, Anthony Palmentieri and I entered a hole in the vicinity behind Tower 2 and east of Tower 1. Before I went in, I told the remaining members of Engine 236 to stay outside and prepare for the removal of the victim. The entrance to this hole was complicated. There was angle iron and rebar bent inward. There was no straight access. We had to shimmy down like a reverse U.

Firefighters and USAR teams had to go down three stories and back up three stories in many areas of the pile to reach their objective.

Once inside it was pitch black. We had the victim continue to yell or call out. At various points along the route there were some areas where you had to crawl, kneel and in some areas you could stand. Without voice communication it would have been impossible to find him. We didn't have any flashlights. We thought we were in the plaza area. We worked our way through some stores. In a couple of areas, natural light came in. In the other 95% of the time, it was total darkness.

Brian Harvey made the first contact. The victim had to be 100 yards inside from where we entered. The man in his mid-40s was buried by a mountain of debris on an escalator halfway up. Brian continued to call out until all of us arrived. It was another area where there was some natural light from above. It wasn't a lot, but it was enough to see. We had to crawl up one to two stories of debris. We could see an enormous hole at the end of the escalator. It dropped off. We didn't know how far it went. The other section of escalator was gone altogether. The victim, Mr. Ardizzone, was in the only area that was left.

Brian had the most medical training when we got around the man. We discussed how we were going to remove him. He is talking. If we remove things too quickly, we might put him into shock. We took a boulder of debris off one at a time. Brian monitored the man. He was coherent and functioning. Moving at a proper pace we were methodical. We moved one boulder and monitored him. Finally he was uncovered. Brian did a quick survey to see the extent of his injuries. He had a broken leg, knee injury. We weren't sure of his back and neck. We were unsure if he had internal injuries. We kept him talking.

Now we tried to figure how we were going to remove him. Where he was located, he was sitting on a two-story pile of debris. We thought about it, we discussed it. We had no tools, sleds, nothing to stabilize him. Brian got down on all fours. We lifted and put the man on Brian's back. One person would take his head and neck. One person took the right leg, arm and right trunk. Same thing occurred with the left side. We would hold him stable while Brian crawled down the 20-foot-high pile.

Firehouse Collection

When the South Tower collapsed, some of the exterior wall laid out over the area. Almost 13 floors of wall are visible near Church Street.

In the background we could smell gas; parts of the building were deconstructing. We could hear water gushing. Once we left the pile we were going to go back into the darkness. When we eventually made it down, it took 20 minutes plus. We were all physically exhausted. If there was a spinal injury, any movement could have been fatal. We went very slowly with a minimum amount of movement. Every step Brian, Pete or Tommy took, some piece of loose gravel gave way. We were committed to go as slowly and carefully as possible. We found a clearing and we rested. We took him off Brian's back and placed him on the ground. I went back the way we came to locate an exit. I said I would be right back. I would let the other guys outside know we had a victim and we would need a Stokes basket, first-aid equipment, ropes and radios. The route was in reverse. Picking out my landmarks I returned and I told the guys inside that the equipment was coming.

Brian said the victim was not as talkative. Brian thought he was going into shock. We lifted his legs to maximize his blood flow. I went back to the original entrance with Pete. I realize we can't go out the way we came in. I went back to the guys inside. I said we don't have a way out. We have to look for another way. We both went to search and had no luck. On the way back we said we had no success in finding another way out. We discussed our options. We all agreed that we would find a new way out and not put the man through the way we came in, whatever that meant, to make sure he got out safe.

Brian said he was slipping away. The most amazing thing I saw, Pete found a damaged orange pumpkin bucket. There was a broken water pipe six to eight feet away. He reached over an opening five feet wide with a two-three-story drop with the pumpkin bucket and let the water drip into it. He then kneeled next to the man's head and wet his lips with the water. I never saw anything like that.

I knew in my heart we had to get everybody out of there. I went back to the entrance. We can't come out this way. I was going to go down and follow the wall. There was a little opening just enough for a Stokes basket to fit through. There

Todd Maisel

was a lot of rebar that was jagged and broken apart. Above us were numerous supports and beams that had to be cleared out. I knew we had a way out and they had all the equipment on the other side for us. I went back and got Pete. We went back to the spot and we looked around and above us. Can we cut the rebar and clear away the metal?

One of the firefighters outside, Steve Razickas, threw a Hurst tool down the hole and jumped in after it. We tried to figure which beams to cut. Anthony and Brian attended to the victim. All three of us agreed on which beams to cut so we wouldn't loosen anything else or create a collapse. We worked that way to get debris cleared at the new opening. Steve handled the tool the entire time, sometimes straight out in front of him. When the tool shifted, he steadied it.

Now the hole was open. We went back and brought the Stokes basket and a utility rope. We also had flashlights and a radio. A chief, Gil Frank, from the 13th Battalion was standing by outside with the remaining members of Engine 236. We loaded the victim onto the Stokes basket. We supported him as best we could with the rope that we had. We moved towards the new exit slowly and carefully. Outside they were evacuating the area around Building 7. We were made aware of it. The remaining members of 236 were waiting to receive the victim. We pushed him through. They received him and we crawled out one at a time to the outside.

Now we were in a crater that was 30 feet deep. We were looking up at the sides of the crater and we didn't have anyway to remove him. Outside, exposed to the debris, I got hit in the head by a metal beam. If we had to lift him up the side of the steep pile of debris, we didn't have enough rope to secure him. If he slipped out, he could land on his back or neck and those injuries could have been fatal. There was a lot more chatter on the radio about Building 7. Debris was still falling and we were still in a 30-foot hole.

I saw a very thin piece of metal from our location to a place that is not as high as we were. It didn't look sturdy. There was a hardhat standing with the members of Engine 236. I asked the hardhat if you throw me a rope, can you pull this basket up on this little piece of metal without it breaking? I thought we would have one try at this. The hardhat says I guarantee it. He threw us a rope and tied it to the Stokes basket. They would pull it up straight and hope that it got up there. We tied some knots and asked them if they were ready above. They pulled hand over hand until we could get him to the top of the crater. They pulled him up and out. He was brought to a triage area.

We wound up 50 yards west from where we entered originally. When we first went in, there was debris about one floor higher than the street. We were able to get out another way. We had been fortunate. Our entry and exit point had been swallowed up by shifting debris when Building 7 collapsed. We went directly to the triage area to see how the man was doing. He took a turn for the worse. He was unresponsive. They ran him out of the triage center to a hospital. We were concerned for him. Then we see people running, a commotion and a long gust of wind. It got black and people ran into the building we were in. They said Building 7 had collapsed.

We took a long break. At one point they thought there was a fire on the 26th floor of the building we were in. Some of the guys walked upstairs. There was nothing there. The members were incredible. Whatever was asked, they did. There was plenty of fire in Building 4 and 5. We got back to the firehouse between 2-3 A.M. The work that Brian, Peter and Anthony did was the reason the man is alive. The care he got from those three guys gave him every opportunity to recover from his injuries. The dozen guys from our unit knew what to anticipate, where to get the equipment, use the equipment. The victim came to our Christmas Party. Everybody was so happy to see him and his family.

Fathers

Retired Firefighter Lee Ielpi
Rescue 2, Bedford Stuyvesant, Brooklyn

I was home in Great Neck, Long Island when my son, Jonathan, called. He was working in Squad 288 and told me to turn on the TV. I saw what everybody else saw. He said they had called the dispatcher. We were on the phone for about 10 seconds when the dispatch tone went off in the background in the firehouse. It was a response to the Trade Center. I told Jonathan to be careful, then I got in the car and headed to the city. My other son, Brendan, came with me. He was assigned at the time to Ladder 110. I dropped him off at his firehouse.

Over the scanner in my car I heard the fire radio and they were talking about a collapse. It didn't make any sense. I went over the bridge and I couldn't go any further than City Hall. I saw Lieutenant Pete Lund from Rescue 2. I ran into a member who was looking for his brother.

Because of the clouds of smoke from the towers you could only see half a block. The walking wounded were coming past me. The first firefighter fatality I saw was right next to the pump panel of an engine company. Someone had placed a turnout coat over him. The North Pedestrian Bridge was down on top of several apparatus. You couldn't see into the site very well. The Hazmat was still running. I got inside and shut it down. It was now obvious that the North Tower was not there anymore.

I was looking for Jonathan. I never found anybody alive. I crawled over beams. I burned my stomach. I only had on shorts and a Rescue 2 T-shirt. As I walked past the World Financial Center, I could see gear and masks with their Vibralerts going off. The open garage doors behind the command post saved a lot of people. I outfitted myself with the gear that was there and went back out to West Street into the piles of debris and crevices.

It was hard meeting people you knew. Did you see my son, I asked. I met some brothers looking for their brothers. At Liberty Street, I met Frank Cruthers, citywide tour commander. I said to him I think we have to open up West Street. He said could you do that?

There were three construction workers standing close by. One of the workers said I heard what you were told. Do you need help, equipment? I can get it. He went with me while the two other construction workers went to get heavy machinery.

At Liberty Street, Squad 1 and Rescue 2 were parked. Rescue 2's rig was stripped of equipment and badly damaged. I said we have to get the rigs out of here and then penetrate into the pile. All of a sudden here comes the lead piece of heavy machinery. Some of the apparatus came out easy and other had to be

Every time a victim was located, be it a firefighter or a civilian, an American flag was draped over the body. A formation of first responders would stand at attention as the body was removed to an ambulance. A prayer was said and all work at the entire site would stop.

AP Photo/Louis Lanzano

Michael Rieger/FEMA News Photo

The fire burned under the pile at over 3,000 degrees Fahrenheit for several months. Firefighters working on the pile could feel the steel shift below them.

towed. I had retired in 1996. I met up with three chiefs. I let them take over. I never left West Street.

A few friends were called to go to my son's home to be with the family. I told them it wasn't looking good. When I arrived at Jonathan's house, one grandson asked if I found Daddy. I said no, but I'm still going to look. Several fathers who had retired and lost sons went to the site every day. They were all senior guys known on the job. We all stayed together. They gave us carte blanche. We were given radios and they told us go do what you have to do. We spent days and a lot of nights with each other. We got to eat and sleep together. We met up every morning. You could tell what kind of night the firefighters working that tour had. If there were smiles, they found people. There were more bad nights than good.

We split into three teams of two. We operated near the North Tower, South Tower and near the firehouse of 10 & 10. Over the handie-talkie would come we think we have a firefighter. I was hoping that they were going to find Jonathan. I wanted to be at the site when they found my son. It was December 11, three months to the day. A chief called me at home very late. He said we have Jonathan.

Brendan showed up at the house a few minutes later. He said he couldn't sleep and was going to sleep in the volunteer firehouse. Someone up there was telling him. We parked on West Street. As we walked down the roadway there was a Stokes basket on the side with an American flag over it. The firefighters started to line up on the side of the road. All work on the entire site stopped. The chief who called me, Paul Ferro, put his hands on my shoulders and said he is all there. Fire department tradition says you carry out your own. Brendan and the members of Squad 288 carried Jonathan up the hill. There was a hand salute by all of those who were there. A chaplain at the top of the hill said some words. They placed him into an ambulance and removed him to the Medical Examiner's office. I was handed Jonathan's Swiss army knife that I had given him.

The first service we had was a memorial service October 27. Jonathan had told me, if I ever got killed I want to shut down the town of Great Neck, NY. He did it twice. After Jonathan was buried I came back to the site and stayed with the other dads until mid-May.

I had spent three months and never had a problem falling asleep. Now I'm coming down to the site with a different attitude. John Vigiano only found one of his two sons that were killed. One was a police officer, the other a firefighter. None of the dads were as fortunate as me. I had recovered a whole body. The searching continued for seven or eight months. The fathers would say, hopefully today. Maybe this week. You could see the toll that is was taking on their faces. It got to a point where there were only two piles left. One father said, could we find just a little something?

Credit Card Info

Firefighter Declan Grant Ladder 48, Hunts Point, Bronx

I volunteered to go down there. There were 14 crews of six working every tour; five firemen and one officer. We were given respirators and hearing and eye protection.

The first day we got there, we got a guy. All we got was a piece of bunker gear with a bone in it, right above the knee, and it was cut at the ankle. It was all yellow and it was charred at the top right above the knee where it had been cut off, I guess. Basically, it was just like a bone inside of it. I guess the other stuff had decomposed.

We smelled it first and then we went in with hand tools and dug it out. The grappler would take a couple of scoops. Someone watched what he was pulling up and what he was dumping out in case you'd see something. A lot of times, you'd see a flash of the yellow striping on the gear. Most of the time, the grappler saw it before you did. Then he'd point and you would look through what he had. He may have seen something. Or once you got an odor, you'd stop him and you'd start hand digging.

Grapplers capable of picking up large loads such as pieces of steel were instrumental in the removal of debris and clean up of the site.

Larry Lerner/FEMA News Photo

This ramp was put in service the second day we were there, our first two days there. They hadn't tested the ramp yet, so they weren't using it. They were still using that road to bring the trucks up and down. But they could see where they were, but they couldn't get to them because they didn't want them digging around at that. There was too much of a collapse hazard.

We found parts of chairs, like the whole back of a chair or the whole seat of a chair or the wheels and the metal on the bottom. All the concrete dust was compacted and it was like clay, digging in it. So I'm digging around in it and I pull out an eyeglass case. The glasses were fine. It was like they were brand new, not a speck of dust or a crack or anything on them. And in the same area I got a lady's purse and I opened it and a calculator was on inside. Nothing in the bag was messed up. The outside of the bag was dirty, but that's about it. It was fine. I found a firefighter's radio case, but it had no markings on it.

We found Battalion 1's car. That was the first week. It was all mangled up and we uncovered a little bit of it. The tires were all mangled up and the axles. We found the license plate and the license plate frame, not a scratch on them, about 20 feet away from the car.

We also found tool boxes. I guess they belonged to guys who worked in the building, tool boxes that were completely crushed flat. Others were half crushed. You opened it up and you found a lot of that kind of stuff. One was an electrician's tool box. All the wire nuts were in it.

We found boxes of MetroCards and I found a guy's credit card. It had expired on 9/11/01, that was the expiration date on the credit card. Literally and figuratively. I thought that was creepy.

We got a civilian. We just got an odor, so we were digging and we got a pant leg first and then you start going gingerly then around. We got his belt and from just above his waist and his full left leg with a construction boot on the bottom and maybe down to just below the knee of his right leg and his wallet was still in his back pocket. We got a name off his AAA card.

When they were finding people. Every time they carried someone out, everything stopped. Every machine stopped on the site.

What happened first was this: If you were digging a person out, the chaplain would come there to whatever spot you found them. They would do a little ceremony there, just the guys, and then they would line everybody up. A lot of times they waited for a fire company to show up or a family member.

A lot of times, if they knew there were other people there, if they knew there was another body, they would bring one to a waiting area at the bottom of the ramp and they would wait until the second recovery or the third recovery was made and then they would take them all out together up the ramp. So we would all line up on the ramp and they would call over the handie-talkie, the chaplain would

Andrea Booher/FEMA News Photo

Message is written on a massive steel beam. Some of the box beams weighed 85 tons.

do another little service at the bottom of the ramp and then uncover and they do the service over the handie-talkie and recover and hand salute. Then they would carry them up to the top of the ramp and put them in an ambulance that was waiting and then you'd finish your salute and then we were dismissed.

I think we got 11 recoveries on one night tour. Seven firefighters and, I think, one was a cop and a few civilians. One of the days I was working, they recovered one EMS guy. But everyone would come, like the cops. If they knew we were doing a recovery, they would come and stand on the ramp with us.

When they took the trains out, not one pane of glass was broken on the train car. It was all charred outside. It looked like they could put it right in service the way it came out. I think there were a couple of trains. A couple of them were flattened down like pancakes. The rest of them were OK.

We found a helmet that was flattened. The whole helmet was flattened. Maybe it was an inch and a half to two inches thick, all the way from front to back, but you could make out the numbers and the company off of the frontpiece. Instead of being put on your head this way, the thing was pushed down all the way down. I don't know if you heard about the civilian they recovered. She was standing up. Her hand was coming up out of the dirt.

There was a guy inside a box beam when we found him. It was maybe a 30-, 25-foot section of beam. Here's the 25-foot, so he just fell and he was down over here. It was when it was lying flat that we saw it. I think they cut it and they moved it out of the way and we were digging through stuff. There was dirt compacted in there too. So whatever way he slid into it, he was inside there. We got wine bottles, full wine bottles, nothing wrong with them. A lot of pictures, a lot of ID cards. They told us not to keep it. They said it doesn't mean they were in the building just because the ID was there.

It was rewarding. At least I wasn't there in vain. If I didn't find anything, I would have felt like I was wasting my time. It was trying being there and just all the work we were doing. A lot of times, you got this little four-pronged rake and you were raking through stuff that was only a couple of inches thick and it just seemed absurd at times and you'd get really frustrated. And then you'd find a bone, maybe, that was only two inches long – and you knew you had to look at it like if that might be the only thing that someone has of someone. And if someone's religious, I thought it was real important because they can't have a funeral without a body part, the church won't give you a funeral without a body part. I guess most of guys all felt the same way.

We put it in a red bag and they would GPS where they found it and EMS would come and take it away. I think all those remains were going to the temporary morgue. I know when I was there someone told me they had 14,000 pieces. They were up to 17,000 the last I saw. It's probably way up higher than that now.

Grim Discoveries

Firefighter Frank Fee Rescue 1, Hells Kitchen, Manhattan

now Special Operations Command

I was off duty and responded to the scene with Paul Hashagen, Jack Flatley and Bruce Newbery — all of Rescue 1. We parked on West Street and were walking south near the Verizon building when the North Tower collapsed. I stopped to watch it come down. Paul and Jack ran north. Bruce crawled to the side of the street and was almost hit by a police car.

After the dust cleared we could see four or five people hanging out the top-floor windows of the building on the corner of Vesey and West streets (Building 6). We helped other firefighters raise ladders to scaffolding around the building. From there other portable ladders were used to reach a walkway around the building.

I made my way under the collapsed walkway. Jack had a handie-talkie. He heard Captain Al Fuentes calling for help. Eventually Jack located him under debris in the street. We climbed on the remains of the North Tower most of the day. Inside the Winter Garden we found 10 victims. Making our way to the pedestrian bridge, we located one or two people there. You couldn't get through the collapsed end.

Two firefighters were located under an engine company south of the North Pedestrian Bridge. Rescue 1's apparatus was crushed under the North Pedestrian Bridge when the North Tower came down. We continued to look for survivors. In a ravine of debris we looked for hours before Building 7 came down.

We had to run off the pile and then went back

Several people were hanging out the top-floor windows after the second collapse.

Steve Spak

The phone company (left) suffered damage after the North Tower collapsed. Note dust and debris.

after the final collapse. Exhausted, I went to sleep in a nearby building. I woke at 4 A.M. With Captain Chris King, we went to the area of the stairway where Captain Jay Jonas was located. After Rescue 2 found a woman alive, I went down the pile to get a Stokes basket. They finished packaging her and she was passed down. We had to continue to leapfrog down the pile to get her to safety. It took eight or nine guys to keep handing her off.

The pile was pretty steep and down some long beams. Some of the steel was smoking hot. Some sections were in good shape others were in real bad shape. Sometimes you could only see 10 feet through the smoke and dust. The bodies we found were heavily pinned. At one point SOC Chief Norman ordered everybody off the pile because it was shifting.

We found Captain Terry Hatton's light and officer's tool and brought them down. One firefighter crawled into a stairway. He found Lieutenant Dennis Mojica of Rescue 1. He still had a spare cylinder hanging on his shoulder with webbing. Chief Downey's car was located. There was so much debris near the driver's door we had to enter through the trunk to search the car. No one was there.

Someone found Firefighter Joe Angelini of Rescue 1 in the street. Airbags from Ladder 113 were found in the hotel where they were working to remove Lieutenant Bob Nagel from Engine 58, who was trapped after the first collapse. The bodies of three or four firefighters were located in the hotel lobby.

Talking With Jay

Deputy Chief Nick Visconti Division 14, Flushing Meadows, Queens

now retired

I was in my car listening to traffic reports and they broke in with a story that a plane just hit the World Trade Center. They're interviewing a woman who said I saw the plane and no, it was a very big plane and oh my God, the plane hit the tower. So they said yeah, we know that. She says no, no, no, another plane hit the tower. They asked if she was sure. She said I'm telling you, another plane hit the second tower.

When I got to the Whitestone Bridge, I could see that both towers were burning, burning fiercely. Cars were slowing down and stopping. When I got onto the other side of the bridge, I pulled over where the Whitestone Expressway meets the Grand Central Parkway. A bunch of cars were stopped. I looked at these towers and I thought to myself, this is the biggest fire in the fire department's history, I've got to go there.

I got back in the car and drove to the 14th Division, which was not five minutes away. I ran upstairs. Everybody was watching the television. They were asking me Chief, Chief, do you know what's going on? Yeah, I said, I'm getting my gear, I want a vehicle and if any of you guys want to come down with me, get your stuff. A couple of the off-duty aides said we'll go down with you. I started getting dressed and the office manager said there's a phone call, they're looking for any off-duty deputy chiefs. I picked up the phone. I was told Nick, we have a recall in, we need a staging area set up at Shea Stadium (in Queens). I said I want to go down to the fire, but I was told we need the staging area, we've got guys coming in, we need somebody to get control of them.

We got into the van and went over to Shea Stadium. All we had were pads and pencils and papers. We didn't have any tables. Thank God, the weather was good because we were able to set up right in the parking lot, right outside the police department office. The police department has a constant presence at Shea Stadium. They gave us access to a phone – we had been using cell phones.

Chief Nick Visconti confers with others.

Steve Spak

People started showing up, firefighters with bunker gear, firefighters with tools, firefighters with masks. They must have stopped at their firehouses. They just kept filling the parking lot and pretty soon we were going to lose control. So we set up some pads on a table and we told the guys to write their names on a pad just to record that they were there.

At that point, we were still getting phone calls. Now, I've got these guys here, what do you want me to do with them? They told me that they have buses on the way, and when they arrive, load up the buses and we'll get instructions. As they're coming in, I decide that I can't just start throwing people into a bus until it's full. We told the company officers to each take five guys, make sure you know them, write their names down on a piece of paper, and we started designating the teams as 1401, 1402, because it was the 14th Division. And we're waiting for the buses, waiting for the buses. It seemed like forever.

Five buses showed up and I started assigning people to get on the buses. I really wanted to go down to the fire. I turned to the battalion chiefs, all the guys from the 14th Division. I said listen, you've got it. I'm going to jump in one of the buses, I'm going to go down with these guys because they've got to have somebody with them.

I went to get my gear just as the buses were starting to pull out. Now I'm thinking, oh, my God, I'm going to miss the buses. Then a cop pulls up in his private car and he says Chief, do you want to go down with me? I jumped in his car. One of my aides jumped in the back seat and he took off. We got separated from the buses because of the traffic they're pushing off the highways. The highways were clear. We eventually made our way down to the ramp. I was told to get the five buses, we'll give you instructions. The instructions they gave me were to proceed over the Triborough Bridge, across 125th Street to the West Side Highway. That way is clear, take your buses down. So that's what we did.

We got to West Street and Canal and there were all kinds of vehicles all over the place. A police officer drove us as close as he could get. We jumped out and started walking down. There were other guys walking down. There were apparatus and police cars and all kinds of vehicles.

We were threading our way through and I got to that bridge near Stuyvesant High School, and (Battalion Chief) Joe Nardone was there. He had the staging area. I walked up to Joe and I said I've got five busloads of guys. He said Nick, we're holding everybody here, but they want the chiefs down at the command post. So I handed him a piece of paper. I said here's the companies or the teams we set up. I said if you want a team or you want teams, just call out 1401, they know who they are, I told them to keep their guys together.

So I walked down. (Assistant Chiefs) Frank Cruthers (citywide tour commander) and Mike Butler were there too. I asked Frank if anybody had gotten killed. And he said it's bad. We don't know where (Chief of Department) Pete (Ganci) is. We don't know where (Special Operations Command Chief) Ray Downey is. We don't know where anybody is. He said (Assistant Chief) Frank Fellini's got the operations post at West and Vesey, I want you to go down there and report in to him.

I walked down to West and Vesey. I got to Fellini and I said Frank, what's going on? He said we think Pete is dead, we think he got killed. He said to me 6 Truck is trapped. They transmitted a Mayday, find out where they are, take care of that.

I got on the radio and for lack of better terminology I said Operations to Ladder 6, Operations to Ladder 6 and (Captain) Jay (Jonas) replied. I recognized his voice and I said what's your location, we need to know your location. And he was very clear, very calm. He said Tower 1, Stairwell B… I said OK, Jay, now explain to me how to get to your location, you've got to tell me how to get there. He said you go into the main entrance of Tower 1. I swear, it was like everybody looked at each other.

I said OK, Jay, after you go through the main entrance, what do you do? He said, very matter-of-factly, you go through the glass doors. What then? Go to Stairway B. Explain to me how to get there. And I didn't hear him getting short or anything like that, but I could hear a little frustration in his voice. At some point during this conversation, somebody said where is Tower 1? I thought to myself, if anything tells him that this is more serious than he thinks, this is going to tell him, but he didn't even

Steve Spak

Heavy fire vents from an upper floor of Building 7. When the North Tower collapsed, it gouged out several floors of Building 7. Fires burned on numerous floors.

realize at the time. I said OK, Jay, we're going to get to you, hold on, just let me get people moving. I picked out five officers. I said to them pick out five guys, get their names, record them here at the command post and then I'm going to give you jobs.

I told one group to go down a side entrance on Vesey Street down into the basement, the lower level of Building 6. Then I gave other people instructions to get up on the mezzanine of Building 6. Then I sent some people over to examine the west pedestrian walkway to see if they could get through. I got these people moving. I just couldn't let Jay think that we forgot about him.

I got on the radio and I said I need to know what your status is. Are you pinned under the debris? No, we're not pinned, we're in the stairwell. I said OK. Do you have any smoke there? No, no smoke. Do you have any fire? No fire. I said all right, is anybody injured, are any of your people injured? He said no, my people seem to be fine, but there's a chief below us, we can't get to him and he's gravely injured. I could hear in his voice the 'I-can't-do-anything-for-him.' I could hear the frustration.

I remember standing there looking over at Building 7 and realizing that a big chunk of the lower floors had been taken out on the Vesey Street side. I looked up at the building and I saw smoke in it, but I really didn't see any fire. I didn't realize that there were people on the other side, on the Church Street side, who had people trying to get to Jay, that there were so many other people involved in this. During my transmissions to Jay I stopped calling him, Ladder 6, Jay, Jay, look, I'm sorry, but I got to repeat this because there was a lot of traffic. I asked him how he was doing. He said 43 Truck is here, we're going to try to get out, we'll let you know.

Now I gave him a few minutes, then I got back to him. I said what's your status? He said we're getting out, we're going to walk out of here, they're helping us. I got back to Jay. I said Jay, I've got to ask you again, are you definitely going to get out of there, is everybody going to be able to get out? Yeah, we're going to be able to get out. I said OK.

Frank Fellini said get those people out of 6. So now with the radio we were walking over to the different locations, starting to get the people out, but we were very concerned about it collapsing. I climbed up to the mezzanine. I wanted to see what it was like. I climbed in the window. I got in as far as the guys who were there. They were outside on a sort of terrace that was around it. I kept telling them come on guys, we're out of here. No, we've got to get to these guys. I said they're taken care of, get your guys out, we're concerned about this building.

A couple of minutes later, I said to Frank, 6 is taken care of, what do you want me to do? He said to me, get a group together, go on the other side of this walkway and find Pete (Ganci). Find Pete. I picked out officers. I said get five guys, report to the command post and then come with me. As I was walking around there, waiting for these guys to get squared away. I heard either there's my buddy or there's my sweetheart or something like that. It was Al Turi and he was sitting on something. I remember him sitting down and I was shocked to see him because I thought that he hadn't made it.

We started hugging and crying and stuff, and he asked me, what are you doing? I said Frank Fellini just told me to go find Pete. And Al said you've got to find him, you've got to find him. He grabbed me by the shoulders and I said OK, we'll get him, we're going to go.

We got the guys and I walked back to Fellini. I said was there a command post outside? He said yeah. He said we've got a guy here who might know where it is. He was a fireman and I don't even know who he was. I said to him do you know where the command post was? He said yeah. I said how do we get to it? Then somebody said we can go through the Winter Garden.

We started walking. It was me and, I don't know, 30 guys, 40 guys maybe. We walked with this fireman up Vesey to the side entrance. We walked through the plaza of the Winter Garden and there were two escalators there. For some reason we went up to the escalators and we walked around.

We were right in front of where World Trade Center 1 was, where this big pile of rubble was. The pedestrian walkway was on our left and I couldn't believe the amount of steel lying there. I was dumbfounded at how much there was and how it was like nothing I had ever seen, piles of it sticking out, little depressions, big, unbelievable.

I said OK, where was the command post? And he looked around. He was a little confused and I could understand because I don't think he had seen what this looked like since he escaped. And he turned around and he said I think it was over here. I asked him if Tower 2 collapsed and they came out, did you see where Ganci went? He said no, I don't know where they went. We had this line of guys that started walking. Almost immediately, we found where we could see 34 Engine and a couple of guys went over there. The first guy down said hey, I've got a couple of guys down here. When he first said that, I was praying that they were alive… And everybody went running over and he said, no, no, no, no, they're not. A couple of minutes passed by, then I said can we get them out? They answered it's going to take time. I said OK, see what you can do.

I turned to everybody else. I said we're looking for live people, guys, we're looking for live people, we can't stop here. We'll get a couple of guys for this, but spread out, we're looking for live people. So guys started looking around. We started moving and to me it felt like maybe 20 minutes or so, somebody said I've got somebody, he's got shoes on. We saw these shoes and work-duty pants, I think. Well, they were blue pants. And somebody said, I think it's Chief Ganci. I thought to myself oh, no. They were picking the stuff off of him and sure enough it was Chief of Department Ganci. We had a moment of silence before we took him out. I said everybody take off your helmet. We didn't say a prayer or anything like that. Everybody was blessing themselves, though, and Al walked him out.

I told the guys, come on guys, we've got people trapped, we're got to find live people, get moving, spread out. And bang, 15 feet away, 25 feet away tops, we found (First Deputy) Commissioner (William) Feehan. I got on the radio. I said we found Commissioner Feehan. And we did the same thing, had a moment of silence, put him in the Stokes and we took him out. I walked out with him and I brought his helmet to the command post because his helmet was really in good shape. I went back.

Again we told the guys to spread out. We started getting hits all over the place, I think there's somebody here, I think there's somebody there. And we realized that we're not getting these people out. The steel was just incredible and the sheet metal was all over the place. And it wasn't just flat. We had to walk around this mound of stuff to get to where some of these places were. The thing started to really spread out. More guys were coming in and at some point they were asking me do you need more people, do you need more people? Yeah, keep sending people. And we just had groups of people out there searching and guys were looking for voids.

Everybody was searching those voids and we realized that we had to do something. We had to mark the locations. Some guys had rags, I guess, with paint. We started painting orange arrows on the beams, pointing down where we found somebody and couldn't get to them. This went on for I don't know how long.

Now, World Trade Center 7 was burning and I was thinking to myself how come they're not trying to put this fire out? I didn't realize how much they had because my view was obstructed. All I could see was the upper floor. At some point, Frank Fellini said now we've got hundreds of guys out there, hundreds and hundreds, and that's on the West Street side alone. He said to me Nick, you've got to get those people out of there. 7 World Trade Center, imminent collapse, we've got to get those people out of there.

I was looking at the mass of people out there. There was no unit identification. I felt that I was losing control over this thing to begin with and now he was telling me to get them out of there. I was thinking, how the hell am I going to do this? There were a couple of chiefs out there who I knew and I called them individually. I said to them listen, start backing those people out, we need them back up to the command post. While this was going on, I saw individual company officers. I was whistling, Captain, bring your guys this way.

I was getting some resistance. The common thing was, hey, we've still got people here, we don't want to leave. I explained to them that we were worried about 7, that it was going to come down and we didn't want to get anybody trapped in the collapse. One comment was oh, that building is never coming down, that didn't get hit by a plane, why isn't somebody in there putting the fire out? A lot of comments, a bit of resistance, understandable resistance. I got a chief. I said stand here, if you see anybody out there, get them back. I had to get the guys away from the North Pedestrian Bridge. There were a lot of people out there.

I walked out and I got to Vesey and West, where I reported to Frank. He said we're moving the command post over this way, that building's coming down. At this point, the fire was going virtually on every floor, heavy fire and smoke... There were a couple of guys standing with me and a couple of guys right at the intersection, and we were trying to back them up – and here goes 7. It started to come down and now people were starting to run.

I said that building is not coming this way, you could see where it was going, but I was concerned about debris. I got over near a vehicle. I sheltered in there a little bit and this dust cloud of debris came up and next thing you know, silence. Guys were all right. Nobody was running, hurt or anything like that. I heard later on that somebody got trapped in the debris of 7, but I don't know.

We started searching there and I think I used 105 or another apparatus that I saw. I started in that place, spread out. I gave up hopes of forming a straight line because of the terrain. I said just start walking and searching and see if we can find anybody. And again, we found people in apparatus, people under apparatus. They were all dead. And that's how the rest of the day went until it started getting dark and then we had to get lights.

I think it was Thursday or Friday, when we had a full-fledged commitment to Tower 1, that at one point I had gotten nervous about it. I asked for a structural engineer to come in. The guy had surveyed it and said look, the sides are not that stable, but if you're on top, it should be stable, I think those guys are good up there, but he wasn't going up there to find out. Anyway, it was reassuring to me because guys were working under my control.

Joe Nardone called me on the radio. It was getting dark. He said I need an assistant chief up here to make a determination of the stability. I said Joe, am I good enough? Yeah. So I went up there. It took me 25 minutes to get up there. I was a little bit winded and I looked at Joe and I said to him there had better be an escalator on the other side. He said, no, there's no escalator, so he took me around to this location where this huge beam was. He said we think it moves a little bit and we sent people in there to check these voids and I'm concerned about it. I said we don't want somebody in there and then have them get sealed in, so we'll just stay away.

He took me around the perimeter of Tower 1. We looked around and down into this hollow and they had lights up there, and there must have been half a dozen guys, with guys backed up behind them in a straight line, working on getting people out of there. They had just found what they thought were five or six people. They were all firefighters. They were on the stairs, but there were big pieces of concrete. We had to break the concrete in some cases and they were using rebar cutters. I was just so impressed with the care and dignity that they used.

Brotherly Concern

Lieutenant Robert Ginley Engine 307, Jackson Heights, Queens

now Battalion Chief covering Battalion 3

I was on vacation on 9/11. I had a third son on September 7. My wife was to come home that morning. My brother John was working Monday night and Tuesday. He was a lieutenant in Engine 40. My brother Joe was a firefighter assigned to Ladder 19. My brother Tim was a firefighter in Engine 94. My other brother was an airplane mechanic. My father was a retired firefighter from Engine 8.

John called me and said did you see what happened? We talked for a few minutes. I asked, are you going to go? He said nothing was happening yet. Engine 40 was located on West 66th Street and Amsterdam Avenue on the Upper West Side of Manhattan. I put my son on the school bus when the second plane hit. At the hospital, I told my wife I'm going to have to go. My mother would come pick up my wife.

I drove to Engine 307 in Queens to pick up my gear. All the units in the 14th Division located in Northern Queens were to meet at the parking lot of Shea Stadium where the New York Mets play. I contacted my brothers while I was at Shea. I called Engine 40 to see what time the company had been dispatched to the Trade Center. They gave me the wrong time. They told me 20 minutes later than they actually responded.

I thought John was down at the scene because he was working. My other two brothers were not. It was decided that we would meet in the Bronx and we would go to the scene ourselves. We went down the West Side Highway. Everything had collapsed. At Vesey and West streets we found the off-duty members of Engine 40 and Ladder 35 who are quartered together.

After working for awhile, we started to look for rigs. Engine 40 was located. It didn't look good. Voids were searched. After 6 A.M. we left the site and went to John's house to talk with his wife. We saw his children. His wife was pretty upset. I said let's hold out hope. The fire department takes care of its own.

The brothers went back together and alone. Engine 40 was observed on a video going into the area of the southeast corner of the complex near Liberty and Church streets. Areas underground and in the subway and plaza were searched. A ramp was put in to facilitate the movement of debris from the site. A probationary member of Engine 40 was found near the ramp several months earlier. The thought was the rest of the company would be under the ramp area. That area wasn't searched until spring.

David Handschuh

A civilian carries an office chair over his head to protect himself from falling debris. He follows firefighters west toward Engine 10/ Ladder 10. The South Tower is just above his chair. Note the debris in the street.

A memorial service was held in Warwick, NY in October. John was found March 19, 2002. I told those in charge as soon as you know give me a call. I went to the site with my father and brothers. Tim was activated in the U.S. Air Force. John was carried from the site. Everything stopped as the family and members of Engine 40 and Ladder 35 carried John up the ramp. John was pretty much intact. He had his gear on.

All the other members of Engine 40 and one other were recovered that night. Whoever else was missing was recovered the next day. They only found a bone from one of the members of Ladder 35. They were supposed to be going upstairs in the South Tower.

John had a little less than 15 years service. My parents were in Korea on 9/11. It took them a week to get back. The family was thinking of running in the Tunnel to Towers run this year. Tim is now a lieutenant in Engine 76. Joe is a lieutenant in Ladder 59. As a firefighting family, we know the job and the danger. John did what he had to do. We didn't expect anything less. I took John's shoes out of Engine 40. We both wore the same size. I wore them until they fell apart.

Executive Order

Retired Firefighter Bob Beckwith Ladder 164, Douglaston, Queens

My grandson was hit by a car on 9/11, so I was busy with him. After he was OK, I wanted to go down to the site. Everybody said you're too old; leave it for the young guys. I found out that the son of past Union President Jimmy Boyle was missing. I was a battalion delegate while Jimmy was president. I knew I had to go down there.

I got up early in the morning of September 14, and set off from Long Island. All the bridges and tunnels were closed. The Williamsburg Bridge was blocked off. I saw a police car and a van, so I pulled behind them and followed them over the bridge and no one stopped me. I parked near Engine 55 in Little Italy. They had lost four members. I told them I was going to Ground Zero. They said good luck.

I was walking with my helmet and came upon several police officers. I talked with them and they said talk to the next group down the street. They let me through. I was stopped next by the National Guard. They said no one is getting in. I told them I was late in meeting another group of firefighters and they let me in.

I came upon the mess and saw the bucket brigade. I started at the bottom and started feeding them buckets for a few hours. I finally saw a few guys I had worked with and they said come on, we are going to get something to eat. We went over near the American Express Building and chowed down. After we were finished they were passing out masks and goggles. I came out and went to work to Vesey and West streets. This was near the North Tower. A fellow had put down a shovel so I picked it up.

I went back to the South Tower, but they didn't need any help. I went back up to the North Tower and they had found Engine 76 in the rubble. A crane lifted it out into the street. Guys were looking for the chauffeur of one of the rigs. The police had dogs searching the area. We dug a little bit. The steelworkers were doing a good job.

I heard that President Bush was coming to the site. They continued to search the area for the missing member. They still haven't located the guy. I heard the President had arrived. I put my shovel down and went out into the street. Engine 76 was in the street. About 30 feet away was a tent that housed a command post. There were numerous microphones in front of the tent. I jumped on the damaged rig and thought I had a great spot.

As the President was walking up the street, a guy comes over next to me and asks if the rig is safe. I figured he was Secret Service. I said yes. He said prove it! So, I jumped up and down and up and down. The guy said someone important is coming over. You help him up and then you get down. I stayed there and I figured it was a politician. Do as you are told. Help him up and get down.

The President was still shaking hands as he walked up West Street. He was headed to the command post when he made a hard right and came right towards me. He put his hand up. It was only a 10-by-10-foot spot. I said you OK? He said yes. I started to get down and he said where are you going? I said I was told to get down. No, no, you stay right here. He put his arm around my shoulder. Someone handed him a bullhorn. He was talking to his right. The steelworkers and firefighters on his left yelled that they couldn't hear him. He said I can hear you and those who did this will hear from all of us shortly!

[New York] Governor [George] Pataki picked me up and placed me in the street afterwards. I said you are going to hurt yourself! and he said no, I am a big guy.

We lost a lot of guys. It was a real shame. They never did find Jimmy Boyle's son.

President George W. Bush and retired firefighter Bob Beckwith stand on the remains of Engine 76 during the president's famous speech a few days after the terrorist attack.

FACT

343 LINE-OF-DUTY DEATHS
equal an estimated
4,400
YEARS OF SERVICE

AP Photo/Doug Mills

Profitable Search

Firefighter Paul Somin Rescue 2, Bedford Stuyvesant, Brooklyn

now Lieutenant Rescue 2

I was off duty on 9/11 and came back to Rescue 2. We commandeered a city bus across from the firehouse, which took us all the way to the scene. We were enroute when the second tower fell. A few firefighters started to dig out our rig, which was covered in debris. Several others went towards Jay Jonas to see if they could find him.

Rescue 2 had responded through the Brooklyn-Battery Tunnel. Half of the firefighters stayed the night and the rest of us left and returned to the firehouse at 6 A.M. Lieutenant Larry Grey conferred with the guys. We decided to go to the area where Captain Jay Jonas of Ladder 6 had survived in the stairwell. If anybody could survive, we thought it might be in that area.

We had Sawzalls, extra batteries, we were loaded with equipment. It took an hour to climb up. We had eight members, all from Rescue 2. As we were going up an I-beam and over steel, a chief said don't go. He saw it was Rescue 2 and said go do what you want to do.

We were going to start looking in voids that were everywhere. Fires were burning underneath. Visibility was OK. Amazingly, we got inside a stairwell that had a few floors intact and found an adjacent elevator shaft. We noted a sign that said 13th floor. I started yelling, hello, hello. I heard a faint voice answering back. I thought it was someone from the firehouse messing around.

I still could hear the voice. We proceeded up the stairs as far as we could go. The voice was fainter. So we went back down. I said my name is Paul. Everything looked the same, so blended in. I said can you stick your hand out. Out came a hand.

A woman was pinned in debris so loaded with dust. She was swollen, she was a tiny girl. Lieutanant Grey said my big mouth finally came in handy. Lieutenant Grey radioed that we found a victim trapped in the rubble. People cheered. Sheet metal, light metal and dust was covering her. It took about 45 minutes to extricate her.

A Stokes basket was brought up close to our position. Her right calf was crushed. After we got her out, she said thank you. She had been working on the 64th floor. She said she fell about 13 floors and lived for 26 hours after the collapse. As soon as she was packaged, we were energized.

Climbing around there were some hairy spots. We marked them as we went with spray paint. We found more than five firefighters who were deceased. We looked around for 10 hours seeing civilians and firefighters who had been killed. In the area of the North Tower we found apparatus crushed.

After a week of searching, we realized it was going from a rescue to a recovery. We didn't think that the woman was the last one to survive. Everything was pulverized. There wasn't any glass. We searched the subways and voids in the pit. The woman survived because Jay Jonas survived. If he hadn't survived, we wouldn't have gone to that area.

Early in the morning of September 12, members of Rescue 2 took one hour to climb to the top of the pile, looking for survivors.

Firehouse Collection

A Rewarding Feeling

Firefighter Mike Fenick
Ladder 48, Hunts Point, Bronx

There were 14 teams of six guys each, on each tour. There were Bronx guys, Brooklyn guys, Harlem guys. We worked with our same team every night. You would get either the transfer station where the excavator would shake out debris in front of you or then you would go through the pit with the rake. They told us to look for any kind of clothing, body parts, of course, and it's common sense, purses and anything that could be related to a human being. We found handbags, attache cases, small bones, sports bags, some clothing, some shoes and sneakers. No fire tools. A couple of radios we found smashed up. We could not tell where they were from. As far as recognizable debris, most of it was pretty crushed. You would find a lot of books. One area was filled with books. It must have been in the library.

When you found a body, usually you could smell it. You would also get a lot of smells and there would be nothing around. If you got by a body, you were going to smell it first.

We used rakes and rebar cutters. It could be difficult. Some of them took quite a while. We had a sifter. They were pouring buckets of dirt into that sifter, sifting it out, finding a lot of bone fragments in there. I did some torch work. That's about it as far as tools. They had a tool shack at 10 & 10 and you would just say send me this or that and the guy would come zipping down.

Somebody said there was like 80 bodies in March. I don't know if that's true or not, 80 bodies they found. I would say close to it. I thought it was more like 50 firemen. Well, it could have been other people, too. There were civilians. Some of them they couldn't identify.

When we did find a firefighter, it was time out, shut down all the machines. Everything shut down. Get the M.E. (medical examiner) down there, the chaplain down there.

The chaplain would say a prayer right over the body. There was a process with the M.E. He would tell you what to do and he would check all the I.D. Then they put the person in the bag, put the American flag over it and put them in the Stokes. Everybody lined up on the ramp, then they would have an honor guard. Guys took a position all the way up on either side and the ambulance was waiting at the top. I think they found nine guys in one day. They took them up three at a time or two at a time.

When we would found a body it's not a happy feeling. It's a rewarding feeling. I know it's a hard emotion to put a finger on. It's nothing to be happy about. But very rewarding.

Most of the guys were volunteers. It seemed like most had at least 10 years and over that I saw down there. The young guys I think were ordered. You could tell who wanted to be there.

September 15, 2001 – the sun streams through the dust over the wreckage of the World Trade Center.

Andrea Booher/FEMA News Photo

Firefighters remarked that at night they could see the lights of the buried apparatus in the debris below. PASS devices going off from airpacks in the debris field were audible.

Michael Rieger/FEMA News Photo

The same process continued, with the M.E. and the chaplain, and then getting the remains boxed up and bringing them out. Sometimes, they would stage them in an area and wait for the company to come. Everything was pretty much shut down. A couple of times, the fathers came down. I saw a wife go down there one time. We had a bunch of women.

Commissioner (Nicholas) Scoppetta led the procession. He would walk in the front with the chaplains and chiefs. And the guys would carry. A construction worker said something about what do you do with the civilians? We told them that we have an honor guard for the civilians when the construction workers carried them out, which I thought was nice.

Everything shut down. They would stop every five minutes if they had to. If they found two guys, that's two recoveries. Then they would carry them up two or three at a time. If they found one, stop everything, honor guard, go back to work. Five minutes later find another one, stop everything.

I was there when they removed the two train cars. They put them on a big flatbed lowboy and drove them up the new ramp. They were both in good shape.

Down in the "bathtub," there were some good cracks. There was some pretty good water seepage here and there. The biggest piece of glass I saw was about two feet by two feet. They must have came from the bottom of the South Tower. Then some big chunks of concrete came out of that too after a while.

One strange thing was we found a bag, an attache. It had the newspaper on September 11, the morning the planes hit.

Most of the time the weather was good, a couple of cold nights. We had a couple of wet nights, a couple of rainy days. Those weren't too bad. There was plenty of rain gear to be had.

We ate in that tent across the street. They had a little area you could take a nap. You could take a shower. They had bathrooms. You could wash up, brush your teeth, eat. We got in there together to chitchat, have something to eat, gather, meet. It was nice. They had lots of volunteers all over the place – what do you guys need, can I get it, do you need this, do you need that?

It was very rewarding, probably the most rewarding thing I've done on this job. The guys going off told us we were going to have a good month. They didn't find much. They were very disappointed. I kind of felt sorry for them. They were full of good advice, pace yourself. They all gave us their lockers with locks and everything. They knew that when they dug up that road, that that's where everybody would be.

FACT

FDNY / EMS RESPONSE

14 ALS, 51 BLS, 2 MERVS

24 OF 31 SUPERVISORS

15 OF 17 CHIEFS

Search & Rescue Operations

When the two 110-story towers of the World Trade Center collapsed, they prompted the largest response of rescuers in the history of the City of New York. Tens of thousands of firefighters, police officers, medical personnel and others immediately recognized the enormity of the calamity that had just occurred and set out to help. Some of these responders worked within the incident command system and sent resources that were specifically requested, while others took it upon themselves to respond on their own. This is the story of how they worked in the wake of the collapses.

By John Norman, Retired Chief of Special Operations, FDNY

Federal USAR teams that responded to the WTC 9/11/01 in three phases:

PA-TF1
MA-TF-1
OH-TF1
IN-TF1
CA-TF1
CA-TF6
CA-TF7
MO-TF1

FL-TF1
FL-TF2
TX-TF1
UT-TF1
AZ-TF1
CA-TF3
WA-TF1
CA-TF8
Co-TF1

NE-TF1
NV-TF1
CA-TF4

Andrea Booher/FEMA News Photo

Michael Rieger/FEMA News Photo

(previous page) A USAR team member and his dog search the rubble. A New Jersey State USAR TF responded.

(above) Members from Salt Lake City, UT, operate near Ladder 79 from Staten Island.

When the planes first struck the towers, the initial response included New York City units and Port Authority of New York and New Jersey Police, as well as several units from the Jersey City (NJ) Fire Department that were part of a mutual aid request by the Port Authority. After the collapses, and the massive response by additional New York City units and off-duty personnel, mutual aid fire units were requested from surrounding counties on both sides of the Hudson River to fill in at vacated NYC stations. These units were often augmented by recalled NYC firefighters from those houses who were familiar with the streets and buildings in the area they were working. EMS units from throughout the region responded to a disaster plan request and were staged on West Street in the vicinity of the Chelsea Piers, approximately two miles north of the disaster site.

When the two 1,350-foot-tall towers collapsed, the debris was flung outward for hundreds of feet in all directions, creating a devastation zone that covered more than 16 acres. Huge chunks of red-hot steel struck numerous nearby buildings, sparking fires in several of them. One of these fires resulted in the later collapse of 7 World Trade Center, which spread the destruction even farther to the north. The scale of the disaster had overwhelmed local resources in several key areas.

One of the first requests for out-of-town assistance was to the Federal Emergency Management Agency (FEMA). Four Urban Search and Rescue (USAR) Task Forces as well as Disaster Medical Assistance Teams (DMAT) and Disaster Mortuary Teams (DMORT) were all requested almost immediately. Eventually, 20 USAR Task Forces would operate at the scene or provide coverage for New York City while its resources were committed to the disaster site. Most of the responders enroute to the incident initially had hopes of being able to do what they were trained to do: save lives, in spite of the obviously catastrophic nature of the fires and collapses. The unfortunate reality of the event, however, was that only the DMORT would be able to practice their specialty.

Andrea Booher/FEMA News Photo

Andrea Booher/FEMA News Photo

Andrea Booher/FEMA News Photo

(above left) California Task Force takes a break on the pile.

(top right) Sacramento USAR members review information at a workstation in the pile.

(above) California TF3 works in the middle of what was the plaza.

The first priority after the collapse was removal of those injured who were lightly buried, while seeking information on the location of survivors deeper in the debris piles. Since the tower below the aircraft impact sites had been nearly evacuated prior to the collapses, the majority of the serious injuries from the collapses were to emergency responders. The walking wounded helped each other from the immediate danger area, while subsequent waves of responders moved into the burning debris piles that were all that remained of dozens of buildings.

Numerous Mayday messages were received from personnel trapped in the collapse zone, including survivors such as Ladder 6 Captain Jay Jonas and the other personnel trapped in the remnants of a staircase in what was left of the North Tower. These early rescues gave hope that many others would soon be removed from the scene. The WTC complex consisted of 16 acres of buildings ranging from the "low-rise" nine-story plaza buildings, to the 47-story 7 World Trade Center, to the twin 110-story towers. Other buildings that were seriously affected ranged from three to 50 stories. All of them would have to be searched.

Thousands of firefighters and other responders plunged into the remains of these structures, searching every accessible void, but finding very few live victims. By the end of the first 24 hours, what would turn out to be the last survivor in the WTC complex itself was pulled from the wreckage, although this would not be obvious at the time. The dead were removed if they could be brought out easily at this stage; otherwise they were left in place while searchers pressed on looking for survivors. The locations of the bodies were marked and recorded for later retrieval as additional resources became available. Many of these victims were pinned by hundreds of tons of steel and concrete and would require months of work with heavy equipment in order to be freed.

The relatively low number of serious injuries compared to deaths was the result of a clear demarcation line between death and survival that existed wherever the steel ended. If one was caught inside this line when the collapses occurred, survival was almost impossible; the falling steel crushed everything in its path. Just feet outside this collapse zone, survival was very likely, although the chronic effects from inhaling the pulverized concrete, asbestos and other materials from the falling buildings is still claiming the lives of those whose lungs were pumped full of this toxic mix.

By the time most of the out-of-town resources arrived on scene and began to be deployed, the accessible void spaces where survival was possible within the complex had been searched over and over again, as firefighters and police officers crawled through every nook and cranny, exposing themselves repeatedly to extreme conditions of heat, smoke, dust and falling objects. That did not mean the task was complete, however. Much more work remained to be done.

One of the first tasks that was undertaken by these units was a systematic search of all the immediately surrounding buildings that had suffered either fire or impact damage. More than 30 high-rise buildings, including some up to 50 stories high, needed to be totally searched, from sub-cellar to roof, including all elevators, and building terraces and setbacks, looking for people who might be trapped.

All of these buildings were without power as a

Andrea Booher/FEMA News Photo

Michael Rieger/FEMA News Photo

The Washington State team resports for duty.

result of the failure of the electrical grid after the collapses. That meant that teams of rescuers comprised of FDNY and FEMA USAR personnel as well as NYPD and Port Authority Police would have to walk every last inch of each building, opening every door to ensure no one was overlooked. This effort paid off in at least one case when a team led by the Ohio USAR Task Force located an elderly woman who had been injured by flying debris in her apartment several blocks from the epicenter of the disaster and who was unable to move or call for help. Telephone service, including cell phones, was disrupted by the collapses as well.

A virtual army of rescue personnel descended on the pile, working hand in hand with construction trades such as ironworkers and operating engineers, trying to uncover additional void spaces in the hopes that other survivors might be located. As each massive steel box beam was raised, the area below was examined for signs of life. If a new void was exposed, it was soon entered. The situation was compounded by a large number of unsolicited volunteers who had managed to enter the disaster site

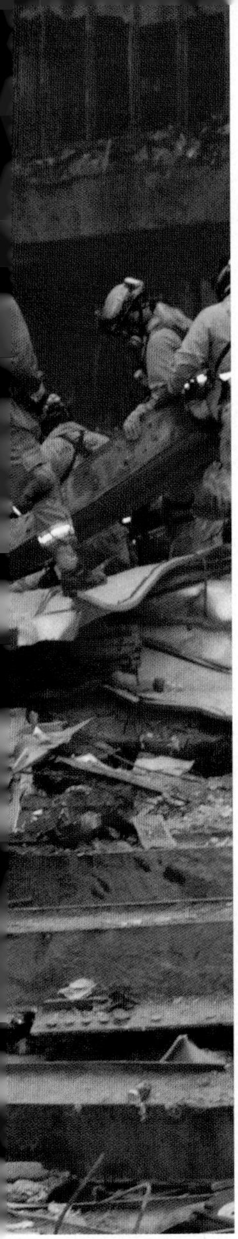

Michael Rieger/FEMA News Photo

Michael Rieger/FEMA News Photo

Michael Rieger/FEMA News Photo

(above left) USAR teams cut up steel sections.

(above middle) Members look to search possible voids.

(above right) Colorado team discusses next move.

Michael Rieger/FEMA News Photo

(left) Miami-Dade team enters void.

Andrea Booher/FEMA News Photo

After making searches and examinations of the structure, USAR teams leave markings on windows.

(above) The team from San Diego County traverses heavy steel.

and were operating outside the incident command system, venturing into areas that had been placed off limits, searching meaninglessly through areas that had already been searched three or four times.

Rescue operations continued in this fashion for a total of 18 days before it became clear that there would be no more survivors. At that point, the risks that rescuers were taking were no longer justified: there was no point in risking death or serious injury to recover a body, though the decision was a heart-rending one. The safety record, however, bears out the decision: in the nine months after the attack, while rescue and recovery operations took place in some of the most dangerous conditions ever seen, no further deaths occurred and only three firefighters and a handful of construction workers suffered injuries that required even overnight hospitalization. Truly a great testament to the thousands of workers who spent tens of thousands of man-hours digging through the 150-foot-deep mountains of steel, concrete and debris in order to provide dignity for the 2,752 people killed in the cowardly attack.

Damaged Rigs

The FDNY has well over 2,000 vehicles in its fleet. Numerous engines, tractor-trailer aerial ladders, rear-mount aerials and tower ladders that were parked close to the towers were destroyed in the two main collapses. A wide variety of special units, chiefs cars and EMS units were also destroyed. Cost of replacement was approximately $50 million. Tools and equipment to re-equip damaged or destroyed hand tools, power saws and airmasks cost another $8 million. Apparatus was ordered and/or donated to replace the units lost. Many of the rigs caught fire or were flattened because of the falling steel. Several rigs were found 30 to 40 feet below the ground close to the original towers.

The only recognizable piece on the apparatus is a discharge pipe on this pumper.

Firehouse Collection

93 FDNY Apparatus Were Destroyed At The World Trade Center On September 11, 2001

- 15 PUMPERS
- 7 REAR MOUNTS
- 4 TILLERS
- 4 TOWERS
- 2 RESCUES
- 7 MISC. UNITS
- 3 HAZMAT TENDERS
- 2 SHOP TRUCKS
- 5 AMBULANCES
- 17 SUBURBANS
- 24 SEDANS
- 3 RESCUE PUMPERS

Burned cab of an engine.

Burned engine on Vesey Street.

Crushed cab of Ladder 101, tractor-trailer aerial ladder.

AP Photo/Kathy Willens

Tower Ladder 18 removed from rubble by crane.

Todd Maisel

The North Pedestrian Bridge collapsed on top of Rescue 1. The complete view of the devastation on West Street was blocked by the collapsed bridge.

Ladder 3's 100-foot aerial ladder after being hit by the collapse of the North Tower.

Donated Rigs

Pieces of first-line apparatus often take up to a year to deliver from manufacturers. Almost 100 pieces of apparatus and cars were needed. Special units were using spare rigs until replacements could arrive. The gravity of the World Trade Center tragedy moved many big businesses, states and corporations to donate cars, vans and apparatus to the FDNY. There were two unusual cases. The State of Oklahoma presented a rescue rig in honor of the Urban Search and Rescue Task Force that had responded to Oklahoma City in 1994 to operate at the Murrah Federal Building after the terrorist bombing. The City of Columbia, SC, donated a 100-foot tractor-trailer aerial ladder, returning a favor from 1865. During the Civil War, in General Sherman's "March to the Sea," his army destroyed everything in its path. The FDNY donated a piece of fire apparatus to the city. The piece was lost at sea in a storm. Another piece of apparatus was sent to help Columbia recover after the Civil War. Columbia returned the favor 136 years later.

Jack Calderone

141 Apparatus Donated to FDNY after September 11, 2001

- 4 AMBULANCES
- 5 ATVs
- 1 HAZMAT TRUCK
- 10 ENGINES
- 1 REAR MOUNT AERIAL
- 3 RESCUES
- 5 STEP VANS
- 1 TILLER AERIAL LADDER
- 4 TOWER LADDERS
- 18 SUVs
- 21 VANS
- 68 SUPPORT VEHICLES

All photos by
Jack Calderone

Collapse Rescue 3 tractor donated by GMC.

A total of 93 FDNY vehicles, with an estimated (2001) replacement cost of $50 million, were destroyed as a result of the attack on the World Trade Center. Most of the damage resulted from apparatus being struck or crushed by heavy debris and structural components during the collapses. Some apparatus were overturned by the displaced air as the buildings collapsed. Other apparatus sustained fire damage, likely from the burning jet fuel spreading as the towers came down. Many apparatus were reduced to barely recognizable twisted, crushed or burned-out hulks as a result. Two apparatus were so badly damaged that they could only be identified by the serial numbers on their axles.

The toll of apparatus destroyed included fifteen pumpers, three rescue-pumpers, seven rear-mounts, four tillers, four towers, two heavy rescues, two high-rise units, a tactical support unit, three haz-mat tenders, the technical response vehicle, a satellite hose wagon, a field communications van, a mask service truck, five ambulances, seventeen suburbans, twenty-four sedans and two shop trucks.

Initially, spare apparatus were assigned to units having wrecked apparatus wherever possible. Scheduled pending delivery of new apparatus was sped up. Emergency purchases were made immediately of demonstrator units available from various manufacturers and emergency purchase orders were placed for the bulk of the replacement apparatus.

Following the attack, patriotism ran high and many groups and organizations throughout the United States looked for ways to help New York City in general and specifically the FDNY. One of the ways this took place was the donation of specific apparatus. A total of 141 vehicles, a trailer, and 4 chassis were donated to FDNY.

Body donated by GMC, chassis donated by Mack.

Kenworth Hazmat Unit donated by Pierce.

Decon Support donated by Ferrara.

Rescue Truck donated by the State of Oklaho

Engine donated by Ferrara.

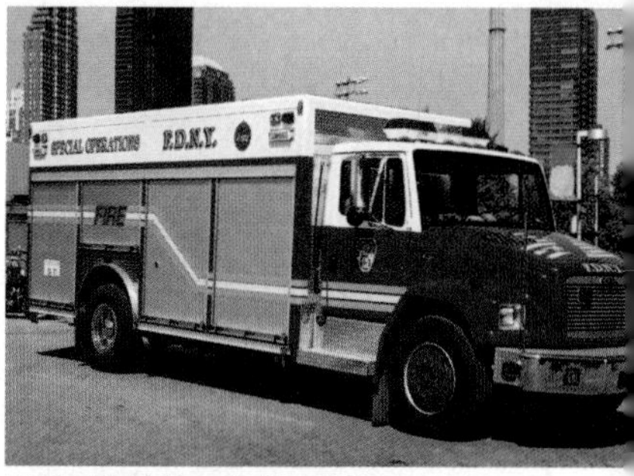

Utility Unit donated by E-One.

Ladder 10/Squad 61

Squad 61. Seagrave Corporation employees donated the artwork.

After Ladder 10's rig was destroyed, this model was delivered. Seagrave Corporation donated the artwork.

Specialized Rigs

By Battalion Chief Jack Calderone

Battalion 22

The terrorist attacks of September 11, 2001, destroyed a large portion of the FDNY's special operations capabilities. More than 90 of the firefighters and officers killed that day were trained technicians assigned to rescue, squad and hazmat units. Many more would subsequently retire as a result of that day. Scores of special apparatus were also destroyed when the towers collapsed.

In the weeks and months that followed, the department identified potential areas of concern in the event of future terrorist attacks, considering the likely potential of multiple, simultaneous incidents. This planning was coupled with an all-hazards approach to deal with natural disasters as well as terrorist incidents. Among the factors considered was the ability to handle multiple, simultaneous large-scale incidents by having each borough capable of sustaining operations independently, as much as possible, without relying on the response of special units from other boroughs. In an effort to rebuild the department with greater special-operations capabilities, extensive training, procurement of tools and equipment and the acquisition of many new apparatus were required.

To accomplish this, units were selected and trained in specific specialty areas and many new special apparatus were acquired. To ensure the optimal availability and distribution of resources, a tiered response system of layered response grades of incrementally higher levels of specialized capabilities was established. This allows for the deployment of an appropriate mix of special units, while simultaneously maintaining adequate capabilities to manage additional incidents citywide. Existing engine and ladder companies, as well as EMS units, took on additional functions and designations, and specialized vehicles were acquired, providing capabilities that did not exist prior to the attacks.

Some of the results of these efforts follow:

Decontamination (Decon) Engines – Twenty-five engine companies have been trained to the hazmat operations level as well as in specialized decontamination. Their purpose is to support hazmat operations and to perform decontamination for responders and exposed civilians. Level B suits, a tent and decontamination equipment are carried in the associated ladder company's rapid response vehicle.

Special Operations Command (SOC) Support Ladders – Twenty-five ladder companies are trained to the Hazmat Technician I level and are equipped with Level A and B suits, meters, mitigation material and limited technical rescue equipment. They are also trained to initiate and support technical rescue operations. This equipment is carried in a utility truck designated as a Rapid Response Vehicle. When assigned as an SOC Support Ladder, the unit responds with both apparatus. During severe storms, or other situations where demand for services increases, these units can be staffed independently to respond to specific incidents. The SOC Support Ladder Rapid Response Vehicles are 2001 Ford/Knapheide utility trucks.

Decon Shower Units – Prior to 9/11, there was one tractor-drawn decontamination unit. During 2003, two tractor-drawn decontamination units, built by Advanced Containment Systems and pulled by 2002 Freightliner tractors, were assigned to Engines 37 in Manhattan and 283 in Brooklyn. They have the ability to process more than 250 people per hour.

Three smaller decontamination units were delivered by Ferrara in 2006, built on Mack chassis. These units are assigned to Engines 4 in Manhattan, 160 on Staten Island and 251 in Queens.

Decon Special Event Units – Two 2006 Kubota ATVs are outfitted with RKO skids having high-pressure pumps, 70-gallon water tanks, five-gallon foam tanks and booster reels. They are deployed to special events where the potential exists for a large number of people to be exposed in an attack and in need of decontamination.

Chemical Protective Ladder Companies (CPC) – Twenty-nine ladder companies are designated CPC and have received specialized training and are equipped with Level A and B suits, antidote kits, detection equipment, patient removal equipment and other specialized equipment. Their function is search, rescue and removal of exposed victims and administering antidotes. These units are also designated Ventilation Support Units and are equipped with high-volume, positive-pressure fans. They are assigned Rapid Response Vehicles (like the SOC Support Ladders) and can also be staffed and respond independently as needed. These rapid response vehicles are 2001 and 2008 Ford/Knapheide utility trucks.

Collapse Rescues – At the time of the attack, there was a single collapse rescue apparatus quartered at Rescue 3. Each rescue company is now assigned a collapse rescue truck. These apparatus carry cribbing, shoring, air shores, trench and hydraulic jacks, saws, carpentry tools, nail guns, concrete-cutting chain saw, air compressor, air knife, surveying transit, ultra-sound listening device, fiber-optic search probe and camera, pavement breaker, welder, dewatering pumps, exothermic torch and a hydraulic tool system. Collapse Rescues 1, 2 and 4 are assigned 2005 Mack/Ferrara apparatus, while Collapse Rescues 3 and 5 have 2009 Spartan/Ferrara apparatus. Collapse Rescues 1, 2 and 4 are quartered with SOC Support Ladder Companies located near the associated rescue company.

Instead of one collapse unit citywide, there are now five – one in each borough.

Jack Calderone

Air Compressor Truck – A 2005 Ford/Reading is equipped with a 250-cfm air compressor, two reels having 100 feet of air hose each, pavement breakers, heavy demolition equipment and flexible and rigid tubes for use with vacuum trucks at trench rescues. It is staffed by one firefighter.

Portable-On-Demand (POD) – There are two 2004 Mack roll-off units and 10 pre-loaded containers of shoring material and collapse equipment. One unit is kept at the Fire Academy, while the other is quartered with Ladder 79 on Staten Island. Both have loaded containers attached. The other eight containers are strategically positioned at facilities throughout the city. Once a container is dropped at an operation, the transport truck will respond to the location of the next nearest container, load it and respond back to the scene.

Mobile Command Centers – At the time of the 9/11 attack, the department operated a tractor-drawn mobile command center. In 2004, two 40-foot Freightliner/LDV units were delivered and assigned to Engines 93 in Manhattan and 233 in Brooklyn. These units respond to third alarms and collapse operations and on special-called assignments. They are staffed by the host engine company. They are equipped with 42-foot camera masts, generator, light towers, televisions, cameras, weather stations, computers, phones and conference areas.

Mobile Operations Center (MOC) – This unit, a 2007 Freightliner/LDV, is a smaller version of the Mobile Command Center and is quartered at Engine 207 in Brooklyn. It is primarily used at special events.

Hazmat Engines – To supplement existing Hazmat Technician Units (squads and rescues), four hazmat engines have been designated and trained. In addition to their normal responsibilities as engine companies, Engines 44 in Manhattan, 165 on Staten Island, 250 in Brooklyn and 274 in Queens are each trained to the Hazmat Technician II level. Level A suits are carried on the pumper. Each company is also assigned a Hazmat Tender that carries Level B suits, absorbent material, drum and leak sealing kits, plugs and wedges, off-loading pump, grounding cables, over-pack drums, meters, non-sparking tools and other assorted hazmat equipment. Engines 44 and 165 have 2004 Freightliner/Utilimaster/LDV hazmat tenders, while Engines 250 and 274 have similar 2005 models.

Dry Chemical Rigs – Prior to the terrorist attacks, there were two dry chemical apparatus in service at Engines 228 and 229, both in Brooklyn. Four additional units were acquired in 2006. They are Ford chassis with 1,000-pound Ansul skids. They are assigned to Engines 33 and 84 in Manhattan, 163 on Staten Island and 326 in Queens.

Rebreather Units – Two 2006 Freightliner/Utilimaster/LDV trucks, each carrying 36 Dräger closed-circuit breathing apparatus, 36 extra oxygen cylinders and scrubbers, freezers to maintain ice blocks and a mask recharging station, were placed into service at SOC Headquarters on Roosevelt Island and at Ladder 20 in Manhattan. These four-hour masks were acquired to extend operating capabilities at subway and underwater tunnel operations. SOC units, as well as SOC support ladder companies, hazmat engines and selected battalions are trained to use these masks.

Planning Vehicle – This vehicle is used by the Incident Management Team (IMT) and/or Planning Chief at major operations. The vehicle is a 2006 Freightliner/Utilimaster outfitted by LDV. It contains a briefing area, data processing area, kitchen, toilet, GIS/reproduction area, two-position operating area, generator, phones, radios, television and image-projection capability.

Command Tactical Unit – This unit operates as a mobile component of the Fire Department Operations Center (FDOC) and is staffed by a firefighter and lieutenant. It responds on all multiple alarms and large-scale emergency operations to furnish the incident commander with on-scene images, video, maps, floor plans, building information and data received from the FDOC while transmitting real-time images back to the FDOC. The apparatus is a 2002 Ford Econoline former Bureau of Fire Investigation surveillance vehicle.

Fire Department Operations Center (FDOC) – Known as the *War Room*, the FDOC is staffed by both fire and EMS personnel. It tracks citywide resources, monitors multiple radio networks and can access maps, building diagrams, photos, building data, floor plans, satellite images, multiple databases of other agencies, live feeds from news media helicopters and other sources to provide information to on-scene incident commanders.

Incident Management Team (IMT) – Approximately 120 members have been trained to national standards to operate as a Type II Incident Management Team. They have been deployed outside the City several times for major national incidents and are used to manage major planned events in the City.

Many of these units are pre-designated to operate as part of specific task forces such as Technical Decon Task Forces, Collapse Task Forces and Rescue Medical Task Forces, to expedite the assignment of specific resources to an incident.

While the terrorist attacks of 2001 took a tremendous toll, decimating the department, these new initiatives and others have helped to currently position the department to deal with future threats and incidents.

One of two Mobile Command Centers citywide.

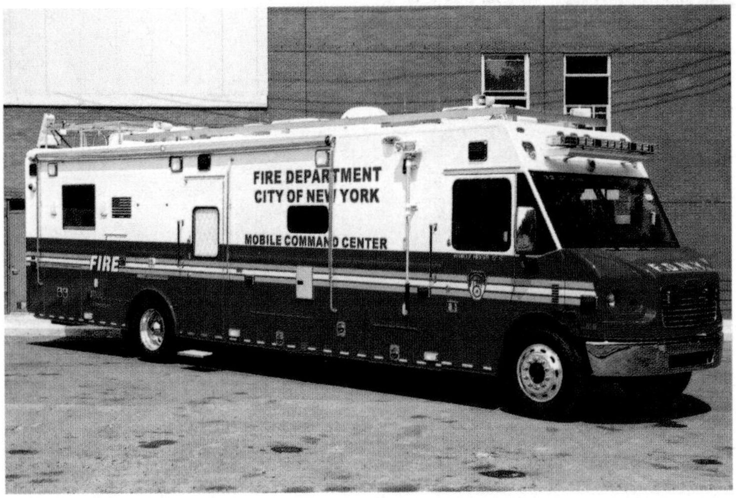

Jack Calderone

The 343

The death toll on 9/11 of the firefighters, officers and chiefs who died in the line of duty was the worst tragedy to strike the FDNY since the department was formed in 1865. There were many sons and brothers, fathers and sons, cousins, and other relations who died. Many of the firefighters listed below were promoted to the next highest rank posthumously. Their original rank remains with their photo. We also pay tribute to the 37 Port Authority police officers and 23 NYPD officers who died in the line of duty on that day.

All photos courtesy of the FDNY

Joseph Agnello, Ladder 118

Lt. Brian Ahearn, Battalion 13

Eric Allen, Squad 18

Richard Allen, Ladder 15

Cpt. James Amato, Squad 1

Calixto Anaya Jr., Engine 4

Joseph Angelini Sr. Rescue 1

Joseph Angelini Jr., Ladder 4

Faustino Apostol Jr., Battalion 2

David Arce, Engine 3

Louis Arena, Ladder 5

Carl Asaro, Battalion 9

Lt. Gregg Atlas, Engine 10

Gerald Atwood, Ladder 21

Gerard Baptiste, Ladder 9

A.C. Gerard Barbara, Command Center

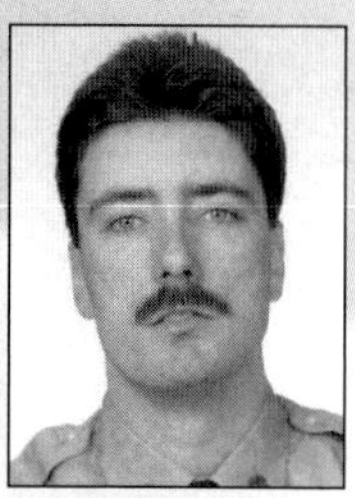
Matthew Barnes, Ladder 25

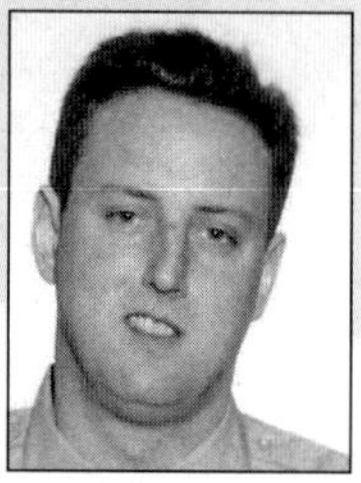
Arthur Barry, Ladder 15

Lt. Steven Bates, Engine 235

Carl Bedigian, Engine 214

Stephen Belson, Battalion 7

John Bergin, Rescue 5

Paul Beyer, Engine 6

Peter Bielfeld, Ladder 42

Brian Bilcher, Squad 1

Carl Bini, Rescue 5

Christopher Blackwell, Rescue 3

Michael Bocchino, Battalion 48

FIRE DEPARTMENT CITY OF NEW YORK 9-11-01

Frank Bonomo, Engine 230

Gary Box, Squad 1

Michael Boyle, Engine 33

Kevin Bracken, Engine 40

Michael Brennan, Ladder 4

Peter Brennan, Rescue 4

Cpt. Daniel Brethel, Ladder 24

Cpt. Patrick Brown, Ladder 3

Andrew Brunn, Ladder 5

Cpt. Vincent Brunton, Ladder 105

Fire Marshal Ronald Bucca

Greg Buck, Engine 201

Cpt. William Burke Jr., Engine 21

A.C. Donald Burns, Command Center

John Burnside, Ladder 20

Thomas Butler, Squad 1

Patrick Byrne, Ladder 101

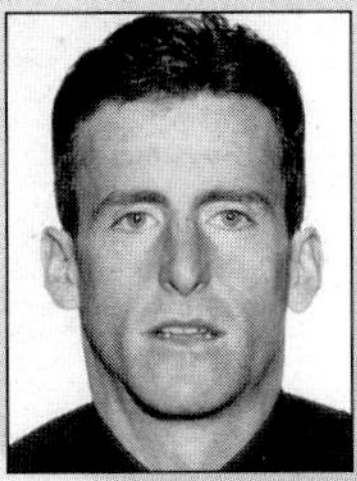
George Cain, Ladder 7

Salvatore Calabro, Ladder 101

Cpt. Frank Callahan, Ladder 35

Michael Cammarata, Ladder 11

Brian Cannizzaro, Ladder 101

Dennis Carey, HazMat 1

Michael Carlo, Engine 230

Michael Carroll, Ladder 3

Peter Carroll, Squad 1

Thomas Casoria, Engine 22

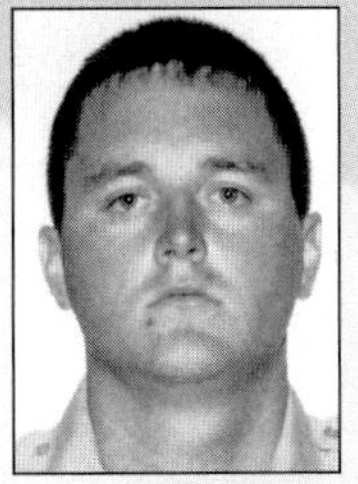
Michael Cawley, Ladder 136

Vernon Cherry, Ladder 118

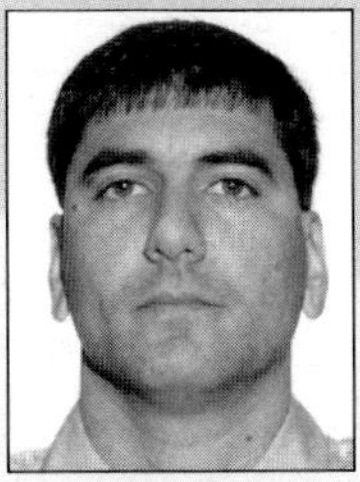
Nicholas Chiofalo, Engine 235

John Chipura, Engine 219

Michael Clarke, Ladder 2

Steven Coakley, Engine 217

Tarel Coleman, Squad 252

John Collins, Ladder 25

Robert Cordice, Squad 1

Ruben Correa, Engine 74

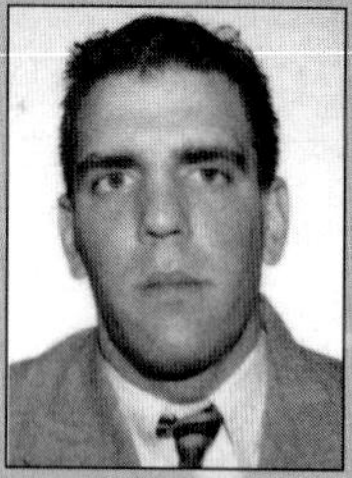
James Coyle, Ladder 3

Robert Crawford, Safety Battalion

Lt. John Crisci, HazMat

B.C. Dennis Cross, Battalion 57

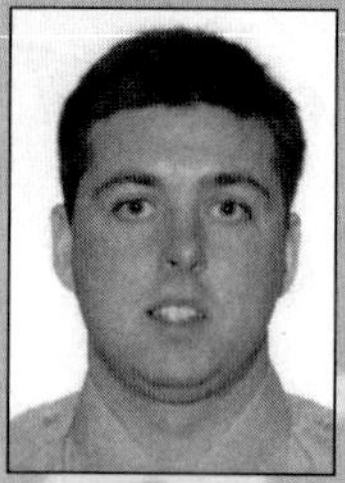
Thomas Cullen III, Squad 41

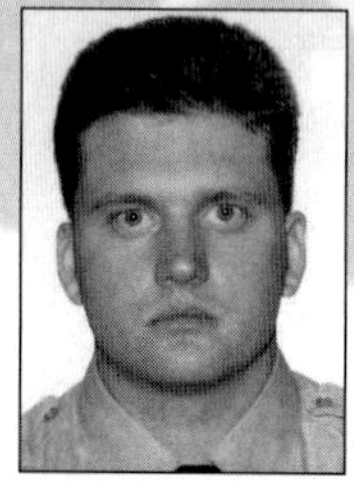
Robert Curatolo, Ladder 16

Lt. Edward D'Atri, Squad 1

Michael D'Auria, Engine 40

Scott Davidson, Ladder 118

Edward Day, Ladder 11

B.C. Thomas DeAngelis, Battalion 8

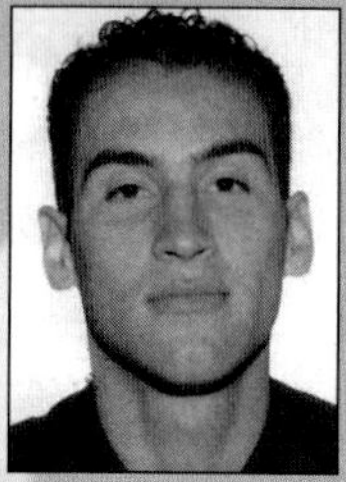
Manuel Delvalle, Engine 5

Martin DeMeo, HazMat 1

David DeRubbio, Engine 226

Lt. Andrew Desperito, Engine 1

B.C. Dennis Devlin, Battalion 9

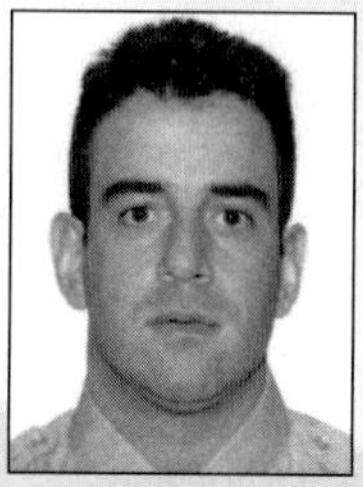
Gerard Dewan, Ladder 3

George DiPasquale, Ladder 2

Lt. Kevin Donnelly, Ladder 3

Lt. Kevin Dowdell, Rescue 4

B. C. Raymond Downey, S.O.C.

Gerard Duffy, Ladder 21

Cpt. Martin Egan Jr., Div. 15

Michael Elferis, Engine 22

Francis Esposito, Engine 235

Lt. Michael Esposito, Squad 1

Robert Evans, Engine 33

B.C. John Fanning II, HazMat Operations

Captain John Farino, Engine 26

Terrance Farrell, Rescue 4

Cpt. Joseph Farrelly, Division 1

Dep. Comm. William Feehan

Lee Fehling, Engine 235

Alan Feinberg,
Battalion 9

Michael Fiore,
Rescue 5

Lt. John Fischer,
Ladder 20

Andre Fletcher,
Rescue 5

John Florio,
Engine 214

Lt. Michael Fodor,
Ladder 21

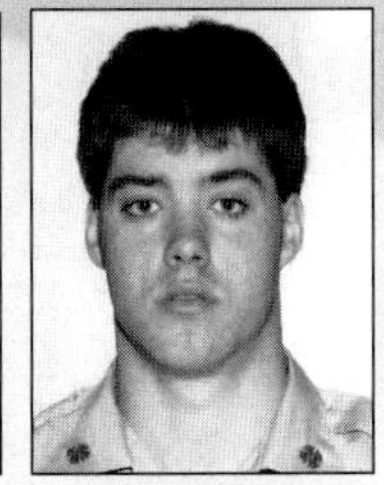

Thomas Foley,
Rescue 3

David Fontana,
Squad 1

Robert Foti,
Ladder 7

Andrew Fredericks,
Squad 18

Lt. Peter Freund,
Engine 55

Thomas Gambino Jr.,
Rescue 3

Chief of Dept.
Peter Ganci Jr.

Lt. Charles Garbarini,
Battalion 9

Thomas Gardner,
HazMat 1

Matthew Garvey,
Squad 1

Bruce Gary,
Engine 40

Gary Geidel,
Rescue 1

B.C. Edward Geraghty,
Battalion 9

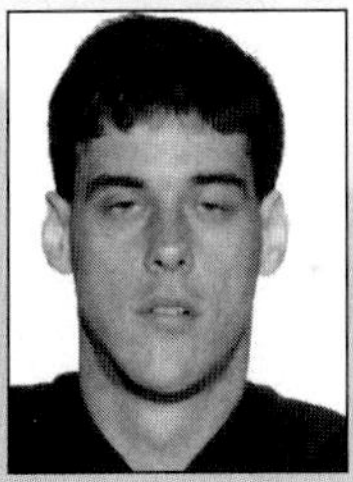

Denis Germain,
Ladder 2

Lt. Vincent Giammona,
Ladder 5

James Giberson,
Ladder 35

Ronnie Geis,
Squad 288

Paul Gill,
Engine 54

Lt. John Ginley,
Engine 40

Jeffrey Giordano,
Ladder 3

John Giordano,
HazMat 1

Keith Glascoe,
Ladder 21

James Gray,
Ladder 20

B.C. Joseph Grzelak,
Battalion 48

Jose Guadalupe,
Engine 54

Lt. Geoffrey Guja,
Battalion 43

Lt. Joseph Gullickson,
Ladder 101

David Halderman,
Squad 18

Lt. Vincent Halloran,
Ladder 8

Robert Hamilton, Squad 41

Sean Hanley, Ladder 20

Thomas Hannafin, Ladder 5

Dana Hannon, Engine 26

Daniel Harlin, Ladder 2

Lt. Harvey Harrell, Rescue 5

Lt. Stephen Harrell, Battalion 7

Cpt. Thomas Haskell Jr., Division 15

Timothy Haskell, Squad 18

Cpt. Terence Hatton, Rescue 1

Michael Haub, Ladder 4

Lt. Michael Healey, Squad 41

John Heffernan, Ladder 11

Ronnie Henderson, Engine 279

Joseph Henry, Ladder 21

William Henry, Rescue 1

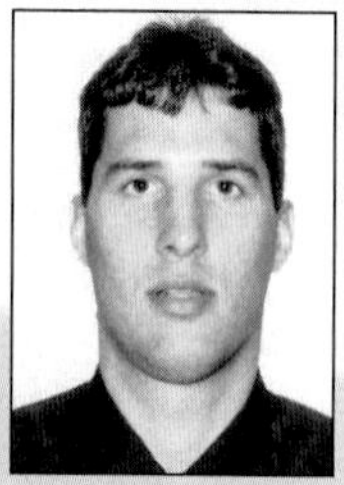
Thomas Hetzel, Ladder 13

Cpt. Brian Hickey, Rescue 4

Lt. Timothy Higgins, S.O.C.

Jonathan Hohmann, HazMat 1

Thomas Holohan, Engine 6

Joseph Hunter, Squad 288

Cpt. Walter Hynes, Ladder 13

Jonathan Ielpi, Squad 288

Cpt. Frederick Ill Jr., Ladder 2

William Johnston, Engine 6

Andrew Jordan, Ladder 132

Karl Joseph, Engine 207

Lt. Anthony Jovic, Battalion 47

Angel Juarbe Jr., Ladder 12

Rev. Mychal Judge, Chaplain

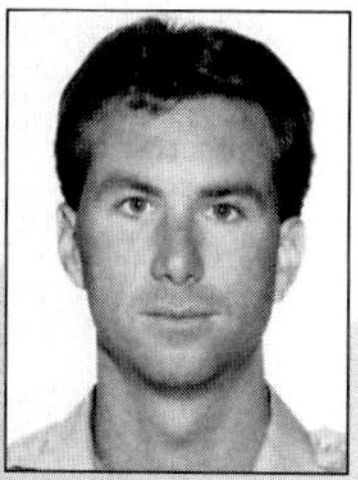
Vincent Kane, Engine 22

B.C. Charles Kasper, S.O.C..

Paul Keating, Ladder 5

Richard Kelly Jr., Ladder 11

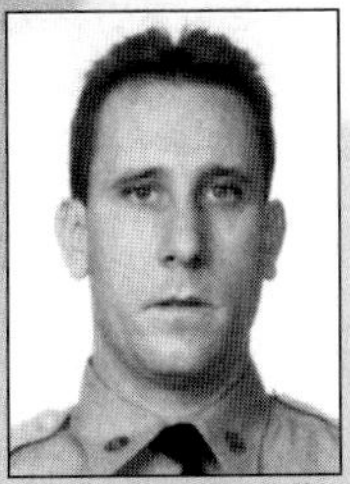
Thomas R. Kelly, Ladder 15

Thomas W. Kelly, Ladder 105

Thomas Kennedy, Ladder 101

Lt. Ronald Kerwin, Squad 288

Michael Kiefer, Ladder 132

Robert King Jr., Engine 33

Scott Kopytko, Ladder 15

William Krukowski, Ladder 21

Kenneth Kumpel, Ladder 25

Thomas Kuveikis, Squad 252

David LaForge, Ladder 20

William Lake, Rescue 2

Robert Lane, Engine 55

Peter Langone, Squad 252

Scott Larsen, Ladder 15

Lt. Joseph Leavey, Ladder 15

Neil Leavy, Engine 217

Daniel Libretti, Rescue 2

Carlos Lillo, Paramedic

Robert Linnane, Ladder 20

Michael Lynch, Engine 40

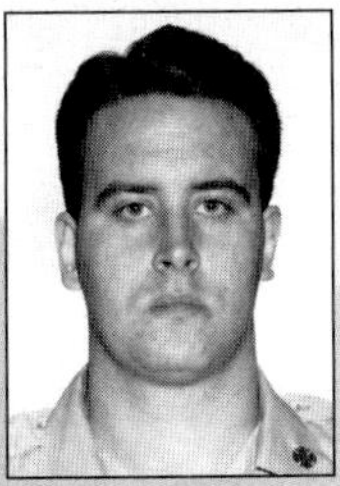
Michael Lynch, Ladder 4

Michael Lyons, Squad 41

Patrick Lyons, Squad 252

Joseph Maffeo, Ladder 101

William Mahony, Rescue 4

Joseph Maloney, Ladder 3

B.C. Joseph Marchbanks Jr., Battalion 12

Lt. Charles Margiotta, Battalion 22

Kenneth Marino, Rescue 1

John Marshall, Engine 23

Lt. Peter Martin, Rescue 2

Lt. Paul Martini, Engine 23

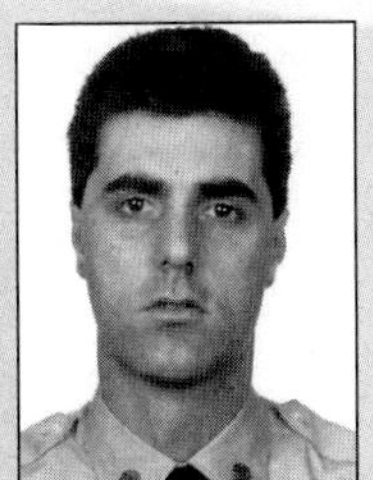
Joseph Mascali, T.S.U. 2

Keithroy Maynard, Engine 33

Brian McAleese, Engine 226

John McAvoy, Ladder 3

Thomas McCann, Battalion 8

Lt. William McGinn, Squad 18

B.C. William McGovern, Battalion 2

Dennis McHugh, Ladder 13

Robert McMahon, Ladder 20

Robert McPadden, Engine 23

Terence McShane, Ladder 101

Timothy McSweeney, Ladder 3

Martin McWilliams, Engine 22

Ray Meisenheimer, Rescue 3

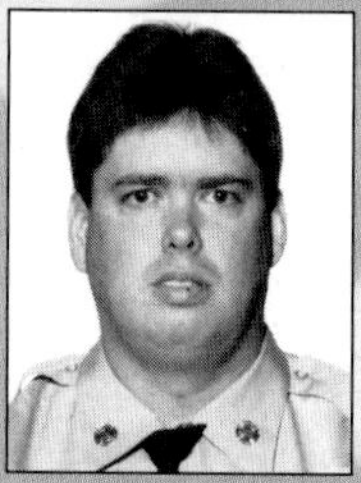
Charles Mendez, Ladder 7

Steve Mercado, Engine 40

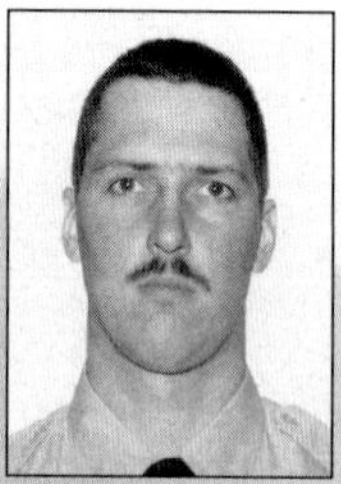
Douglas Miller, Rescue 5

Henry Miller Jr., Ladder 105

Robert Minara, Ladder 25

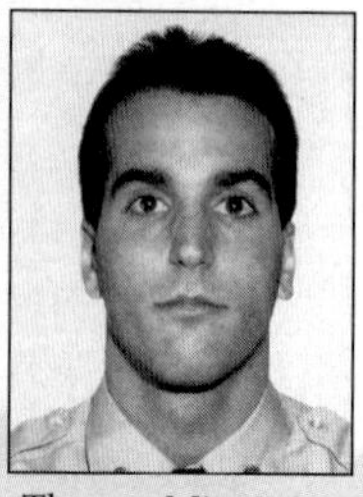
Thomas Mingione, Ladder 132

Lt. Paul Mitchell, Battalion 1

Cpt. Louis Modafferi, Rescue 5

Lt. Dennis Mojica, Rescue 1

Manuel Mojica, Squad 18

Carl Molinaro, Ladder 2

Michael Montesi, Rescue 1

Cpt. Thomas Moody, Division 1

B.C. John Moran, Battalion 49

Vincent Morello, Ladder 35

Christopher Mozzillo, Engine 55

Richard Muldowney Jr., Ladder 7

Michael Mullen, Ladder 12

Dennis Mulligan, Ladder 2

Lt. Raymond Murphy, Ladder 16

Lt. Robert Nagel, Engine 58

John Napolitano, Rescue 2

Peter Nelson, Rescue 4

Gerard Nevins, Rescue 1

Dennis O'Berg, Ladder 105

Lt. Daniel O'Callaghan, Ladder 4

Douglas Oelschlager, Ladder 15

Joseph Ogren, Ladder 3

Lt. Thomas O'Hagan, Battalion 4

Samuel Otice, Ladder 4

Patrick O'Keefe, Rescue 1

Cpt. William O'Keefe, Div. 15

Eric Olsen, Ladder 15

Jeffrey Olsen, Engine 10

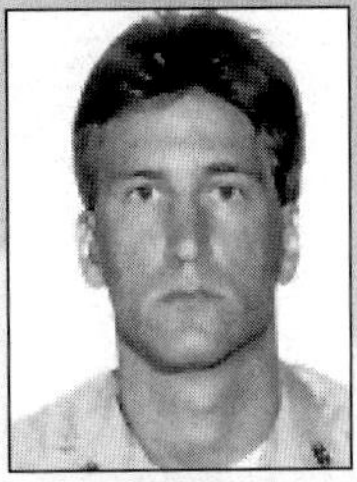
Steven Olson, Ladder 3

Kevin O'Rourke, Rescue 2

Michael Otten, Ladder 35

Jeffrey Palazzo, Rescue 5

B.C. Orio Palmer, Battalion 7

Frank Palombo, Ladder 105

Paul Pansini, Engine 10

B.C. John Paolillo, Battalion 11

James Pappageorge, Engine 23

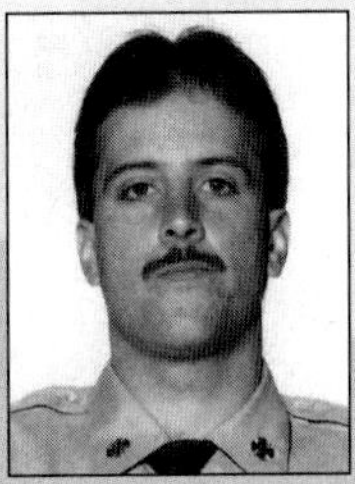
Robert Parro, Engine 8

Durrell Pearsall, Rescue 4

Lt. Glenn Perry, Battalion 12

Lt. Philip Petti, Battalion 7

Lt. Kevin Pfeifer, Engine 33

Lt. Kenneth Phelan, Battalion 32

Christopher Pickford, Engine 201

Shawn Powell, Engine 207

Vincent Princiotta, Ladder 7

Kevin Prior, Squad 252

B.C. Richard Prunty, Battalion 2

Lincoln Quappe, Rescue 2

Lt. Michael Quilty, Ladder 11

Ricardo Quinn, Paramedic

Leonard Ragaglia, Engine 54

Michael Ragusa, Engine 279

Edward Rall, Rescue 2

Adam Rand, Squad 288

Donald Regan, Rescue 3

Lt. Robert Regan, Ladder 118

Christian Regenhard, Ladder 131

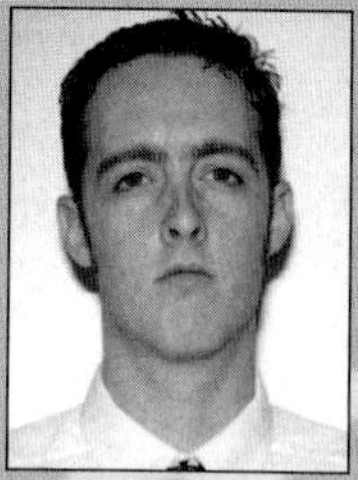
Kevin Reilly, Engine 207

Lt. Vernon Richard, Ladder 7

James Riches, Engine 4

Joseph Rivelli, Ladder 25

Michael Roberts, Engine 214

Michael E. Roberts, Ladder 35

Anthony Rodriguez, Engine 279

Matthew Rogan, Ladder 11

Keith Roma, Fire Patrol 2

Nicholas Rossomando, Rescue 5

Paul Ruback, Ladder 25

Stephan Russell, Engine 55

Lt. Michael Russo, S.O.C.

B.C. Matthew Ryan, Battalion 1

Thomas Sabella, Ladder 13

Christopher Santora, Engine 54

John Santore, Ladder 5

Gregory Saucedo, Ladder 5

Dennis Scauso, HazMat 1

John Schardt, Engine 201

B.C. Scheffold, Battalion 12

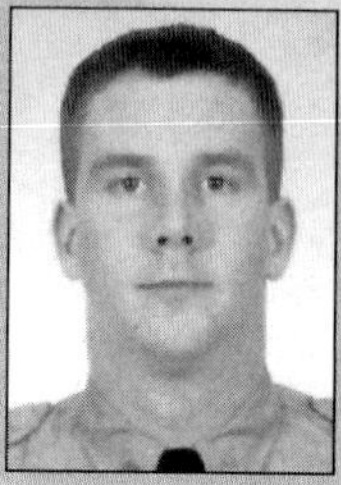
Thomas Schoales, Engine 4

Gerard Schrang, Rescue 3

Gregory Sikorsky, Squad 41

Stephen Siller, Squad 1

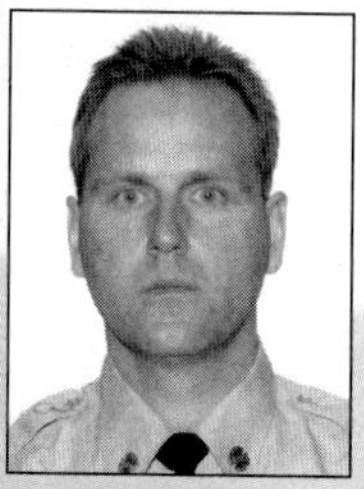
Stanley Smagala Jr. Engine 226

Kevin Smith, HazMat 1

Leon Smith Jr., Ladder 118

Robert Spear Jr., Engine 26

Joseph Spor, Rescue 3

B.C. Lawrence Stack, Safety Battalion

Cpt. Timothy Stackpole, Division 11

Gregory Stajk, Ladder 13

Jeffrey Stark, Engine 230

Bemjamin Suarez, Ladder 21

Daniel Suhr, Engine 216

Lt. Christopher Sullivan, Ladder 111

Brian Sweeney, Rescue 1

Sean Tallon, Ladder 10

Allan Tarasiewicz, Rescue 5

Paul Tegtmeier, Engine 4

John Tierney, Ladder 9

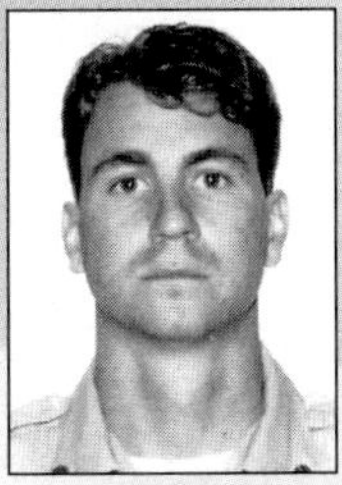
John Tipping II, Ladder 4

Hector Tirado Jr., Engine 23

Richard Vanhine, Squad 41

Peter Vega, Ladder 118

Lawrence Veling, Engine 235

John Vigiano II, Ladder 132

Sergio Villanueva, Ladder 132

Lawrence Virgilio, Squad 18

Lt. Robert Wallace, Engine 205

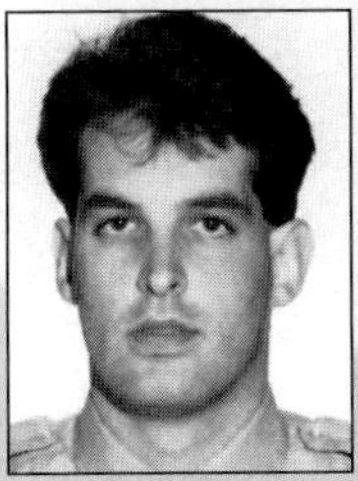
Jeffrey Walz, Ladder 9

Lt. Michael Warchola, Ladder 5

Cpt. Patrick Waters, S.O.C.

Kenneth Watson, Engine 214

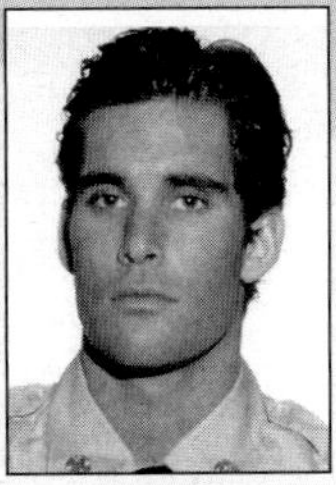
Michael Weinberg, Engine 1

David Weiss, Rescue 1

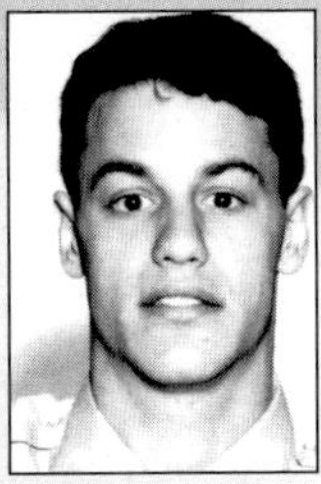
Timothy Welty, Squad 288

Eugene Whelan, Engine 230

Edward White, Engine 230

Mark Whitford, Engine 23

Lt. Glenn Wilkinson, Engine 238

B.C. John Williamson, Battalion 6

Cpt. David Wooley, Ladder 4

Raymond York, Engine 285

Memorials

There were numerous memorial services and funerals after 9/11. On some days there were as many as 15 funerals. The Emerald Society Pipes and Drums had to split members to cover all of the services. Retired members of the band had to fill in so all services received the proper attention. Firefighters constructed memorials within and outside of their firehouses. Streets where firefighters lived were dedicated in their memory by adding their names to street names. Right after 9/11, people dropped off flowers, candles, posters and cards at their neighborhood firehouses where firefighters were lost. Firehouse doors were painted and riding lists for 9/11 were saved in memory of those lost in the line of duty.

Todd Maisel

Funeral of Firefighter Stephen Siller of Squad 1.

459 FDNY Funerals/Memorials were held after September 11, 2001

Cards, posters, flowers and memorial candles outside Engine 10 and Ladder 10. Numerous firehouses received similar tributes.

Andrea Booher/FEMA News Photo

(below left) Funeral of Captain Terry Hatton, Rescue 1.

(below right) Funeral for Firefighter Durrell Pearsall, Rescue 4, at St. Patrick's Cathedral.

Todd Maisel

AP Photo/Ed Bailey

Memorial outside of Engine 10 and Ladder 10.

Line-of-Duty plaques and photos of members from Rescue 5 of Staten Island. Jack Calderone

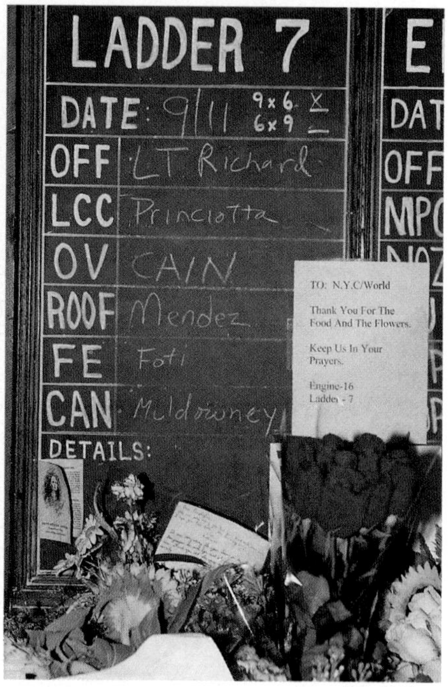

Peter Matthews

Original riding list for Ladder 7 on September 11, 2001.

A portion of the memorial inside Rescue 5's firehouse honoring members of "Blue Thunder." Jack Calderone

Jack Calderone

Street sign for Lieutenant John R. Fischer from Ladder 20, who was promoted posthumously to the rank of captain.

Courtesy of the Uniformed Firefighters Association

Andrea Booher/FEMA News Photo

Emerald Society Pipes and Drums play at the World Trade Center. The band played at 459 funerals and memorial services.

Street sign for chief depicted on the cover of this book.

Jack Calderone

Firehouse doors of Rescue 5 and Engine 160 of Staten Island with painting of 11 boots from missing members.

Steve White

AP Photo/Matt Rourke

A flag is seen in view of the Tribute in Light as it rises above New York on Saturday, Sept. 11, 2010. In an annual tradition, the two bright-blue beams of light rise from lower Manhattan in memory of the fallen Twin Towers.

(below) Messages left by grateful civilians on Ladder 24 apparatus.

AP Photo/Amy Sanceta

Glossary

10 & 10 – The firehouse of Engine 10 and Ladder 10

10-60 – The code for a major emergency

10-8 – A radio signal that signifies a fire company is back in service and ready for another alarm

ABC – Acting Battalion Chief

ABC Chart – The fire department went from a 40-hour work week to a 24-hour-on/24-hour-off schedule after 9/11. The schedule was changed to 24 hours on and 48 hours off.

Box – Usually a first-alarm assignment of three engines, two ladders and a battalion chief to a predetermined location

Box 8087– The fire-alarm box number specific to the North Tower

Can Man – Usually a junior firefighter who carries a 2½-gallon water extinguisher

CFR – Certified First Responder

Circle Line – A popular sightseeing vessel

Command Board – A device that allows the incident commander to keep track of where units are operating at scene

Con Ed – The major electric company in New York City

Cribbing – Wood used to stabilize an object that is unstable, typically a vehicle or an object to be lifted

Cross-Band Repeater – Transmits on a five-watt VHF radio to a 40-watt UHF radio for use in high-rise operations to boost the radio signal

Decon – Decontamination

DMAT – Disaster Medical Assistance Team

DMORT – Disaster Mortuary Operational Response Team

DOA – Dead on arrival

ERS – Emergency Reporting System

ESU – Emergency Service Unit (NYPD)

FEMA – Federal Emergency Management Agency

FEMA Team Cache – About three tractor-trailer loads of equipment brought by one of 28 FEMA Urban Search and Rescue Teams

Field Comm – Field Communications

GPS – Global Positioning System

Grand Concourse – A major thoroughfare in Bronx, NY

Grappler – Piece of machinery used to move heavy loads. The use of grapplers at the WTC site allowed the removal of heavy objects quite easily

Handie-talkie (HT) – Walkie-talkie fire department radio

Housewatch – A firefighter who receives alarms and greets the public

HOV – High Occupancy Vehicle

LIE – Long Island Expressway (Route 495) allows drivers to travel from Long Island to Manhattan via the Queens Midtown Tunnel

Light Duty – A firefighter working in a modified assignment after being injured

Mask Service Unit – The unit repairs over 4,000 masks and 15,000 cylinders used in firefighting operations. They refill empty air cylinders every day. A unit is dispatched on the third alarms, high-rise incidents or special-called assignments

OAD – Officer Assignment Desk

OEM – Office of Emergency Management

OV – A firefighter who performs outside ventilation

PASS Device – Personal Alert Safety System

PATH – Port Authority Trans-Hudson Railway

The Pile – The debris-filled 16-acre site following the collapses

Probie – A probationary firefighter just out of the academy

RAC – Recuperation and Care

Riding List – A document with the officer and on the truck of who is working that tour and what assignment each firefighter has been given

Rollups – Sections of 2½-inch hose in 50-foot sections carried by engine company firefighters in high-rise buildings to operate off a standpipe system

Roof Man – A firefighter from a ladder company assigned to operate on the roof by providing ventilation of stairway bulkheads, cutting the roof and providing information on conditions on the roof and from what is seen from above

Satellite – A hose wagon with a large-diameter hose that responds with an engine to multiple-alarm fires.

SEMO – State Emergency Management Organization

Sergeant-at-Arms – A Uniformed Firefighters Association Union official

SOC – Special Operations Command

Standpipe Kit – Usually a wrench, wheel and fittings to hook up 2½-inch hose to a standpipe in a building taller than 75 feet

Stang Nozzle – Large-caliber nozzle capable of throwing 1,250 gpm of water, usually located on top of an engine or in a tower ladder basket

Super Radio – A high-powered radio capable of reaching the borough fire dispatcher

Tactical Support Unit (TAC) – An apparatus that carries an inflatable boat, 28-foot light tower, generators (fixed and portable) and responds to second alarms, building collapses and water-related emergencies

Technical Services Division – The division that handles budgeting, procurement, maintenance, repair and relinquishment in three areas. It is responsible for procurement of breathing apparatus, Special Operations equipment and grant equipment. Fire Tools handles 975 items issued to the field. The Medical Equipment Unit handles 275 inventory items of biomedical equipment. The Medical Supply Unit manages more than 600 inventory items

Tender Smoke – A 52-foot-long fireboat capable of supplying 2,000 gpm (retired in July 2008)

Tormentor Controls – Controls used to operate the jacks and tormentors of a tower ladder to keep the apparatus steady while operating at 75 or 95 feet above the street

Transit – A device used to measure movement of an unstable building

Truckie – A firefighter assigned to a ladder or a truck company

USAR Task Force – A Task Force made up of 62 positions and transports over 58,000 pounds of equipment

Winter Garden – The area next to the World Financial Center in lower Manhattan